History of Economic Thought as an Intellectual Discipline

To Julia and Juliet

History of Economic Thought as an Intellectual Discipline

D.P. O'Brien

Emeritus Professor of Economics, University of Durham, UK

Edward Elgar

Cheltenham, UK • Northampton, MA, USA

Published by
Edward Elgar Publishing Limited
Glensanda House
Montpellier Parade
Cheltenham
Glos GL50 1UA
UK

Edward Elgar Publishing, Inc.
William Pratt House
9 Dewey Court
Northampton
Massachusetts 01060
USA

A catalogue record for this book
is available from the British Library

Library of Congress Cataloguing in Publication Data

O'Brien, D.P. (Denis Patrick), 1939–
History of economic thought as an intellectual discipline / by D.P. O'Brien.
p. cm.
Includes bibliographical references and index.
1. Economic thought–History. I. Title.

HB75.O32 2007
330.09–dc22 2006034677

ISBN: 978 1 84720 259 8

Printed and bound in Great Britain by MPG Books Ltd, Bodmin, Cornwall

Contents

Preface

In the preparation of this book I owe an enormous debt to John Creedy. First, it was he who undertook the arduous task of welding together my essays into a coherent whole in the form of camera ready copy, providing along the way all sorts of advice and encouragement as he asked me to look at the intermediate versions which emerged. The reader of the volume will be able to see just how much work John did, and the extent of my debt to him concerning this and the companion volume *The Development of Monetary Economics*.

But the debt is much greater even than that. For every essay was first read by John, commented on by him, and amended in the light of his criticisms. This is true not only of the previously published items but also of those which are new to the book. In particular I have benefited from his comments on the full length essay on classical economics, chapter 5 (only a highly abbreviated version of which had previously appeared), and the lengthy essay on Hayek's place in the history of economic thought, chapter 10, during the course of the writing of which I found my own perspective on Hayek's macroeconomic theory altering somewhat.

I have certainly been fortunate in the development of modern communications; we have been able to engage in more or less continuous intellectual dialogue over a distance of 12000 miles, without any of the difficulties which previous generations, whose work is discussed in this book, had to endure when all that was available was the postal system and, more recently, the telephone.

I must also thank my wife Julia, who has not only had to put up with a house full of papers and books but who has also read all of the papers appearing in this volume from first draft onwards. Though an intellectual historian herself, economics is not her field, yet she has managed to make valuable comments in every case.

In the course of the work on this book, I have enjoyed reacquainting myself with the intellectual issues arising in the essays which it contains. I hope that the reader too will feel that the history of economic thought as an intellectual discipline, a discipline the value of which would not have been considered to be in question in earlier generations, is still of value.

Acknowledgements

Chapter 2 appeared in A.E. Murphy and R. Prendergast (eds.) *Contributions to the History of Economic Thought: Essays in Honour of R.D.C. Black*. London: Routledge, 2000. I am grateful to the publisher for permission. A version of chapter 3 appeared in *The Journal of Economic Methodology* **5**(1), 1998, pp. 23–41. I am grateful to the journal and to Taylor and Francis (*http://www.tandf.co.uk/journals*) for permission. Chapter 4 appeared in N.J. Foss and B.J. Loasby (eds.) *Economic Organisation, Capabilities and Co-ordination*. London: Routledge, 1998. I am grateful to the publisher for permission. A very short version of chapter 5 appeared in W.J. Samuels, J.E. Biddle, and J.B. Davis *A Companion to the History of Economic Thought*. Oxford: Blackwell, 2003. I am grateful to Blackwell Publishing for permission to draw upon the shorter essay. Chapter 6 appeared as 'Marshall and his Correspondence', *Economic Journal* **107**, 1997, pp. 1859–1885. I am grateful to the Royal Economic Society and to Blackwell Publishing for permission. Chapter 7 appeared in *Research in the History of Economic Thought and Methodology* **17**, 1999, pp. 1–21. I am grateful to the journal and to Elsevier for permission. A version of Chapter 8 appeared in *Proceedings of the British Academy* **84**, 1993, pp. 347–66. I am grateful to the British Academy for permission to reproduce material from the article. Chapter 9 appeared as 'Hayek: Economics and Law', in P. Newman (ed.) *The New Palgrave Dictionary of Economics and the Law*, vol. **2** pp. 217–28, London: Macmillan, 1997. I am grateful to Palgrave Macmillan for permission. Chapter 10 will also appear in *The Elgar Companion to Hayekian Economics*, edited by Norman Barry. Chapter 11 appeared as an introduction to the reprint by Pickering and Chatto (London, 1995) of the six volumes of McCulloch's splendid *Select Collections* of economic literature and I am grateful to the publisher for the original appearance of this essay. Chapter 12 appeared in *The International Journal of Applied Economics and Econometrics* **10**(1), 2002, 1–29. I am grateful to Transaction Publishers for permission.

In addition to the help from John Creedy and Julia Stapleton mentioned in the Preface, I am grateful to Roger Backhouse for comments on chapters 2,3 and 7; to Mark Blaug, Terence Hutchison, and Richard Lipsey for comments on chapter 3; to Peter Johnson for comments on chapters 3 and 4; to Richard Morley for comments on chapter 4; to Bob Coats for comments on chapter 7, to R.C.O. Matthews for comments on chapter 8, and to Paul Samuelson for comments on chapter 12. I am also grateful to the editors of the books and journals in which my work first appeared, particularly Warren Samuels and Roger Backhouse.

Part I

Introduction

Chapter 1

Introduction

The essays in this book are all, in one way or another, concerned with the wider intellectual issues which once did, and still should, concern economists. All of the writers who are considered are people whose own scholarship was – or in one case still is – exemplary, and who set an example to their professional colleagues through their concern to avoid subjective originality and indeed to learn from, rather than peremptorily discard, so much that has been achieved by economists of earlier generations.

I begin, in Chapter 2, by attempting to restate the case for history of economic thought as an intellectual discipline. In earlier times, such an attempt would have been regarded as superfluous; most of the great economists of the past, though their interpretations of the wider literature may have been sometimes idiosyncratic, regarded knowledge of that wider literature as a professional requirement.[1] But now two different forces have interacted to bring an end to this healthy state of affairs. On the one hand, increasing specialisation and the huge increase in the literature of economics, an increase itself partly driven by the top-down imposition of a publish-or-perish regime, has made keeping up with the wider contemporary literature, let alone famil-

[1]Ricardo admittedly was not widely read and in the area of monetary economics, in which he first came to prominence, is not immune to accusations of subjective originality (Fetter, 1969, p. 74). But he seems to have relied upon James Mill and McCulloch to provide him with information on the work of previous authors. Keynes, as is well known, was not merely widely read but a collector of economic literature.

iarising one's self with the great works of the past, ever more demanding. On the other hand, for reasons which have never been publicly articulated, an active policy of marginalising the study of the history of economic thought and, with it, the scholarly education of the next generation of economists, has been pursued. Yet the very expansion of the literature, and of the number of practising and writing economists, has made more necessary than ever some attempt to produce an orderly picture and to stabilise a situation rendered unstable by the transience of passing fashions which, as they pass, attract enthusiastic but temporary disciples.

Passing fashions lead to detours. Such detours are given impetus by a methodological fashion which, though never clearly stated (for obvious reasons), may be described roughly as follows. First, state an economic problem in ways which can be handled by mathematics. This is an important first step. It is not merely that the mathematics enables a problem to be set up as a tractable theoretical one; it is that the available mathematics itself dictates what is regarded as an approachable theoretical problem. Second, in order, as W.S. Gilbert might have it, to give verisimilitude to an otherwise bald and unconvincing model, some 'stylised facts' may be introduced. In Chapter 3, I deal both with the question of detours and that of stylised facts – which are not facts in the normally accepted sense of the word. Rather they are essentially myths – as in the case of lighthouses mentioned in the chapter – which acquire a factual aura through being repeated endlessly by people working in a particular field. The detours themselves are assisted in their development by invocation of the pernicious doctrine (one not unrelated to the concept of the stylised fact) that the truth of assumptions is irrelevant. Such a doctrine predates Friedman by many years; although writers of an a priorist bent have paid lip service to the idea of 'verification', by which they meant checking whether the assumptions of a theory made it applicable to a particular situation, it is evident from the work of the Austrians in macroeconomics, in particular, that such an injunction was more honoured in the breach than the observance.

One of the areas in which what was tractable mathematically has determined permissible theory, throughout at least most of the twentieth century, was in the treatment of competition – 'perfect' competition. The attack upon this by G.B. Richardson, which is discussed in Chapter 4, has been widely appreciated – but only within a very small subset of the economics profession considered as a whole! In the chapter I consider the importance of Richardson's now classic book *Information and Investment*, and the wider issues which need to be considered when adopting his approach to the problems raised by the dominance of the 'perfect competition' approach – and problems there certainly are – in the literature of economics.

'Perfect competition' is a creation very largely of inter-war microeconomics, though the roots lie further back in general equilibrium. Viewed within the literature of economics as a whole, it may seem to represent a minor issue, just as much of inter-war microeconomics now looks antique. However, to an extraordinary extent, modern economics owes a much larger debt to earlier writers – to the eighteenth and nineteenth century writers. Nowhere is this more true than in the areas of macroeconomics and trade. Although I have written at length upon the content of that literature elsewhere (O'Brien, 1975, 2004), I attempt in Chapter 5 to give an overall view of its strengths, as well as its limitations. It was produced by several generations of outstanding individuals, including one of the greatest of monetary writers, Henry Thornton.

Modern research by Ronald Coase (1990) has established the startling fact that Henry Thornton was a distant relative of the great Alfred Marshall. It is Marshall's work which is considered in Chapter 6. With the publication of Marshall's *Correspondence* we now have much more detailed evidence about the man who, as George Stigler remarked, wrote the second greatest book in the history of our subject (after Smith) and – and this is worth emphasising – has been, since his death in 1924, endlessly traduced on both an academic and a personal (even on a marital) level, especially in the university which he loved. In Chapter 6 I raise some questions about the basis for that abuse.

One of Marshall's intellectual (though not personal) critics was Edwin Cannan. Yet though he was critical of Marshall, he greatly respected Marshall as well, as his pupil Lionel Robbins was later to relate. In Chapter 7, I explore Cannan's own work as an economist, and the way in which he developed his incisive critical discussions of economic literature, with his refreshing emphasis on the important question of whether an argument was actually right or wrong. I also deal with his strangely obscurantist approach, as it seems to me, to monetary theory.

Cannan was the first Professor of Economic Theory at the London School of Economics. He approached his subject through the history of economic thought. A successor at LSE was Friedrich Hayek, invited to lecture at LSE by the young and dynamic Lionel Robbins, and subsequently appointed to a chair. Hayek too, like Cannan and like Robbins, delighted in, and was a formidable scholar of, the history of economic thought. As his interests widened beyond economics to questions of social and legal philosophy, he deployed his formidable scholarship over a huge literature in several languages, with results which are still impressive and influential today. Chapter 8 attempts to provide an overall view of Hayek's contributions, and shows how his work came to cover a huge range of subject areas, very largely through scholarly study (his Vienna education having been limited). His devastating and scholarly analysis of the intellectual traditions of historicism and scientism led to an analysis of socialism which was even more devastating. It also led to his becoming a non-person, both as an economist and, in many circles, even as an academic, for daring not merely to confront but to criticise most damagingly the cherished preconceptions of the academic establishment.

In particular, his analysis of the interweaving of law and economics, which is dealt with in Chapter 9, stressed the idea that individual intelligence is limited, and that we have to understand the way that economic, legal and social institutions have evolved – and evolved in such a way as make individual plans compatible and social progress possible. Such an analysis resulted in Hayek arriving at a position which was - and is - a deep affront to the social engineering aspirations of the dominant left-liberal establishment in academic life.

Hayek's economic thought, more narrowly defined, and its influence upon other economists, is explored in Chapter 10. In particular I discuss his approach to macroeconomic theory which was so important in the debates of the 1930s, but was to be eclipsed by the rise to complete dominance of Keynes's *General Theory* – or rather of a particular interpretation of the *General Theory* by Keynes's self-proclaimed disciples and co-workers. Essentially, Hayek was developing the Wicksell-Mises approach, analysing the effects of monetary expansion in terms of over-expansion of investment goods industries. I argue that the approach was vulnerable to criticisms of writers such as Hawtrey, Wilson and Kaldor, and suffered – as also noted in Chapter 3 – from the a priorist approach. Hayek essentially neglected key facts and relied upon 'stylised facts' about the investment process which had limited correspondence with reality. Nonetheless, his approach had the merit of treating money as important, while the so-called Keynesians were so successful in eliminating money from discussion that its importance had to be (painfully) rediscovered by the economics profession in the 1970s.

Throughout, Hayek's approach is scholarly. The final two chapters return to the opening theme of the book, by discussing the work of two very different economists who have both, in their individual ways, done so much, by their example, to instruct their colleagues in the wider literature of the subject. The first of these writers is John Ramsay McCulloch, arguably the first major historian of economics, a bibliophile and self-taught scholar whose achievements were long overlooked because of his short-lived (and in many ways ill-advised) association with Ricardo.

McCulloch was not primarily a theorist, and he believed that theory should be brought to the test of empirical information – that data mattered. This alone should (but did not) have made clear to writers that he could not be a slavish follower of Ricardo (O'Brien, 1970). His writing, taken as a whole, is full of references to data. It is also full of references to the wider literature of economics. (This again provides a strong contrast with Ricardo.) In Chapter 11, I look at McCulloch's involvement in the literature of economics, his discoveries, his collections, and his reprinting of historic texts.

The subject of the last chapter Paul Samuelson is, in contrast to McCulloch, very much a theorist. But he is not merely a theorist but probably the leading pure theorist of the twentieth century. In contrast to his successors he has been, throughout his career, a scholar. He has written extensively on the history of economic thought – more extensively indeed than he may himself have recognised. Starting as a graduate student of the great (but, to graduate students, terrifying) Jacob Viner, and perhaps having both the quickness of mind and the self-confidence to respond to Viner on the latter's own terms, he absorbed from Viner not only an emphasis, like that of Cannan, on whether an argument was right or wrong, but also a breadth of reading and of scholarly care and concern which has been exemplary.

In writing the essays which make up this book, I have tried to adhere to the scholarly standards which I learned from the writings of men like Jacob Viner, Lionel Robbins, Bob Black and others; and which I learned too from friends and contemporaries, who still, against prevailing fashion, believe that knowledge of the wider literature is important. If the reader in turn absorbs some of this influence which I have inherited and attempted to pass on in my teaching and writing, perhaps it may help to delay the total introversion of at least some of the economics profession.

Part II

Methodology

Chapter 2

History of Economic Thought as an Intellectual Discipline

The study of the history of economic thought dates back to the early years of the nineteenth century and, in particular, to the work of J.B. Say (1817, pp. xv-lx) and J.R. McCulloch (1824a, 1845a).[1] These two can really be regarded as the founders of the study of the history of economic thought and McCulloch's work was praised by Schumpeter in his early book (1912, p. 3). The study of the subject developed rapidly in other countries. In Italy it dates from the 1820s, and a succession of notable Italian writers followed, with the work of Pantaleoni and Einaudi at the end of the 19th century particularly noteworthy (Barucci, 1983). Both Einaudi, and another Italian economist Cossa, have been cited as not merely precursors but possible influences on the later work of Schumpeter (Barucci, 1983, p. 88; Perlman, 1983, p. 127). In Germany the subject seems to date largely from 1830s; by the 1850s there were systematic histories in German (Schumpeter, 1912, pp. 3-5; Cossa, 1893, pp. 115-25) and anyone studying the bibliographical details in Cossa's 1893 book cannot but be impressed by the extent of the literature that had already sprung into existence by the mid-1870s.

For practical purposes, then, the study of the history of economic thought

[1] On McCulloch's extraordinary pioneering work see O'Brien (1970, p. 55, 1995a, 1995b) and Chapter 11.

is as old as the widespread cultivation of the subject of economics itself. Indeed some of the greatest names in economics have been associated with the study of the history of the subject.

2.1 Eminent Practitioners

The great economists of the last quarter of the nineteenth century, who participated in the development of economics as an academic subject, were all, as Robbins has observed, 'truly learned in ... the scholarship of the subject' (1952, p. 1). Jevons's enthusiasm for the work of his predecessors, from Cantillon onwards, is well known, and he encouraged the history of economic thought work of Cossa (see Cossa, 1893, p. v). Marshall and Edgeworth were thoroughly well versed in the work of their predecessors; and leading figures in the next generation of economists, notably Keynes, H.L. Moore and Wicksell all displayed more than a passing interest in the history of economics (Jaffé,1965b, p. 225).

Of course not all of the work of great economists in the history of economic thought was above criticism, to put it mildly. Marshall's adulation of Ricardo, and corresponding downplaying of the achievement of J.S. Mill, is notorious. Keynes's work could be described as idiosyncratic at best. Later on the American economist John Commons treated the history of economic thought as an extended prelude to his own work, (Coats, 1983a, p. 154) while Wesley Mitchell advanced a version of the history of economics of such extreme relativism (Hirsch, 1983) that he was forced to neglect the intellectual development of theoretical work and, stressing its purely passing significance in relation to the kind of statistical work which was his own forte, coupled with a naive 'scientism', laid himself open to the charge of measurement without theory (Koopmans, 1947).

For many of the leading figures in economics during this century, history of economic thought has been an abiding concern. Indeed for Jacob Viner, economics and the history of economic thought were integral (Winch, 1983, p. 1). Frank Knight taught the history of economic thought throughout his entire career (Howey, 1983, p. 170) and, in turn, taught George Stigler (Rima, 1983, p. 272). Despite what might be described as an 'anti het phase' (Winch, 1962, p. 193), Paul Samuelson has done distinguished work in the history of economic thought; and other modern leaders with genuine and considered appreciation of the historical literature of the subject include Buchanan, Musgrave, Hicks, Baumol and Friedman.

Indeed several of these distinguished figures – Stigler, Samuelson, Buchanan and Hicks, as well as Hayek – have been the recipients of Nobel Prizes. One of these – Stigler – will surely be remembered primarily as an historian of economic thought (though see Mincer, 1983; Schmalensee, 1983).

Subsequent generations, however, have displayed a much greater intellectual narrowness – with the very important exception of Harry Johnson – and the process of narrowing has continued to the point where those interviewed by Klamer (Klamer, 1984) (selected for interview on the grounds that they are current leaders in the subject, moreover) seem, for the most part, to have no interest in the history of the subject at all. This is partly symptomatic of a decline in the subject, as well as being, in all probability, a significant cause.

2.2 The Decline in the History of Economic Thought

As early as 1965 Donald Gordon was reporting a decline in the subject, although it has to be said that he himself regarded this decline as being from a high – even possibly an abnormally high – level. Viewed from the perspective of the end of the twentieth century, the figures reported by Gordon can now only be seen, with regret, as a reflection of a lost world. At that date, 86 per cent of the institutions which he surveyed offered graduate work in the history of economic thought, and in 70 per cent it was required (this was the main case) or chosen by graduate students (Gordon, 1965, p. 120). A huge increase in the size of the profession, as measured by American Economic Association membership, had been accompanied by a process of increasing specialisation (which was to be expected) and marginalisation of the history of economic thought (Spengler, 1968, p. 6). The process of decline has continued (De Marchi and Lodewijks, 1983).

It is perhaps worth considering the details of what happened. Firstly, the history of economic thought became harder and harder to place in journals. In response, specialist journals began to appear, but this perhaps hastened the decline of the history of economic thought in more general journals.[2] In Britain this problem seems to be particularly acute; the history of economic thought has very largely disappeared from the leading British journals and academics specialising in the field routinely avoid sending material to such journals, resulting in a possible 'adverse selection problem'.[3] In North America, despite the praiseworthy diversity of the universities, there have been discernible problems (Barber, 1998, p. 182; Hollander 1995, pp. 299-302) though some remain optimistic (Samuels, 1996, p. 59). Anderson and Tollison (1986) have offered the ingenious explanation for decline that history of economic thought work involves difficulty over property rights, resulting in most of the benefits being external rather than captured by the researcher.

In the process of decline from the late 1960s onwards, some history of economic thought was pushed out of economics departments into the newly formed specialist economic history departments. But these economic history departments have themselves now almost entirely disappeared, and have not

[2]There is an earlier parallel; the emergence of specialist economic history journals resulted in the almost complete disappearance of economic history articles from economic journals.

[3]This has a number of aspects. In particular the main journals are denied the best specialist work in the history of economic thought, receiving only a small, and unrepresentative, selection, some of it the product of non-specialists who are perhaps unaware of the journals' general attitude towards the field, while most of the specialists hold back.

been reabsorbed into economics departments but joined up with history departments.

The process of decline seems inexorable at least in Britain and the United States – continental Europe seems to be different (Backhaus, 1986). A decade or so ago it seemed to some that perhaps the tide was turning (Coats, 1983c, 1987; De Marchi and Lodewijks, 1983); but, unfortunately, this proved a false dawn.

The regime of Research Appraisal in British universities has produced particular local problems. The emphasis on journal articles, for which much history of economic thought, requiring work in depth, is ill-suited, has been a considerable handicap to the pursuit of scholarly work; and there are some kinds of work in the history of economic thought, notably in the editorial and biographical field, which seem to be, for practical purposes, ruled out by Research Appraisal. Indeed it seems that, without any real public debate, scholarship has been not so much downgraded as eliminated under the RAE regime. Viewing the matter from the perspective of the history of economic thought this is doubly unfortunate; not only does it prevent the subject being pursued, but it elevates the journal article, which a longer-term perspective shows to be almost an entirely transient form,[4] to a position of complete dominance.

Further difficulties for history of economic thought are posed by the increasing tendency amongst universities in Britain to regard inputs (the obtaining of research grants) rather than scholarly output as the test of academic merit. Historians of economic thought come low in the priorities of grant-giving bodies. Yet there is a very serious case for continuing with the

[4]In this connection, it is instructive to consider two points. Firstly, it is a common experience that one cannot even *give away* back numbers of journals, let alone sell them. Secondly, one can apply and extend the test suggested by George Shackle – looking at the grease marks on bound volumes of journals. It quickly becomes apparent that very few articles are widely consulted. Extending this to pencilled marginalia, one finds very little of this in journals; books in the stack are full of it. I exclude here recent citation practice as being part of the 'journal game'.

study of the history of economic thought.

2.3 The Case for the History of Economic Thought

The grounds for studying the history of economic thought, and, more particularly, for imparting a knowledge of it to succeeding generations of economists, are numerous. Firstly, as Taylor has pointed out, general truths get lost with the progress of time because they become confused with specific applications in specific times and conditions (Taylor, 1955, p. 13). One has only to look at the different messages which succeeding generations have taken from Smith's great work (Black, 1976), and the salutary rediscovery of so much of Smith in later times, to realise the truth of this observation. Moreover, as Stigler has argued, 'time identifies the economists who were worth reading properly. Most of the articles, and probably all of them, in the next issue of the professional journal are not worth a careful and costly reading' (1969a, p. 221).

W.R. Allen has written eloquently of the dangers of relying on the '(momentarily) definitive textbooks':

> Who are to be the authors of these ...? I shall believe that they have been appointed by the Deity only when they appear to me from out of the mountain mists carrying their opera writ on tablets of stone. Until then, is no one to check up on these seers to make sure that no pearls of any sort from the past are lost? Even those in charge of summarising, improving, and teaching the best (and only the best) thought will occasionally find useful the contemplation of some things written prior to, say, last Thursday. How far back are we allowed to go before entering the realm of 'history'? Is it really never nothing more than sheer antiquarianism – to be both pitied and scorned – to read the writings of

> Keynes himself? and Fisher? and Wicksell? and Smith? (1965, pp. 143-4).[5]

The history of economic thought has a number of other benefits. In particular it is, as Edgeworth, said, corrective of one's estimate of authority and 'corrective of the narrower prejudices and deceptive associations which are sure to be contracted by those who have been confined to a single school or system' (1891, pp. 6, 11). It enables the economist to stand back from the fashions of the day, which can be almost as transient as the latest version of a word processing package, learning the intricacies of which has been instructively compared in usefulness to dodo-sexing. History of economic thought can act as an antidote to the 'pap culture' produced by the expansion of economics and the other social sciences, by planting the subversive suggestion that there may be more to learning than memorising sections of textbooks. It may – and one hopes it has – have the power to at least moderate that 'provincialism in time' of which Lionel Robbins complained (1952, p. 2); and just as there is none more blinkered in outlook than the metropolitan sophisticate, so there is none more provincial in time than the devotee of the latest theoretical development.

But in any case the history of economic thought should be a basic part of scholarship (Gordon, 1965, p. 125) – and, until recently, it has not been thought necessary to argue that scholarship is an important part of life in a university. The historian of economic thought may well indeed be the interpreter of the past to the profession; but without the specialist interpreter, and without the systematic cultivation of the history of economic thought, it will simply be invented ad hoc, as Terence Hutchison has pointed out (1951, p. 130). People will insist on referring to past economists, and such references, as one sees increasingly frequently with the decline in specialist

[5] As Roger Backhouse has shown, one needs to know the history of economic thought to read a textbook, for what is presented is akin to geological layers of accumulated ideas – as Backhouse argues, economics itself is a historical process (Backhouse, 1996).

study of past economists, are typically inaccurate (Grampp, 1965, p. 134). Loose references to 'Adam Smith's conjecture' as (like Fermat's Last Theorem (Singh, 1997)) waiting centuries for proof by modern mathematicians (in the case of Smith, Arrow and Debreu (cited by Hutchison, 1994, p. 300)) are, in their cavalier style, typical enough of what can be expected in the absence of proper specialist work.

Such cavalier references are often associated with those pressing the merits of the latest as the best; the lessons which a study of the history of economic thought provides, from Ricardo's work onwards, concerning highly generalised theory claiming policy relevance, is clearly at odds with the 'latest is best' school. The great economists who studied the history of economic thought have understood this; Viner was as distrustful of theoretical fashion as of ideological enthusiasm (Winch, 1983, p. 6) while Stigler noted that a sense of disengagement from current controversies, after studying previous ones, was inevitable (1969a, p. 222).

At the same time, studying the development of a theory, and the controversies which its development has occasioned, can be a valuable aid to understanding the modern theory, as Stigler himself noted in the case of utility theory (Stigler, 1965b, p. 66; Rima 1983, p. 274). More generally, the history of economic thought can be of considerable use in the professional training of economists who have to go out into the world with some idea of the weight which theoretical tools bear and of how important particular ideas may be in the broader scheme of things rather than in the latest textbook.

Of course the historian of economic thought has to face the fact that both the history of natural science and the flourishing history of medicine are not part of the training of natural scientists and of doctors and are pursued as academic disciplines in other contexts, such as philosophy departments. But this is only a problem if we insist on maintaining that economics is a science. The truth of the matter is that it is apparent, first of all to the historian of economic thought, that it is, as Hicks himself always maintained, a discipline not a science (Hicks, 1983, pp. 4, 365-75), and it is characterised by a lack of that linear progress which characterises natural science pursuits for long periods in their history. As G.B. Richardson has put in, 'there is no orderly inheritance of ideas; the gains of one generation are frequently jettisoned by the next according to the swing of the doctrinal pendulum ... [and] many ideas find their way only belatedly into the corpus of knowledge, having been entirely ignored when first expounded' (1955, p. 146).

The truth of the matter – though it is an unpopular truth with the 'latest is best' school – is that the world, and the historical literature of economics, is much too complex for such Whiggishness. In truth, the literature of economics is replete with examples of lost insights. Thus George Stigler, an enthusiastic endorser of neo-classical microeconomics nevertheless wrote that:

> The theory of marginal utility was revolutionary in another sense. It led to serious retrogression in important parts of economics, more by neglect than repudiation. The study of the supplies of factors of production other than capital virtually disappeared from economics, and the theory of economic growth vanished. The neat equations of marginal utility and general equilibrium had less to say on these subjects than the Smithian and Ricardian models (1978, p. 598).

Indeed the loss was greater than Stigler seems to have appreciated; he was confident that there were no microeconomics to be learned from Marshall (1969a, p. 217), yet, as Brian Loasby (1978) has shown, Marshall's demand theory was so old fashioned as to be avant-garde. Again it was Stigler who pointed out that while Adam Smith drew attention, extensively, to the role of self-interest in legislation, twentieth century economists like Pigou continued to write about a wise, impartial, benevolent state, and it was only with the advent of American writers like Niskannen in the 1960s that the focus of attention shifted and the whole literature on rent-seeking developed (Stigler, 1971, 1982, p. 9).

Whole areas of macroeconomics have at times been abandoned, including the business cycle literature which flourished up until World War II (O'Brien, 1997b), and even economic growth, the staple of economics from Smith to Marshall, disappeared from consideration under the influence of a 'Keynesianism' which – as is painfully evident from the advice given to successive British governments in the 1960s and 1970s – was founded on the belief that inflation of aggregate demand was sufficient to produce real economic growth.

These are big examples, but there are smaller, though no less illuminating, ones. For instance, in the field of international trade theory anyone familiar with Heckscher and Ohlin (Flam and Flanders, 1991) knows that what they argued is certainly not the same as the so-called Heckscher-Ohlin-Samuelson model, which is really dedicated to a single proposition – that, in general equilibrium, it can be shown that trade with identical technologies can increase welfare in the presence of differing factor endowments. Another example is provided by the history of monopolistic and imperfect competition literature; the mistaken assimilation of the work of E.H. Chamberlin (1933) and Joan Robinson (1933), whose 'classic' books are treated as containing the same analysis, is a nice illustration of Harry Johnson's dictum that a 'classic' is a book that everybody has heard of and nobody has read. In the context of that kind of analysis one might also observe that there is a lesson to be learned concerning the kinked demand curve. Endlessly, the invention of this is attributed to Sweezy. In fact it is to be found in Joan Robinson's *Imperfect Competition*; but it turns out that it originated in work by Hayes published in 1928 (Spengler, 1965). Those citing Sweezy also systematically ignore the fact that Hall and Hitch, who published in the same year as Sweezy, and also employed a kinked demand curve, explicitly acknowledged Chamberlin's two demand curves (Hall and Hitch, 1939, p. 122), which in turn actually date from the filing of his Ph.D. thesis in 1927.

At an anecdotal level things get even worse. I recently read a paper by a young economist which claimed that economists in the past had paid no attention to the effect of occupation on income distribution. I suspect that the author had not even heard of John Stuart Mill. Given the increasing ignorance of economists of past literature, it is far from inconceivable that such a claim could get past journal referees. Walter Eltis has a nice story of battling with fellow examiners in Oxford in the 1960s when self-styled 'Keynesians' wished to penalise students who wrote that interest rates rose during inflation (Eltis, 1993, p. xxi). This is doubly ironic. Not only is there a huge literature on precisely this point, but it was named by Keynes himself as the 'Gibson Effect' after an author of part of the literature (Keynes, 1930, II, 177-86). The truth is probably that most 'Keynesians' have not even read the *General Theory*. But at least the attitude to Keynes is appreciative; Hayek on the other hand has suffered endless denigration by people who have never looked at his work.[6]

Some knowledge of the history of economic thought is thus highly desirable to prevent not just bad scholarship but also bad economics. But the job which the history of economic thought can do is much wider than this. Firstly, history of economic thought can be a very good way of teaching theory, as shown successively by Edwin Cannan (1929), Lionel Robbins (1970, 1998) and Mark Blaug (1985). It is also possible to teach history of economic thought through theory, as demonstrated by Viner (1937) and Seligman (1925, 1926). A recent excellent text on macroeconomics has shown that this approach is far from dead (Snowdon *et al.*, 1994).

Secondly, the historian of economic thought has techniques which can be employed in a modern policy context. Terence Hutchison has demonstrated this admirably in *Economists and Economic Policy* (1968) and *Knowledge*

[6]The gradual emergence of the new and splendid edition of Hayek's works, with volumes edited by W. Bartley, Stephen Kresge and Bruce Caldwell, may help to rectify this situation.

and Ignorance in Economics (1977). As Stigler has remarked, 'Professor Hutchison has written two mordant volumes on the treatment of macroeconomic policy by contemporary British economists. They are unattractive tales of unjustifiably dogmatic recommendations, quick changes of direction, and convenient loss of memory. The tales could be matched in other countries' (1978, pp. 598).

In this connection we might note a methodological point. As Mark Blaug (1994, pp. 119, 132) has pointed out, the same economists who deplore methodology itself, and make ludicrous claims for the power of, for instance, general equilibrium theory, are also to the fore in making sweeping policy recommendations and claiming, both by implication and explicitly, the 'authority' of the subject. The now notorious letter signed by 384 economists in 1982 is a case in point. It is in disentangling the kind of mess that results in these circumstances that history of economic thought techniques have a clear role to play.

On a more modest scale, two other examples from macroeconomics of valuable work employing an het approach might be cited. Firstly, there is the work which Tom Humphrey (1992; 1993, pp. 303-12; 1997) has done in articulating Wicksell's policy rules for price stability – highly relevant when both the Federal Reserve and the Bank of England appear to be followers of Wicksell; and, secondly, a recent study of the economic thought of Arthur Burns has been able to explain convincingly the apparent paradox that this anti-inflation economist presided over a time of high inflation while a presidential adviser (Hetzel, 1998).

2.4 Approaches to the History of Economic Thought

Given that there is clearly a case for the cultivation of the study of the history of economic thought, it seems right to ask what kind of history of economic thought we want. Perhaps the easiest way into this is to indicate first of all some approaches which do not seem to me either helpful or likely to advance the case for studies in the history of economic thought.

Firstly, there is the search for respectable precursors for an idea that somebody wishes to advance. This kind of approach has been quite rightly condemned by Bob Coats (1983a, p. 148) as likely to involve either casual or wilful distortion of the historical record. I can myself remember, as a young academic, being asked to provide raw material for such an exercise, preferably finding a precedent in Ricardo; when all I could offer was James Wilson, of whom, it emerged, my interrogator had never heard, interest cooled rapidly. This kind of exercise can broaden out into the creation of spurious alternative 'traditions'.[7] Two examples which spring to mind (or at least spring to my mind) are Sraffian economics, and the enthusiasts for free banking. Involved in such an exercise may be a furious critique of all the other 'traditions' in which the underlying aim – to leave the ground clear for the one 'true' tradition to flourish – can be hard for the reader to pick up.

In general, this kind of exercise does not seem to me helpful. As Terence Hutchison has written, 'There is, perhaps, something rather questionable in the sort of intellectual generosity which assumes that Ricardo's interests and purposes, rightly understood, must certainly have been the same as one's own, when, after all, Ricardo was as explicit as he could have been that they were distinctly different' (1952, p. 423).

I am dubious, too, about history of *opinion*. This may be satisfactory as a starting point for research, and as presented it often contains a good economic history background. But it seems to me only a prelude to analytical work. As Bob Black has written, 'the question remains whether any survey, however exhaustive, of *opinions* about the workings and effects of a financial mechanism can conclusively support or contradict any theory about them'

[7]On the pressures exerted on the editor of the Keynes edition by competing 'traditions' of this sort see Moggridge (1997, p. 40).

(1965, p. 60; italics in original).

Then there is the 'lucky dip' or 'cor look at that' approach, as it might be called. In an age dominated by the requirement to publish journal articles, such an approach can well pay dividends; it provides the basis for a short, and apparently novel, piece and the claims for its novelty made by its author are increasingly unlikely to be constrained by any awareness of the full picture on the part of referees. But as Jaffé has written:

> Those who dabble in the history of economics may crow over finding a forgotten book by an obscure economist; ... but they rarely have any idea of seeking after original sources, of *systematic* documentary research, of pursuing elusive evidence of the efficient cause, not the sufficient reason, underlying the emergence of a new theory. ... The answer to such questions requires patient historical research and disciplined historical judgement, for the exercise of which economists in general are ill prepared (1965b, pp. 224-5).

Then there is the approach which, in its single-minded concentration on textual reading, is redolent of nineteenth century biblical scholarship (and which may, indeed, as in the work of the late Barry Gordon (Gordon, 1989; Ohrenstein and Gordon, 1992), involve actual biblical scholarship). Such an approach can result, as Stigler (1981) observed in reviewing Hollander's *Economics of David Ricardo* (1979), in a 'highly personal document' of a 'partisan' nature. The problem essentially becomes one of deciding what weight is to be attached to particular quotations, including, in this particular case, private letters, and parliamentary speeches. Stigler's position was that quotation-selection could distort seriously the record, 'Why should we allow the hand picked quotation to carry an interpretation when we would reject the hand picked fact as an empirical test of a hypothesis? In fact the two problems are basically the same' (1965a, 69).

Stigler's solution was that quotations should be tested by their consistency with Ricardo's model: 'The test of an interpretation is its consistency with the main analytical conclusions of the system of thought under consideration' (1965a, p. 69). Unfortunately, Stigler's solution is essentially circular – the theoretical structure to which he appeals is not independent of the weight attached to quotations. Thus Hollander, by attaching weight (and indeed emphasis) to sources other than Ricardo's published opus has managed to arrive at a fundamentally different interpretation of Ricardo's theoretical structure.

In dealing with problems of this sort it is necessary that there should be a body of scholars actively working in the history of economic thought. Essentially the decision on which is the correct theoretical structure to interpret Ricardo depends upon there being a 'scientific community'. This is particularly so because the history of economic thought regularly throws up examples of work which most scholars would regard as aberrant. Ronald Meek's view that the adoption of the marginal utility theory 'set the seal upon the incorporation of certain important elements of ideological illusion into bourgeois economic theory' (1957, p. 13) is by no means an isolated example; and readers of Roll's venerable textbook encountered a schizophrenic text in which the earlier part was 'written while Roll was clearly an ardent Marxist, and the latter part, when he clearly was not' (Perlman, 1983, p. 121). Sometimes the unusual views to some extent cancel out each other, as in the tense exchanges between Samuel Hollander (1973, 1975) and John Eatwell (1975); but more often this is not the case. Many of the curiosities of Schumpeter's great *History* were remarked upon at the time of its publication, by reviewers, but have since become, in some sense, part of the intellectual landscape. In particular Schumpeter's 'scientism' (in praising Walras's achievement Schumpeter asserted that Walras's was 'the only work by an economist that will stand comparison with the achievments of theoretical physics'; it was 'the outstanding landmark on the road that economics travels towards the status of a rigorous or exact science' – 1954, p. 827), and his denigration of Adam Smith and of Alfred Marshall, might have had considerable influence, perhaps, were there not a community of historians of economic thought who take different views. The denigration of both Smith and Marshall was part and parcel of Schumpeter's approach to the history of economics; it appeared in his 1912 book, long before the *History* and it was remarkable for its lack of balance (Schumpeter, 1912, pp. 64-5, 185-6). Indeed it is ironic that Schumpeter criticised Smith for his attitude to 'political Arithmetic' despite the lack of attention to econometrics in Schumpeter's own book, and despite the fact that, as one reviewer observed, Schumpeter's strengths as an economist were not dissimilar to Smith's own (Taylor, 1955, 17).

2.5 The Mainstream Approach

In order to provide a balancing role, when faced with aberrant interpretations, it is essential that the history of economic thought is cultivated by economists who are not seeking to advance particular private agendas but rather to interpret the literature of economics in terms of the mainstream training which an economist both receives and gives. At the heart of this must be Rational Reconstruction. However this term seems to be susceptible of a variety of interpretations and so it is necessary to indicate the meaning attached here. By 'Rational Reconstruction' I mean that the central concern is with the internal logic of a theory. Where there are gaps in the reasoning, the historian of economic thought can legitimately seek to ask what is required to fill the gaps, and what can reasonably be assumed as implicit knowledge on the part of the historical figure being studied. Thus it is reasonable to ask, as Walter Eltis has done, what Quesnay could have assumed about the returns to horse culture and oxen culture respectively (Eltis, 1984, pp. 3-21). A historical dimension enters directly via the plausibility of the assumptions made by the original writer. But at the heart of the argument is the theory.

This was the approach adopted by Jacob Viner in his *Studies in the Theory of International Trade* (1937), which has provided a model for so many subsequent historians of economic thought. The approach is essentially critical, rather than relativist, but is fair and not in any sense triumphalist. An approach which concentrated on the theory also characterised Viner's contemporary Frank Knight. Indeed Knight, having started off, so we are informed, with the intention of pursuing a relativist approach along the lines of the French writer Blanqui (Howey, 1983, p. 172), pursued an ultra-critical approach towards Ricardo (Knight, 1935). In turn, Knight's pupil George Stigler put theory (though not in any extreme sense) at the centre of his concern. This proved beneficial and illuminating; it was concentration on the theoretical content which led to Stigler's correct reappraisal of John Stuart Mill as an economic theorist:

> There have been only a tiny handful of enormously fertile theoretical innovators in the history of economics, and Mill has full rights to membership in this regal circle along with Smith, Marshall, and Edgeworth (1982, p. 97).

Concentration on the theoretical content becomes all the more important when extravagant claims are made for a certain historical economist as being an important 'predecessor'. This has been particularly the case with Malthus and other writers concerned with problems of aggregate demand, and Bob Black's (1967) disentangling of the issues involved demonstrates, without formality, how this can be done.

Concentration on theory does not rule out other approaches. In particular the history of analysis is not enough on its own, because policy attitudes are also extremely important. At the same time there is a need for treatment of analysis separate from policy attitudes. The long-standing denigration of the

Austrian trade cycle theory, for instance, has little to do with the internal merits of the theory and everything to do with the policy attitudes of Hayek, Robbins, and others in the 1930s which, I have argued elsewhere, were based upon a fundamental mistake of fact (O'Brien, 1998a, pp. 33-5; and Chapter 3). It is also possible, though I think it requires special skills, to produce a study of the interaction of theory and policy of the kind which Bob Black produced in his *Economic Thought and the Irish Question* (1960a). To study the two-way interaction between theory and policy is an intriguing research project; but it requires enormous amounts of scholarship and perseverance, and is certainly not something to be undertaken lightly or in the spirit of a 'quick raid'. A quick raid would not enable us to answer the question of how far theorists and policy makers realised the problems created by uniting a developed and a backward economy, nor enable us to find out how far the economists of the time were prepared to admit that the relative role of the public sector might differ between the English and Irish economies. Such work is very difficult; but when it is done well, as in Bob Black's study, it can be highly illuminating.

Concentration on theory thus does not rule out wider concerns. What it does rule out is a retreat into relativism. As Donald Gordon has reported, relativism frequently gives rise to what can only be described as 'atrocious economics' (1965, p. 127). In its most extreme form relativism does little more than insist that economic theory is a 'Reflection' of contemporary historical events. The relativist historian of economic thought then sets about examining the historical record to find out which historical events can be selected to explain the theories. The results can be frankly risible. After discussing one such treatment in which the diametrically opposed approaches of Mill's *Principles* and *The Communist Manifesto* were both found to be reflecting the historical circumstances of the late 1840s, Terence Hutchison asked sardonically whether it was 'all done by mirrors?' (1978, p. 252).

Of course historical circumstances do influence both the questions addressed by economists and the assumptions they make – and it is part of the task of the historian of economics to tease out the implicit assumptions. But after its inception, a theory becomes detached from its historical origins (Sobell, 1983, p. 246) and undergoes its own internal development – and, as Terence Hutchison pointed out, in criticising Wesley Mitchell, a purely relativist approach debars the historian of economic thought from examining the logical development of the theory (1951, pp. 125, 129).

2.6 Qualities Needed by Historians of Economic Thought

So concern with theory is at the core of the history of economic thought. But examination of theory has to be conducted in a sympathetic and scholarly way, taking account not merely of historical circumstances but also of wider intellectual considerations. What sort of qualities does the historian of economic thought require?

2.6.1 The Paragons

Any historian of economic thought confronted with the list of qualities attributed, by reviewers of his *History*, to Schumpeter, could be forgiven for throwing in the towel and pursuing something simple. According to Viner:

> This is a history of theory written on the grand scale by an economist who was an original, a powerful, and a versatile theorist on his own account. Schumpeter, moreover, was interested, deeply interested, in apparently the entire range of matters intellectual, was learned beyond the normal capacities of economists, could exercise with facility and with power the whole range of skills which the economic theorist employs, static analysis, dynamic analysis, historical analysis, mathematical and statistical analysis, partial

> – and general-equilibrium analysis, and so forth without visible end. He was able to deal familiarly with all ages and with the materials of a wide range of disciplines, physics, psychology, history, sociology, mathematics, philosophy, jurisprudence, and perhaps still others. This is a work written in the polymath manner by perhaps the last of the great polymaths (1954, p. 894).

Or consider the comments of I.M.D. Little:

> Schumpeter's intellectual range was very remarkable. He comments extensively on, among other subjects, Roman law, theology, political philosophy, ethics, epistemology, aesthetics, the history of science, sociology, psychology, not to mention economic history throughout the ages, and the proper subject of the book. The author index must contain about 1,500 names; and Schumpeter could and did evidently read almost every European language, ancient and modern, though he apologises for his lack of Russian. He balked at understanding no branch of economics in the wider sense, from history to mathematical theory, from statistical theory to the intricacies of *Das Kapital.* Besides all this, he was himself an original theorist of the first rank not lacking in the 'vision' which he rightly claims as essential for anyone who is to advance scientific knowledge (1955, p. 91).

The result is widely agreed to be a remarkable book, at once inspiring and illuminating, despite a comprehensive list of faults to which various reviewers drew attention. The breadth of Schumpeter's vision is astonishing; as Frank Knight remarked in reviewing the work, 'So far from being confined to "economic analysis", the book is more like a history of western thought from the standpoint of ideas relating to economics' (1955, p. 261).

While Schumpeter is arguably in a class of his own, other leading scholars have attracted similar descriptions. Thus Donald Walker writes of William

Jaffé that, in order to conduct work on Walras, 'he had to be thoroughly versed in neo-classical economics and to be familiar with modern theoretical developments. He had to know English, French, German and Italian. He needed a detailed knowledge of the social, political, philosophical, and economic history of the 19th century. He had to travel widely in Europe and have entry into many foreign homes and institutions' (1983a, p. 19).

For mere mortals, these descriptions imply an unattainable standard. However Stigler's description of the qualities of Lionel Robbins is more down to earth. Indeed it serves as a very good description of the basic requirements of a historian of economic thought: 'Lord Robbins unfailingly has shown analytical rigour, thorough and honest scholarship, understanding of alien minds, and unshakeable common-sense – a bundle of virtues that few rivals in his craft have approached' (Stigler, 1970). These are indeed the qualities to be looked for in a historian of economic thought. What sort of intellectual background would help to produce such qualities?

2.6.2 Requirements

Good work in the history of economic thought is hard. Viner is reported to have believed that it was an arduous and difficult art, calling for unintermitting self-discipline (Winch, 1983, p. 11). My own list of the qualities required would include physical stamina (particularly now that pre-1800 works are no longer available through the inter-library loan system, thus increasing the amount of travel required), which is particularly necessary with editorial work; a retentive memory which serves not only as a filing but as a sorting system; a genuine interest in ideas – where they originated, how they fit together and where they have led; an instinctive interest in the history of the subject; and an unwillingness to take as gospel the ruling fashion.

In addition to these personal qualities it is necessary, at least in my view, since I believe analytical history of economic thought is at the core of the discipline, that historians of economic thought should have a mainstream economics training.[8] Such training, which forces the economist to cope with modern analytical techniques, is not only valuable in developing analytical skills but it makes it possible for the historian of economic thought to communicate with economists who are not concerned directly with the subject.

Ideally the training of a historian of economic thought should also include some philosophy, some economic history, and, if possible, some wider subjects such as law or political history. Although such degrees can still be found in Britain by those who search diligently, they are not heavily subscribed, and are widely believed to offer few employment prospects – although, seeing the ease with which English literature graduates slot into stockbrokers offices, I find this hard to understand. It is however certainly true that such a degree might make it difficult to secure a place on a masters programme, thus shutting off one potential source of further training.

In practice it is thus necessary for historians of economic thought to be economics graduates, albeit ones prepared to undertake subsequent on-job training. Such on-job training should include a willingness to try to learn some languages other than English. The linguistic skills of economists seem to have deteriorated quite sharply even in the last four decades; and a comparison of work reviewed in mainstream journals in the 1990s with the reviews to be found in journals at the start of the century provides some evidence in support of this. Of course, as in the case of Keynes, there are some questions concerning how far the works in foreign languages were fully understood (O'Brien, 1998a, p. 34; and Chapter 3); but other economists, including Dennis Robertson, reviewed works in French and German, while Robbins fought a long battle to keep a language requirement in the London

[8] I taught International Economics (a subject which itself became increasingly technical with the passing of the years) throughout my entire time as an academic, as well as other mainstream subjects. I found this invaluable as analytical background when dealing with the history of economic thought itself. History of economic thought was not a majority of my teaching.

degree and Hicks has left an account of his learning of Italian (1983, p. 356).

The matter of languages is particularly important because translations can be both difficult and unsatisfactory. Schumpeter's German is widely recognised to have been particularly difficult to translate, both by professional translators and by academics more or less equally fluent in English and German[9] (Aris in Schumpeter, 1912, p. 1; E.B. Schumpeter in Schumpeter, 1952, p. xiii). Similarly, the version of Mises's *Socialism* (1936), in the excellent translation by Kahane, is pretty much a paraphrase when the text is compared with the author's *Gemeinwirtschaft* (1932). Thus some linguistic investment on the part of the historian of economic thought is highly desirable.

But the character of work in the history of economic thought has changed, as anyone comparing Blaug's *Economic Theory in Retrospect* (1985) and Cossa's *Introduction to the Study of Political Economy* (1893) will see immediately. This change makes it inevitable that there should be greater emphasis on technique. Technique is not optional for historians of economic thought. Mathematical, and indeed econometric, techniques can now be applied to the historical literature and the circumstances of its time with illuminating results.

But such investment in technique, while it requires time, does have the benefit of helping the historian of economics to survive and to work in other areas than the history of economic thought as well, as many of the great figures have done in our time, notably Baumol, Samuelson, Stigler, Patinkin, and Viner.

2.6.3 The Wider Intellectual Canvas

The philosophical background to economic writing poses particular problems for historians of economic thought. An economist who becomes too

[9] I can vouch for this from the viewpoint of someone with less fluent German, having translated some of Schumpeter (1908) into English as an exercise.

immersed in philosophical literature risks becoming separated from his colleagues (Tarascio, 1975, p. 37). Yet to attempt to tell the story without any reference to philosophical issues is to miss important aspects. The historian of economic thought is faced with a choice between getting out of depth and producing a lopsided account.

Essentially, historians of economic thought have got to be prepared to take their courage in both hands and to 'get in over their heads' just as mathematical economists are occasionally prepared to admit to doing (Klamer, 1984, pp. 32-3, 74-6). Philosophy cannot be ignored. Schumpeter's contention that the philosophical background was so much surplus baggage (1954, pp. 28-32, 780) is contradicted by the content of his own *History*, with more than half the book occupied by material which he apparently believed to be irrelevant to the history of economic analysis (Viner, 1954, p. 897; Little, 1955, p. 94). Ironically enough, commentators have pointed to deficiencies in Schumpeter's appreciation of philosophical issues, despite this. Taylor has argued that Schumpeter's treatment of Plato and Aristotle is defective (1955, p. 15) while Little has pointed to unsatisfactory aspects of Schumpeter's treatment of Utilitarianism and of Natural Law (1955, pp. 94-5). It is certainly evident that Schumpeter exhibited a sweeping tendency to see eighteenth century natural law and medieval natural law as equivalent (Taylor, 1955, p. 16). If even an economist so superbly equipped as Schumpeter, and so determined to write a history of economic analysis, ended up producing a work which was neither the history of economic analysis nor a work in which the philosophical issues were thoroughly explored, it is clear that the philosophical background has to be taken seriously.

Schumpeter apparently believed his claim that the philosophical background was superfluous – even making the extraordinary claim that Hegelianism was 'unessential' to Marx (1952, pp. ix, 10). But one has only got to look at more balanced treatments to see that this is unsustainable. Bob Black's essay on Bentham and the nineteenth century economists is a case in point

(Black, 1988a). Indeed broader intellectual history can be of great value, as Hayek's extraordinarily scholarly work on Saint-Simon displayed (O'Brien, 1994a, pp. 355-8). His material on Marx's youthful studies – which were far from 'unessential' to what Marx finally produced – shows what is to be gained from a patient examination of the philosophical background (Hayek, 1941b, II, pp.129, 131, 139, 145; III, pp. 287, 289-92; 1942-4, II, p. 45).

Of course it is true that spreading the intellectual net too widely carries with it particular dangers. In particular the analytical issues can be lost sight of. Indeed there seems to be a connection between this and the kind of extreme relativism exhibited by Wesley Mitchell which, in turn, influenced Spengler (Sobell, 1983, pp. 95-9; Spengler, 1968).

2.6.4 Philosophy of Science

Despite such dangers, philosophical issues cannot be avoided. Moreover, it seems to me that some sort of background in the philosophy of science is necessary for economists who write on the history of economic thought, at least in a twenthieth century context. It may well be that, as George Stigler (1978) has argued, there are either no revolutions in economics or, if they exist, they are of small importance compared with the cumulative progress of the subject. It may thus be that a Kuhnian approach (Kuhn, 1962) is not helpful. At the same time it is worth pointing out that Stigler's position was based upon a high level of confidence in the standing of microeconomics. He criticised Terence Hutchison's *On Revolutions* (1978) for paying too much attention to changes in macroeconomics in support of the idea of revolutions. But in fact the date of Stigler's criticism is telling – he was arguing, in 1978, on the basis of citation practice, that microeconomics was much more stable in intellectual content. But after that date microeconomics changed radically with the rise to dominance of game theory.

Nonetheless, there certainly are severe criticisms to be made of a Kuhnian approach. Yet *some* framework seems to be required.[10] I understand fully that there are real difficulties in identifying Scientific Research Programmes (since few authors agree on precisely the same delineation – c.f. Goodwin 1980) and in agreeing on the content of the Hard Core and so on, if we adopt a Lakatosian approach. But the value of the concept of a Scientific Research Programme can be demonstrated from something written long before the work of Lakatos. For it is precisely the concept of a SRP which is at the heart of Schumpeter's contention – which is in my view valid, despite the criticisms of Viner and others – that Ricardian economics was a detour.

2.6.5 Economic History

That economic history is intermittently linked with the history of economic thought is something which should not need emphasis although, with the disappearance of economic history from economics departments and from economic journals, it appears to do so.[11] It is clearly necessary to take account of the historical setting in which a theory was formulated, while acknowledging that theories then assume a life of their own. Not all economists accept this; Stigler extrapolated from his (valid) rejection of a 'Reflections' approach, of the kind referred to above, to all other 'environmental influences', treating these also as merely incidental (1960, p. 37; 1969b, pp. 336-7). Such a message is of course welcome to many economists because many economists now lack any knowledge of economic history. But, as already indicated, one fundamental question in a rational reconstruction approach (in the sense in

[10] My own experience, in attempting to make sense of microeconomic literature dealing with the firm in the inter-war period (O'Brien, 1983a) is that a Lakatosian framework can be extremely helpful – I vividly remember this coming to me on a footbridge high above the River Wear as I struggled in my mind to find some order in the inter-war microeconomic literature while walking to the university library. I am here talking about the Lakatosian framework as viewed in O'Brien (1983a, 1983b). For much fascinating material on the later critics of such an approach (and much else) see Backhouse (1997, 1998).

[11] It is sad that Hollander (1995, p. 301) reports a 'deafening silence' from the economic historians at Toronto when moves were in hand to reduce the importance of history of economic thought there.

which this term is used in this essay) is the realism of assumptions, or at least what assumptions a theorist could reasonably have made – and here some knowledge of economic history is indispensable. For those historians of economic thought who venture into econometric work, a care for the quality of data (which is more typically displayed by economic historians than it is by economists) is also highly necessary.

Economic history is not the history of economic thought but neither is it something which can simply be ignored by the historian of economic thought in the way that Stigler suggested. For some specialised kind of study, such as that of Bob Black on Ireland already referred to, it is completely indispensable.

2.7 Biography

The subject of what may loosely be called biographical work undertaken by historians of economic thought is worthy of particular discussion, not least because its value has been a matter of controversy between leading historians of economics. Although there have been recent, and outstanding, examples of biographical work relating to Keynes (see Skidelsky, 1983, 1992, 2000) and Marshall (see Coase, 1984, 1990), the writing of full biographies is not something which can any longer be undertaken by someone in full-time employment in a department of economics, and not all the biographies written have been so successful. Rather I am concerned with biographical work of a broader sort and, in particular, with editorial work. Editorial work is extremely hard, although it typically receives little credit. Economists, engaging in the kind of long-run scholarly work which was once associated with universities before the dominance of the journal article, have produced editions of the correspondence of Ricardo, Walras, Jevons, Overstone and Marshall as well as the huge quarry for scholars provided by the Keynes *Collected Writings*.

The road of the editor is a hard one. As Bob Black has observed, 'Editing ... is a form or aspect of literary scholarship; as such, it is a type of intellectual activity about which the great majority of modern economists know little and care less, because they do not see it as relevant to their science' (1988b, p. 20). For this reason economists are reluctant editors. As Bob Black, again, has put it, 'an edition of the works and papers of a leading economist is perhaps not so much something which people are likely deliberately and advisedly to decide to do as to have happen to them' (1988b, p. 25).

The struggles which Jaffé had to undergo to persevere with his Walras edition are well-known amongst historians of economic thought, though not fully acknowledged in print so far as I know (Hollander, 1995, p. 299); but virtually every editor can recall the difficulties that such perseverance presents.

Yet at the end of the day, as a result of Jaffé's activities, we do understand a lot more about Walras. As Jaffé himself insisted, biography helps us to understand the balance of the artistic creation which is a theoretical structure (Jaffé, 1965b, p. 226). Walras's *Correspondence* shows us what was driving him (Walker, 1983a, pp. 44-6). At a more detailed level we learn about Walras's reluctant embracing of the idea of variable coefficients of production (Walker, 1983b, pp. 46-7) and we can see how his relations with Picard and Amstein, and his reliance on Poinsot, explain both the form and limitations of his theory (Jaffé, 1965b, p. 229).

Jaffé had himself found much value in the imperfect selection of Marshall's letters published in the *Memorials* (Walker, 1981, p. 1013). We now have a full and comprehensive edition of Marshall's *Correspondence* (Whitaker, 1996) and much that was before unclear is now clear. In particular, as the editor of Marshall's *Correspondence*, John Whitaker, has observed, we can now see the letters which in the past have been quoted from, or referred to, with such telling effect (1996, I, p. ix). Indeed in some cases we can see that the letters do not even exist (O'Brien, 1997a, p. 1864; and Chapter 6).

From Marshall's *Correspondence* and *Early Economic Writings* (Whitaker, 1975) we can evaluate Marshall's later claims to priority and thus gain insight into the process of the Marginal Revolution. For both works throw light on the troubled question of the relation between Marshall's thought and that of Jevons, and on Marshall's strange writings on the question of rent and value. The *Correspondence* also throws light on the sometimes strident attempts to depict Marshall as some kind of politically incorrect ogre. In addition, his letters provide a good deal of information on his relations with his Cambridge contemporaries, especially the elder Keynes, and Foxwell (O'Brien, 1997a; and Chapter 6), and, as Jaffé himself has argued, the whole question of Marshall and the so-called 'oral tradition' requires biographical study (1965b, p. 228).

There is a particular value in the editing of correspondence. As John Henry Newman argued long ago, the case for letters is that 'Biographers varnish – they assign motives, they conjecture feelings – they interpret Lord Burleigh's nods, but contemporary letters are facts'.[12]

But from biographical work considered more widely we can learn about Jevons's unusual intellectual background, and in particular his thoroughly scientific one, which certainly helps to explain much about the particular nature both of Jevons's contribution and of his particular lines of attack on economic problems (Black, 1972c). Learning about the nature of an intellectual community can also be extremely helpful in understanding the path which particular developments followed, as at Trinity College Dublin (Black, 1947) and indeed to understand that, though Jevons and Cairnes were very much at odds over marginal utility, they were still fellow economists who could discuss other economic issues in a professional way (Black, 1960b).

Biography can also be a fruitful source of hypothesis. For instance the

[12] I chose this as the motto for the *Correspondence of Lord Overstone* (O'Brien, 1971). For the original see Newman (1970, pp. 442-4). The version quoted is the one given by the editor of the volume in a note as an earlier draft – Newman, 1970, p. 443n.

knowledge provided by the Sraffa edition about the relationship between Ricardo and James Mill provided the background to W.O. Thweatt's provocative thesis concerning the origins of the idea of comparative advantage (Thweatt, 1976; 1979, pp.14-15; O'Brien, 1988a, pp. 191-2).

Such insights are provided by scholarly work of high quality. It is unfortunate that the professional pressures now faced by economists make this very hard to pursue. For without professional and scholarly biography there will be what might be called 'ad hoc biography' – ad hominem arguments based on selected facts culled from places like the *Dictionary of National Biography*.

However we cannot avoid the fact that one of the twentieth century's leading historians of economics rejected the idea of biography as being in any way useful or valuable. According to George Stigler biography does not help us to understand economic theory. Science consists of arguments and evidence marshalled by a person and, so Stigler maintained, whether or not these arguments are accepted depends entirely upon the intellectual content and not upon the intellectual environment. According to Stigler 'biography distorts rather than illuminates the understanding of scientific work' (1970, p. 426).

It is then rather ironic that it is evident from Stigler's many asides that he was in fact well acquainted with biographical details. He contradicts Marshall's claim that J.S. Mill lacked free time to write on economics, and he refers confidently to W.T. Thornton and Mill as being friends and colleagues in the East India company (1982, p. 163). One may ask why, if it was all so useless, he was so effortlessly acquainted with the biographical material.

Stigler's attack upon biographical work (1976c) is extremely strong, referring to 'the Implicit Absurdity, the Hand-Picked Example, the Abhorrence of Evidence'. Yet none of the 'Hand-Picked Examples', which Stigler himself uses (and it is ironic that he in turn should resort to hand-picked examples, in view of his opinions upon textual exegesis) actually stands up very well to detailed examination. Moreover, specifically in the context of the life of J.S. Mill, which occasioned these strong comments from Stigler, it is not true that Mill's thought existed in a vacuum independent of, say, Mrs Harriet Taylor whose influence on Mill's attitude both to socialism and to women (I mean in an economic sense) is evident to the reader.

In any case, as Jaffé has argued, the faulty use of biographical material provides no case for abandoning this source of information (Walker, 1983b, p. 43). The respectful tones in which Stigler, not a habitually respectful reviewer, discussed Sraffa's Ricardo, indicates that, perhaps in his heart of hearts, he felt the same (Stigler, 1953). Stigler would maintain, and in this essay I have argued that such a view is correct, that analytical considerations and the logical structure of theory must be at the centre of the study of the history of economic thought. But this should not be taken to mean that biographical work, broadly understood, is in any sense redundant.

2.8 Conclusions

There is always room for good new work in the history of economic thought. Although much of Cannan's work has stood the test of time wonderfully well, the history of economic thought as a subject does not stand still. There have been important changes in the relative importance of different countries as sources of economic literature (Barber, 1998, p. 188) which are largely unexplored. Above all there has been an explosion in the literature of economics. The AEA Index for 1950-54 has 204 pages listing articles, or only slightly over 40 per annum; by 1981 the index required two volumes per year, and by 1987 the list of articles covers 876 pages for one year.

There is also a constant need for new discussion informed by the current concerns and techniques of economists. This means that at least some of the literature on the history of economics is going to get more technical (this does not imply, of course, any lowering of scholarly standards – c.f. Creedy

1986, 1989, 1992) – 'raising the quality of doctrinal history several notches' as one reviewer has put it (Collard 1992, p. 334). But this is a process which has been going on for a century, as the reference above to Cossa and Blaug makes clear. It cannot be avoided if historians of economic thought are to continue to communicate with the wider profession.

There is, or there should be, room both for the grand sweeping work of the kind at which Schumpeter was so good, and for the waspish short essay which was George Stigler's forte. Of course we should try to learn from both the strengths and also the defects of what has gone before; most basically we have a duty to be clear rather than bombastic – Schumpeter's tone has much in common with that of Marx when discussing other economic writers, and there is simply no basis for Schumpeter's lordly awarding of grades to past economic writers.

The previous literature shows us the competing dangers of arrogance (of which Schumpeter seems to have had more than his fair share) and of ancestor worship (perhaps Alfred Marshall's besetting sin in this context). To put it another way (as Stigler did) there are the twin dangers of hyper criticism and adulation (1969a, pp. 219-20). In warning against the latter, Stigler was able to cite particularly embarrassing pieces on Stalin by Meek and by Lange.

But I would argue that both these dangers can be guarded against by the kind of rational reconstruction which I have advocated in this essay. I would suggest that in this context model building pays dividends – not the kind of 'Ricardo-like' or 'Smith-like' model building which (to be unfair) attempts the *Wealth of Nations* in three equations, but model building which sticks as closely as possible to the original author's own model, as I attempted with Thomas Joplin (O'Brien 1993, pp. 256-70). There are serious reservations to be expressed about, in particular, Smithian modelling, as Spengler (1959) has shown; but there are much lesser economists whose work can be modelled more easily, and, even in the case of Smith, a serious attempt to disentangle the intellectual issues does pay dividends.

I believe that the history of economic thought as a subject will survive. But it will survive with difficulty. Some aspects of it will survive within the discipline of history, and the modelling and theoretical aspects on which I have laid such stress will, necessarily, be pushed to one side. Some of it will survive really in an underground form, as publication becomes more difficult. There will always be those who are fascinated by the literature of their subject; and those historians of economic thought who have published autobiographical material, notably John Whitaker, have made this clear to a wider world (Whitaker, 1998, p. 12).

It will also survive in less desirable forms, of the kind which I have discussed above, such as the creation of spurious alternative traditions. But where history of economic thought has a propagandist element there will always be those who, in the end, will step forward to put the record straight – as Patinkin (1976) did with regard to the claims of the so-called Cambridge Circus, as Mark Blaug (1987) did with regard to the Sraffians and other rather specialised interpretations of classical economics, and, arguably, as Alan Meltzer (1988) did with regard to the so-called 'Keynesians' and fiscal fine-tuning.

But 'in the end', like 'in the long run', has a certain resonance for economists – even if it is only the history of economic thought specialists who appreciate that the resonance of the latter phrase comes from the *Tract on Monetary Reform* (Keynes, 1923, p. 65) not the *General Theory* – and that resonance is not reassuring. In the long run – in the end – we are all dead; and I hope that the starvation of, and pressures on, scholarship, which would have been inconceivable 15 years ago, and in which so many academics have willingly or unwillingly participated, will not result in the death of the history of economic thought. History of economic thought is actually very hard; it involves a range of qualities which are not common in combination, and a degree of dedication – and of 'long-termism' – which should be of value to an academic community. If that community creates, as has happened in this and other countries, a situation in which these qualities are not valued, academics – and the students who might have been educated by those possessing these qualities – will be the poorer, as they have indeed become in recent years.

Chapter 3

Five Methodological Detours

This chapter considers five examples of apparent progress in economics, each of which proved illusory. In the first four cases the problem stems from factual errors. The fifth case deals with an episode of theory replacement on grounds almost entirely unconnected with factual shortcomings. The first four cases relate to: treatment by Arrow of scientific research; the obliteration of industrial economics by game theory; Pigou's use of legal cases to buttress his arguments about externalities in market failure; and the macroeconomic disputes leading to Robbins's *The Great Depression* of 1934. The fifth case concerns the replacement of the Mundell-Fleming model by monetary models of exchange rates.

I take the theme of 'detours' from Schumpeter, who argued that Ricardian economics was a detour which had effectively ended by 1830. Ricardo developed what Schumpeter calls a new 'engine' of analysis. 'This spelled decisive advance. But, of course, if a defective engine meets with success, that advance may easily prove to be a detour. And let me state at once: *a detour Ricardian analysis was*' (1954, p. 474). The implication of this view is that Ricardian economics illustrates an episode in which economists went astray; and I would draw the further lesson from this that they went astray for two identifiable reasons – an acceptance of the argument that assumptions do not matter; and an ideological drive which led Ricardo (was he snubbed by his neighbours at Gatcombe?) to attempt to construct a model which would prove to his satisfaction that the interests of the landlords were opposed to those of the rest of the community. On the first point Mark Blaug has written that 'Indeed, the divorce between abstract theory and empirical work was never more complete than in the heyday of Ricardian economics' (1956, p. 42).[1] Subsequent revisionist discussions (de Marchi, 1970; Hollander, 1979) do not seem to me to have damaged the essential correctness of this conclusion, although much has been made of the ambiguities, especially over time-frame, concerning 'prediction'. On the second point, Ricardo's association with the James Mill brand of philosophical radicalism would have provided enough motivation without any necessity to speculate on anti-Semitic (or anti-Arriviste) sentiment amongst the English aristocracy. At all events the first four detours do exhibit ideological elements as well as mistaken assumptions, and it is upon assumptions rather than predictions that this paper focuses.

These cases have been chosen because they illustrate clearly the nature of the problems; but they are not in any sense intended to be exhaustive. They all contain some illustrations of the danger of using 'stylised facts'; not only do stylised facts frequently turn out not to be facts at all, but the choice of such stylised facts not infrequently has an ideological basis, as illustrated by Terence Hutchison's brilliant discussion in *Economics and Economic Policy*, most notably when dealing with the work (or rather opinions) of Balogh (Hutchison, 1968).

Other possible cases will come to the mind of any reader. In particular the reconstruction of macroeconomics on a 'Walrasian' basis could provide another case. The claim that all the exciting developments in macroeconomics in the last 10 years have been Walrasian is extremely depressing. I agree with Mark Blaug's appraisal of general equilibrium (Blaug, 1994, pp.

[1] McCulloch has clearly to be exempted from this stricture; see O'Brien (1970, especially pp. 84-98).

124-6)[2] (though I think it is useful as a critical tool, especially in relation to partial equilibrium welfare economics); and I agree with David Laidler that Walrasian macroeconomics does not take money seriously (Laidler, 1990, p. 1). But the ideological basis of this development has been well documented in Mayer's recent book *Doing Economic Research* (Mayer, 1995, pp. 26-36, 73-91). It is hardly surprising that the idea of the neutrality of money in a world of economic actors with Rational Expectations seems at variance with monetary history – not only is money illusion all-pervasive in the histories of inflation (at least short of hyper-inflation) but changes in the money supply do produce changes in income, at least in the short run, despite the conventional wisdom concerning policy ineffectiveness. But these issues will not be pursued here.

3.1 Arrow

Arrow's work on scientific research has been enormously influential (Cosimano, 1981). Even where the results obtained by researchers do not seem to support his position, they are sometimes given an Arrow twist. Arrow's basic case is that first-mover research – above all, basic research – is underperformed by the private sector and that significant additional government finance is required (Arrow, 1962).[3] The argument is that a second-mover, benefiting from the work done by a first mover, enjoys costs that are so much lower, and returns which are correspondingly higher, that industry will only finance second-mover research and not basic research: 'Thus basic research, the output of which is only used as an information input into other inventive

[2] 'This is not to say that highly aggregated computable GE models (such as IS-LM) are pointless or that a GE formulation of an economic problem may not prove illuminating, but simply that Walrasian GE theory ... has turned out to be an utterly sterile innovation' Blaug (1994, p. 124).

[3] Arrow does not himself use the now conventional terms 'first-mover' and 'second-mover' (see e.g. Lieberman and Montgomery, 1988; Scherer and Ross, 1990) but these convey the essence of his argument.

activities, is especially unlikely to be rewarded' (Arrow 1962, p. 618).

Of course most basic research does indeed already appear to be done by the public sector (and by non-profit organisations) – but this is a statistical tautology, because basic research is typically *defined* as that not done for commercial purposes (Scherer and Ross, 1990, p. 616). Thus basis research (in a scientific sense) undertaken by a firm would not be classified as basic research.

Arrow's case is theoretically faulty, as Demsetz was later able to show (Demsetz, 1969).[4] But, much more seriously, it turns out that the case is based upon a fundamental misunderstanding of the nature of scientific research.

Arrow's background was primarily in mathematics and statistics (Harcourt, 1984; Feiwel, 1987). It is indeed tempting to speculate that, had his early work led him more in the direction of the huge economic literature on firms and technical progress, his ideas might have taken a different direction.[5] In particular, as later studies by Mansfield (1980) and Griliches (1986) have shown, firms that do basic research prosper. At the same time, it is also true that firms that do second mover research find it extremely expensive. Crucially, it involves basic research being done at the same time as second-mover research. The reason for this is that the only people who can do second-mover work satisfactorily are first-rate scientists. So firms that wish to do second mover research have to employ first rate scientists, and to retain them it is necessary to allow them to do basic research.

[4]As a theorist, Arrow naturally approaches the matter from the viewpoint of perfect competition (used interchangeably, in the conventional theoretical manner, with 'competition') and apparently had in mind comparison with an 'ideal socialist economy' (1962, p. 617). (A favourable reference is made, on the basis of information supplied in a 'verbal communication', to the ostensible separation of invention reward and charge for use, in the Soviet Union (ibid., p. 617n).) The main discussion is, however, in terms of Pareto optimality, in which it is argued that the optimal price of information is zero (ibid. p. 618). In truth, this is not necessarily the case when, as here, we are concerned with maintaining a *flow* of additions to the stock of information.

[5]For a summary of that literature available in 1962 see Scherer (1970, pp. 346-99).

Thus Arrow seems to have been misled on both counts. On the one hand basic research allows firms to prosper; on the other, second mover research is not cheap.

Kealey, a distinguished natural scientist,[6] illustrates this by reference to the cases of Tagamet and Zantac (Kealey, 1996, pp. 226-8). Tagamet was the product of a commercial organisation – and it involved basic research for which James Black was awarded a Nobel Prize. Zantac was directly inspired by Tagamet, but its development involved a team of top-ranking scientists. Neither product provides support for the idea either that first-mover research has to be financed by government or that second-mover research is cheap and easy.

So far from second-mover research being cheap, Japanese drug firms spend very large sums employing high-quality people scanning the literature (Kealey, 1996, p. 133). Certainly these Japanese firms find second-mover research is expensive. But second mover research can even cost dramatically more than first-mover research. Alexander Fleming was the first mover in the case of penicillin; but it was the second-movers (Florey and Chain and their team) who developed penicillin, and it could only be developed with the aid of a grant from the Rockefeller Foundation, the Medical Research Council having declined the application (Wilson, 1976, p. 150). Moreover the idea that basic research is for gentlemen financed by government, and should not be patented, can have serious economic implications. Chain fought a furious battle against this, but lost, and Britain paid large sums in royalties to the United States (in the immediate post-war years, when sterling was under particular pressure) (Kealey, 1996, pp. 136-7; Wilson, 1976, pp. 236-7).[7]

Yet sometimes economists seem to be extraordinarily naive about the

[6] I am grateful to John Ashworth who first drew my attention to Kealey's book.

[7] Wilson disputes this view, and it is true that the majority of licence payments were for the deep fermentation mass production technique developed by the Americans. But the basic point in the text is still valid and indeed material quoted by Wilson (1976, p. 237) supports it.

factual basis of their subject. One study of the Japanese drug industry which found that *first-mover* research produced a return on research and development expenditure of no less than 19 per cent (Odagiri and Murakami, 1992, p. 343) still felt 'tempted to argue that measures should be taken to protect the inventor's interest further' (p. 344) because the return on second-mover research and development was higher.[8] As Kealey commented:

> The arguments of Arrow and Nelson are so ingrained within the souls of academics who investigate the economics of research that Odagiri and Murakami, like everyone else in the field, just parrot them. Arrow and Nelson argued that, because companies can only sequester a small proportion of the benefit of their research, they therefore underinvest in it – hence their call for government funding. Odagiri and Murakami drew the same conclusion in their paper. ... But this is nonsense. Second-mover advantages are not free; they are very expensive, and that expense is dedicated to research, much of which is first-mover, or basic. While Zantac was being discovered, Glaxo's profits fell from £87 million (1977) to £60 million (1980) as research costs rose from £17 million (1976) to £40 million (1981) (Kealey 1996, pp. 227-8).

Further support for Kealey's claim about the mind-set of economists is to be found in the excellent text by Scherer and Ross which, despite reporting the huge literature on invention and innovation (Scherer and Ross 1990, pp. 613-60), still manages to endorse the Arrow-Nelson orthodoxy (p. 636) on which – inevitably – a game theory structure has now been built.[9] Game

[8] Odagiri and Murakami do however qualify the argument in various ways, contenting themselves with saying that one may be 'tempted' to argue for greater protection or assistance for first-movers, noting both the limitations of their study and the possibility of different kinds of external effects of which they have taken no account.

[9] In fairness it should be said that the same text also reports the extensive advantages also accruing to first-movers in a genuine market (as distinct from an imagined perfectly competitive structure), noting that 'The links between image advantages, market share,

theory figures prominently in our next story.

3.2 Industrial Economics and Game Theory

To be critical of the way in which industrial economics has been taken over by game theory during the 1980s, a decade now apparently celebrated as the decade of game theory (Rubinstein, 1990, p. ix), is to risk a great deal of personal unpopularity. Virtually all economists have now made some investment in game theory. Nonetheless it seems to me that the criticisms of game theory put forward both in methodological writings (Blaug, 1994, pp. 120, 127; Backhouse, 1992, p. 4) and more widely (Fisher, 1989) seem justified. Real industries do not have one-shot games; repeated games produce a wide range of possible equilibrium positions. As Fisher says: 'the full rich contextual story of how multimarket contact affects the ability to get to joint maximisation cannot be told by concentrating on Nash equilibria' (1989, p. 122).

There is also the basic problem that, in the intoxication of intellectual knitting patterns for which game theory provides scope, important information has to be pushed to one side – indeed suppressed – because game theory seems to have very little capacity for dealing with industrial data. With very limited exceptions, the striking characteristic of game theory treatments of industrial economics is the lack of contact with reality. Even exceptions to this, such as the important work done by Gavin Reid and his collaborators (Bhaskar *et al.*, 1991, 1993; Bhaskar and Machin, 1993) turn out to be of limited scope. It has proved possible to restate the kinked demand curve approach in game theoretic terms, in order to confront the reformulated theory with data; but while this is a valuable exercise on its own (and it is nice to see questionnaires making a comeback (Blinder, 1991) – two decades ago,

and a history of having been a first-mover have received impressive statistical confirmation' (1990, p. 585).

a suggestion of this sort (O'Brien, 1973) met with disfavour), this is only a very small part of the kaleidoscope of 'results' and 'insights' claimed for game theory in the literature of the firm.

Instead, the game theorists have to resort to 'experimental economics'. This originated with Chamberlin in the late 1940s (Chamberlin, 1948), but it seems to have attracted little attention at the time, and little emulation subsequently. This may well reflect good judgement on the part of the economists of that era; and it also reflects the fact that the original work of von Neumann and Morgenstern (1944) attracted little support as a research programme initially, within the field of economics. Game theory had an intellectual interest of its own; I have to admit to having read parts of von Neumann and Morgenstern as an undergraduate in the late 1950s. But its aims were relatively modest, and although there were distinguished exponents like Martin Shubik, and a host of others covered in the volume edited by Ariel Rubenstein (Rubinstein, 1990), it was a specialist interest. But now it has colonised an important area of economics, and its need for data has in turn reactivated the idea of 'experiments'.

Yet these 'experiments' produce oddly paradoxical results. They even lead to suspicions of irrationality on the part of participants. To some extent the suspicion simply reflects the failure of academics to employ common-sense evaluations of the costs and benefits of equipping oneself to take decisions with no real pay-off, as Demsetz has pointed out (1995, pp. 86-91, especially pp. 86-7). Some of these peculiar results have even apparently helped to provide natural scientists with a comforting feeling of superiority to ordinary people – 'There is some evidence that the scientific mode of thought is neither natural nor comfortable' (Wolpert and Richards, 1988, p. 2). On closer examination, however, it turns out that this judgement of the capacity of ordinary mortals is based upon a fundamental failure to understand what the ordinary mortals actually mean, and that the latter are perfectly correct in their intuition.[10] But both because of the limitations of 'experiments', and of the academic approach to decisions, the microeconomic literature contains plenty of examples of paradoxical results – including the finding of Schotter, Weigelt and Wilson that they got totally different results when they used two different sets of 20 pairs of subjects for an experiment (Schotter, 1994, pp. 217-8).

But there is no need to despair. Such paradoxes provide endless openings for yet more experiments. For such experiments, research grants can be obtained. Thus an enclosed process has developed its own momentum, while economists seem to have disengaged from industry.

The evidence for this disengagement is everywhere. In the 1960s the *Economic Journal* published (literary form) articles by Swann and McLachlan on competition policy (Swann and McLachlan, 1963, 1964). Nowadays not only would that journal not look at such material, but economists do not seem to have any views on competition policy.

Yet the origins of this are not intellectual but – at least in my view – ideological. The story I would tell would go something like this. The structure-conduct-performance literature, drawing not just on Chamberlin but also on J.M. Clark, and Workable Competition, had built up an impressive body of research with substantial empirical content. This was indisputably an area of

[10] Wolpert and Richards (1988, p. 2) continue: 'Experimental work by psychologists shows that people rely on a limited number of principles which reduce the complex task of assessing probabilities to simpler judgmental operations. In a very simple example, people expect that a sequence of random events such as tossing a coin is more likely to yield H-T-H-T-H-T than H-H-H-H-H-H, which is, in fact, not the case. The studies show that thinking statistically is not only difficult for many people, but an alienating activity'. However, this judgement of the capacity of ordinary mortals is based upon a fundamental failure to understand what the ordinary mortals actually mean. The sequence of 6 heads has a (classical) probability of $\left(\frac{1}{2}\right)^6 = 0.015625$. What ordinary mortals are contrasting is the probability of a run of 6 consecutive heads with a run containing some tails. Now there are many ways in which we can get a run with some tails and the probability of each of these (independent) sequences can be added. Thus there are 2^6 possible sequences of 6 tossed (fair) coins (=64) so that each sequence has a 1/64 chance (=1/2)6 = 0.015625. So ordinary mortals are perfectly correct in their intuition – a sequence containing some tails is 63 times as likely as one containing none at all.

economics in which the United States led the world. The work, in particular, of Bain was outstanding (O'Brien, 1983a, pp. 282-4). An excellent picture of the merits of this work can be found in the first edition of Scherer's *Industrial Market Structure and Economic Performance* (Scherer, 1970).

Of course there were, necessarily, imprecisions in the resulting intellectual structure, and policy applications needed to be tempered by common sense – as in practice they were, by the US legal system operating such broadly sensible pieces of legislation as the Sherman Act, the Clayton Act and the Celler-Keefauver Act.

But then, rather in the spirit of Ralph Nader, along came the 'Neal Task Force' and Senator Hart's Industrial Reorganisation Act.[11] This proposed taking a structural approach, without much reference to either conduct or performance, and was designed, more or less, to take a bulldozer to the existing American industrial structure, breaking up large firms on the grounds that their existence was not required by economies of scale. This would have created a legal framework for wholesale divestiture – the breaking up of American industry on the grounds simply that there existed positions of market concentration.

This was clearly an interventionist measure of an unprecedented sort. Divestiture powers had been allowed only sparingly, and with care, by American courts under the existing legislation (O'Brien, 1986, pp. 175-84). But the new approach could be viewed as an attack on the whole structure of private property.

The intellectual origins of this attack lie in previous academic discussions, and in particular in an influential book by Carl Kaysen and Donald Turner (1959). At about the same time there also appeared a revisionist form of economic history concerning Standard Oil, Rockefeller, and the origins of the Sherman Act (McGee, 1958). This was later to find favour with the

[11]The Hart Bill is contained in appendix B (pp. 444-8) and the Neal Report is in appendix C (pp. 449-56) of Goldschmid *et al.* (1974).

Chicago forces (e.g. Posner, 1976, p. 185).

It must be emphasised that the approach proposed to move from structure-conduct-performance simply to structure. For instance, the Neal Report proposed that in any industry with sales of $500 million, and a four-firm concentration ratio of 70 per cent, divestiture proceedings should be undertaken to reduce individual market shares to a maximum of 12 per cent.

Not surprisingly, such proposals caused economists, especially those associated with Chicago (notably Brozen and Demsetz), and some of the lawyer-economists (notably Posner), to question the whole intellectual basis of competition policy. (References can be found in Scherer, 1980, p. 337 and in Goldschmid *et al.*, 1974, which contains some of the important contributions.) The Chicago counter-attack was so effective that the Chicago economists managed to persuade the profession as a whole that predatory pricing was a myth, and that barriers to entry were unimportant. In particular, Brozen argued, with success, that the statistical association between entry barriers and profits was an illusion created by small samples and limited time periods, while Demsetz argued that large firms become large simply because they are more efficient. In McGee's view, the existing structure was the efficient structure. Ultimately, as Eisner has demonstrated (1991, p. 105), the Chicago version succeeded in virtually defining away barriers to entry, arguing that all market positions enjoyed by firms were subject to threat. The conflict between this mentality and a more traditional one can be seen in the disagreement between Brozen and Mann, during a conference convened to discuss these issues, in which Brozen argued that advertising *facilitated* entry while Mann argued that it was a *barrier* to entry (Goldschmid *et al.*, 1974, pp. 115-61).

The counter-attack was astonishingly successful. The Chicago economists were so good that they not only blew away the intellectual basis of the Neal Task Force's position, they also blew away industrial economics and, with it, competition policy. Indeed Kaysen recanted his former position (Posner,

1974, p. 414) and even provided a foreword to the book which recorded the successful outcome, from a Chicago point of view, of the IBM case, which is discussed below.

Thus it came to be very largely accepted, at least for policy purposes, that concentration reflects efficiency (Eisner, 1991, p. 105), that there is no welfare loss from concentration (Bork, 1978, p. 178), and that, if there were any possible benefits from deconcentration, these were certainly outweighed by the costs (Posner, 1974, pp. 393-400). The calculations by Scherer of minimum efficient scale in relation to total market size were subject to a highly effective critique by McGee, on the grounds that many cost dimensions were excluded from Scherer's calculations (McGee, 1974, pp. 55-97). McGee was undoubtedly assisted by the fact that most economists do not know much about industry, even though, at that date (1974), industrial knowledge was not actually regarded as a handicap. When McGee, Brozen and Demsetz confronted those favouring the new structural approach, the new school undoubtedly won, as the record of the conference shows (Goldschmid, *et al.*, 1974).

Perhaps the most heavy blow dealt to the intellectual basis of industrial economics and competition policy was the response of Fisher and McGowan to the anti-trust investigation of IBM. They used the new Chicago positivist approach to destroy the case put forward by the prosecution so completely that one feels considerable sympathy for their wretched opponents (Fisher *et al.*, 1983). Even though there is a different account of the IBM case, reflecting the views of the prosecution side (DeLamarter, 1986), the performance of the economists hired by IBM, together with the change in intellectual climate produced by the Chicago counter-attack against structuralism, resulted in the IBM case being dropped as 'without merit' in 1982, after 12 years of proceedings (Scherer and Ross, 1990, pp. 459-60). The government economists – McAdams, Preston and Weiss (subsidiary roles were played by Scherer and Houthakker) – were given such a hard time over their use of accountancy data as representing economic profit (Fisher *et al.*, 1983, pp. 254-7) that their opponents were ultimately able to record a sad capitulation (ibid., p. 257).

It is indeed ironic that, it having been established that IBM had no market power, the world then observed the loss of the (non-existent) market power with the rise of personal computers.

However, the episode had done enormous damage to the conventional approach to industrial economics, and cleared the way for game theory. I think it is apparent that Fisher, as his subsequent discussion of game theory makes clear (Fisher, 1989), did not intend to destroy industrial economics – but to that destruction he undoubtedly made a significant contribution.

The outcome for competition policy in the United States has been well summarised by Eisner:

> The intellectual dominance of economic structuralism was successfully challenged by the Chicago school. A body of expertise that supported the multiple goals of policy and an activist enforcement agenda was replaced by a school of thought that questioned the logic of state intervention in general and the mission of anti-trust in particular. As the economic staffs at the two agencies [Federal Trade Commission and Department of Justice] adopted Chicago-based enforcement criteria and as court doctrine embodied the new consensus, agency case loads evolved to reflect Chicago school priorities (Eisner, 1991, p. 230).

Indeed, as Eisner notes, 'politics, in essence, lagged behind policy. ... any discussion regarding the merits of a Chicago-based enforcement agenda was immaterial, for the changes in policy and administration were well in place and unlikely to prove responsive to the demands of political officials' (1991, p. 233).

It was, of course, not only the United States which was affected in this way. In Britain there was, in the 1980s and 1990s, little active competition policy. The government appeared unwilling to interfere with most mergers in practice, the reports of the Monopolies and Mergers Commission (not to mention implementation of the recommendations of these reports) were in no danger of being regarded as consistent, and competition policy was been largely replaced by ritual exercises such as the abolition of the Net Book Agreement. With a change of administration there was some revival, althought in practise this amounted to little more than long drawn out (and sometimes pretentious) examinations of the structural implications of merger proposals.

In summary, then, this section of the paper is arguing that game theory filled a vacuum left by the destruction of industrial economics; that that destruction was ideological in origin; and that the very detachment of game theory from genuine industrial data was part of its attraction as a device for filling the vacuum.

3.3 Pigou and the Factual Background

The lack of correspondence between Pigou's account of the factual background, and in particular of the legal framework, to his writings on welfare economics and the actual situation, is well-known since Ronald Coase's attack on Pigovian welfare economics in 1960. But it is perhaps worth reminding ourselves of Coase's view that Pigou's recommendation that the State should interfere in the case of railway engine sparks 'is based on a misapprehension of the facts' (1960, p. 29). For the State itself was responsible for the fact that *statutorily authorised* railways enjoyed protection from larger claims for damage to agricultural crops; and the State had itself chosen to make some limited provision for compensation, such limit being a deliberate choice of the legislature. It had nothing whatever to do with the consequences of an unregulated 'state of nature' in the market.

Steven Cheung also noted the extraordinarily thin factual basis for Pigou's structure of a divergence between private and social costs, noting that, apart from the case of a polluting factory (and Sidgwick's lighthouse, of which more below) convincing examples were hard to come by until Meade's 'apples and bees' example (taken over in turn by Bator).

Two points stand out from Cheung's discussion. Firstly, 'Most of Pigou's examples, however, were drawn from land tenure arrangements in agriculture, but an exhaustive check of his source references has revealed no hard evidence at all to support his claim of inefficient tenure arrangements' (1973, p. 11). Secondly, the 'apples and bees' example turns out, again, to have no real factual basis, as Cheung is able to demonstrate in considerable detail. Essentially Meade had invented a 'stylised fact' of the kind so beloved of economists. The bees and apples case is introduced as if it were obviously true (Meade, 1952, pp. 56-8) and a laborious mathematical model is then constructed on this supposed foundation. Meade is then able to conclude that, 'Capitalists in apple-farming should be subsidised because the unpaid benefits which they confer upon the bee-keepers more than outweigh the unpaid benefits which they receive from labour and capital employed in bee-keeping' (1952, p. 61).

As Cheung says of Meade and other economists in the Pigovian tradition: 'My main criticism ... concerns their approach to economic enquiry in failing to investigate the real-world situation and in arriving at policy implications out of sheer imagination. As a result, their work contributes little to our understanding of the actual economic system' (1973, p. 33).

Perhaps the splendid setting of Cambridge encouraged what I have called elsewhere 'Ivory Tower Empiricism' (O'Brien, 1984, p. 252). At all events there is no doubt that a significant intellectual structure, which was held to have policy implications, was built on a basis which involved a less than adequate acquaintance with the facts.

Pigou himself may be less to blame than some of his successors. In the main part of his discussion of externalities (1932, pp. 172-203), it is true that he posits the existence of 'the general divergences between the values of marginal social and marginal private net product that occur under simple competition' (1932, p. 174); but he does refer to empirical sources such as Bonn (1906) as well as to second-hand accounts of such divergences such as Nicholson (Nicholson, 1902; Pigou, 1932, pp. 174-5).[12] Yet two things stand out; firstly, there was a substantial literature on this going back to Adam Smith, and the topic had been explored in detail by McCulloch, whose knowledge of agriculture was enormously greater than that of Pigou (e.g. McCulloch, 1859d, pp. 165-222; O'Brien, 1970, pp. 374-8). (McCulloch is not mentioned by Pigou.) Secondly, in so far as the divergences cited by Pigou – notably under-investment by tenants, because landlords get the land back at the end of the lease – existed, they could not only be remedied by a redefinition of property rights but they had, at the time that Pigou was writing, mostly been remedied in that way.

As is well known, Pigou (1932, pp. 213-228) also built a substantial part of his argument on propositions concerning the welfare implications of increasing and decreasing supply prices. Not only was this argument logically confused as is also well known (Young, 1913; Knight, 1924; Ellis and Fellner, 1943) but there were no empirical counterparts to the intellectual constructions, as was pointed out by Clapham (1922). The whole structure really again involved stylised facts. Had Pigou considered the matter seriously (and it would seem from his reply to Clapham – Pigou, 1922 – that he did not) he might in turn have noticed that the whole apparatus was logically faulty. Instead he made a vague appeal to future statistical developments (1932, pp. 227-8).

[12]Nicholson as a source was, in any case, seriously outdated; the material to which Pigou referred was a reprint of chapter 8 of Nicholson's book of 1883, *Tenant's Gain not Landlord's Loss*.

But the most striking 'stylised fact' in this context is the lighthouse case (Pigou, 1932, p. 184). For even Cheung, in his otherwise highly critical article, had accepted this as a valid case. Yet only a year later Ronald Coase showed that this also was a product of the imagination (Coase, 1974). As Coase noted, in quoting Gilbert and Sullivan's *The Mikado*:

> The question remains: how is it that these great men have, in their economic writings, been led to make statements about lighthouses which are misleading as to the facts, whose meaning, if thought about in a concrete fashion is quite unclear, and which, to the extent that they imply a policy conclusion, are very likely wrong? The explanation is that these references by economists to lighthouses are not the result of their having made a study of lighthouses or having read a detailed study by some other economist. Despite the extensive use of the lighthouse example in the literature, no economist, to my knowledge, has ever made a comprehensive study of lighthouse finance and administration. The lighthouse is simply plucked out of the air to serve as an illustration. The purpose of the lighthouse example is to provide 'corroborative detail, intended to give artistic verisimilitude to an otherwise bald and unconvincing narrative' (Coase, 1974, pp. 374-5).

The robustness of Coase's demonstration that the lighthouse example was based on fantasy is shown by the unconvincing nature of the later attempts to criticise his work.[13] Indeed in all this there are two exquisite ironies relating

[13] Thus Zandt (1993) questions the public/private dichotomy in the provision of lighthouses, but stretches the definition 'public' (via government) to include the establishment of property rights and in his section (pp. 50-53) on excludability misses the point that exclusion could work (Coase, 1974, pp. 361-2), with tolls collected at by ports by agents (Coase, 1974, pp. 364-5, 375), relying instead on J.S. Mill's statement of the conventional wisdom – which Coase had already quoted at the start of his demolition of the conventional wisdom (1974, p. 357).

this section of the paper to that dealing with Arrow. Firstly, the Arrow hypothesis concerning first-mover research is actually to be found, long before Arrow, in Pigou's *Economics of Welfare* (1932, p. 185). Secondly, Arrow also figures in the lighthouse story; as Coase notes, Arrow offers a picture of lighthouse operation (where he side-steps excludability and instead treats the problem as a small number, indeterminate price, case) which Coase rightly describes as 'surrealistic' (1974, p. 376).

3.4 Hayek, Robbins and the Great Depression

The conflict over macroeconomics – not merely macroeconomic policy but the fundamental theoretical basis of macroeconomics – in Britain in the late 1920s and 1930s was the product of several different forces. On the one hand there were indeed pressing policy questions, especially following the Wall Street Crash, the succeeding banking failures in Europe, and the breakdown of the reconstituted gold standard (Yeager, 1976, pp. 335-6). But there were also very fundamental personal tensions, most notably between Robbins and Keynes, Keynes having treated the younger man with little ceremony in the Economic Advisory Council Committee (Robbins, 1971, pp. 151-2; O'Brien, 1988b, pp. 13-16). In addition to this, Robbins, unlike most of the Cambridge economists, read German and was widely read in recent macroeconomic literature published in that language.

As is well known, Keynes claimed to be unable to understand German unless he already knew what the argument was (1930, I, p. 178). Hayek for his part accepted this as true, commenting that 'The world might have been saved much if Lord Keynes's German had been a little better' (1992, p. 131). Keynes's ignorance of German certainly raises some puzzles; as has recently been pointed out, he published a review of Mises's long and complex book on money *Theorie des Geldes und der Umlaufsmittel* in the *Economic*

Journal 1914 (Keynes, 1914). This has naturally led to the suggestion that he had mastered the art of reviewing a book without reading it (Haberler, 1995; Saffran, 1996, p. 188). Even more puzzling, perhaps, is the fact that Keynes, in his obituary of Wilhelm Lexis, cites a number of works in German, and refers to some of the content (Keynes, 1933, pp. 317-8).

Whether linguistic incapacity or intellectual resistance lay at the root of the matter is thus unclear; but at all events it is apparent that Robbins was aware of the Austrian followers of Wicksell (whose own work had only been published in German and was not, at that time, available in English), in particular Mises, Hayek and Haberler, in a way which Keynes certainly was not. Persuaded of the importance of this work, Robbins can be said to have been looking for allies, and indeed it was on his initiative that Hayek was invited to LSE to deliver the lectures which resulted in *Prices and Production* (Hayek, 1931a). Hayek was subsequently appointed to the Tooke Chair at LSE (Hayek, 1994, pp. 77-8).

Robbins essentially adopted the trade cycle theory developed by Mises and Hayek, and it provided the theoretical structure of his *The Great Depression* (Robbins, 1934c). But in expounding this theoretical structure, Robbins did not do so in a data-free way; he did not go as far in an a priorist direction as either Mises or Hayek (Stewart, 1979, pp. 118-21, 233) – or, if we accept Terence Hutchison's view, Hayek up to 1937 (Hutchison, 1981, pp. 210-24). The methodological position in Robbins's *Essay on the Nature and Significance of Economic Science* (1932) is a priorist but also verificationist – under the influence of Cairnes, Robbins accepted that it was perfectly appropriate to check that a theory could be used in a particular factual setting (Blaug, 1980, pp. 53-93, especially pp. 77-81, 86-91; O'Brien, 1988b, pp. 36-7). It is this verificationist element which explains the substantial amount of empirical material (36 pages of tables) with which the book ends.

Yet in Robbins's and Hayek's interpretation of the factual setting there was a fundamental error (O'Brien, 1994b, p. 360; and Chapter 8). The crisis is blamed on monetary expansion in the United States (Robbins, 1934c, pp. 73-4). Believing this to be the case, the Austrian recommendation was to 'sweat out' the depression, on the grounds that depression was the inevitable concomitant of the preceding boom, and that things would return to normal once the fever had passed. The depression was being prolonged precisely because governments would not face the necessity for monetary rectitude: 'We eschew the sharp purge. We prefer the lingering disease. Everywhere, in the money market, in the commodity markets and in the broad field of company finance and public indebtedness, the efforts of Central Banks and Governments have been directed to propping up bad business positions' (1934c, p. 73).

But even on the data in Robbins's own appendices, the basic factual assumption was wrong. In particular table 3 (showing shrinking capital issues) is inconsistent with the idea of monetary expansion, and there is some indication in table 17 (bank loans and discounts) that the money supply was contracting. Part of the problem may lie in the fact that Robbins did not assemble his own appendices – there is really no substitute for getting one's hands dirty with data. Another part of the problem lay in the fact that the data which he was employing was not really that most appropriate for the purpose (Steindl, 1995, pp. 55-7). We now know, from the work of Friedman and Schwartz, that the United States money supply fell by one-third over the years 1929-33 (Friedman and Schwartz, 1963, pp. 299-419; Steindl, 1995, pp. 47-53). Indeed, from August 1931 to January 1932 the money stock fell at the astonishing annual rate of 31 per cent (Friedman and Schwartz, 1963, pp. 317-18). On this basic factual matter, Robbins was simply wrong (Steindl, 1995, pp. 128-30).

In all of this there is an element of personal tragedy. For Robbins, a deeply honourable man, felt that he had no alternative but to espouse an equally deeply unpopular position on the basis of his understanding of the data – the understanding which was the basic assumption on which the Mises-Hayek model was applied to depression. Yet his basic factual starting point was in error.

3.5 Models of Exchange Rates

The final case considered in this paper is one where a model which was fundamentally unrealistic, the Mundell-Fleming model, which had been the standard model of exchange rates in the 1960s, was abandoned in favour of monetary models of exchange rates. The process simply involved exchanging one flagrantly unreal set of assumptions for another. The Mundell-Fleming model, which was an orthodox Keynesian model, assumed a fixed price level since it was developed from the IS-LM framework. It also analysed balance of payments equilibrium in terms of balancing flows on capital account. Yet it was not the fixed price level which caused the model to be abandoned during the greatest world-wide explosion in inflation in human history:

> The model was largely rejected on a priori grounds as a serious contender for the explanation of exchange rate movements at the beginning of the recent float. This was because it was judged to contain a fundamental flaw – it is cast almost entirely in flow terms. In particular, the model allows current account imbalances to be offset by flows across the capital account, without any requirement of eventual stock equilibrium in the holding of net foreign assets (MacDonald and Taylor, 1992, p. 3).

The monetary models which, in a variety of variants, replaced the Mundell-Fleming one, did indeed allow for varying price levels; but coupled this with the astonishing assumption that purchasing power parity held instantaneously and at all times (e.g. Mussa, 1976, 1979). It was not until the second generation of monetary models, beginning with Dornbusch (Dornbusch, 1976), which partially reinstated the Keynesian type of framework while abandoning the idea of a fixed price level, that this problem was addressed.

The choice of model of exchange rates has thus been driven more by the search for theoretical consistency than by any regard for empirical shortcomings. It is thus hardly surprising that a succession of researchers, starting with Meese and Rogoff (1983), should have found poor 'out-of-sample' performance of these models.

3.6 Conclusions

I have deliberately painted each of these episodes in rather strong colours to bring out the key point that economists theorise – especially if they draw policy conclusions from their theories – in the absence of a firm empirical foundation, at their peril. This does not mean that I take this aspect of the empirical nature of theories to be the only important one; rather I am arguing that it is an important one. Several of the cases discussed illustrate the truth of George Stigler's dictum that the greatest mistake economists ever make is to believe other economists. The empirical basis of a theory really is relevant.

The role of prediction is still of fundamental importance. If we set aside that discipline, we open the door to mountains of economic literature which, as in the Sraffian case, conceal an ideological programme beneath a mathematical structure which is rhetorical – persuasion through demonstration of expertise – in intent and which is spared painful confrontation with the real world. Indeed I am reminded by Sraffianism of the story told by Hogben about Diderot and Euler. Diderot, staying at the Russian court, was, it was feared, undermining the religious faith of the courtiers.

> Diderot was informed that a mathematician had established a proof of the existence of God. He was summoned to court without being told the name of his opponent. Before the assembled court,

> Euler accosted him with the following pronouncement, which was uttered with due gravity: '$\frac{a+b^n}{n} = x$ donc Dieu existe' (Hogben, 1936, p. 1).

But if we accept the importance of testing, and accept what Mark Blaug once called constraints on what we allow ourselves to believe, we necessarily run the risk of encountering falsification. If theory does not forbid anything then we are wasting public money – engaged in the intellectual equivalent of publicly financed origami. I subscribe entirely to the view that a theory must forbid the existence of some sets of circumstances if it is to be either interesting or useful. The capacity for universal retrodiction is not – and this applies to game theory.

Of course the critics of falsificationism have made much of the so-called Duhem-Quine problem. If a theory is falsified, we do not know at what point the argument has broken down, to put this in its most straightforward terms. But if we have paid sufficient attention to the factual basis on which the theory was constructed – if we have the courage to defy both Friedman and Popper on the question of what may be called, for shorthand purposes, the realism of the assumptions – then we have a far better chance of discovering where the breakdown has occurred.

For, in the last resort, assumptions do matter. It is extremely unfortunate that Friedman's flamboyant claim to the contrary, based on a confusion between 'negligibility', 'domain' and 'heuristic' assumptions (Musgrave, 1981), should have been accepted at face value by the majority of economists. Acceptance has been greatly assisted by Popper's attack on induction, which is actually a separate issue; but even Popperians now accept that Popper's rejection of induction was too sweeping – indeed that it went so far as to damage the case for Popper's own approach (Hands, 1993, pp. 126-30; Blaug, 1994, p. 112).

The belief that assumptions do not matter has also facilitated that retreat into sterile mathematical formalism which has been such a feature of economics in recent decades. Of course economists are not alone in this: biologists, frustrated at the impossibility of explaining the irreducible complexity of cells in Darwinian terms, have resorted instead to complex mathematical models of evolution which simply *assume* that the insoluble problem of such explanation can be solved (Behe, 1996).[14] But the problem really does seem to be worse in economics than anywhere else, and the urge of those who conduct, in economics, activities similar to the mathematical biologists, to attempt to have their cake and eat it, by claiming real-world policy applications, seems to be uniquely strong. Essentially economists do need the discipline of a well-attested factual basis for their structures. Stylised facts are not merely inadequate; they are almost always not facts at all.

[14]'Hard nosed chemists have begun to drown their frustrations in mathematics' (Behe 1996, p. 161); 'Although useful for understanding how gradual processes behave over time, the mathematics *assumes* that real-world evolution is a gradual, random process; it does not (and cannot) demonstrate it' (Behe, 1996, p. 174).

Chapter 4

Information and Investment in a Wider Context

It can fall to few authors to succeed in generating, with a single work, a sub-culture in which professionals, familiar with the work, all acknowledge both its importance and its neglect by the wider intellectual community. Yet this is precisely what George Richardson achieved with *Information and Investment.* Nonetheless, precisely because it is a sub-culture that is involved, the real nature of the book's importance and influence remains shadowy, and it may well be that for others, as for me, the matter has required some further reflection. It is with gratitude that I recognise that the invitation from Brian Loasby has enabled me to engage in such further reflection.

I first read George Richardson's classic *Information and Investment* in the 1960s when working with Dennis Swann on information agreements (O'Brien and Swann, 1966, 1968). The argument of the book has continued to nag away at me over the years. On the one hand, as Dennis Swann and I made clear in a number of publications (O'Brien and Swann, 1966, 1968; Swann and O'Brien, 1967; Swann, O'Brien *et al.*, 1974), it was hard to accept Richardson's favourable attitude towards cartels (1960; see also 1965, 1966, 1967), an attitude which we believed – increasingly, as we studied these organisations – was fundamentally misconceived. On the other hand it was clear that Richardson had identified a fundamental problem with conventional analysis. It is only with the writing of this paper that I think that I have finally identified the nature of the difficulties which have been nagging away at me over these years.

One problem, I shall argue, which relates to Richardson's profound and entirely valid criticism of general equilibrium, is the fact that his critique failed to include time, a neglect of which is, I believe, at the heart of the incoherence of attempts to employ general equilibrium in the analysis of concrete competitive situations.

This neglect of the role of time in turn led Richardson to fail to allow sufficiently for time, except as a possibly beneficial friction in permitting adjustment to take place, when he came to consider *actual* competition – as distinct from *perfect* competition which I once heard Leijonhufvud call a perfect contradiction in terms. For it is time which, in real competition, solves many of the problems which Richardson believed cartels might be needed to solve.

To avoid both misunderstanding and accusations of nihilism, I should say that general equilibrium does have a valid role to play, as a critical device designed to show the limitations of conclusions – especially welfare conclusions, most especially those relating to taxation – drawn from a partial equilibrium framework, and in this form was employed successfully by authors as disparate as Edgeworth and Robbins. Richardson's criticisms seem to me much more damaging to the idea of general *equilibrium* than to that of analysing the interactions within the economy in a general equilibrium framework.

It was in considering genuine competition that a second very real difficulty arose. For Richardson seems to have allowed himself to be bemused by what might be called the 'Perfect Competition Shuffle'. This requires some explanation. In the debates over competition in the 1930s, and especially in the 1930 exchanges between Sraffa, Shove and Robertson, one group consistently took propositions from *perfect* competition and then argued as if they were the concomitants of *all* competition. This 'shuffle' was performed with particular virtuosity by Sraffa; and although it did not fool the acute Gerald Shove, Dennis Robertson does seem to have been taken in (O'Brien, 1984, p. 253). But one cannot draw any conclusions about how *industrial* competition may or may not work, from *perfect* competition – in which competition does not exist. It is the word 'competition' which permits the verbal trick. Inter-war economists were by no means universally deceived – a notable exception is Chamberlin (1933, pp. 6, 25-9). Moreover Richardson himself at various points, like P.W.S. Andrews, agrees that there is no actual competition in perfect competition (Andrews, 1949, 1964). Yet throughout the book he slips repeatedly, at least as it seems to me, between perfect competition and actual competition; and it is this which leads to his endorsement of cartels and cartelisation.

The order of the discussion is as follows. After considering Richardson's criticism of general equilibrium I go on to consider his attempts to graft elements of Marshall's analysis on to the general equilibrium model in an attempt to remedy the defects that he had correctly identified. I then discuss the way in which Richardson proceeded from this to endorsement of both cartels and national planning. Finally I note contributions from the wider literature which Richardson did not discuss but which were, and still are, relevant to his argument. But let us begin by looking at Richardson's very real achievement.

4.1 Richardson's Criticism of General Equilibrium

Richardson's key insight was that general equilibrium is impossible because perfect competition could not provide enough information (1960, pp. 1-2; a preliminary statement is in Richardson, 1959). As Richardson elegantly put it:

> It [perfect competition] shows that a particular economic configuration, if associated with a particular set of beliefs, can be regarded as self-perpetuating so long as the ultimate determining conditions remain unchanged. No explanation was given, however, of how these beliefs could come to be established, no account was offered of the information upon which, if rationally held, they would have to be based, and no proof was given that this information would, under the conditions which define the model, be available. The analysis cannot therefore be regarded as offering sufficient grounds for the conclusion that, if once the general equilibrium were attained, it would persist. Far less ... does it entitle us to claim that, under perfectly competitive conditions prices and outputs would actually tend to their equilibrium values (1960, p. 9).

As Richardson argues, equilibrium cannot be defined without reference to knowledge (1960, p. 5); and, paradoxically, 'there is clearly no presumption that the general equilibrium of production and exchange would be reached provided that all the members of the system had full information about its ultimate determinants' (1960, p. 6). The identification of a perfectly competitive equilibrium 'represents a system in which entrepreneurs would be unable to obtain the minimum necessary information' (1960, p. 2). Thus identification is a long way from the prospect of attainment. In turn, as Richardson argues, there is little point in having a perfectly competitive equilibrium as an ideal if there is no indication that it could ever be reached (1960, p. 89).

Richardson also correctly identifies the device which Leontief (1937) had discerned, notably in Cambridge theorising, as 'implicit theorising' – what Richardson refers to as a procedure which 'merely presumes the existence of functional relationships between different variables in the system and then proceeds to work out the consequences' (1960, p. 24).

Building on these perceptions, Richardson is able to show that the problem of circularity, which is widely recognised to dog oligopoly theory, extends also to perfect competition and is simply evaded therein by assuming it away. The form of the evasion, as he explained in the Preface to *Information and Investment*, is the assumption of perfect knowledge. Yet in actual competition the acquisition and processing of knowledge is crucial. Beliefs and plans are central to economic activity. Entrepreneurial expectations are the pivot of economic decisions. There is a vital need for horizontal information (about competitors at the same stage of production) and, as Richardson recognises later on in the book (1960, pp. 75-9), for vertical information (about suppliers and customers).

Richardson focuses his critique upon the key problem of the way in which firms, under perfect competition, would respond to a product market demand shift (1960, pp. 13-14). Richardson's argument, brought into stark relief both by his neglect of time and by his decision to ignore all adjustments which do not involve investment (1960, p. 15), is that, under perfect competition, the volume of extra investment in response to a demand increase is infinite. Those familiar with the perfectly competitive model will immediately recognise that, in using and expounding the model, they themselves implicitly assume that extra investment will, initially at least, be made by those firms already in the industry and that, in so far as supernormal profits give rise to entry, this will take time. But these are implicit assumptions which have to be tacked on to the perfectly competitive model to hide its central incoherence; and Richardson recognised their inadequacy. At a later stage he extends his critique to the idea that the increase in output under perfect competition might be infinitely large as well (1960, pp. 33-4).

Not content with identifying the central problem in the perfectly competitive model, Richardson also identified similar difficulties existing in the imperfect competition variant (1960, pp. 108-12); and, as Lancaster (1972) pointed out when reviewing Arrow and Hahn, general equilibrium analysis has failed to deal, even on its own terms, with genuine imperfect competition.

4.2 The Origins of the Problem of Knowledge

The acceptance of perfect competition as an ideal really only dates from the 1930s. Although Richardson referred to the origins of this idea in the work of the Lausanne school, it was only in the 1930s that Pareto Optimality entered the mainstream of economics, with Robbins's attempt at LSE to encourage an alternative to Pigovian welfare economics, leading to the development of the 'New Welfare Economics'. Joan Robinson, indeed, initially believed that equality of price and *average* cost was the key welfare criterion, until corrected by Lerner (1933-4; O'Brien, 1983a, p. 285); and in the 1930s' debates there were important dissidents from the idealisation of perfect competition, notably (again) Chamberlin (1933, pp. 25-9). I have documented elsewhere the process whereby the abandonment of Marshallian economics was involved in the welfare economics programme of which Joan Robinson's *The Economics of Imperfect Competition* was the outstanding example (O'Brien, 1983a); but it is worth emphasising this point because it was the 1930s' writers who drew welfare implications from a model which, as Richardson showed, could never have a real world counterpart.

Earlier writers on general equilibrium, especially Walras and Edgeworth, both knew – and made some attempt to rectify the matter through '*tâtonnement*' and 'recontracting' respectively – that there was a fundamental problem about the attainment of equilibrium, as Richardson recognises (1960, pp. 10-13). He is perhaps less appreciative of the fact that Edgeworth's attitude towards general equilibrium was more than a little detached; as Stigler (1941, p. 228) has noted, Walras devoted a book to general equilibrium, and Edgeworth did general equilibrium in a footnote (Marshall devoted an appendix to it). But nonetheless it was clear to Richardson that the founders of general equilibrium were less culpable than their successors (and one could argue that this is a trend which has continued beyond the 1930s) in an apparent willingness to avert the eyes from a fundamental flaw in the whole construction.[1]

Although the driving force behind Joan Robinson's work was, in the last resort, ideological – the inherent misallocation of capitalism as she saw it – there were other forces at work which helped to ensure the widespread acceptance in the 1930s of exchanging the real world for a model (as Shackle has put it (1967, p. 47)). Richardson himself refers to 'scientism'; and this is a perfectly valid point (1960, pp. 40-1; Hayek, 1942-4). It perhaps arises because economists feel that what they are doing is in some sense scientific – it deals with relationships between observable phenomena – but then feel unease when confronted by the disdain of natural scientists. This striving after 'scientific status' is very evident in the work of Pigou, to parts of whose welfare economics, Edgeworth's jibe about 'a profusion of algebraic foliage', originally directed at Walras, could well apply. It was Pigou who, in 1928, introduced the concept of the 'equilibrium firm' (Pigou, 1928), replacing Marshall's very different Representative Firm, and clearing the way for the assumption of uniformity of firms which was an essential part of Joan Robinson's model of industry equilibrium (1933, p. 98).

It was in the 1930s that the most blatantly unreal assumptions about knowledge – the centre of Richardson's concern – were introduced into economics. In particular, Joan Robinson felt able to draw average revenue curves which incorporated the reactions of all other firms (1933, p. 21). Although the circularity of such a procedure is blatant, it seems to have taken econo-

[1] John Creedy has pointed out to me that while *tâtonnement* and recontracting are highly artificial mechanisms for dealing with the problem of information, modern readers wonder why such attention is paid to these artificial constructs – without appreciating the issue with which they were trying to cope. Marshall also employed a special case so that disequilibrium trading did not affect the final price, and while that too was a very special case he was extremely upset by criticism from Edgeworth (Marshall, 1920, II, pp. 791-8).

mists a long time to realise the difficulty (Triffin, 1941, pp. 68-70).

4.3 Attempts to Mend the Model: The Marshallian Elements

Having established his central thesis, Richardson went on to explore other aspects of the working of competition. Unfortunately he then encountered the very real difficulty that different parts of competing 'paradigms' (to borrow Kuhn's term which, in this context at least, is most helpful) do not fit together – the concepts, even where they have similar labels, do not match.

This was pointed out with particular clarity, in discussing the case of general equilibrium, by Alan Coddington. In a paper dissecting some of the more ambitious modern claims for general equilibrium, Coddington discussed the difficulties of *translating* other theoretical approaches into general equilibrium (Coddington, 1975). Although the criticism was directed, with accuracy, at one particular writer (Hahn), Coddington's point is more general – and it is precisely this difficulty which dogged Richardson. For Richardson tried – and failed – to use elements of Marshall's analysis to supply the deficiencies in general equilibrium; and he failed because of a lack of appreciation of the fundamental difference between a theoretical structure grounded in time, real as well as logical, and a definitional ('axiomatic' as Coddington has it) approach which is general equilibrium.

4.3.1 Time

Time is central to Marshall's analysis of competition. Time is required for both the firm and the industry to adjust, and for the entrepreneur to gather, assimilate, and act upon knowledge. The central role of time in Marshall's analysis has long been recognised (Opie, 1931). Yet, despite the attempt to remedy the shortcomings of perfect competition analysis by the importation of Marshallian elements, the most fundamental difficulty which a reader of

Richardson's book encounters is that the matter of time is unresolved. Yet the absence of time is a central difficulty with both perfect and imperfect competition analysis. As George Shackle pointed out (1967, p. 59), perfect competition has no time, whether logical or historical, but entry and exit take time.

It is true that Richardson does make the occasional brief reference to time (e.g. 1960, p. 36). There is also an implicit recognition of time in the reference to 'restraints on competitive activity which are essentially short lived' (1960, p. 125); and at other points in the book there is arguably a confusion of time with what Richardson considers to be 'imperfections' (1960, pp. 68-71). Of Marshall's perception that the expansion of output takes time – and thus that cost curves have a time dimension – there is no sign. Nor is there any sign of the recognition that the need for management to 'digest' phases in the growth of the firm, to which Richardson refers (1960, pp. 59-60) is an aspect of time.

4.3.2 The Perfect Competition Shuffle

It is the neglect of time which makes possible the 'perfect competition shuffle' noted above. For time is entirely absent from perfect competition, and if we neglect its importance in genuine competition we enable elements of perfect competition to be smuggled in to a discussion of the latter. Thus, limitations on the expansion of an industry resulting from the economic history of that industry are of course inconsistent with *perfect* competition (Richardson, 1960, pp. 58-9); but they are certainly not inconsistent with genuine competition, and thus it is not necessary to argue that, because such limitations are inconsistent with (perfect) competition, there is some need for cartelisation.

4.3.3 Markets as Information Mechanisms

Following from the failure to distinguish genuine competition from a series of axioms going under that name is an apparent failure in Richardson's work to perceive that genuine markets – and there are no genuine markets in perfect competition – are information mechanisms. Active competition involves gathering and assimilation of information. At an academic level this lack of appreciation may be traceable to an unfamiliarity with the Austrian tradition as embodied recently in the work of Kirzner (1973) and, earlier, in that of Mises (1932) and Hayek (1949).

Yet even those unfamiliar with the Austrian literature can gain such insights from Marshall. The Representative Firm in Marshall's work is an information device – it gives an idea of the supply response of an industry to a change in demand, and it tells potential entrants whether entry is worth while.

However there are particular aspects of the Austrian literature of which we do need to take particular account in the context of the present discussion, and Richardson's reliance on Marshall's work as a source of remedies for the ills of perfect competition may have led to a neglect of this. Firstly, the Austrians stressed that a price *contains* a good deal of information. This is the very reason that markets work (and planning does not). Now it was open to Richardson to argue that the information could be misleading; but the initial point needs to be recognised, particularly as Richardson showed apparent enthusiasm for planning. Secondly, some of the Austrians stressed *general* rather than *equilibrium*; and it could be argued that Richardson's critique was really directed at the idea of equilibrium, not at the objections to going outside the context of partial analysis to understand the transmission of economic information.

At a more practical level, Richardson's neglect of the role of markets as information mechanisms may reflect the ignorance of many academic economists of the operation of informal means of transmitting information which may be generally classified as 'gossip'. (I once worked for a firm which employed an economics department – of which I was a member – one of whose tasks was to distil the economic significance of such 'gossip'.) It is this same academic innocence of the way in which industry operates which could lead to the belief that in genuine (as distinct from perfect) competition there is likely to be a recurrent problem of over-investment. Here the role of the capital goods industry is vital; firstly, it is through the suppliers of capital goods that firms learn of investment plans by other firms and, secondly, capacity in the capital goods industries is itself limited and the strength of demand is reflected in the variability of quoted delivery times.

4.3.4 The Entrepreneur

The (unconscious) importation into discussions of *actual* competition of aspects of perfect 'competition' leads also to a neglect of the role of the entrepreneur. An understanding of this role is present in the Austrian tradition (as manifested by Kirzner, 1997) and it is *central* to Marshall's work. It is true that, half-way through Richardson's book (1960, p. 105), we find a Marshallian kind of entrepreneur searching for technological best-practice; but, for the most part, the entrepreneur is conspicuous in this discussion only by absence.

4.3.5 The Emphasis on Investment

Richardson ignored, apparently deliberately, Marshall's 'time period' solution to a change in demand – the celebrated fishing industry example (Marshall, 1920, pp. 369-80, pp. 331-6; see also Opie, 1931). The whole thrust of the book is on the expansion of output as a result of increasing capacity rather than of working capacity harder. It is thus easy to respond – as indeed Swann and I did – to the thesis of Richardson's book, as applied to actual competitive situations, in the following way: firms initially expand along their marginal cost curves, and the process of expanding in this way gives them some feel for the desirability or otherwise of extra investment (O'Brien and Swann, 1968, pp. 118-19). The neglect of this form of response by firms to an increase in demand leads to an overstatement not merely of the problem which concerns Richardson – at least it is an overstatement once we step outside perfect competition – but to the introduction of investment variations into situations where they do not take place. An example is Richardson's discussion of the cobweb theorem, which in truth involves acreage variation not investment (1960, pp. 27-8). The significance of the distinction is that acreage variation can be reversed without writing off fixed capital.

4.3.6 Richardson's Interpretation of Marshallian Competition

Richardson recognised that Marshall was not concerned with perfect competition (1960, pp. 14-15) – how could he be indeed, given his obsessive concern with industrial realities? He recognised too that Marshall had been misapplied (it might be more accurate to say that his name had been misappropriated) by later generations. Richardson acknowledged that Marshall 'far more than either Walras or Edgeworth, was deeply concerned with the problems of adjustment and of time, and his treatment of them is much more profound' (1960, pp. 14-15). He recognised the role which Marshall saw for buyers' preferences (because firms sold both in a general and in their own particular market) in limiting over-entry into an industry (1960, pp. 62-4).

Yet in developing his analysis he failed to appreciate the content of what Marshall had to say. The reader is left with the impression that Richardson himself had been deeply affected by the programme of perfect competition which he was criticising – to the point where he defined uncertainty as a result of incomplete information about preferences and production functions, (1960, pp. 81-2) even though knowledge of preferences is, by definition, unobtainable and production functions were, in Marshall's view, not fixed. On the matter of preferences the Austrian tradition is quite clear; preferences are non-observable. On the second matter, Marshall was, as always, instructive; in his view, factor combinations were the result of the continuing knowledge-assimilation process. But both these sources of insight do not seem to have affected Richardson as deeply as the perfect competition he was criticising. It is true that, having stated the problem in terms of preferences and production functions, Richardson then retreated some way from it (1960, pp. 82-3); yet the initial statement is itself instructive. It explains why Marshall's careful discussion of the way in which firms respond to increases in demand seems to have made little impact, and his discussion of entrepreneurial expectations to have been largely ignored. Whereas Marshall's entrepreneur studies technical and market information, and assimilates this in the process of choosing factor combinations and outputs, a form of activity regarded as entirely superfluous in the perfectly competitive model, Richardson's entrepreneur is apparently incapable of doing this and requires a cartel to do it for him.

4.3.7 The Representative Firm and Costs

The Representative Firm finds no place in Richardson's discussion, even though this was Marshall's central device for studying the response of an industry to a change in demand conditions. But even Marshall's partial equilibrium reasons for expecting cost curves to rise after a certain point disappear – managerial diseconomies are dismissed without evidence (Richardson, 1960, pp. 211-14). For Richardson, cost curves are expected to rise only because of general equilibrium considerations in the form of rising factor prices for the industry as a whole (1960, pp. 16-21). At this point one suspects an incipient confusion between partial and general equilibrium in the argument; and this suspicion is reinforced by the failure to consider how large an *industry* has to be in relation to the *economy* before this rise in factor prices – and the consequent increase in costs – can be expected. In fact, as Lionel Robbins (1934a) pointed out, the problem makes little sense as formulated; factor prices cannot be considered in isolation from demand changes. If firms attempt to expand output without an increase in demand, they will have to bid factors of production away from more highly valued uses, and thus costs will rise; if however firms expand output after a shift in demand has freed resources in another industry, there is no reason for factor prices to rise.

The attempt to remedy the defects in perfect competition by introducing Marshallian elements was always doomed to failure. While Richardson had correctly diagnosed the fundamental incoherence of perfect competition as a theory of actual competition, a system which exhibits fundamental incoherence cannot be patched up by the introduction of ad hoc expedients: and the attempt to marry Marshallian competition with a fundamentally different research programme was bound to fail – as Coddington's critique implies.

But, having got this far, Richardson went on to use the failed marriage between Marshallian and perfect competition in two ways, the discussions of cartels and of planning, which were, in my judgement, unfortunate.

4.4 The Defence of Cartelisation

The 1956 Restrictive Trade Practices Act seems to have acted as an unacknowledged background to Richardson's book. Certainly this is the suspicion raised by a reading of some points in it. It is also apparent that Richardson believed that the 1956 Act was predicated on the basis of perfect competition (1960, pp. 70-1; 1965, pp. 434-6, 440; 1967, p. 369). At all events, the stages in the argument outlined so far led in *Information and Investment* to a favourable attitude towards cartels (1960, pp. 67, 76-9, 95-6). The non-sequitur involved should be clear. It is that, because perfect competition cannot work, real competition needs cartels. While he was prepared to concede that there might be some sub-optimality involved in cartelised industries, he believed that the severe restriction of cartels – as envisaged by the 1956 Act – could make things worse by increasing uncertainty.

Richardson saw cartels as institutions embodying those 'frictions' which made competition more stable than his attempts to apply the perfectly competitive model to the real world would suggest it would otherwise be. He recognised that, in the real world, investment and expansion might take place as established firms increased output to maintain their market share (1960, p. 55), and that, if this were the pattern followed, the result would be predictable. He also recognised that capital market imperfections and managerial limitations could constrain expansion and be stabilising (1960, pp. 58-60). But he clearly believed that the existence of these stabilising forces was accidental and that it was better to stabilise matters through a cartel. Firstly, he did not believe that firms in cartels engaged in joint profit maximisation (since if they did, marginal revenue would be positive and elasticity of demand greater than one, yet Richardson indicated that elasticity of demand facing cartels was low, e.g. 1960, p. 13; 1965, p. 444). Secondly, he believed that the conduct of firms in cartels was compatible with efficient allocation (1960, 130-2). Not only did he believe that it was possible for a cartel to improve selection of efficient firms – through the avoidance of price cutting – but he also believed that cartels would not achieve supernormal profits.

He buttressed his faith in this argument – though without reference to any actual cartels – with discussion of what he conceived to be the inadequacies of the market in achieving both the selection of efficient firms and the competitive constraint of profits to a normal level. There was, he believed, a significant role for chance in the availability of both internal and external finance to firms, and thus in firm-selection, this element of chance being in turn related to chance variations in the supply of adequate information. He also – though the reasoning here is not entirely clear – seems to have doubted that the market would, unaided, constrain profits to a normal level; again the implication is that market selection was affected by risk associated with inadequate information. In all this Richardson does not discuss the question of whether such imperfections were quantitatively sufficient to justify cartels.

Consistently with the perfectly competitive model, Richardson ignored the open economy aspects of the problem. If the possibility of imports is allowed for, then shortages – particularly of produced inputs – can be made good by imports, which in turn signal the extent of the shortfall in the market to all the existing participants. It is perhaps an interesting reflection on the nature of progress in economics that a nineteenth century economist, J.R. McCulloch, not only anticipated Richardson's thesis about over-entry but pointed out that, in an open economy, the availability of imports would prevent such over-entry (McCulloch, 1826a).

Richardson felt able to argue that cartels would be beneficial in preventing what he later called 'short run competition' (1965, 1966, 1967; see also 1960, pp. 130-40 and for criticism see O'Brien and Swann, 1968, p. 234) and also that co-operation between firms might lead to operations at minimum efficient scale (1960, pp. 91-4). There was also the possibility of vertical integration or joint subsidiaries as a way round uncertainty affecting business decisions (1960, pp. 83-4). He even suggested that cartels could somehow or other co-ordinate new products (1960, p. 115) – even though cartels more often than not, in practice, interpreted 'co-ordination' as suppression which removed even the vestiges of competition through product variation. They also impeded technical progress; but an appreciation of this aspect of competition is absent not only from *Information and Investment* but also from later work by Richardson (1965, 1966, 1967).

Apart from outright cartels, Richardson also later came to defend information agreements (1967) even though, as pioneered in the United States by A.J. Eddy, they had a long (collusive) history (Scherer, 1980, pp. 224-5, 521-3; Neale and Goyder, 1980, pp. 43-50) and, as it turned out, were also cartels in all but name in this country (O'Brien and Swann, 1966, 1968; Swann and O'Brien, 1967). Richardson's belief in the need for industrial co-ordination through cartels led him to adopt a position distinctly favourable to such ill-fated 1960s' developments as indicative planning and the National Economic Development Office (1960, pp. 36-7, 99, 115), but to explore that issue here would take us too far away from the main path.

4.5 The Planned Economy

Richardson made clear in *Information and Investment* that he did not subscribe to totalitarianism (1960, pp. 217-20). Yet throughout the book there are comments which suggest a naive attitude towards central planning – and above all to its knowledge problems (e.g. 1960, pp. 45, 70). Richardson's basic argument against perfectly competitive general equilibrium theory actually supports directly Hayek's criticism of the use of such general equilibrium, by people like Lange, to 'justify' planning – Hayek pointed out that these people had shown only that *any* (statically) efficient economy must meet the Lausanne conditions for such static efficiency, without showing how, under planning, this could be done (Hayek, 1949, pp. 92-106, 148-80). Yet Richardson, while pointing out the fundamental problems of knowledge as applied to perfect competition, appears to assume that in that context where the knowledge problem is completely *insoluble* – central planning – it does not even *exist*. Thus according to Richardson, 'It is perfectly possible to conceive of conditions under which the adjustment of capacity, whether to an increase or a reduction in demand, would be best accompanied by central planning, whether by the government or by the industry itself' (1960, p. 70).

One might interpret this to mean a reference to activities pursued in the 1960s by Britain's National Economic Development Office, were it not for chapter 10 of *Information and Investment* which appears to be a late insertion into the book. In this, the naiveté about planning becomes very marked; and costs are held to be higher in a decentralised economy than in a planned one, because of the greater degree of uncertainty (1960, p. 198). Falling into the trap into which micro textbooks still sometimes fall, Richardson had earlier in the book asserted that 'in principle' Pareto optimality could be brought about by central planning (1960, p. 45).[2] Of course it could not, both because a knowledge of preferences is required and because there are no proper factor markets in a planned economy. Mises (1932) had, long before *Information and Investment*, shown that, without competitive markets, there was no way of registering the preferences of consumers in the form of factor prices, although this was necessary to ensure the allocation of factors between the satisfaction of different wants in a way which reflected such preferences. The knowledge problem was insoluble. Similar problems occur at various points especially towards the end of the book. In particular we find the curious argument that a redistribution of gains and losses would increase certainty (Richardson, 1960, pp. 207-8) – which would only be true if the redistributing authority were provided, by magic, with the information to undertake this.

4.6 Considerations From the Wider Literature

As indicated already, *Information and Investment* proceeded from a critique of a hypothetical axiomatic construct – perfect competition – to the consideration of actual competition and of potential problems which could arise in the course of its operation. It is, however, rather surprising that much earlier literature with a direct bearing on these problems does not seem to have impinged on Richardson's formulation of them. Given the subject matter of Richardson's book, some of the omissions seem rather remarkable.

[2] A poignant example of this kind of thing may be found in a widely distributed textbook by Chacholiades (1986, p. 462), 'In a centrally planned economy, a planning bureau could intentionally allocate resources at some point on the contract curve'.

Particularly noteworthy, given Richardson's stress on the possibility of over-investment in the absence of 'frictions', is the omission of any reference to over-investment theories of the trade cycle, associated with writers like Aftalion, Spiethoff, and even Robertson (Haberler, 1937, ch. 3; Presley, 1978, 1981). The lack of discussion of alternative approaches to competition – some of which one might have expected Richardson to find sympathetic – is also striking. P.W.S. Andrews receives only one mention, and not in this context. Yet Andrews insisted that the characteristic of 'perfect competition' was the absence of competition. The roles of belief and plans in the operation of the price system figure in the work of Mises and Hayek; Mises is not referred to at all, and Hayek only once (1960, p. 6). The Austrians, as well as Smith and Marshall, stressed that markets generate knowledge; yet Smith is mentioned only once (and as a historical figure), though Richardson has, in later work, repaired this gap (Richardson, 1975). In the context of discussions of the firm, it is even more remarkable, since an issue of co-ordination is involved, that the name of Ronald Coase does not appear in the book.[3]

The most prominent omission is that of any reference to empirical material. The apparent innocence of the practical operation of information agreements has already been alluded to; but this is symptomatic of a much wider problem. Scherer, after an excellent summary of Richardson's thesis, has pointed out that collusive agreements are as apt to *destabilise* investment as to stabilise it – *and there is empirical evidence on this.* Market sharing and cartels can actually produce investment races – again there is empirical evidence. Oligopolistic price fixing can lead to competition in capacity. Scherer himself provides further econometric evidence that investment *instability* is *positively* related to concentration (1980, pp. 370-4). A subsequent investigation found that neither the level nor the variability of investment was adversely affected by the ending of cartels (O'Brien *et al.*, 1979).

[3]The only reference to Coase in the work of Richardson appears as a footnote appended right at the end of Richardson (1972).

Richardson's book suggests testable propositions; but the author seems to have been inhibited at the time of writing by what I have called elsewhere 'Ivory Tower empiricism' (O'Brien, 1984, p. 252), peculiarly Oxbridge in form. Indeed Walter Eltis has recently documented the Oxbridge resistance to the suspiciously new-fangled econometrics as late as the mid-1960s (Eltis, 1993, p. xi). Observations like the one that 'one may wonder' if adjustment to a common joint price 'might not involve a degree of instability' (Richardson, 1960, p. 134) cannot substitute for empirical research.

4.7 Conclusions

There seems little doubt that Richardson's work has been seriously neglected. There have been fruitful later manifestations of his influence, notably in the work of Brian Loasby (1991), but the very fundamental difficulty which he identified in the axiomatic 'perfectly competitive' model has been largely ignored. Even Coddington's incisive critique of some extravagant claims made on behalf of general equilibrium failed to make the point which was at the centre of Richardson's concern. Part of the reason for the neglect of the message must lie in the belief that, by specifying a full set of contingent markets, general equilibrium theorists had somehow solved knowledge problems – as distinct from assuming them away. Part of the problem may also lie in Richardson having become sidetracked into an endorsement of cartelisation. Yet the economics profession as a whole has lost a good deal by this neglect. *Information and Investment* contains an outstanding discussion of demand in terms of attributes (1960, pp. 102-4).[4] It contains an analysis of uncertainty which is highly suggestive, even though the discussion tails off and the various coefficients formulated are unused (1960, ch. VIII). It introduces

[4]Lancaster's classic 1960 article appeared only in the same year that *Information and Investment* was published, having passed through the process of publishing, so Richardson's contribution deserves independent recognition. (John Creedy however has pointed out to me that the characteristics model was first produced by Alan Brown).

the important idea of dislocation effects for both producers and consumers; and it contains an outstanding chapter on risk (1960, ch. IX) – with a critique of Friedman and Savage – which could have been the basis for much further work. Finally, it contains a most interesting suggestion of the way in which information affects the yield of an investment because of the need for an *adaptable* programme (1960, pp. 188-90). A certain outcome is preferred to an uncertain one with the same expected value. All of these issues deserved further exploration and – since Richardson's original background was in maths and physics – there is no reason why that exploration should not have been pursued. Even so, the fundamental perception of *Information and Investment* remains one of the greatest importance.

Part III

History of Economic Thought

Chapter 5

Classical Economics: An Overview

Classical economics was the ruling body of economic thought during the great explosion of economic growth which began in the second half of the eighteenth century. For this there was no historical precedent; population rose from about six million to well over twenty million within a century, and while the total was still modest by modern standards, it was reached by very high rates of growth – as high as 17 per cent – which were unprecedented. National income rose from perhaps £50 million to more than £900 million, and almost all of this increase was in real terms, with rising real wages, at least from 1820, and a fundamental change in the balance of economic activity – the Industrial Revolution – and in the role of the State (Mitchell and Deane, 1962).

The focus of the classical literature is squarely on macroeconomic issues and, above all, on economic growth. Because the growth was taking place in an open economy, with a currency which (except in the years 1797-1819) was convertible into gold, the classical writings were necessarily concerned with the balance of payments and its links with the money supply and the price level. Thus monetary theory occupies a central place. The achievments of the classical economists in this area were substantial, and extremely long lasting – indeed they are still with us today. The same is true of the trade theory. The desirability of freedom of trade is a starting point in the literature from Adam Smith onwards; and there developed a complex and sophisticated theory of the gains from trade and their division, which is a fundamental part of the modern literature of economics.

Most of this literature developed in the context of an international economy free from major wars. However the French wars of 1793-1815 had a pwerful influence on the classical literature; not only did they lead to major problems with public finance, and the development of a significant national debt but, because convertibility of the note issue into gold was suspended for much of this time, it was necessary to develop a theory of the operation of an inconvertible paper currency.

We begin by examining the intellectual foundations of this literature. Then the issues of value and distribution, including distributional shares in a growing economy, are covered. The four great areas of money, trade, economic growth and public finance then follow. Finally we take a brief look at the classical attitudes to some policy issues.

5.1 Foundations

The intellectual basis for the classical literature is to be found in Adam Smith's *Wealth of Nations* of 1776; and the era of classical economics lasted for a century until the rise of marginalism in the 1870s. Smith's great work is of key importance: not only did it lay the foundations for virtually all of the subsequent literature, but earlier work, including that by Smith himself (his *Moral Sentiments*, 1759, and his *Lectures*, 1763) and of David Hume (1711-76) are seen in the context of the research programme which Smith established.

Apart from Adam Smith (1723-90), who is the most important figure in the entire history of economics, the most famous and influential figure was David Ricardo (1772-1823). Of Ricardo there are several views. Schumpeter

(1954) regarded Ricardo's work as essentially a detour. The Sraffians regard it as the start of the only valid tradition in economics, running from Ricardo to Marx and thence to Sraffa; characterised by a sort of sectarian spirit, this has led to distortion of the historical record, as commentators have noted (Blaug, 1987, 1988, 1999; Peach, 1988, 1999), with a picture of an omniscient and infallible Ricardo surrounded by intellectual pygmies. Anyone disagreeing with Ricardo simply failed to understand him properly, in this view. Others, including such diverse figures as Alfred Marshall and Samuel Hollander (1979), have interpreted Ricardo as some kind of neo-classical economist – and in Marshall's case for good measure, credited him with theoretical advances that were achieved by J.S.Mill, thus again distorting the historical record.

Ricardo excelled in model building: but his restrictive type of model grafted uneasily on to the main part of classical economics, and the work of McCulloch (1789-1864) and J.S. Mill (1806-73) – two later writers who both covered the whole range of economics – owed much more to Smith than to Ricardo, despite Ricardian obeissances.

But to interpret classical economics in terms of Smith and Ricardo alone, treating all the other classical writers as also-rans, is a major mistake (O'Brien, 1988a). Contemporary with Ricardo were Malthus (1766-1834) (who made valuable contributions to the literature on population and on aggregate demand), James Mill (1773-1836), Nassau Senior (1770-1834) (the first professor of economics in England), Robert Torrens (1780-1864) (a superbly agile theorist), and a host of writers on special topics especially money where the achievements of classical economics were the most long-lasting.

The classical economists were not specialist economic writers in the modern sense, with the exception of McCulloch. Most had other intellectual interests, such as law and philosophy, and few of them had academic employment. Journalism, the law, and business, especially banking, were the occupations of most of the classical writers though Smith, McCulloch (for nine years) and Senior (twice) occupied university chairs, as did Montifort Longfield (1802-84) in Dublin. Yet at a time when the educated classes formed a much smaller proportion of the population than today, these writers did form in some sense a scientific community, though much of the work done in Ireland made little impact in England. With the exception of the French economist J.B. Say (1776-1832), who had in any case spent time in England, and was a correspondent of Ricardo, the writers with whom we shall be concerned lived in the British Isles. They read not academic journals but the literary reviews of the day, especially the *Edinburgh Review*, and there was an active circulation of pamphlets which could be published cheaply with the aid of a bookseller. The core group was to a considerable extent Metropolitan, meeting each other at the Political Economy Club, as well as in other societies such as the [Royal] Statistical Society.

The diverse backgrounds and interests of the classical economists are hardly surprising, given that economics grew out of philosophy, and remained linked to it throughout the classical era. Smith, and his friend David Hume, were the products of a distinctive Scottish philosophical school. Smith's teachers had a background in the Protestant version of the European natural law tradition, which led, in the work of Francis Hutcheson (1694-1746), to the idea of an innate moral sense – 'benevolence'. This led in turn to Smith's vision of economic actors constrained not only by a framework of law, religion, and custom, but by a kind of fellow feeling which he called 'sympathy'. In addition, the Utilitarian strain in the classical literature, which is usually associated with Jeremy Bentham (1748-1832) actually has its origins in this Scottish philosophical tradition, leading to Smith's stress on the welfare of the labouring classes as the majority of the population – the greatest number, whose greatest happiness Hutcheson had stressed. Smith's friend Hume is of course chiefly famous as a philosopher, despite the enduring contributions he made, in compact form, to economics; and he was part of the same Scottish philosophical tradition, advancing a pain/pleasure psychology, the idea of a sense of justice based on respect for fellow men, and sympathy with general happiness.

Absorbed into this philosophical background were ideas from more narrowly economic literature which had been developing for the century before Smith's great work. The most important example of this is the work of the Physiocrats in France, with whom both Smith and Hume became personally acquainted. It is probably true that the particular form of the classical focus on economic growth, untrammelled by State regulations, owed much to the Physiocrats; and their emphasis on freedom of trade, for which there were only a few English precursors, was important. It is arguable that they also influenced Smith's approach to distribution, and the stress he laid upon the importance of agriculture, as well as his use of the distinction between productive and unproductive labour.

Associated with the Physicrats was A.R.J. Turgot (1727-1781) whose emphasis in his *Réflexions* (1769) on resource allocation, resulting from mobile capital responding to profit opportunities, undoubtedly harmonised with Smith's views. Yet in some ways what was borrowed from France merely reinforced ideas which Smith had developed before he went to France in 1764, as much of the *Wealth of Nations* is present in skeletal form in notes on lectures which he delivered in 1763.

Smith's debt to some of his English predecessors is not always so clear. Yet it is hard to ignore the likely influence of Bernard Mandeville (1660-1733) whose *Fables of the Bees* (1714) made him a scandalous figure, for he argued that from private vices came public benefits. Smith's emphasis on individual motivation and self-interest as productive of social benefit reflects Mandeville's own, though Smith studiously avoids mentioning Mandeville. Nor does he mention Sir William Petty (1623-87). There was undoubtedly much of Petty's work of which Smith disapproved: and 'Political Arithmetik' – of which Petty was a pioneer, ably satirised by Swift (Letwin, 1963) – is the subject of adverse comment in the *Wealth of Nations*. But the whole of the fifth book of the *Wealth of Nations* is about public finance: and there is no doubt that Petty had an influence on Smith here, if only on the treatment of equality in taxation.

It is against this background that the *Wealth of Nations* has to be seen. Its basic concepts are so wide-ranging as almost to defy summary, and they set the agenda for the next century of economic writing. The individual pursues self-interest which, because it is constrained by a framework of law, religion and custom, and an inherent moral sense (sympathy), brings about a coincidence of private and public satisfaction. Competition in response to price signals allocates resources, as capital pursues profit opportunities, and the search for greater ouput from the resources commanded by capital leads to specialisation and division of labour (again, an idea to be found in the French literature and also in Hutcheson) which is the mainspring of technical progress. Freedom of trade provides both the stimulus to technical progress and the widening of the market which is necessary to dispose of the increased output – division of labour depends on the extent of the market.

But though Smith set the agenda, Ricardo, reading Smith with the mind of a natural model builder, was to have a huge, if ultimately transient, influence on the way that agenda was developed. For Ricardo was concerned with two immediate practical problems – inflation, and agricultural protection; and he found the material in the *Wealth of Nations* failed to provide the clear-cut answers which Ricardo's model-building mind sought. Indeed he concluded that Smith was in error.

In the Bullion controversy, the role of the price level was critical, in relation to the balance of payments. Now Smith had argued that a rise in wages would ultimately raise the price level. But Ricardo, in the monetary conroversies, applied Hume's theory. He thus perceived that, in an open economy on the gold standard, the price level could not rise permanently; though it might increase initially, a balance of payments deficit would ensue, gold would flow out as Hume had explained, the money supply would be reduced, and prices would return to the initial level. This insight, it has been plausibly argued (Hollander, 1979, though see Peach, 1988) led Ricardo to argue that profits would be compressed by a rise in wages.

Applying the argument to agricultural protection, it was possible to predict dire consequences for economic growth, if wages and profits moved inversely, and if real wages were constant at subsistence but (due to diminishing returns) required increasing amounts of resources – and thus a rising level of money wages – to provide them. Protection involved rising agricultural costs as inferior land was brought into use to feed a growing population; rising agricultural costs meant a rising price of corn. To enable the labourer to purchase the same amount of corn as before, to receive the constant subsistence wage, money wages would have to rise. Profits would consequently fall, accumulation of capital would slow, and it would ultimately stop. The economy would cease to grow and there would be a stationary state.

All this had important implications for social shares. The landlords' share, as rent, would increase in Ricardo's model, as diminishing returns ensured a growing gap between total product and the net product shared between proft and wages. With wages at subsistence, profits would be reduced to a minimum. So it was the landlords whose interests conflicted with the rest of society – to the extent, as Ricardo argued (quite wrongly, because he neglected the economic interests of *individual* landlords) that improvements in agricultural technology were against their interests.

As we shall see, the apparatus which Ricardo constructed made a very considerable impact on the thinking of economic writers over perhaps two decades. But there was an element of misunderstanding. Ricardo was believed to have developed theorems which fitted into the basic programme developed by Smith, and in some instances corrected the conclusions which Smith had drawn. But it eventually became apparent, in one area after another – value, distribution, economic growth in particular – that Ricardo had constructed a whole framework of analysis which was qualitatively of a different kind from that of Smith, a framework from which sweeping policy conclusions could be drawn by piling up simplifying assumptions. As this became clear, the literature of classical economics developed along a path increasingly divergent from that laid down by Ricardo, though so powerful was his intellectual personality that his name continued to be invoked, and some of his mistakes – notably the idea that rent did not enter into cost of production – continued to be repeated. Thus McCulloch and J.S. Mill both attempted to incorporate Ricardian material into broader, eclectic, approaches that had much more in common with Smith than Ricardo. Ricardo's sweeping policy conclusions – especially the emphasis on diminishing returns in agriculture leading to the stationary state – were seriously weakened.

Ricardo was not the only writer whose work enjoyed this ambiguous position in relation to the main body of classical literature. The same is true of Malthus. The theory of population growth, as dependent on the power of increase of food being relatively less than the power of increase of population, so that population was always pressing up against the limits of available food supply, was not invented by Malthus; at the very least, it goes back to Cantillon, writing about 1730. But Malthus provided the population theory underlying much classical economic literature, articulating it as a conflict between a geometric rate of increase of population and an arithmetic increase in food supply. This had the analytical advantage, especially for Ricardo, of leading to the conclusion that population would increase to the point where wages were at subsistence – and thus the wage level could be treated as a constant in Ricardo's model building.

However, from the second edition of his *Essay on Population* (1803), Malthus removed this certainty. He introduced the idea that population might, or might not (if moral restraint, as distinct from vice, limited procreation) press up against the limits of the available food supply. In this slightly ambiguous form the population theory was incorporated into nineteenth century economic writings. According to Senior, population might be limited not by actual shortage of food, but by the anticipation of it, and even by the anticipation of losing social status. McCulloch distanced himself even further from the mechanical version of Malthus's theory, spotting that the claim that population had a 'tendency' to outrun subsistence was simply a tautology – if population were not doing so, it could still be claimed that the tendency existed but was being restrained by a non-observable 'fear' of losing decencies. J.S. Mill, the great reconciler and synthesiser of classical literature (though he was much more than this, an economist of powerful originality as well), allowed Malthus an honoured place in his *Principles* (1848), while denying that Malthus had attached any importance to his arithmetical and geometric ratios, and restating the tautological 'tendency' as an economic law which could only be modified by the spread amongst the multiplying classes of methods of family limitation.

But to understand how all these threads fit together, it is best to look at the classical treatment of particular aspects of economic analysis. We begin with value and distribution.

5.2 Value and Distribution

5.2.1 Value

Adam Smith's approach to value theory was designed to produce a theory of relative price, on the basis of adding up the per-unit cost of the labour, capital, and land inputs into production, the valuation of the inputs being determined separately. Thus, after a brief exposition of valuation according to labour input in a labour-only economy, he explained the value of commodities in long-run equilibrium, in terms of wages, profit and rent. Around this long run equilibrium price there fluctuated market price, with departures from long-run equilibrium being eliminated by the mobility of capital (in command of labour) in response to profit opportunities (where market price was greater than the long-run equilibrium one) or losses (where market price was lower than equilibrium).

Ricardo then attempted to replace Smith's adding-up approach with a labour theory of value; and in so doing he caused endless problems for his contemporaries and successors. Even if capital amortisation were treated as payments to stored-up labour (stored-up in machinery), it quickly became apparent that relative values could change, without any change in labour input, if the capital/labour ratios were not uniform across all commodities. This would happen when wages rose and profits accordingly fell as, in the Ricardian model, they were supposed to. Ricardo was reluctant to accept this, but it was an inescapable consequence of his model, so he claimed that it would only produce variations of 6 or 7 per cent (it turns out that this was very optimistic – Barkai, 1967), leading to Stigler's famous dictum that Ricardo had a 93 per cent labour theory of value (Stigler, 1958). But the problems were all tied up with the basic Ricardian model: for money wages were supposed to rise with the growth of population and the rising cost of obtaining food, at the margin. Wages should rise, and thus values should alter.

Ricardo seems to have made two startling assumptions to take the argument forward. Firstly, he posited an average capital/labour ratio, and the existence of a commodity produced under such conditions – the 'Invariable Measure': he then decided that gold would fit that specification. Then he treated agriculture as operating with the same capital/labour ratio. Thus a rise in wages would not, of its own, alter the price of corn in terms of money. Then if the price of food did rise in terms of money, this must signal the existence of diminishing returns in agriculture, and thus progress towards the stationary state.

But what about rent as an element in cost of production? Here, Ricardo introduced one of the longest-lasting fallacies in the whole history of economics. Rent, he argued, was an intra-marginal surplus, due to the existence of diminishing returns in agriculture – in now conventional terms we can envisage this as a rising agricultural supply schedule, with an area of producer surplus lying between the supply schedule and the ruling market price which is itself equal to marginal agricultural cost. Because it was a surplus, Ricardo argued that it did not determine price but was determined by price. The argument was fallacious, because it neglected transfer earnings: to grow one crop, land had to be paid sufficient to prevent it being turned over to another crop. Thus the cost of the land used certainly did enter into the cost of production where there was a variety of agricultural products, rather than the single product 'corn' which featured in Ricardo's model.

There were other problems with Ricardo's analysis. While Smith had paid considerable attention to the question of wages in different occupations, which was highly relevant to Ricardo's approach since relative quantity of labour could only mean relative quantities of wages, Ricardo simply pushed the problem aside by assuming that wage differentials were fixed.

All of these intellectual efforts have to be seen in the context of Ricardo's overriding aim – to produce a model of growth and stagnation. This is clear in his *Essay on Profits* of 1815, before he had been pushed by James Mill into writing a full-length book, his *Principles* of 1817, in which the value material appeared. Yet this was not understood by his contemporaries, who were concerned with relative price, and saw no role for 'Absolute Value' in terms of the 'Invariable Measure'. McCulloch, who gave Ricardo's *Principles* two ecstatic reviews, in the *Edinburgh Review* and the *Scotsman* (O'Brien, 1970, p. 34), clearly believed that what was on offer was an improved cost of production theory: accepting the elimination of rent from cost, he wrestled vainly (as did James Mill) with the problem of capital, and indeed with the nature of the profit reward. At one stage he even argued that labour embodied in maturing wine stocks goes on working, and thus earns a reward. Finally (as late as 1838) he arrived at the conclusion that the limit on supply of capital (because of waiting for a return) and the demand for its services (because of productivity) combined to allow it to earn a positive reward which entered into price. Torrens, always original, adopted a different approach and argued that relative amounts of capital , rather than relative amounts of labour, determined relative price. However, since the valuation of the capital turned out to depend on the number of days labour 'stored up', this was no advance. But, again, he was simply trying to produce a theory of relative price.

The same is true of J.S. Mill, whose treatment of the cost of production approach to value represents the high point of this part of classical theory; and it provides an interesting insight in relation to Ricardo's influence. For, firstly, Mill insisted that value was only a relative term – he had no use in his approach for Ricardo's 'Invariable Measure'. Secondly, Mill emphasised, in the Smithian manner, the fluctuation of market price around the long-run natural (cost of production) price; but the latter was not assumed to be constant over attainable output variations. He also conceded that there were a number of products which were not produced in this way but commanded a scarcity value. Cost of production itself was made up of wages and profits (depreciation being classed as wages and profits incurred in the past) and rent was not an element of cost of production. Things could only differ in relative value if they required more labour, or labour paid at higher wages, differed with respect to the capital/labour ratio, or were the products of industries requiring a higher rate of profit. Ricardo's influence is apparent in the 'getting rid of rent' and in the recogntion that varying capital/labour ratios would produce changes in relative values if average wages rose and average profits fell: but his contributions are treated only as modifying a basically Smithian cost of production approach.

But there was, in the classical literature, a wholly different approach, stemming from a French tradition, in particular from the work of J.B. Say. It was one which was consistent with the post-1870 approach to value theory, in terms of subjective valuation (as underlying demand) and of limitations in supply. Say himself argued that not only goods, but also the productive services involved in producing goods, derived their value from the utility of the final product. Price was determined by the intersection of a negatively slopped demand curve, described verbally, and a rising supply schedule.

Say's performance was incomplete, if much superior to that of Ricardo. For he explained the declining demand schedule in terms of income distribution, not in terms of the utility which he stressed. However two other writers were able to develop the argument further and to fill this gap. Nassau Senior explained clearly the idea of diminishing marginal utility, though he did not relate it to a demand curve (Senior, 1836). It was the Irish economist Mountifort Longfield who provided the decisive step. Longfield was certainly influenced by the idea put forward (somewhat unclearly) by Malthus of 'intensity of demand': and he was probably influenced by Say, though there is no clear evidence of this. At all events, Longfield, in 1833, having started from a conventional cost of production approach (even 'getting rid of' rent) put forward a complete subjective value theory which is strikingly modern (Longfield, 1834). Value depends on demand and supply: cost of production limits supply, and demand depends on diminishing marginal utility. Marginal utility varies not only between units of a commodity but between persons. So, rather than relying upon income distribution, as Say had done, to derive a negatively sloped demand schedule, Longfield derived it explicity from diminishing marginal utility: it was explained by intensity of demand, and intensity of demand was explained by diminishing marginal utility. Longfield was followed at Trinity College, Dublin by other writers in this tradition (Black, 1945), and in England a mathematician called W.F. Lloyd, who was appointed to the Drummond Chair of Political Economy at Oxford, put forward a clear analysis of utility, distinguishing total and marginal utility (Lloyd, 1833). However he conducted the analysis in terms of a Robinson Crusoe economy, and thus did not relate it to market price.

5.2.2 Distribution: Wages

The cost of production theorists, if they were not to explain prices by prices, had to provide a theory of the valuation of factor services. While Smith, with his usual appreciation of the complexity of economic relationships, provided a number of different approaches to wages, the main classical development followed two main lines. Firstly, there was the concept of subsistence wages. There is disagreement amongst commentators about how far the subsistence was physical, though if it were merely conventional (psychological) subsistence, with some allowance made for luxuries, it is difficult to see why a fall in wages below that level should reduce population, unless perhaps it led to postponement of marriage. The nature of the consumption basket is not clear, and this ambiguity conceals important problems, especially in the case of Ricardo, for if allowance is made for technical progress in the production of non-food items (as Malthus, impressed by the cotton industry, pointed out) then this could, in terms of the workers' budget, offset the rising cost of food, and thus enable subsistence wages (however defined) to remain constant despite diminishing returns in agriculture.

The concept of subsistence provided a theory of the long-run equilibrium wage. But the bulk of the emphasis in the classical literature is on the market period, and the so-called wage fund. This determined wages in the process of clearing the labour market. In the market period, the supply of labour could be taken as fixed; the wage rate was then determined by the intersection of a vertical market supply of labour and a demand curve for labour of unit elasticity, its position dependent on the size of funds pre-accumulated to employ labour. Thus it was capital, not demand for commodities, which constituted demand for labour, as J.S.Mill insisted.

As a snapshot of labour market clearing this approach perhaps had some merits: but it left open many questions. These included the determination of the size of the labour force (the participation rate) given the population, the determination of the size of the wage fund itself (particularly as, in the classical analysis, a tax on wage goods was generally to be passed on, implying that it increased the size of the wage fund), and the division of a given stock of capital between fixed and variable capital. This last was particularly important, as the wage rate would affect the choice of technique both within an industry and (by altering the relative price of different commodities) within the consumption basket.

The average level of wages was of course the mean of a distribution, and the theory of relative wages was supplied for classical economics by Smith, borrowing, from Richard Cantillon (c. 1680-c. 1734), the idea of equalisation of the net advantages of different employments (Cantillon c. 1730). While this affected only the supply of labour to different occupations, the implication was that the supply to each occupation would be perfectly elastic in the long run: in the short run, with barriers to labour mobility (not least the capital requirements of investment in training), the theory was incomplete without reference to the demand for labour in different kinds of employment – which was a corollary of the theory of market value already discussed. But even in the long run, as J.S. Mill and Cairnes (1874) pointed out, there were non-competing groups in the labour market, so that market segmentation on the supply side acted as a barrier to perfect elasticity of long-run supply.

5.2.3 Distribution: Profit

Profit in classical economics, as distinct from wages of management, was the return on capital, identified as interest plus a risk premium, from Smith onwards. Some writers, notably McCulloch, anticipated the twentieth century (Knight, 1921)concept of non-insurable risk. The source of the interest element in profit still needed analysis. A number of writers recognised that capital increased total output, thus sensing that its reward must be linked in some way to productivity – Lord Lauderdale (1759-1839) was an early example of this. But it was Samuel Bailey (1791-1870) and, more importantly, Nassau Senior who developed the idea of time preference, which limited the supply of this productivity-enhancing (and thus demanded) factor (Bailey, 1825; Senior, 1836). Then the combination of limited supply and positive demand gave rise to a positive price for the services of capital.

This development provided the basis for a more elaborate treatment by J.S. Mill, in which the motives for saving this limited supply of capital were analysed, the power to save out of income was considered, and the rate of interest was equated with the marginal supply price of saving. Longfield had earlier made the point that demand for capital at the margin could be identified with the marginal product of capital, and Mill (who was unaware of the work of Longfield) advanced the same argument.

The level at which the profit reward settled was thus dependent on both the demand for investment (in relation to the available supply of investment funds) and on the demand for consumption goods (which influenced the productivity of that investment), as the classicists from Smith onwards recognised. Ricardo, however, pursued his own agenda, and argued that the rate of profit for the economy as a whole was determined by the marginal rate of profit in the agricultural sector. This was consistent with the basic aim of his model, which sought to show how diminishing returns in agriculture would bring the economy to a stationary state. Not without reason, his contemporaries were unable to see why increasing manufacturing productivity should not offset diminishing returns in agriculture. Examination of Ricardo's model shows that Ricardo's view was arrived at, at least partly, by dividing the whole economy into one giant farm and a series of manufacturing tributaries. Then the profit-raising effect of innovation in any of the tributaries would be swamped by capital inflow and also (notably in his *Principles*) by the effect of rising wages (due to agricultural diminishing returns, and neglecting manufacturing increasing returns), which both raised costs and lowered the relative value of (capital-intensive) manufactures.

5.2.4 Distribution: Rent

The classical analysis of rent as an intra-marginal surplus has already been indicated. It blended (and confused) declining marginal product of factors combined with a fixed factor (land), with diminishing returns to scale, both of which produced rising agricultural costs at the margin and an intra-marginal producer surplus which was appropriated by the landlords, as farmers competed for the fixed supply of land. In competing, the farmers drove up rents until they were left only with the minimum acceptable level of profit on their agricultural capital. This analysis, though usually referred to as the Ricardian theory of rent was actually due at least equally to Sir Edward West, Malthus and Torrens, who all published at the same time as Ricardo in 1815: but it had been put forward, at least in terms of decreasing returns to scale, as early as 1777 by the Scottish writer James Anderson (1739-1808), as a later Scot, McCulloch, emphasised (O'Brien, 1970 p. 397).

Since the landlords gained the rents, and since agricultural improvements, at least in the short run, before population feedback, would reduce marginal cost and lower rent, the analysis was used by Ricardo as the basis of a class-conflict thesis. Agricultural improvements, while in the interests of the rest of the community, were, he held, against the interests of the landlords. In fact Ricardo's analysis was flawed in a number of ways, including the manner in which he treated technical change (absolute rather than proportional upward shifts in the marginal product curve, for instance) in agriculture. But in fact the whole argument was bogus. The agricultural sector was not one giant collective farm, and individual landlords had every interest in improvements which would increase the rents that farmers were prepared to pay for the particular land owned by the individual landlords. McCulloch deserves credit for having advanced this criticism (1849 p. 508), as well as a number of others, of Ricardo's thesis.

Given the classical treatment of rent, wages and profits, the treatment of relative shares was fairly easy to discern. Wages would eventually reach subsistence (though some, especially J.S. Mill, envisaged this as being greater than physical subsistence); but wage-earners would enjoy spells where wages were greater than subsistence (however defined), as capital accumulation ran ahead of population increase. Profits would fall to a minimum, both as a result of capital accumulation in relation to investment opportunities (Smith, Malthus, J.S. Mill) and as a result of diminishing returns in agriculture (as stressed by Ricardo). Rent would rise both as a share of national income and in absolute amount.

5.3 Money

5.3.1 Background

Classical monetary theory focused on commodity money (gold and silver) and bank notes, treating bank deposits as devices for increasing the velocity of circulation, even though the concept of the deposit multiplier was put forward in the 1820s by James Pennington (1777-1862) (Pennington, 1826-40), and by Robert Torrens (1837).

The basic theory stemmed from one of Hume's beautiful and concise essays. This put forward what has become known as the price-specie-flow mechanism, which may be summarised as follows: the price level of a country is a function of its money supply; the equilibrium price level is that at which there is no net flow of commodity money over the exchanges – there is balance of payments equilibrium. If the price level is too high, an outflow of metal will reduce the money supply (and the price level) to equilibrium, and vice-versa. World-wide, the value of gold and silver depends on its cost of production – Ricardo emphasised this. But the relative value of gold and silver on the one hand, and of commodities on the other, within a country, was defined by balance of payments equilibrium.

For reasons which have been debated by scholars, Adam Smith (it is generally, though not universally, agreed) did not put forward the price-specie-flow mechanism in the *Wealth of Nations*, even though it is clear from his *Lectures* that he understood it. Nonetheless it proved the pivotal idea in the two great monetary contoversies of classical economics – the Bullion controversy and the Currency and Banking controversy.

5.3.2 The Bullion Controversy

In 1797 the Bank of England was allowed to suspend the convertibility of its notes into gold. This effectively freed it from any immediate constraint on the quantity of bank notes which it issued – it no longer had to find gold to honour them. The resulting regime of inconvertible paper currency set the scene for a major monetary debate.

This was, if not the first, certainly the first major controversy between those who believed that causality ran from the money supply to the price level and those who believed the money supply to respond passively to the price level. Those in the first camp, the Bullionists, blamed the Bank of England for generating inflation once it was freed, as it was from 1797 to 1819, from the obligation to give gold in exchange for its notes. Basing themselves on Hume's analysis, the Bullionists were clear about the direction of causality running from the money supply to the price level. But their policy prescriptions differed. On the one hand there were those Bullionists who held to this position rigidly. The most famous member of the group – though certainly not the most original – was Ricardo, and their position is captured in what has come to be called the Ricardian Definition of Excess. This holds that whenever there are two symptoms of excess (paper) money supply – a high value of gold bullion (a low value of bank notes) and a depreciated exchange rate – then, by *definition*, the currency supply (Bank of England notes) is excessive, and the Bank should contract its issues.

The other group of Bullionists, of whom the most important was Henry Thornton (1760-1815), argued that while these tests were valid if the symptoms were sustained, they could, in the short run, arise from other causes (Thornton, 1802). Thus a depressed exchange could be due to harvest failure, for instance, and the high price of bullion could be due to an internal demand for gold because of financial panic. Severe damage to the real economy could be caused by contracting the note issue in the face of such transient causes of pressure.

Nevertheless, both groups of Bullionists agreed that in the long run the Bank must restrict its note issue sufficiently to permit a return to convertibility of its notes into gold.

The Anti-Bullionists, by contrast, argued that the Bank's note issue was simply responding to 'the needs of trade' as indicated by the 'real bills' presented to it for discount, the Bank issuing notes in discounting. The 'real bills' were bills of exchange resulting from real transactions in goods and services.

Unfortunately their position was not sustainable. Firstly, many of the notes issued had nothing whatever to do with 'real' transactions, but were ultimately a consequence of the Bank's position both as the government's bank and as lender of last resort to the financial sector, a position recognised since statements of it by Francis Baring (1797)and Thornton, and endorsed by the famous Bullion report of 1810 (Cannan, ed. 1925). Secondly, as Thornton pointed out, even had the Bank confined itself to 'real bills', the transactions to which they related had to take place at some absolute price level – and in the Bullionist analysis, the price level depended on the money supply. Thirdly, the Anti-Bullionists argued that the Bank could not over-issue its notes because it charged interest (discount) when issuing notes, so that no one would demand notes for which they had no need. But as Thornton – again – pointed out, there was an indefinitely large demand for loans and discounts if the rate charged by the Bank was less than the marginal rate of profit.

Ultimately the Bullionist case triumphed. Convertiblity of the note issue into gold was progressively restored from 1819. But, crucially, convertibility turned out not to be able to guarantee its own continuance, as most of the Bullionists had assumed it would.

For the 1820s and 1830s witnessed a series of financial crises. Although the first of these, that of 1825, was essentially a liquidity crisis, those of the 1830s brought the convertibility of the note issue into question, as the Bank of England found itself hard pressed for gold. The critics of the Bank charged it with bringing this about by aggravating an inherent trade cycle through pro-cyclical issue of its notes. The charter of the Bank was due for renewal in 1844, and the debates over the terms on which it should be renewed – and especially over what limits there should be on its discretion to issue notes – formed the basis of the Currency and Banking controversy.

5.3.3 The Currency and Banking Debate

Many of the issues from the Bullion controversy, and basically the same theoretical structure, are to be found in the literature of the Currency and Banking debate in the 1830s and 1840s. The two labels indicate what was at stake. The Currency School, positing that there was an endogenous cycle of real income, argued that if the money supply (by which they meant Bank of England notes, which they saw as the high-powered monetary base of the system) were regulated in accordance with the Ricardian definition of excess – and, specifically, contracted whenever there was a balance of payments deficit – this could act countercyclically. A balance of payments deficit was due to a rising price (and income) level, so it indicated the need for monetary contraction. According to the Currency School, the Banking School's prescription of allowing the money supply to respond to the 'needs of trade' would, on the other hand, magnify the cycle and even, by intensifying the price level rise which had produced the balance of payments deficit, result in such a gold outflow as to put convertibility of the note issue into gold in danger.

The Banking School, for its part, denied the basic causal association that underlay this analysis. It maintained that the money supply depended on the price level, that the balance of payments did not depend on the price level, and that deficits were self-reversing. Over-issue of notes was impossible as long as the Bank adhered to discounting only 'real bills' – any over-issue would automatically return to the Bank under the so-called Doctrine of Reflux.

However, both parties to the dispute shared a number of common assumptions. These included an acceptance of the need for convertibility, and of the key role of the Bank of England note issue in the money supply. Neither of these assumptions went completely unquestioned. Thomas Joplin (c. 1790-1847) argued cogently that the country bank notes were not, as both the Bullionists and the Currency School believed, controlled by the high-powered money base of the Bank of England notes; even more damagingly, he argued that the predominant influence on the price level was these very country bank notes rather than those issued by the Bank (O'Brien, 1993).

Joplin did however accept that the link with gold should be maintained under normal circumstances, though he was prepared to see it suspended in an emergency. The members of the Birmingham School, however, notably Thomas Attwood (1783-1856), did not even go this far (Attwood, 1816-43). In their view, an inconvertible paper currency could be used to inflate aggregate demand, with the aim of reducing unemployment, and they urged this. This idea had respectable antecedents in classical literature: Hume, in his essay 'Of Money' (1752) had put forward the idea that increases in the money supply would increase output and employment, though he certainly did not advocate an inconvertible paper currency. The mechanism involved was the spending of cash balances; and Malthus (who also did not advocate inflation) added to this the idea that forced saving in inflation would redistribute income to the productive classes. But though the inflationary mechanisms were recognised, inflation as a policy had few supporters – the experience of the Assignats in Revolutionary France had demonstrated the lurking danger of hyper-inflation, and the consequent damage to real economic activity.

It was not that the matter of aggregate demand was ignored by the classical writers. The misnamed Say's Law – in truth a distillation from Say's justification of economic growth, by James Mill, who used it to argue that markets must clear, using a barter formulation – was certainly used as an explanation of the underlying circularity of the economic system. But the classical writers, especially J.S. Mill in his *Unsettled Questions* (1844), as well as McCulloch, recognised that outside a barter system there could be excess demand for money, and that market clearing in a monetary, as distinct from a hypothetical barter, economy was an equilibrium proposition. Monetary changes were not neutral – if the classical economists had believed they were, the Bullion and Currency and Banking controversies would have been pointless.

5.4 Trade

5.4.1 Smith and the Gains from Trade

Perhaps the single most prominent feature of classical economics is the central importance attached to trade, and the corollary that trade should be free of restrictions. Yet the intellectual underpinnings of this position are complex.

It was Adam Smith who set the tone for classical economics by offering in the *Wealth of Nations* a critique of existing restrictionist trade policy, sustained and defended as it was by interest groups. The basic grounds for Smith's position, however, involved a blurring of the distinction between home and foreign trade. Specialisation and division of labour increased output per head, and thus produced increased national income, but were limited by the extent of the market. Freedom of trade increased the extent of that market, allowing greater division of labour. International trade, like interregional trade, was thus based upon the source of supply being the one with the lowest resource use – the producer with absolute advantage. An international outlet for the increased output was offered by trade – this was later called the Vent-for-Surplus doctrine – in exchange for goods (and raw materials) produced more efficiently abroad. But for sources of supply to be absolutely the most efficient, it was necessary for factors to be able to migrate to where they could work most efficiently. This was patently not the case with labour, even though capital might be footloose, as Smith's successors (with the exception of McCulloch who stuck with Smith's trade model) pointed out. In particular J.S. Mill explained that for trade to be based upon absolute advantage, labour would have to migrate (in his example, from one bank of the Thames to the other) in search of its highest productivity, as its output would have to be sold in the same market wherever it worked, but the return to capital would be higher, the lower the resource input.

5.4.2 Comparative Advantage

But if resources were not fully mobile internationally, it was still possible for trade to take place and to yield advantages for all parties, even though some of them were not the most efficient in terms of resource use. This idea, developed as the principle of comparative advantage, is usually associated with Ricardo's *Principles* of 1817. However its origins are not clear. Certainly Robert Torrens published the idea two years before Ricardo (Torrens, 1815; Robbins, 1958), and it has been plausibly suggested that Ricardo received the idea from James Mill, who had been anxiously scouring the literature for arguments in favour of freedom of trade (Thweatt, 1976) – even though in Ricardo's case the freedom of trade sought was not the generalised Smithian one, set in the context of a complex vision of economic growth, but that in corn.

At all events the argument was basically that if one country were generally more efficient than another, it would initially run a balance of payments surplus and gold would flow to it. This would inflate its money supply, and raise its price level, and this process, with the corresponding balance of payments deficit and money supply loss for the less efficient country, could continue until both countries were in balance of payments equilibrium, the price level of the less efficient country having fallen far enough that it could export those commodities in which it was least inefficient. Correspondingly, the more efficient country would import those commodities in which its productivity advantage was least, and export those in which its superiority was greatest.

The model, as put forward by Ricardo and other classical writers, assumed constant costs, and was stated in terms of labour resource use. But it has been shown to be easily generalisable to opportunity cost and to cases of increasing cost (Leontief, 1933; Viner, 1937). The model was normally stated in terms of two commodities, though Longfield made important steps in the direction of producing a model with a range of commodities, those of which were exported and those imported depending on the level of relative international prices.

5.4.3 Productivity Differences

This still left the question of the sources of differences in comparative advantage. On this the classical literature is much richer than the modern general equilibrium trade literature. Thus classical writers, especially Torrens, considered natural resource endowment, geographical position, stages of economic development, and technical development. Longfield and others considered the quality of the labour force, the degree of liberty and security, and differences of soil and climate.

5.4.4 Welfare Issues

The welfare gains from trade were not always fully explored in the classical literature, which tended to concentrate on the rise in income per head which trade produced. This is essentially Adam Smith's approach. In the case of Ricardo, there is a welfare gain (in terms of increased levels of wages and profits) from the postponement of the stationary state through corn imports. This idea is also present in Smith, though in the more general form that trade increased investment opportunities and thus the exhaustion of such opportunities was postponed by trade. But, as later writers, especially Jacob Viner (1937), were to stress, any removal of protection results in both winners and losers. The classical economists were no more able than later generations to avoid making interpersonal comparisions of utility – aided, at least implicitly, by the utilitarian maxim (which pre-dated Bentham) of securing the greatest happiness of the greatest number. There were, in particular, income distribution changes to be taken account of, and the general judgement in the classical literature is that the immediate loss of rent by landlords and protection lobbyists was significantly less than the gain to society as a whole while, in the long run, all parties would benefit from economic growth, even the landlords, who would benefit from increased population and thus increased demand for food.

5.4.5 The Terms of Trade

The forces which determined the levels at which the terms of trade settled were left unexplained by Ricardo, though he did offer a mechanism by which differing efficiencies could be translated into differing price levels, through specie flows. But the issue was of considerable importance in the context of the gains from trade: for the division of the gains between countries depended on the terms of trade. In the limiting case where a small country traded at a larger one's internal price ratio, a case explored by J.S. Mill, all the gains went to the smaller country.

Senior attempted to explain the terms of trade via relative labour productivity in export industries – which left unresolved the question of which were the export industries, since this actually depended on the terms of trade. Both Torrens (1827) and Joplin (1828) perceived that the key must lie in the reciprocal demand of each country for the products of its trading partners, and James Pennington identified the outer limits of the terms of trade as being the different comparative cost ratios of the trading countries. But it was J.S. Mill, in a performance which placed him in the first rank of economists (though he may have received some help from studying Whewell's work – Creedy, 1989) who explained the analysis of reciprocal demand so completely that it was left only for Alfred Marshall to translate it into geometric terms and pass it on to later generations (Marshall, 1879). Although Mill drew no curves himself, his analysis is permeated by a complete understanding of the importance of the elasticity of offer curves (as they are now called) for the terms of trade, and he explored the way in which shifts in production conditions shifted the 'Equation of international demand' so as to alter the terms of trade, in ways dependent upon the elasticity of the curves. He even extended the analysis to multiple equilibrium.

5.4.6 Trade Policy

These developments had important implications for the analysis of trade policy, and to some extent they undermined the Smithian case for free trade. For Torrens was able to show, in his celebrated Cuba case, that unilateral free trade would turn the terms of trade against a country: it would lead to a balance of payments deficit, which would cause an outflow of metal, reducing the money supply, and lowering the price level, thus turning the terms of trade against the free trade country (O'Brien, 1977). Moreover, the fall in the price level would increase the weight of fixed charges, such as taxes, and produce economic depression. Conversely, a country would benefit from protection.

Torrens's work was comprehensively criticised. Senior (1843) pointed out that a country which imposed protectionist duties would lose the advantage of specialisation; the reduction in output per head, and thus loss of competitiveness, could lead to a balance of payments deficit with third countries, to offset the gain of metal from the country whose products were now dutied. George Warde Norman (1860) showed that the effects assumed by Torrens would be much reduced if the assumption of constant outlay (a reciprocal demand curve of unit elasticity) were abandoned; indeed, in showing that part of the burden of an import duty would fall on home consumers, Norman anticipated the so-called Metzler case (1949) in twentieth-century literature. Norman also made the point that the logic of Torrens's case led to retaliation on the part of a country faced with new import duties on its exports, with the prospect of a tariff war, the original terms of trade restored, but international trade at much reduced levels – a welfare loss for all participants.

5.4.7 Unilateral Transfers

In general, the classical economists looked to balance of payments adjustment via relative price levels, consistently with their monetary theory, though there was often an implication that both the price and the income components of money income moved together, and the importance of income changes was stressed by John Wheatley (1772-1830) (Wheatley, 1807-22). The adjustment in relative prices would come about either through a change in the general price level, as under the Gold Standard, or via a change in the external value of the paper currency under convertibility. However the application of this analysis to the case of Ireland posed a problem.

There was a continual flow of rents to absentee landlords who owned property in Ireland but lived abroad, usually in England, and there was no price adjustment which could bring the balance of payments of Ireland into equilibrium – there was very little gold and silver in Ireland to start with, and the paper currency was shared with England.

It was in this context that there developed the concept of demand transfer which was, in the twentieth century, to prove a central issue in the controversy between Keynes and Ohlin over German reparations (Moggridge, ed., 1983). The idea was put forward initially by Irish writers – J.L. Foster (d. 1842) and Sir Henry Parnell (1776-1842), but it was most fully developed by McCulloch. He argued that the payment of rents to absentee landlords transferred the power of demanding commodities from Ireland to England; this enabled Ireland to generate sufficient extra exports to keep payments in balance, and thus a financial transfer was transformed into command over real resources.

5.5 Economic Growth

It seems to have come as a shock to many economists after 1950, when modern growth theory developed, to learn that the *Wealth of Nations*, and the subsequent classical literature, are all about growth. Yet economic growth is at the core of the classical literature. In laying the foundations for classical economics, Adam Smith established its focus on economic development.

5.5.1 Adam Smith

The *Wealth of Nations* takes as its starting point the idea that economics is about economic growth. The treatment pays attention both to the required institutional framework and to the mechanics which operate within that framework.

The required framework included well-defined and secure property rights, diffusion of agricultural property through control over the concentration of inheritance, and the provision of an infrastructure. Here government had a key role to play, in addition to its duty of providing defence and a legal system.

Within this framework, individuals pursued their self-interest, but as limited by law, religion, and custom (Robbins, 1952; Samuels, 1966). In so doing they allocated capital to where the return was greatest. Capital employed labour: and the output per head from a given population then determined national income. The determinants of output per head were the proportion of the labour force employed productively, and its productivity when employed.

The distinction between productively and unproductively employed labour in Smith's work is basically that between labour which adds value (and/or produces a vendible or storeable product) and labour employed in such areas as government and the law. Of course it could be objected that, at least in principle, the activities of lawyers are productive of growth, through increasing security of property, as are those of soldiers in the course of the defence of the realm. But Smith saw the big picture well enough: the State accumulated no capital, and had an apparently endless capacity for inventing sinecures; and its appropriation of labour, which might otherwise be employed productively, was not conducive to economic growth.

The productivity of productive labour depended on capital which supported specialisation and division of labour. In addition, Smith, and here he was influenced by the Physiocrats, believed labour to be most productive if employed in agriculture where the efforts of Nature assisted. Next came manufacturing (which, unlike agriculture, did not enjoy the gratuitous assistance of Nature), after that trading, and finally distribution. The ranking is far from convincing, though Smith was probably concerned to avoid artificial stimulation of manufactures (as in France) or trading. Perhaps most importantly, he recognised that, without an agricultural surplus, towns could not develop to serve their vital role.

But at the core of the argument was the idea that specialisation and division of labour – the mainspring of technology – depended on the supporting capital and the extent of the market. Smith's examples, of the increase in output per head in pin manufacturing, through specialisation of tasks, is immortal; but it has tended to obscure the bigger point that division of labour was of even more importance between occupations: it thus required a developed market system, and it proceeded to the point where the invention of machinery became a specialised occupation.

As output per head rose, wages were slow to adjust, capital was accumulated, extra labour was demanded, wages then rose, and population increased in response to this. The larger population, in receipt of increased wages, in turn increased the extent of the market. Thus economic growth involved simultaneous supply-side and demand-side mechanisms – which is what Say, following Smith, was to argue in his *Traité* (Say, 1817).

Welfare improved with rising wages, and the psychological subsistence level increased, so that subsistence in England would, as Smith observed, seem the lap of luxury to an African chief. Nonetheless the welfare effects of rising national income were not completely unambiguous; division of labour raised output per head, as Smith stressed in Book I of the *Wealth of Nations*; but it also had harmful effects in confining people to monotonous and dulling work, as he was to explain in Book V.

Nonetheless, for as long as economic growth continued, it had a tendency to raise wages and to accustom people to small luxuries. However Smith did not believe that economic growth would continue indefinitely. He did not anticipate the immediate arrival of a stationary state; he believed that it would only come about through the exhaustion of investment opportunities – which was a fairly distant prospect, given technical progress, the establishment of colonies, and security of property which allowed accumulation to continue till the minimum acceptable rate of profit was reached at a low absolute level. But in the end, growth would cease.

5.5.2 Smith's Successors

It was Smith's great achievement to set the whole agenda for the classical treatment of economic growth, and the content of his book dominated all later discussions, with the exception of Ricardo. The latter focused instead on the mechanics of his model, in which economic growth was going to come to an early halt because of the existence of agricultural protection. But for the rest, we find a continuation of Smith's research programme, though now bearing Ricardian scars.

Malthus stressed similar elements to Smith – security of property, capital accumulation, natural resources and trade; and, living after the technical explosion of the Industrial Revolution had made such a major impact, he naturally added material concerning invention. His treatment of population, as both responding to wages in excess of the minimum acceptable level, and also as stimulating development through widening the market, went beyond Smith, but the most novel element in his approach (one also stressed by Lauderdale) was an emphasis on the importance of ensuring sufficient aggregate demand, an important element of which, he contended, was the existence of what Smith had classified as unproductive labour.

McCulloch too stressed the importance of accumulation of capital, resources, division of labour, and security of property (especially after the political turbulence of the 1830s and 1840s); and he added to this, religious tolerance, an expanded (and extensive) role for government, and a banking system. His approach went further than Smith, reflecting the later era in which he wrote in stressing the importance of invention, and especially in introducing the concept of human capital (which he held to assist invention), leading in turn to emphasis on the importance of education. He also, like some other writers (notably Say), rejected Smith's distinction between productive and unproductive labour – in his case, on the grounds that the desire for the products of unproductive labour could stimulate activity.

However McCulloch also made some uneasy Ricardian additions to the picture, especially the idea that diminishing returns in agriculture would ultimately lower profits. But in the end he rejected this, basically on empirical grounds – profits were not, after all, declining, and diminishing returns in agriculture were offset by technical progress in manufactures.

J.S. Mill's treatment of economic growth also exhibited uneasy incorporation of Ricardian elements. He stressed the ultimate inevitability of diminishing returns in agriculture, despite asserting that technical progress had put them in abeyance for the 20 years before the appearance of his *Principles.* He invoked not only this Ricardian reason for the ultimate decline to be expected in profit, but also the Smith-Wakefield thesis of exhaustion of investment opportunities. There was certainly the prospect of a stationary state; but it was not to be as miserable as Ricardo had envisaged – family limitation would ensure that wages were not unduly depressed, and there could be redistribution of wealth by means of legacy duties.

Despite these Ricardian scars, the majority of Mill's treatment could, however, be described as *The Wealth of Nations* updated to the 1840s, following the impact of the Industrial Revolution. Thus he borrowed material relating to technology, scale, organisation and joint stock companies from the book by the mathematician Charles Babbage (1792-1871) *On The Economy of Machinery and Manufactures* (1832). From John Rae (1796-1872) he borrowed not only material on invention but a remarkable treatment of capital (Rae, 1834), covering both the motives for saving and the ranking of investment opportunities by pay-back period, to arrive at a theory of investment due to the interaction of time preference and the marginal productivity of investment.

5.5.3 Machinery and Aggregate Demand

Thus the treatment of economic growth in classical economics is overwhelmingly due to Smith. Nor did Ricardo's views on technological unemployment find much support. Ricardo, drawing on John Barton (1789-1852), had advanced, in the third edition (1821) of his *Principles*, a numerical example in which the introduction of machinery resulted in unemployment which was not temporary (Barton, 1817; Ricardo, 1817-21). As usual with Ricardo, there was something special about the arithmetic; and in this case it was the assumption that aggregate demand fell in proportion to the technological unemployment initially produced. Most of the other classical writers regarded the argument as unconvincing because it was obvious, on the most casual inspection of recent economic history, that employment had increased hugely in parallel with the employment of machinery. In addition, several writers, including Malthus, McCulloch and J.S. Mill, all noted the special nature of another of Ricardo's assumptions, in his arithmetical example – the investment of wage capital in machinery. This was an aspect of another typically Ricardian peculiarity: Instead of one giant farm to represent the agricultural sector, we had here one giant firm. Otherwise, as the Swedish economist Wicksell was later (1934) to point out, machinery installed by one firm would displace labour, wages would be depressed by the initial unemployment, and this would make the old technology profitable again, so that the displaced labour could be absorbed.

But if technological unemployment was not regarded as a serious problem, there was more concern over the possibility of demand-deficient unemployment. Malthus, in particular, was concerned, like the eccentric Scottish peer Lord Lauderdale, that capital accumulation would proceed so fast that there could be no market for the output of the expanding industries. Malthus and Lauderdale were thus not concerned with over-saving but with over-investment. Too much investment at one time could come on stream together, depressing prices to the point where the marginal return on capital was negative. They both looked to 'unproductive consumption' – an expanded public sector and its employees – to maintain a sufficient level of aggregate demand and to keep some resources away from production. Malthus in particular envisaged a role for public works.

Of course a number of writers, notably Ricardo in correspondence with Malthus, argued that a fall in the marginal productivity of investment would choke off saving, and would thus be self-correcting. But, as Malthus sensed, reliance on long-run equilibrium did not rule out disequilibria between successive equilibria.

5.6 Public Finance

Adam Smith devoted the whole of the final book of the *Wealth of Nations*, Book V, to public finance, and after him an extensive literature on taxation developed (O'Brien, 1999b). This included a substantial volume by McCulloch (1845b), his *Treatise on Taxation*, which ran to three editions (1845, 1852, 1863). The literature revolved around taxation and debt; there was little support for public enterprise (with the exception of Bentham) or for public ownership of land (with the exception of James Mill).

5.6.1 Taxation

The starting point for tax analysis was Smith's four maxims of taxation – equality, certainty, convenience and economy. The first of these, equality, could mean taxation according to equal benefit received, or according to equal ability to pay, and Smith did not distinguish these concepts. He seems to have been following Petty here. But later classical economists adopted one or other standpoint. The benefit theorists included Hume, Bentham and J.B. Say. The most important writers on taxation after Smith, McCulloch and J.S. Mill, both favoured an ability to pay approach, though they meant different things by it. For McCulloch it meant equality of burdens on different sectors of the economy, so as not to distort the process of economic growth, although he also looked at equality in a narrower sense when considering how an income tax might work. For Mill, ability to pay meant that taxpayers should suffer equal sacrifices of utility, though whether these sacrifices should be equal absolute ones or equal proportional ones was not clear. Equal marginal sacrifice would have involved levelling down of incomes from the top, of which Mill would not have approved, because he was opposed to progression.

Although both direct and indirect taxes were considered in the literature, the majority opinion, from Hume and Smith onwards, favoured indirect taxes, despite recognising that they distorted relative prices, gave rise to smuggling, and could be levied in an oppressive way. McCulloch, who had, in any case, severe reservations about direct taxation, since he believed it could not be levied in accordance with ability to pay, thought indirect taxes, at least at low levels, avoided investigation, were convenient, could be used for sumptuary purposes, and stimulated effort and ingenuity. He adopted Hume's idea of tax stimulation of technical progress, illustrating it with the history of distilling. He also believed that indirect taxes, since they discouraged consumption, could stimulate saving.

The main exception to the general approval of such taxes was Ricardo, who believed that a tax on wages (which in his model would be passed on and paid out of profit, a conclusion arrived at by telescoping the long run and short run together), together with a tax on rent, and one on interest on government securities, was the ideal tax system. J.S. Mill, while recognising that government would have to rely chiefly on indirect taxes, favoured a limited use of direct taxes on houses, land, and increments of rental value.

The classical economists approached the analysis of taxation itself in two different ways. Firstly, there was discussion of the taxation of different kinds of factor rewards – wages, profits and rent. Secondly, they discussed particular modes of taxation, such as the income tax. While the majority of writers (with the exception of Ricardo, who concentrated very largely on the first approach) covered taxation in both ways, the more empirically orientated ones, especially McCulloch, paid particular attention to forms of revenue raising.

5.6.2 Functional Rewards

While Smith and Ricardo believed that a tax on wages would be passed on (because in the long run wages could not be pressed below subsistence) Hume, and later, McCulloch, could see that this was not the case. But, with the exception of Ricardo, there was general opposition to such taxes. Nor was there any enthusiasm for taxing profits – hardly surprisingly, given the failure to do so under the 1799-1816 income tax. In Smith's view, profits were undiscoverable and they contained a necessary reward to risk bearing, which was part of the supply price of capital to different occupations. He did not believe that this was a fit subject for taxation. Taxes on profits might also affect resource allocation; Ricardo argued that a tax on profits in particular trades would alter relative prices through capital mobility, reducing the supply of commodities which generated taxed profits to the point where price had risen far enough to restore profit to the same level as in other employments of capital. Although this was a neat theoretical result, both McCulloch and J.S. Mill were critical of it, noting the barriers to capital mobility and the possibility that technical progress might offset the tax. But it was generally accepted, in accordance with the Ricardian model, that a tax on agricultural profits, which was not offset by technical progress, would increase rent by raising marginal cost in agriculture.

A tax on rent itself was theoretically ideal, in that it would not affect factor allocation, being levied on an intra-marginal surplus. James Mill was particularly keen to tax increments of rental value. But in practice there was a serious problem: the analytical argument applied to economic rent, but this could not be distinguished as a payment within gross rent, which also included a return on capital invested in improvements. Thus a tax on rent would act as a disincentive to improvements in agricultural technology. (However a tax on houses, part of which fell on the ground landlord, did not suffer from this disadvantage).

5.6.3 Revenue Raising

The income tax was a matter of serious controversy during the classical era. Introduced in 1799, it was abandoned in 1816, and the records burned. The civil service kept quiet about the fact that there was a duplicate set of records (Hope Jones, 1939). But it was reintroduced in 1842, and eventually became a mainstay of public revenue, despite attempts by Chancellors of the Exchequer, including Gladstone, to abolish it. In operation, it was characterised by widespread fraud and evasion, and it found little support amongst the classical economists.

There was little enthusiasm for progression in such a tax, apart from that implied by the exemption of a subsistence minimum. McCulloch famously said that once proportionality was departed from, we were 'at sea without rudder or compass'. Of the major figures who did show some sympathy for progression, at very low levels it should be said, Smith and Say dealt with the issue only briefly, and it was mainly discussed by pamphleteers (O'Brien, 1999b).

A related issue was the question of whether permanent and temporary incomes should be taxed at the same rates. On the grounds of ability to pay, McCulloch and others argued that the tax should be a proportion of an income imputed to a capitalised value of an income stream. Capitalisation of an income stream involved such problems over the use of life tables, and the arbitrary interest rate applied to the capitalised value, that McCulloch himself thought an income tax unworkable.

Taxation according to capitalised value implied different tax rates for nominal income streams of the same value, depending on the expected duration of the stream – essentially whether it was permanent or temporary. The tax itself was expected, until 1860, to be a temporary tax; had this not been the case, the problem would have been less pressing as the ratio of the capitalised value of tax to the capitalised value of income would be the same in both the temporary and the permanent income cases. A second argument for differentiation of tax rates between permanent and temporary incomes (basically, income derived from capital and income derived from work) was that offered by J.S. Mill and also McCulloch – the desirability of allowing some margin for saving out of temporary income, to make it possible to accumulate capital and thus to receive some permanent income. Mill also advanced the 'double taxation of savings' argument – the idea that, because the income out of which savings were made was taxed, and the income from the savings themselves was taxed, this amounted to double taxation of savings – though in truth it was taxation of two separate income streams. Finally there were those, notably J.G. Hubbard (1805-1889) of the Bank of England, who argued that income earned by mental or physical exertion should be taxed at a lower rate than rentier income.

There was less discussion of legacy duties. Bentham and J.S. Mill both favoured steep progression, but McCulloch favoured proportionality. The former looked to legacy duties as a means of redistribution; but the latter, despite his expressed dissatisfaction with the distributional consequences of the factory system, did not seek redistribution by means of the tax system, and was more consistent than his opponents in recognising that the disincentive argument against progressive taxation also applied to legacy duties, unless people were completely unconcerned about their successors.

One particular tax discussed at length was tithes – the ecclesiastical 10 per cent tax on output. Ricardo, assuming zero elasticity of demand for agricultural output, argued that tithes raised marginal agricultural cost by the full amount of the tax. Others, notably Smith and McCulloch, doubted this – output might be reduced instead, given more reasonable demand assumptions, and there could be a switch of output to untithed land as well. But tithes, which were a nineteenth century scandal, were generally condemned by the classical writers. Smith pointed out that they interfered with improvements, and Ricardo argued that, because they were proportioned to gross rather than net output, they were an increasing burden as diminishing returns in agriculture occurred, hastening the onset of the stationary state by reducing the amount left for profit.

There was pragmatic acceptance of a range of miscellaneous duties, such as stamp duties (and McCulloch favoured a tax on postage, opposing Rowland Hill's Penny Post), though stamp duties on leases, and law taxes, were resisted. Lotteries were roundly condemned.

Commodity taxes were seen as the major source of revenue, however. This was indeed for long the case. It was generally argued that these taxes should be at low levels (to avoid the obvious disadvantages such as their regressive nature, and the danger of smuggling) and some writers, particularly McCulloch, argued that such taxes should be on both home and imported sources of commodities, to avoid a protective effect.

Such taxes on home-produced commodities were generally held to raise price by the full amount of the tax. (Say, it is true, saw that with a rising supply schedule, and a negatively sloped demand schedule, this should not be the case.) McCulloch, consistently with his retention of the Smithian absolute advantage trade model, also held that import duties were paid entirely by the home consumer; and this enabled him to argue for the balancing of duties on home produced and imported commodities. The reciprocal demand analysis of J.S. Mill and of Torrens showed that this symmetry did not necessarily exist, however.

It was generally agreed that such taxes had to be on 'luxuries' – tobacco, tea, beer and sugar – rather than on 'necessaries' (basic foodstuffs), taxes on which might raise wages even if not fully passed on. Since these 'luxuries' were widely consumed by lower-income groups, however, taxes on them were still in practice regressive.

5.6.4 National Debt

With the advent of the Revolutionary and Napoleonic wars with France from 1793 to 1815, the National Debt, which had been dismissed by mercantilist writers as merely something owed by the right hand to the left hand, became a problem which could no longer be ignored. Debt service charges assumed a significant relationship to national income, and cost well over half of gross tax revenue.

The objections put forward by the classical economists to the creation of public debt rested not just on opposition to the creation of a rentier class (Hume's complaint) – though Malthus approved of such a class, as a way of maintaining aggregate demand – or even the possibility, envisaged by Hume, Smith and Say, of public bankruptcy. Rather, the core idea was that debt involved a future burden. Firstly, it consumed productive capital, so that future output would be lower. Secondly, output would be depressed in future by the taxes levied to service the debt (although Ricardo, unlike Say, rejected this). Thirdly, the taxes led to capital export, and, again, to lower output in future. Even J.S. Mill, more attuned than most to the Ricardian idea of abundant capital and lower profit, accepted that if public borrowing raised the rate of interest it was crowding out productive investment.

Thus public borrowing was suitable only for emergencies – chiefly war with France. Ricardo, however, went further and argued that even in this case tax finance should be used. It would discourage wars, and avoid the capital consumption involved in borrowing. The necessary taxation would admittedly fall on property rather than on professional incomes; but, startlingly telescoping the long run and short run together, Ricardo held that entry into professions would depress earnings far enough to compensate for this. The burdens of debt and taxation were equivalent, he held, because taxpayers would write down the future value of income streams in the light of future taxes to service debt, by an amount equivalent to the tax that would have to be raised if debt were to be avoided – assuming that taxpayers were prepared to capitalise beyond their own life expectancy.

But this left the existing large debt. A capital levy plan dated from an essay of 1714 by Archibald Hutcheson (d. 1740). It had been criticised by his contemporaries, notably Hume, for just the sort of distributional inequities (it would fall largely on visible property) that Ricardo, who put forward a similar plan, ignored. McCulloch (who had in 1816 supported debt interest reduction, until learning from the calculations of Robert Mushet (1782-1828) that the fund holders had been robbed during wartime inflation through receiving interest payments in depreciated paper currency) lent his support to Ricardo, but later rejected the scheme because of the distributional inequities. J.S. Mill was also opposed to the scheme on the grounds that those not owning property would be relieved of a tax burden at the expense of property owners.

But if a capital levy was rejected, there was no enthusiasm for a Sinking Fund either – the British version had proved a sham. It had increased total borrowing in order to maintain payments into the fund at a time when government revenue was straitened, and it was conceptually based upon bogus compound interest calculations – there was no source of revenue other than tax – due to, amongst others, the eighteenth century writer Richard Price (1723-91) (Price, 1774).

In the end, the only solution was for government to budget for a surplus to repay the debt although, until the income tax became a permanent weapon of government, such surpluses proved elusive.

5.7 Policy Prescriptions

The classical economists were the first group of writers to appreciate fully the allocative role of the market. But the market operated within a framework of law, religion and custom, and the first of these was properly subject to development, pragmatically, as needs were discovered. Thus the classical economists exhibited no die-hard adherence to a dogmatic laissez-faire. From Smith onwards, a legitimate role for the State was recognised. Bentham and J.S. Mill distinguished between the list of things that the State should do (the agenda) and the things which it should leave alone (the non-agenda), the contents of each list depending on the stage of economic and political development.

But the classical economists did not suffer from the delusion of neo-classical welfare economists that there was an omniscient, benevolent, State; government intervention had to be justified, and it posed dangers to economic progress because progress depended upon variety and competition. Moreover there was the ever-present danger of abuse of public authority for rent-seeking – the mercantilism which Smith had attacked so vigorously in Book IV of the *Wealth of Nations*.

Smith had indeed stressed the role of the State in the provision of defence, justice, a legal system, infrastructure and coinage, and even advocated the regulation of inheritance and of leases. He defended shipping restrictions (the Navigation Laws), and legal limitations on the rate of interest (the Usury Laws). In these matters he was not followed by later classical writers, all of whom believed in letting the market clear. However his advocacy of public health regulation and banking regulation was supported, and a number of writers went much further – McCulloch advocating employer accident liability and supporting Samuel Plimsoll's campaign to prevent the overloading of ships. Even the regulation of public utility charges was approved both by McCulloch and J.S. Mill.

Of course in part they were, as some have argued, simply following the trend of public opinion. But, firstly, they were not hampered by any laissez-faire dogmatism from responding to revelations about, for instance, the risks faced by sailors; secondly, they examined the economic implications of possible legislative remedies.

It was legislation to amend and regulate a functioning price system. Socialism, though J.S. Mill flirted with what he called socialism (more accurately, co-operation) under the influence of Mrs Harriet Taylor, held no attraction for them and centralised and totalitarian socialism was completely foreign to their outlook.

5.7.1 Factories

In general, the classical economists were reluctant to endorse intervention in industrial organisation. Thus although they (especially McCulloch) supported the regulation of child labour (and in McCulloch's case explicitly stated that there was no objection founded on economics to this) they were ambiguous about separate regulation of women's work, and opposed to the limitation of factory hours – Torrens and Senior famously, opposed the Ten Hour Bill, though on reasoned economic grounds (that the resultant increase in costs would lead to a fall in exports, a balance of payments deficit, an outflow of metal, a fall in the price level, and a reduction in profitability).

5.7.2 Machinery

They had, however, no objection to measures to cushion unemployment resulting from mechanisation through the provision of alternative employment (Bentham), unemployment relief (Torrens), or even slowing the pace of mechanisation if necessary (J.S. Mill). Even when intervention was not recommended (as in the report on the plight of the handloom weavers, written by Senior) there was no belittling of the hardships involved, and what was presented was an economic analysis of the likely effects of intervention. There was no objection in principle to intervention; merely pessimism about the likely outcome.

5.7.3 Poor Relief

There were, however, some who objected in principle to the provision of poor relief, notably Ricardo and Malthus. The basis for the objection was the idea that poor relief subsidised population growth out of net rent. Other writers, led by Senior, favoured making poor relief available, but only in the workhouse, a view which triumphed in the New Poor Law of 1834. The disincentive to seeking relief which this 'indoor relief' provided was held to neutralise the adverse effects on labour supply and population control of providing poor relief, which would otherwise be on an 'outdoor' basis. A third group, of whom McCulloch was the most important, favoured retaining the existing system of outdoor relief, though abolishing wage subsidies paid under the so-called Speemhamland system, and instead providing relief straightforwardly for those not earning wages.

5.7.4 Education

A major check to population growth could be provided through education, which would help to raise the psychological subsistence level; and all the classical economists favoured public provision of education – though not a State monopoly. There was, however, a difference of view over whether fees should be paid. Smith and McCulloch argued that reliance upon income from fees was a necessary incentive for the teachers – a market test. But Senior and J.S. Mill believed that education was an instance of market failure – those paying fees could not tell the difference between a good and a bad supplier – and so they argued for State-funded education. But both groups emphatically supported the provision of schools, and McCulloch stated quite explicitly that there was no laissez-faire objection to this.

In addition to the beneficial effect on population, education would provide investment in human capital. This was a theme of both Smith and, more particularly, McCulloch, and also of J.S. Mill who saw education as supplying potential managers as well as increasing equality of income through erosion of the rents enjoyed by those with favoured access to education. Education would also have the benefit of enabling people to understand the need for security of property, and it would thus favour economic growth.

5.7.5 Trade Unions

If education discouraged population growth, it would help market wages to rise. The same was true of the removal of the Speenhamland wage-subsidy system. But trade unions themselves were of limited value, in the view of the classical economists, though (with the exception of Senior) they did not favour restricting them. Indeed McCulloch took part in the campaign for the repeal of the Combination Laws (designed to prevent the establishment of unions) in 1824. Trade unions could not raise wages above the market equilibrium, at least in the long run, but they had a valuable role in raising wages to equilibrium in the short run. This avoided unnecessarily depressed wages, which themselves reduced productivity and altered the distribution of income – wage earners were, as Smith had argued, the majority of the population, and wages below equilibrium implied a welfare loss. The trade unions rectified the balance between employers and employees.

5.7.6 Ireland, Colonies and Emigration

Of course wages were also depressed by immigration from Ireland, and, partly with this in mind, the classical economists devoted a good deal of attention to Ireland, pressing the case for agricultural, governmental, and social and religious reform. This was partly in the hope of raising the psychological subsistence level and checking the astonishing Irish population growth which, it was correctly recognised, lay at the heart of the problem.

One solution to the problem of Irish population was emigration, and a number of writers, especially McCulloch and Torrens, favoured this, though J.S. Mill regarded it as a very inferior solution when compared with peasant proprietorship. Those favouring emigration also favoured a reform of landholding and agriculture in Ireland, envisaging the introduction of large scale English-style capitalist farming. Some also favoured the introduction of a Poor Law like that in England, though this was opposed by Senior (who favoured public works), Ricardo and Torrens (who was Irish).

If emigration were to be a solution, it would be desirable to set up colonies to take the emigrants. From the time of Adam Smith onwards, it had been argued that it was a mistake (following the North American experience) to try to retain control of colonies, forcing them into restrictive forms of trading with the mother country, which was a form of mercantilism – government in the interests of merchants. But the establishment of colonies was seen as beneficial by Smith, since it could raise profits by increasing investment opportunities, and colonies permitted increased specialisation and division of labour.

However, the view that colonies could be an outlet for population really only came to the fore in the 1820s and 1830s. Initially the advantage perceived was the transfer of population from a margin of low productivity to one of high productivity; but, under the influence of Edward Gibbon Wakefield (1796-1862), this developed into the case for 'scientific colonisation'. The argument was that if colonial land were charged for, this would both provide funds to finance further emigration and produce a concentration of population, as new emigrants sought, through paid employment, to accumulate funds to enable them to buy land. Concentration would produce economies of scale – specialisation and division of labour within a concentration of population or, as the twentieth century came to call it, a 'growth centre'. Interestingly, those who supported Wakefield – and they included Torrens, Senior and J.S. Mill – seem to have moved also in the direction of Smith's argument abour raising the profit rate through increased investment opportunities, thus quietly side-lining the last vestiges of the Ricardian model in which only corn imports could do this.

5.8 Conclusions

The literature of classical economics is enormously rich and varied. It covered virtually all areas of concern to later economists, and laid the foundations for the development of economics ever since. Some parts of what it contained – essentially the microeconomics – were submerged in the course of that development; but the work on trade, growth and money has proved to be extremely durable and has outlived scientific revolutions, and changes of economic fashion. It is a literature which is still worth our attention today.

Chapter 6

Marshall's World in His Correspondence

Marshall's work continues to fascinate economists. His name has been appropriated, via the term 'Marshallian', for a whole range of views which he not only never held but of which he certainly would not have approved; but there is also a genuine and substantial interest in the content of his writings which offer a salutary perspective on the excesses of modern economic literature and sometimes, as Brian Loasby (1978) has recognised, contain material going beyond developments in modern theory. While the Marshall industry does not begin to compare, either in scope or in ideological fervour, with the Ricardo or Keynes industries, it is still true that, as George Stigler (1962, pp. 283-4) remarked, 'no man could live long enough or read fast enough to read everything written on Marshall, and no sensible man would want to'. However, amongst the contributions to literature on Marshall since Stigler wrote those words have come items of real value to economists. These have included Whitaker's exemplary *Early Economic Writings of Alfred Marshall* (Whitaker, 1975) and we now have his edition of Marshall's *Correspondence*. In addition, we have, edited by Groenewegen, a new supplement to the *Official Papers*, the main volume of which, edited by Keynes, appeared in 1926.

6.1 Whitaker's Edition of Marshall's Correspondence

There are 1148 letters in this edition, together with related documents. Compared with the 555 letters in Sraffa's *Ricardo* (which, unlike the Marshall *Correspondence*, was designed to be exhaustive) this is a substantial tally; at the same time it is significantly less than the three huge volumes of Walras correspondence and the seven volumes of Jevons. The edition is nonetheless the product of enormous efforts, although only the tiny number of people who have actually undertaken work of this sort can have any idea of the personal costs involved. It is true that Whitaker has been aided, at least in some of the later *Correspondence*, by the existence of typewritten copies, and does not seem to have had to struggle, like Jaffé, with the full-scale horrors of Walras's handwriting, and that he has had help at various times from no fewer than six research assistants. Even so the task must have been huge.

The assembly of the raw material alone has clearly been a major undertaking – 37 collections are listed, of which only 11 are in Cambridge, and there are inevitably gaps – which Whitaker no doubt made efforts to fill. In particular, there is no Hawtrey correspondence (though Marshall and Hawtrey were actually related) and most of Foxwell's replies to Marshall's letters also appear to be missing. But search is necessary if only to avoid the fate which befell Sraffa – the Ricardo edition was already in type when the Ricardo-Mill correspondence was discovered (Sraffa, 1951, pp. viii-x). Despite Hayek's view (formed during an earlier era when the pressures on academics were somewhat different) that it is the search for papers which is the enjoyable part (Hayek in Mineka, 1963, p. xxiv) no reader should underestimate the efforts which Whitaker has made. Even then he has clearly been faced with difficult decisions on inclusion; a letter referred to (1996, II, p. 121, n. 4) as being in the Foxwell papers is excluded, while another letter to Foxwell of the same date is included. Whitaker (1996, III, pp. 419-20) contains a list of Marshall material not used by him.

Even amongst specialists in the history of economic thought there are significant differences of opinion about the value of enterprises such as this (Coats, 1973, p. 51). At one extreme, George Stigler was dismissive. But I take the view – and not, I hope, simply because I have been involved in this kind of enterprise myself (O'Brien, 1971) – that there is considerable merit in this kind of work if only (though not only) because it enables us to tease out the implicit assumptions which lie behind an economist's reasoning. In the case of Marshall, whose taste for the elliptical verged on the Delphic, this is particularly valuable – indeed essential. One could not know what Marshall was really trying to say about rent (and his reasons for perpetuating a confusion stemming from Ricardo) without knowing that his antipathy (or, at best, highly ambiguous attitude) towards Jevons lay behind this reluctance to set the analytical record straight. Yet so powerful was Marshall's influence in this regard that as late as 1959 Samuelson could complain that the matter was still confused (Samuelson, 1959, p. 8).

It is true that, within these volumes, there is much that is of limited interest outside the Byzantine world of Cambridge (on which Kadish and Tribe (1993) have been able to shed some light). But there is much else here which enables us to obtain a more rounded picture of Marshall than that which can be extracted from the existing secondary accounts; and Whitaker can also reply to critics of an enterprise of this sort that he has already made substantial analytical pieces by Marshall available elsewhere in his earlier editorial work.

As Whitaker notes, Robbins (in reviewing that earlier work) said that a comprehensive edition of the correspondence was an 'essential desideratum' for Marshall scholarship. As Whitaker points out, Marshall's letters have often been quoted or referred to previously 'and offered as telling evidence' (1996, I, p. ix). There is now considerable value in seeing what Marshall actually wrote – which, in not a few instances, produces a picture which is a good deal less negative than that of the secondary accounts.

Whitaker has searched extensively, included letters which Marshall published in the press, pointed to inaccuracies in transcriptions by others, supplied names omitted from earlier versions of a letter (including in the Keynes edition) and produced what is in some ways a portrait of a Victorian intellectual community – even Silvanus P. Thompson (the author of perhaps the most famous introduction to calculus (Thompson, 1910), though Whitaker does not make this connection – makes his appearance (Whitaker, 1996, II, p. 379).

Whitaker has attempted to cater for different kinds of readers, by the provision of a detailed index subdivided into an index of letters by correspondents, an index of persons, and a subject index with eight divisions. Each of the subdivisions contains in turn further divisions. There is a biographical register at the beginning of each volume – 140 individuals for volume I alone. These are quite well done, with the length of the entry varying in relation to the content of the volumes. Thus Ricardo gets three lines, Smith three, and F.A. Walker gets thirteen.

The footnotes are at the end of the letters, rather than at the foot of the page (this can be frustrating in the case of long letters), and the presentation has a couple of idiosyncrasies. Marshall's address (Balliol Croft), of which the first line at least could have been supplied, so as to give the sense of a correspondence, has been suppressed throughout and replaced by a footnote referring to it. At the same time, for reasons which it is hard to imagine, the full names of every correspondent are spelled out at the head of every letter on every occasion (though the vice-chancellor of Cambridge has to make do with his title (1996, I, p. 203)). Thus endlessly we have Herbert Somerton Foxwell; we have Edwin Robert Anderson Seligman, and even Langford Lovell Frederick Rice Price. We also have a correspondent 'Beatrice Potter' and it is only with the second letter in the exchange that the uninitiated get a clue that the correspondent is Beatrice Webb (1996, II, pp. 45-8).

Of course much – almost 20 per cent on my count – of the *Correspondence* has already appeared, above all in the *Memorials* (Pigou, 1925) but also in work by Coats, McCready and others[1]. The references to the previous appearances in the notes are somewhat unpredictable, though Whitaker deserves credit for signalling these. But it is still worth having the originals, in unexpurgated form where possible. It is clear that Pigou had the plums for *Memorials* – many of one's favourite quotations from that volume can be found here. At the same time, it is not true that all the interesting letters had already made an appearance there; in particular there are two interesting letters to Foxwell on wages (1996, I, pp. 95-7) which did not appear there. The letters which did appear in *Memorials* are very largely reproduced from that volume. The vast majority of the originals seem to have disappeared, which is rather puzzling, although a few have survived (e.g. III, p. 321). In number, if not in interest, the *Memorials* letters are, however, very much in the minority in this remarkable collection.

6.2 The Official Papers: A Supplement

Groenewegen's volume is a by-product (an external economy which Marshall would have enjoyed) of his work on Marshall's biography (Groenewegen, 1995). The contents are as follows: Marshall's evidence to the committee on higher education in Wales and Monmouthshire (1880); a note to the Gold and Silver Commission (1888); extracts from the final report of the Royal Commission on Labour (1894); Marshall's examination of witnesses before that Commission (1892); a memorandum on trade disputes (dated by Groenewegen at 1893); and a Treasury document which has in the past been attributed to Marshall.

The work (for which Groenewegen had three research assistants) has been

[1]Whitaker cites previous appearances (in secondary sources) for 56 of the 332 letters in Vol. I (17 per cent), 86 of the 400 in Vol. II (21.5 per cent) and 85 of the 416 letters in Vol. III (20 per cent).

well done. Each extract has a separate introduction, and the notes are accurate and informative.

This material has already been drawn on, for the most part, by others – the Bristol evidence on higher education has been used notably by Kadish (1989) – but there is considerable value in having the material available in a single volume. There are also considerable merits in reprinting Marshall's examination of witnesses before the Labour Commission, not least because his examination has been misrepresented in the past. The extract from the report of that Commission is however more doubtful, and I will return to the matter later on.

The inclusion of the Treasury document poses difficult questions, though I think Groenewegen was right to include it. The original is not in the Marshall papers, nor is there any overlap between it and Marshall's 1908 memorandum on the same subject. Groenewegen in his introduction weighs the evidence concerning the document judiciously, but concludes, like Whitaker (1996, III, p. 245), that the attempt by J.C. Wood to attribute this document to Marshall is mistaken. A critical point noted by Groenewegen is that there are no duplicate passages whatever between the 1903 and 1908 documents, despite Marshall's tendency to reuse material. But the truth of the matter is apparent to anyone familiar with the Civil Service; it is in fact a 'briefing paper', one of those internal pieces written by a civil servant, drawing (mostly without acknowledgement, though there is one give-away footnote (p. 352)) on a number of sources, to impress his superiors. But as a document which represents part of the debate going on at that time (ably summarised by Groenewegen) it is worth including.

Whitaker's three volumes and Groenewegen's one together enable us to form a picture of Marshall and of his relationships with his contemporaries. It is worth exploring this in more detail.

6.3 Marshall the Man

One of the things which emerges very clearly from these volumes is Marshall's total immersion not merely in his work but indeed in some kind of a mission. His zest for travel, and for observation on his travels (so nicely brought out by Mary Marshall , 1947) is evident in these volumes. Frail as he felt himself to be in Cambridge, he was apparently quite happy to come home from Austria via Budapest so as to broaden his experiences (Whitaker, 1996, III, p. 47). Those who have wondered how Marshall managed to work during his long absences from Cambridge may be reassured to know that when he went to Palermo after leaving Bristol he had 7cwt of books sent by sea (1996, I, p. 148). He later (1996, II, p. 95) reports having 3cwt sent to the Tyrol. From the letters written to his mother during his visit to the United States, which feature in Whitaker's first volume (1996, I, pp. 36-84), it is apparent that he was a shrewd observer of both people and events. Indeed, given Marshall's evident later struggles at literary composition, it is surprising to find how well he wrote in his letters home. His account of a debate with an Irish priest will strike a chord with anyone familiar with the pre-1960s Catholic priesthood, with its articulate, and frequently well-read, membership – the shrewd (and agnostic) Marshall however putting his finger both on limitations in the priest's reading and on ambiguities in Irish attitudes to England (1996, I, pp. 40-42). Some of his letters are the same as the entries in Whitaker's earlier volumes, including his account of his interview with the American economist Carey (1996, I, p. 82; 1975, II, pp. 92-3). There is also the remark that 'there is scarcely a virtuous woman in the state of Nevada' (Whitaker, 1996, I, p. 73; 1975, I, p. 54). One assumes that this remark was not made on the basis of extensive research; shrewd though he was, there was a naiveté about some aspects of his personality which well-matched that of Jevons who, in a visit to the gold fields in Australia, reported encountering 'an extraordinary wooden construction of considerable size, inhabited almost entirely by a number of females, in a way not easy to understand the reason of' (Black, and Könekamp, 1972, I, p. 227).

It was not only in foreign countries that Marshall was a keen observer, as Mary Marshall has testified. He was concerned about the problems of towns, a supporter of the Garden Cities movement, and extremely critical of the housing conditions in urban slums, not only in this country but also in Germany (Whitaker, 1996, II, pp. 302-4; III, p. 81). In fact he was probably as opposed to slums, in his own way, as the much more strident Beatrice Webb (Webb, 1928). He had a genuine concern with poverty, like Jevons who also walked extensively in London observing the conditions (Black and Könekamp, 1972, I, p. 17 and n), and he had a deep regard for the work of Charles Booth. In fact the picture which emerges is one which confirms the view expressed by Keynes in his obituary that Marshall was simply too anxious to do good (1933, pp. 171, 220).

Yet there is no avoiding the fact that there is a large literature, almost all of it connected with Cambridge, which seems intent on denigrating Marshall. The great founder of the Cambridge economics Tripos is the target of remarkable hostility. For example the references to him in Joan Robinson's *Imperfect Competition* are almost all negative (Robinson, 1933). In part the hostility to Marshall seems to be ideological in origin – he was insufficiently critical of the capitalist system and was himself critical of Christian Socialist types such as F.D. Maurice (1996, II, p. 295; see also Shove, 1944, pp. 51-61). This would certainly explain why Sraffa was in the vanguard of the critics (Sraffa, 1926). But even Robbins, though he sought to distance himself from those who exhibited a generalised hostility to Marshall (Robbins, 1928, p. 387n) delivered himself of the remark that Marshall 'was obviously a bit of a Turk at home' (1955, p. 64). This remark, so 'politically incorrect' to modern-day readers, does however offer, at least on the surface, a clue to some of the denigration of Marshall. For the idea of Marshall as a domestic tyrant has become established; and as it became established, stories – which lost nothing in the telling – got repeated and enlarged to the point that even a man so fundamentally generous as Robbins could deliver himself of this opinion.

Whatever the truth of the matter, those hoping to follow the long and deplorable Cambridge tradition of depicting Marshall as, maritally and in all matters relating to women, possessed of horns and a forked tail (even if falling remarkably short of what might be called in the context of a rather wider world the Picasso-Marx standard in these things) will find little support in these volumes.

It is noticeable that the denigratory material written about Marshall often relies, indeed, not on Marshall's own words, but on those of individuals such as (especially) Beatrice Webb who strongly disliked him (and who had her own very particular agenda) or even, in one case, a condemnatory article on women and cycling which appears to have *no connection with Marshall at all* (Groenewegen, 1995, p. 249). Indeed Marshall writes with evident pleasure of cycling with his wife (Whitaker, 1996, II, pp. 182, 199).

But poor Marshall cannot win. If he did say or write something 'incorrect' this would prove he was a monster (at least by the standards applied, uniquely, to him); if he fails to oblige in this respect, as in these volumes he does, this is due to his deceitful nature (McWilliams-Tullberg, 1975, pp. 88-9). If he expresses himself in a painfully 'correct' manner in a letter to his mother, on the need for female emancipation, it can be 'proved' that he later radically changed his views – this on the basis of a diary entry by Beatrice Webb written no less than six months after the event (ibid., p. 236; Webb, 1928, pp. 397-8).

Indeed, it is highly beneficial that Whitaker has printed letters which had previously been used in support of this general position. Thus the letter to Foxwell which refers to a letter of Marshall to the Vice-Chancellor of Cambridge has been used as evidence about the content of the letter to the Vice-Chancellor which does not seem to have survived; and the Foxwell letter

(1996, II, pp. 120-1) does not provide evidence for the weight placed upon it but is written in the most general terms (Groenewegen, 1995, pp. 247-8). The fact that the female lecturer who apparently aroused Marshall's ire in this episode was a very close associate of his sworn enemy William Cunningham is somehow lost sight of.

All this is not to argue that Marshall was a paragon of all virtues. He was clearly vain, as his portrait painter William Rothenstein avers (1932, II, p. p. 130); he was distinctly touchy over priorities and, as we shall see, his behaviour towards Jevons was, at best, ambiguous. But there is really nothing in these papers to compare, on the scale of Political Incorrectness, with the recent sensational release from the Keynes papers (Toye, 1997).

Beatrice Webb has managed to convey to posterity the picture of a misogynist. Yet the *Correspondence* here shows that Marshall encouraged Helen Bosanquet (who as Helen Dendy had been one of his pupils) in her writings (1996, III, p. 66) and there is a distinct contrast between the courtesy of his exchanges with her and his bluntness towards Beatrice Webb who, he had no hesitation (it would seem) in pointing out, had plagiarised other people for her book on co-operation:

> Your voice is far sweeter, and true, and more eloquent than Mitchells; but your arguments are his. I do not think you have omitted one on wh[ich] he does not lay stress, or that you have laid stress on one on wh[ich] he does not also insist. And I believe that nearly all of them are true & important in their way; but that scarcely any one of them is the complete truth, & that in nearly every one you have suppressed ... those that make for hope & life (Whitaker, 1996, II, p. 45).

I do not think that there is any doubt that, as his more sympathetic critics have recognised, Marshall was not a misogynist but was driven by a social philosophy about the importance of women in the home which was grounded in his own harsh upbringing (Coase, 1984), protected from his Calvinist father by his mother, as he recounts in the *Correspondence* here, indeed (1996, II, p. 118). This led him to have an extraordinarily strong belief in the social role of women, a role which he feared would be fundamentally damaged by the 'masculinisation' of women (1996, III, pp. 230, 248). We may smile patronisingly at such beliefs; but the attitude which they represent is hardly demonical.

6.4 Letters as Evidence

Whitaker offers a very timely warning against the weight sometimes placed on letters (notably by parts of the Ricardo industry (O'Brien, 1981), although Whitaker does not make this explicit) in interpreting a writer's position: 'Readers need to be reminded that hasty scribblings – although often revealing – are less accurate than carefully honed publications in representing a writer's *conscious* position. Too often, casual phrases from a letter are made to bear too heavy an evidential weight, a risk enhanced by over-polished editorial transcription' (1996, I, p. x,). As it happens Marshall himself was unusually eloquent on the same subject:

> But may I venture to expostulate against your having allowed anyone to publish the contents of my private letter to you. A new terror is introduced into life by the notion that loose emotional phrases wh[ich] one has written with a free & careless hand in a private letter may appear in print without notice (1996, II, p. 124).

Indeed, in these volumes there is a marked contrast between the informal letters and the formal letters which Marshall wrote, which are polished, elliptical, and sometimes allusive to the point of impenetrability, such as his letters to the press on trade policy (II, pp. 309-11) or even letters to public figures such as Lloyd George – his letter of 1908 (1996, III, pp. 196-7) is correct analytically, although no one without considerable familiarity with international trade theory would know this.

6.5 Diaries as Evidence

But if these questions arise in relation to letters, which at least one other person was supposed to see, they arise *a fortiori* in relation to diaries – and this is highly relevant in the present context since Marshall's critics have lighted on the extracts from Beatrice Webb's diaries in her *My Apprenticeship*, and Whitaker here uses the diary of J.N. Keynes for footnote material. It is clear that such diary extracts should be treated with considerable reserve. It seems evident that the diary of J.N. Keynes was essentially a safety valve, written as a release for day-to-day feelings of frustration rather than as an exercise in considered long-time judgement.[2] An interesting modern parallel is provided by the celebrated diaries of Alan Clark whose off-the-cuff references to the then Defence Minister, Tom King, and indeed the record of the day-to-day frustrations which King caused Clark, seemed to Clark himself, on cooler reflection, uncalled for.[3]

The nature of Beatrice Webb's diary is rather different – often malicious in content, it was sometimes (as in the extract referred to above) written up months after the event, and with a view to publication, albeit in expurgated form where necessary (Webb, 1928, p. 367-8). Indeed insulting material about Marshall was published from the diary after his death, while parts of the same entry relating, also insultingly, to Mrs Marshall, were omitted – pre-

[2]For a contrary view see Maloney (1985). However, it is clear, even from the extracts used by Whitaker, that it is not true that there is a 'complete absence of friendly references' (Maloney, p. 64) to Marshall in J.N. Keynes's diaries.

[3]'Clark refers in his introduction to 'Tom King ... whom I still regard with affection in spite of the way in which we treated each other in the heat of our political careers ... And there are many others to whom references coloured by the irritation of the moment are ill-suited' (1993, p. xii).

sumably because she was still alive.[4] It is evident that Beatrice Webb found Marshall (whose work she also had the greatest difficulty in understanding, seeking help from Sidney (Webb and Webb, 1978, pp. 163, 165-6)) rather tiresome at best. But her vitriolic pen ranged more widely. Consider the following description of Mary Marshall: '... badly dressed with protruding teeth, weak eyes and quickly changing colour ... who sits by his [Marshall's] side, selects his food and guards him from obtrusions' (Webb, 1982, p. 285).

She was even more vitriolic about poor Edgeworth, who had the misfortune to have found her attractive – for which she despised him.[5] (As Creedy (1986, p. 13) has remarked, the diary entry probably sheds more light on Beatrice Webb than it does on Edgeworth.) She was particularly infuriated by Marshall's acknowledged reluctance (1996, II, pp. 385) to state his moral position and by his claim to be in some sense Socialist but not to have followed in the path of herself and Sidney (Webb, 1983, p. 109). (In view of the direction in which that path led – Webb and Webb, 1935[6] – there is much to be said for Marshall's caution). In truth, Marshall's 'Socialism' was indeed nothing more than traditional British Puritanism, shorn of its nonconformist religious rationale, so that his references to 'my semi-socialistic

[4]Compare Webb (1928, p. 415; 1982, p. 285).

[5]'Francis Edgeworth (nephew to Maria Edgeworth) Professor of Political Economy at King's College, London: eminent statistician of the mathematical type, a gentle-natured and intellectual man with queer cramped nature, excessively polite and diffident in manner, formal and exact in phraseology – an old admirer and a present lover! Even if I had not my work, the prospect of matrimonial engagement, and the preliminary receipt of addresses, bores me intolerably, a horrible sense of unreality in a relationship which seems to spring from chance and ripens without occasion for intimate knowledge on either side. This man is pathetic: his somewhat pedantic and thoroughly conventional conversation, his starved affections, the furtive glance of unsatisfied desire peering through the old bachelor habits and appearance of forty-four years of celibate continence, the little stories from Punch, the correct literary reminiscences, the greenness in all that appertains to emotional experience – and yet, withal, a hidden fire burning within, which might burst forth and burn down conventional barriers and dry sticks and leave the ground free for a new spring growth of thoughts and feelings. Poor fellow! He bores me' (1982, pp. 283-4).

[6]As is well known, the question mark in the title of Webb and Webb (1935), *Soviet Communism: A New Civilisation?*, was dropped for the second edition – published in 1937 at the height of Stalin's terror.

principles' (1996, III, p. 375) should be understood in that context.

6.6 The Marriage

Since so much of the hostility to Marshall involves claims – based on remarkably little evidence – concerning his marriage, the subject is unavoidable in the context of this *Correspondence*. In particular nothing more than a single sentence, itself capable of a variety of interpretations, originating with Mrs Sidgwick – certainly one of Marshall's enemies – has been used as the basis for speculation.[7]

However there is really very little in this collection which bears directly on the marriage and what there is does not do so in a negative way. It is quite clear that Marshall himself encouraged Mary Paley, and that both husband and wife were anxious that she should teach at Bristol (Whitaker, 1996, I, p. 94). Foxwell was persuaded to provide a testimonial in her support in this endeavour (1996, I, p. 97). The internal evidence concerning the co-operation of Alfred and Mary Paley on *The Economics of Industry* is, at least in my judgement (O'Brien, 1994c, pp. x, xxi, xxx), such as to suggest that Marshall showed considerable patience when faced with the reality of the gap between his rapidly evolving ideas on such issues as marginal productivity theory – at that time he was clearly working towards the idea of wage equal to the present value of marginal revenue product (1996, I, pp. 105-6) – and the classical analysis of Mill which provided Mary Paley's intellectual frame of reference. Indeed he seemed to have allowed her to have considerable freedom in dealing with such matters as co-operation (1996, I, pp. 110-111). He expressed a hope that he would be able to continue working with

[7] Groenewegen (1995, pp. 248-9). The passage comes from E. Sidgwick (1938, pp. 168-169). 'Mrs Marshall visited her friend in the evenings too, and brought her difficulties to be talked over at the Newnham fireside.' Given that Mrs Sidgwick was five years her senior, and at the time both women were well into middle age, it seems rash, to say the least, to conclude that the only source of such troubles was what Groenewegen refers to as 'her increasingly mysoginistic husband'.

her (1996, I, pp. 140) and encouraged her work on the history of economic thought (1996, I, pp. 153). He was clearly devoted to her, and in 1891 sent, by mistake, to Seligman a letter intended for Mary which began 'My own dear darling' (Webb and Webb, 1978, p. 310). On her part there seems no doubt that she was perfectly sincere when she wrote to J.M. Keynes that 'To have been for so many years his companion, & to have helped, however little, such a life as his is an enviable & delightful lot' (1996, III, pp. 385), and it seems patronising to doubt her sincerity.

6.7 Marshall and his Contemporaries

6.7.1 J.N. Keynes

It was Ronald Coase (1975, p. 25) who drew particular attention to the doubts cast upon the idea that Marshall and his contemporaries were what Coase called a 'little band of brothers' by J.N. Keynes's diary – although, as suggested above, diary entries of that kind may be taken with a pinch of salt.[8] Nonetheless there were clearly considerable tensions in Cambridge – as in any university – and not least between Marshall and the elder Keynes. Keynes did comment, extensively, on the *Principles* (1996, I, pp. 251-6) and, to some extent, the tensions were not intellectual but administrative – Marshall felt ill after committee meetings (1996, I, p. 250) – though Keynes was wont to let off steam to his diary and wrote that Marshall's literary style was 'often atrocious' (1996, I, p. 256, n. 4). Marshall made efforts, which at times seem to have been almost frantic, to persuade Keynes to go to Oxford (1996, I, pp. 182-196); while Kadish has interpreted this as meaning that Marshall wanted to get Keynes out of Cambridge (1989, 149-50), it is also the case that Marshall made a distinct effort to forward Keynes's career by attempting to

[8]The quotations used by Coase (1975, pp. 26-7) rather exaggerate the degree of tension because – necessarily, given the confines of a journal article – they include only extracts from letters which, taken as a whole, are kindly in tone and clearly well meant (I, 299-300, 338-40), especially the second of these letters.

secure for him the founding editorship of the *Economic Journal* (1996, I, pp. 264, 287), that he provided a most generous testimonial for Keynes which Keynes described in his diary as 'wonderful' (1996, I, p. 131, n. 1), and that Keynes did appreciate Marshall's encouragement over his book on methodology – again, if the diary entry is to be believed (1996, I, p. 341, n. 6).

Inevitably, however, there were also difficulties; Keynes found Marshall overbearing at times in conversation (1996, I, p. 268, n. 1), and there is no doubt that Marshall was concerned to establish his pre-eminence in Cambridge – understandably perhaps, since J.N. Keynes was to oppose the introduction of the Economics Tripos.

6.7.2 Cunningham

Marshall's troubles with William Cunningham are very much in evidence in the volumes – and indeed Cunningham was described by Jowett as a 'troublesome & unscrupulous fellow' (1996, II, p. 84). Marshall, it is true, supported Cunningham for the Tooke Chair in London (which he got) in 1891 (Cunningham, 1950, p. 69) – but in this case this may truly have been to get him out of Cambridge. Cunningham had actually attended Marshall's lectures – and, according to his daughter, had found them stimulating and enjoyable (Cunningham, 1950, p. 19). But, before Marshall returned to Cambridge in 1885, Cunningham had established himself there and seems to have been teaching economic history without any reference to economic theory. Indeed he had hopes of the Chair when it was vacant in 1885, only to have these hopes dashed by the news of Marshall's candidacy (ibid., p. 64). Once Marshall was established in the Chair, he did indeed take steps to ensure that Cunningham's course included some economic theory; and this, Cunningham's daughter reports, the historian greatly resented. Nonetheless this hardly excuses the extraordinarily intemperate tone of Cunningham's

1892 attack on Marshall in the *Economic Journal* – his article is offensively entitled 'The Perversion of Economic History' – and he was enraged by the refusal of Edgeworth, as editor, to accept further missives from him after Marshall had replied to the attack (1996, II, pp. 82-3; Cunningham, 1950, p. 66; Coats, 1967a, p. 712). Subsequently Cunningham seems to have waged a campaign against Marshall from the stronghold of his position in London (Kadish and Tribe, 1993, p. 40). In the mid-1890s there seems to have been some co-operation, according to a letter cited by Kadish (1989, pp. 182, 285 n. 81) (which does not seem to have been selected for the volumes); but Cunningham was later to fight Marshall's introduction of the Economics Tripos (1996, II, pp. 317 n. 2, 361; III, pp. 12, 24 n. 1, 25 n. 6, 28, 404 n. 5; Kadish and Tribe, 1993, pp. 158-9). All this is particularly unfortunate because Marshall clearly attached considerable importance to history and to historical studies; but he sought a balance between history and theory, while Cunningham did not.

6.7.3 Ashley

Marshall's relations with Ashley were ambiguous. Unlike the intemperate Cunningham, Ashley's criticisms of Marshall, which had appeared in the *Economic Journal* after the publication of the first edition of the *Principles*, were temperate, and extremely well aimed. In his 'The Rehabilitation of Ricardo' (1891) Ashley exposed very effectively the extent to which Marshall had rewritten intellectual history so as to credit Ricardo with far greater achievements than were his due. There are undoubtedly signs within the *Correspondence* of tensions with Ashley concerning whom Marshall, initially at least, seems to have had reservations (1996, I, p. 174). But when Ashley went to the United States, relations seem to have become cordial (1996, II, pp. 99, 130, 141, 175). Later on, Ashley was one of the candidates for the Chair at Birmingham and, according to Whitaker, Marshall 'gave Ashley the nod' when asked to rank candidates for that appointment (1996, II, p. 327, n. 4). Ashley was also the editor of a remarkably fine edition of John Stuart Mill's *Principles* (Mill, 1848) and, given both Marshall's initial debt to this book and his irritation with Jevons's attitude towards Mill, this may have helped to incline him towards Ashley in the longer term. However Ashley's own attitude is also uncertain; it was Ashley who told Foxwell how Marshall had engineered his defeat in the 1908 election to the economics chair (1996, III, p. 383, n. 3).

6.7.4 Jevons

Marshall's attitude towards Jevons can also most charitably be described as ambiguous. On the one hand he maintained proper professional relations with Jevons, who was one of the external examiners for Mary Paley (1996, I, p. 29) and he lent him a copy of Rau (1996, I, pp. 107-108). Jevons in turn provided a testimonial for Marshall when he went to Bristol (1996, I, p. 88). But Jevons's attitude to Ricardo still rankled with Marshall – indeed it rankled even after Jevons had died (1996, I, p. 164; Black, 1970, p. 30) – though there is nothing in the *Correspondence* to explain Marshall's idolisation of Ricardo.

Marshall's tone towards Jevons hovered between the ambivalent and the patronising. Thus he expressed pleasure to Jevons at criticism by George Darwin of the first chapter of Cairnes's *Leading Principles* (Cairnes, 1874) – but since this chapter involved an attack on Jevons, the tone of his letter could be viewed as making a dig as well. In some respects his letter could be regarded as something of a snub to Jevons; he thanks him for sending his paper on a mathematical theory of political economy – 'I read it with interest some time ago in a newspaper' (1996, I, p. 32) – and although he apologised to Jevons for the failure to make proper acknowledgement of Jevons's priority in the treatment of capital used in *The Economics of Industry*, (1996, I, p.

122) the apology was somewhat inadequate and half-hearted (O'Brien, 1994c, p. xx). Indeed Jevons would really have been justified in being a little paranoid about Marshall – under the civilities, the tone of the letters seems frequently condescending, and this is reflected in his comments to Foxwell, as Whitaker notes (1996, I, p. 33, n. 4). The fact is that Marshall denigrated Jevons on technical grounds (1996, I, p. 255), was condescending about his mathematics (1996, I, p. 164) and was critical of Jevons as a theorist (1996, II, p. 71). Despite his own acknowledgement of Jevons's priority concerning capital, he was critical of Jevons on the matter of distribution (1996, I, p. 105) and he accused Jevons of confusing the hedonic and the economic (1996, I, p. 307).

Though he had a genuine regard for Jevons's statistical work, encouraging Foxwell in the editorial work on *Investigations in Currency and Finance* (1996, I, pp. 150-1, 164; Jevons, 1884) he made several claims – which do not seem to be substantiated by the content of his *Early Economic Writings* (Whitaker, 1975, I, pp. 37-52) – to have anticipated Jevons's theoretical contributions (1996, I, p. 167; and see Whitaker's note, I, p. 170, n. 3). This tendency seems to have become more marked as he got older (1996, III, pp. 182-4, 227-8).

Of course it is true that, whatever the subsequent attempts to downplay Marshall's own mathematical expertise, he had come second in the mathematical Tripos to Lord Rayleigh, who won a Nobel Prize for Physics in 1904. A study of the Tripos papers for 1865 would certainly indicate that, the old-fashioned nature of the mathematics notwithstanding, Marshall was a properly trained mathematician (Creedy and O'Brien, 1990, p. 142) while Jevons, by his own account, struggled with the work which De Morgan gave the students at University College London (Black, 1973, pp. 403, 406, 422). But though this may explain much of Marshall's attitude, it is possible to feel that the same attitude leaves a slightly bad taste.

Jevons was, as a product of the University of London, and a one-time staff member at the University of Manchester, someone very much outside the charmed circle of Oxford and Cambridge. There is however one character who was very much inside that charmed circle, with whom Marshall's relations deserve the closer scrutiny which these volumes make possible. The long story of his relationship with Foxwell is in the volumes for all to see.

6.7.5 Foxwell

There are more letters to Foxwell in these three volumes than to anybody else. Marshall was clearly close to Foxwell in the 1870s, and some of his particularly warm letters begin 'Beloved Fox' (e.g. I, pp. 94). When he went to Bristol he gave Foxwell his rosewood reading desk ('I love it too much to sell it & cannot use it at Bristol' – I, pp. 91) and there is a shared understanding in the letter which he wrote to Foxwell about the death of the latter's mother (1996, I, p. 101).

Foxwell was not merely consulted extensively during the writing of the *Economics of Industry* (1996, I, 86-114); he seems to have been able to act as a buffer in some of the tensions between Mary Marshall's decidedly Millian approach and Alfred's rapidly developing neo-classical analysis. Unfortunately hardly any of the letters *from* Foxwell to Marshall seem to have survived; the excellent Index of Letters by Correspondent shows that there were no letters from Foxwell in volume I and two each in volumes II and III. This in itself would seem to require some explanation, although there is no basis for such an explanation and Marshall has already suffered too much from speculation without evidence, so I will not add to the list of speculators.

The exchanges over the *Economics of Industry* continued even after publication (1996, I, pp. 116-120, 147), and Marshall also had extensive discussions over book recommendations (1996, I, pp. 96-100) with Foxwell, whose enormous bibliographic achievements should never be underestimated (Keynes, 1933, pp. 283-92).

It was Foxwell through whom Marshall, while at Bristol, seems to have retained his contact with Cambridge, and indeed his hopes of securing a lectureship there (1996, I, pp. 114-116). Foxwell for his own part offered to resign half his salary to Marshall to enable him to return as a lecturer in 1879, (1996, I, p. 116); and two letters which Whitaker reproduces in appendix III to volume I show that in 1881 Foxwell again pressed Marshall's case and suggested foregoing £50 of his own College stipend towards Marshall's salary (1996, I, pp. 360-362).

Letters still start 'Beloved Fox' occasionally, as late as 1894 (1996, II, p. 119). While Marshall's testimonial for Foxwell (1996, I, p. 133), written to support his application to University College London in 1881, is perhaps a little reserved on Foxwell's intellectual qualities, they do seem to have worked well together for many years, and Marshall had Foxwell's support over the establishment of the Economics Tripos, although by that time there had been severe difficulties over teaching.

But then, in 1908, Foxwell, who was so confident of succeeding Marshall in the Chair at Cambridge that he had begun preparing his lectures (1996, III, p. 191), found that he had been defeated in the election by the young Pigou. This episode has been examined at length by Coase and Jones and it seems clear that Marshall did indeed engage in what Whitaker refers to as 'blatant manoeuvring in Pigou's favour' (1996, III, p. 190 n. 1; Coase, 1972; Coats, 1972; Jones, 1978). Foxwell was not merely exceedingly bitter at the time; his bitterness was exceedingly long lasting. Whitaker quotes a letter from Foxwell to J.N. Keynes of 1912 which shows the resentment after four years to have been as strong as ever (1996, III, p. 292, n. 3); even more remarkably, another note to Keynes quoted by Whitaker (1996, III, p. 383, n. 3) shows the bitterness to have been undiminished 14 years after the event.

Of course one might take the view that Foxwell had not only been over-confident but also that he in his turn had been rather lucky to get the Chair at UCL when Edgeworth was a contender (Kadish and Tribe, 1993, p. 31). It could also be argued that the later personality of Foxwell, as reflected in the volumes, shows signs of being both tense and increasingly difficult to work with – rather insecure, and a university politician to his fingertips.

But that said, there really do seem to have been some remarkable ambiguities in Marshall's dealings with Foxwell, although the absence of the replies to Marshall's own letters makes it difficult to arrive at a balanced judgement. Certainly, just as with J.N. Keynes, Marshall seems at times to have been trying to be both overbearing and confusing – there is a letter to Foxwell on rent which merits both these descriptions (1996, I, pp. 92-3). There were intellectual difficulties too; Marshall and Foxwell did not see eye-to-eye on bi-metalism (1996, II, p. 108ff.) and there were undoubtedly differences over the matter of free trade, particularly after Marshall had come off the fence on this question (1996, III, pp. 55, 69). Indeed Foxwell attacked the Free Trade Manifesto to which Marshall was a signatory (1996, III, p. 55).

However, this does not seem, to judge from the *Correspondence*, to be the nub of the matter. Rather it was to do with the whole development of economics in Cambridge. Marshall had not found Cambridge to be particularly fertile ground for the recruitment of young followers (Kadish, 1989, p. 125). Moreover, in trying to develop the teaching of economics in Cambridge, difficulties with Foxwell had undoubtedly been encountered. In one letter Marshall set out at length his version of these difficulties (1996, II, pp. 319-21). Treating this as an isolated matter, Marshall would certainly have preferred to arrive at an accommodation with Foxwell, as indeed he did at the time that Foxwell was an unsuccessful candidate for the Chair of Commerce at Birmingham (1996, II, pp. 324-7). But it seems to have been the advent of Pigou which brought matters to a head. For Pigou seemed both able and willing to undertake the kind of teaching which Marshall considered necessary but which Foxwell declined to get involved in. As Marshall wrote to Foxwell: 'I put on Pigou solely to do that which I had three times implored you to do' (1996, II, p. 320).

Foxwell of course knew Pigou – indeed he had been one of the examiners for Pigou's thesis (1996, II, pp. 341-2). But what he had failed to take account of was Marshall's desperate feeling of need to build up the succession – his mission. It was this which led to Foxwell's baffled rage – 'If I had had the slightest idea that I should have been rejected in favour of an untried man young enough to be my son ... I would never have put up. I could have well understood the preferance [sic] of Ashley or Cannon [sic]' (1996, III, p. 191). But Marshall had found somebody who, though not a product of the mathematical Tripos, showed a distinct bias towards analytical matters even though, ultimately, his mathematics were to prove distinctly laborious and, on one occasion, to let him down.[9] (Pigou thus came from a different intellectual background from that of Bowley and the younger Keynes, whom Marshall favoured. Both were mathematicians by training. But Fay, whom Marshall was also cultivating, was not.) Marshall felt sufficiently confident of Pigou's capacity that he informed the hapless Foxwell that 'Pigou is in my opinion likely [to] be recognised ere long as a man of quite extraordinary genius' (1996, III, p. 190).

The episode of the election to the Chair must thus be seen in the wider context of Marshall's concern with his successors. Whether this is attributable to vanity, or to a quite extraordinary singleness of purpose in being 'anxious to do good' is, in the last resort, a matter of taste and temperament.

When he wrote to the Vice-Chancellor of Cambridge in October 1907, giving notice of his resignation the following year, he did indicate that he planned to be professionally active after retirement, as indeed he was; and this activity certainly involved the continued cultivation of likely successors,

[9] 'The mathematical argument by which Professor Pigou establishes his final formula is rather confusing: not only are there a number of obvious slips in the presentation, but also the steps in the derivation do not seem to follow logically one from another' (Johnson and Carter, 1950, p. 837).

notably the younger Keynes whom Marshall got involved in a joint attack on Karl Pearson (1996, III, pp. 256-60, 263-7).

6.7.6 Edgeworth

Marshall's acquaintance with Edgeworth began when Edgeworth sent him a mathematical paper 'The Hedonical Calculus' from *Mind*, 1879. Marshall at first wrote to Foxwell asking who Edgeworth was (1996, I, p. 124), but then wrote a polite letter of acknowledgement to Edgeworth, praising the work (1996, I, p. 124). This was followed by another one which seems to have been occasioned by comments made by Edgeworth as a result of receiving, via Jevons, a copy of Marshall's *Pure Theory* (Marshall, 1879; I, pp. 124-5). Marshall then received from Edgeworth a copy of his great work *Mathematical Psychics* (1881), and (foolish fellow) on the basis of this receipt, rather than of careful reading, he wrote a testimonial in support of Edgeworth's application for the Chair at University College London (1996, I, p. 135). He then discovered, like so many subsequent readers, as Whitaker notes (1996, I, p. 135 n. 8; see also Creedy, 1986) that the book was so allusive, not least to the mathematical techniques being used, as to be baffling. He was also flabbergasted to learn that Edgeworth was not, as Marshall had previously believed, a young man, but somebody of 40 years old (1996, I, p. 137).

Yet a close friendship developed, and there is no doubt of the respect in which each held the other. Marshall provided testimonials for Edgeworth, not only for University College London but also for the Tooke Chair at King's College, London and subsequently for the Drummond Chair at Oxford (1996, I, p. 328). When Edgeworth succeeded, Marshall was delighted – his congratulatory letter began 'Hurrah! Hurrah!! & Hurrah!!!' (1996, II, p. 7).

Yet there was an underlying tension between them, particularly as Edgeworth for his part did not always appreciate the carefully worked out theoretical underpinnings of Marshall's apparently bland text, while criticising material in the *Economics of Industry* in terms of the rarefied apparatus of *Mathematical Psychics* (1996, I, pp. 135-7, 149-50). There were further exchanges over mathematical items in the Principles (1996, II, pp. 6, 26) and there was some considerable difficulty between them over an article on indeterminacy which Edgeworth published in an Italian journal (1996, II, pp. 27-8). (The matter is discussed in Creedy, 1986, pp. 96-7, and in much more detail in Creedy, 1992, pp. 145-55, though Whitaker does not refer to these, and in Guillebaud's supplementary volume for the *Principles*). There were also difficulties between them over Giffen goods (1996, III, pp. 220-224; Creedy, 1990, pp. 33-35; Newman, 1990, pp., 119-121). As is now fairly well known, Marshall considered Edgeworth to be at one extreme in the spectrum running from the historical school to pure theory, and this comes out both in letters to Edgeworth (e.g. 1996, II, p. 391) and in letters to other people about Edgeworth (1996, I, p. 314; II, pp. 307, 350). One of the things which seems to have exercised him in this respect is the very static nature of the analysis to which Edgeworth's mathematics drove him (1996, I, pp. 124-5).

But though there were underlying tensions with Edgeworth, there is no doubt of Marshall's respect for Edgeworth's powers of analysis (1996, I, p. 314).

6.7.7 Böhm-Bawerk

It is much more doubtful whether Marshall had that much respect for the Austrian economist Böhm-Bawerk. Volume III contains the letter, already known from Gårdlund's book about Wicksell (1958, p. 342), in which Marshall denounced Böhm-Bawerk for what could most kindly be called 'subjective originality' (1996, III, pp. 86-7), though it has to be said that Wicksell did not accept Marshall's view on this (1996, III, pp. 88-9, 101-2; see also O'Brien, 1990b, p. 134, n. 21)). There was undoubtedly disagreement between them, and indeed Mrs Marshall records that she was fearful of a meeting between Marshall and Böhm-Bawerk when the Marshalls were on holiday, although in the event the meeting passed off without incident (M.P. Marshall, 1947, p. 48).

6.8 Analytics

As already noted, Whitaker has rightly warned against placing too much weight on the treatment of theoretical topics in hastily written letters. However it is the case with this *Correspondence* that there is little in it which is new when judged from an analytical point of view. Pigou had the best of the letters, and most of the letters with economic content have already appeared in the *Memorials*. There are a few topics which, however, merit mentions.

6.8.1 Rent

The content of some of these letters is bound to raise in the mind of the reader the possibility that Marshall really was, at least intermittently, confused on the subject of rent, rather than merely engaging in verbal gymnastics so as to avoid any concessions to Jevons (Marshall, 1961, vol. I, p. 437n). Edgeworth made patient efforts to untangle the confusion, which arose from ignoring transfer earnings and reasoning largely in terms of a single crop ('corn'), that lay behind Marshall's insistence that rent did not enter into cost of production. But Marshall clouded the issue with vague references to the importance of time, and claimed to be quite unable to understand Edgeworth's clear statement, even returning his letter to him (1996, II, pp. 85-93). Even J.B. Clark, who had clearly understood the problem, found Marshall obfuscatory (1996, II, pp. 412-13, 415-18). Poor Foxwell, whose strengths were not analytical, received several letters on the subject, including one that claimed that the question of rent and cost depended on the concentration of ownership (1996, I, p. 126) and another which said that rent did not depend on diminishing returns, and then went on to say that it did (1996, I, pp. 92-3).

Most of the confusion can be disentangled from other sources; the argument about ownership turns out to relate to a very special case which is dealt with in Marshall's *Early Economic Writings* (1975, I, p. 249); and the question of transfer earnings is neatly sidestepped in a mathematical model (which Marshall never published) in which outputs are determined simultaneously (and, by implication, there is a sole producer) and the pricing of land services does not appear (1975, II, pp. 319-22; see also 1961, I, pp. 434-7).

But the impression remains that Marshall was not completely clear on the matter, as exemplified by his responses to Edgeworth; and a later letter to Edgeworth in which he says that it is 'wicked' to say that rent enters into cost of production (1996, II, p. 392) suggests that there was even an emotional problem involved.

6.8.2 Mathematics and Methodology

Although Marshall was a properly trained mathematician, there is no doubt that he struggled with Edgeworth's *Mathematical Psychics.* While Marshall wrote flatteringly to Edgeworth about the book (in a letter designed to serve as a testimonial – 1996, I, p. 135) he confessed to Foxwell a couple of months later that he had not been able to understand all of it (1996, I, p. 137). Since it involved calculus of variations (Creedy, 1986, p. 87), a technique with which many professional mathematicians were unfamiliar, and which Edgeworth took no trouble to explain, this is hardly surprising. Marshall had the capacity to master such a technique, had he considered it valuable. But he was pursuing a very different research agenda from that of Edgeworth, and the development of a workable, synthesised, theoretical structure with empirical counterparts was what concerned him.

This is clear from a number of the letters in the volumes, and the famous letter advising Bowley to burn the mathematics if they cannot be translated into English is here (1996, III, p. 130). He also objected strongly to the tedious use of mathematics to prove things which he considered to be obvious. In a letter to Foxwell, he wrote:

> As to the sort of Bimetallism that Fisher established by his two tanks & acres of Mathematics: that drives me furious: I'd a deal sooner wade through a long treatise to prove that two & two are four, or that the whole is greater than the half &c (1996, II, p. 318).

But more generally he had reservations about what could be regarded as mechanical (as distinct from philosophical) economics, a view he set out in a letter partially reproduced in the *Memorials* and which is printed at full length here, being one of the very few to have survived the process of assembly of Pigou's volume (1996, II, pp. 305-7). It is this which undoubtedly explains his less than generous letter referring to Cunynghame, who excelled in the exposition of technical matters (1996, II, p. 72). This letter appeared previously not in *Memorials* but in Guillebaud's supplementary volume to the *Principles* (Marshall, 1961, II, pp. 811-13).

Marshall's cautious attitude towards advanced mathematical treatments of economics seems to have stemmed in part from his belief that this distracted attention from the more important task of building up and using data. Marshall is known to have been an avid reader of economic statistics (1996, II, p. 306), and indeed to have compiled his 'Red Book' with each page containing a different time series but with a common time axis throughout the book. For some time this was thought to have been lost. It has now however fortunately surfaced, and is in the Marshall Papers (1996, II, p. 308 n. 4). Marshall described the book both in a letter of 1901 to Bowley (who was clearly familiar with it – 1996, II, p. 306) and in a letter to H.L. Moore of December 1921 (1996, III, p. 380). It was, as he testified, important in forming his own thinking, and the importance which he attached to it is a manifestation of a tension in Marshall's work between the theoretical and the 'realistic', a tension which led to his disdainful attitude towards advanced mathematics in economics and even towards the ingenious geometry of Cunynghame.

6.9 The Educationist

It is sometimes forgotten that Marshall was concerned not merely with economics, and not merely with education in economics, but with educational issues much more broadly. The *Correspondence* provides ample evidence of this – it even begins with letters to the *Cambridge University Gazette* proposing improvements in both the courses which students were required to take and in the employment position of their teachers. In his first letter indeed he suggested a reform of classics teaching, although he was later to be dismissive of classics as a form of education (1996, I, pp. 1-2; III, pp. 91, 103-7).

We also find here Marshall's doubts about examinations, which were bad both for examinees, at least after the age of 22! (1996, III, p. 21), and for examiners, a matter on which Marshall seems to have felt strongly, (*Official Papers* supplement, p. 36). To some extent Marshall looked upon examinations as a necessary evil for the classification of the elite – an Oxbridge tradition which apparently dies hard (Johnson and Johnson, 1978, p. 97; see also Kadish in Kadish and Tribe, 1993, pp. 137-43). Indeed there are times when Marshall seems to regard classification as more important than education (1996, II, p. 357).

6.9.1 Degrees for Women

As is well known, Marshall opposed the introduction of Cambridge degrees for women – although, as Whitaker points out, his was the majority view, and his statement of his position was temperate (1996, II, p. 154, n. 1). The volumes contain a good deal of material about this episode, and it is extremely valuable to have Marshall's own words which the reader can evaluate without gloss. There are clear statements of his grounds both in 1887 (1996, I, p. 244) and in 1896 (1996, II, pp. 147-92). His 1896 speeches on the subject (unfortunately misindexed) are included at the end of Volume II as well as his 'flysheet' (1996, II, pp. 147-54). The tone is much more temperate than some secondary accounts might lead one to believe.

Given the subsequent literature on this issue, and the fact that Marshall was so clearly fighting a lost cause, it is perhaps worth stressing that both the *Correspondence* and the *Official Papers Supplement* contain much balancing material. For one thing it is clear that Marshall was enthusiastic about higher education for women, making a public statement on this in 1887 (1996, I, p. 226). He was one of the 'runners' who brought the examination papers to the women students in Cambridge in the 1870s when the then Mary Paley was a candidate (M.P. Marshall, 1947, p. 17). Exhibiting a contrasting attitude to that of Foxwell, who would not even admit women to his lectures (1996, III, p. 125), Marshall favoured degrees for women during his time at Bristol (*Official Papers Supplement*, p. 46 – Groenewegen's note is informative here) – where, and this is of key importance, the women continued to live at home (*Official Papers Supplement*, pp. 15, 38, 46-7, 50-1; 1996, I, p. 128).

It is much to be regretted that Marshall got involved in the controversy over Cambridge degrees for women. He did not have the temperament for it, and the cost in terms of his own output was clearly considerable. Although he worked at volume II of the *Principles* in the 1890s, and even turned down an invitation to the United States in order to be free to work on it, (1996, II, pp. 129-30), he failed to deliver it, and for this his involvement in the controversy over degrees for women must take a significant part of the blame.

He was also unwise to get involved in a controversy in which the very upper class Mrs Sidgwick (A.J. Balfour's eldest sister) was on the other side. Her self-assurance indeed contrasted with the socially insecure Marshall who seems to have been uncomfortable about his humble origins (Coase, 1990).

Unlike Marshall, she was eloquent; and she was also exceedingly tough, having already seen off the spiritualists from the Society for Psychical Research (E. Sidgwick, 1938). There had already been some tensions between Marshall and Henry Sidgwick on Marshall's return to Cambridge (A. and E.M. Sidgwick, 1906 pp. 394, 401-2) and, earlier, over the use to be made by the latter of notes, taken by J.N. Keynes, on Marshall's lectures (1996, I, pp. 131-2); and Mrs Sidgwick herself, even though Marshall wrote to her in the most polite manner at the time of the controversy over degrees for women (1996, II, pp. 158-160), seems to have disliked him thoroughly – she is indeed the source of one of the unkind stories about him which appeared subsequently (E. Sidgwick, 1938, pp. 168-9).

6.9.2 The Economics Tripos

Marshall's achievement in securing the establishment of a degree in economics at Cambridge has already been discussed extensively, notably by Kadish (1989). It is evident from the *Correspondence* that it involved him in immense struggles, and it also no doubt contributed to the failure of his second volume of the *Principles* to appear (1996, II, p. 360). But, driven by his evident sense of mission, he persevered. As already noted, he had the support of Foxwell; but not only did he encounter the opposition of Cunningham (which was to be expected – Kadish, 1989, p. 207), but also the opposition of J.N. Keynes (1996, II, p. 350).

Marshall's determination to persevere in the face of this opposition seems to have been explained in part by his worries about the implications for Cambridge of the development of the London School of Economics. This indeed is evident from the *Correspondence* (1996, II, p. 368). His worries stemmed also from what he regarded as the protectionist influence at LSE (1996, III, pp. 33-5) – by this time, free trade was assuming for Marshall a test of moral character (1996, III, pp. 39-41), a test which Hewins, the LSE director, failed – and he was concerned about Sidney Webb whose control over LSE seemed set to become complete (1996, II, p. 379).

The Cambridge degree which Marshall envisaged was extraordinarily broad by modern standards. It partly reflected Marshall's own interests and methodological preconceptions, and partly the existing and potential competitive pressures, not only from LSE but also from Birmingham (1996, III, pp. 95, 118-21).

In the end he was successful, though clearly at considerable personal cost; and his efforts have to be seen in the context of the aim of setting economics in Cambridge on the right course to be followed after his departure from the Chair.

6.9.3 Bristol

No account of Marshall as an educationist would be complete without some mention of his time at Bristol, and valuable material on this is contained in the evidence which he gave about higher education while he was Principal at Bristol and which is reproduced in the *Official Papers supplement.* But the overwhelming impression which emerges from the *Correspondence* is of somebody who wishes he had never gone to Bristol. He was not suited to university administration, and his depression at the frustrations he encountered, especially frustrations to the writing of the *Principles*, is evident in the *Correspondence* (e.g. 1996, I, pp. 129, 139). By 1879 he was already attempting to leave Bristol (1996, I, pp. 111-12), and indeed while there he seemed unable to shake off concerns about events in Cambridge (1996, I, p. 107). He stayed in Bristol until his resignation in July 1881 (1996, I, p. 138) but his heart had clearly not been in the job for at least two years before that.

6.10 Macmillans

Many of the details of Marshall's dealings with Macmillans are already known, as a result of work by Guillebaud (1965) and indeed by a member of the publishing family (Macmillan, 1942). What however comes out from the *Correspondence*, in a way which was not previously apparent, is the extraordinary patience which the firm showed, and their tact in dealing with Marshall. It was Frederick Macmillan himself who was very much to the fore here. He tried to get the writing of the *Economics of Industry* improved (1996, I, pp. 86-7), and he showed great patience with Marshall's haggling over the pricing of that book (1996, I, pp. 89-90) and indeed of other books, including *Industry and Trade* (1996, III, pp. 365-6). The firm's flexibility was however rewarded when this product of Marshall's old age proved a highly successful publication (1996, III, p. 369). Macmillan also showed considerable tact when Marshall, having called the *Principles* volume I, and failed ever to produce volume II, wanted to call *Industry and Trade*, volume I (1996, III, pp. 357-8).

Of course in Marshall they had one of the world's leading authors in his field, and one with a large American readership of which the author himself was very appreciative, going to great trouble to get complimentary copies of the *Principles* widely distributed in the United States (1996, III, p. 162). Nonetheless, Marshall must have tried Macmillan's patience sorely, with his endless over-optimism over volumes and completion dates (e.g. 1996, I, pp. 97-8), the evidence for which is scattered through the three volumes of *Correspondence*. In the end even Marshall felt called upon to apologise to the firm for the delays and for endlessly keeping matter in type (1996, III, pp. 347-8).

6.11 Editorial Matters

6.11.1 The Correspondence

Whitaker's standpoint has been in favour of inclusiveness when dealing with marginal cases in his compilation of correspondence (1996, I, p. x). However the reader should be warned that this inclusiveness is limited. Thus we find a letter from Marshall to J.N. Keynes which is sufficiently interesting to be quoted in a footnote (1996, II, p. 406) but not included; and for some things, notably Marshall's 'Plea' of 1902, leading ultimately to the Economics Tripos, we have to turn to Guillebaud (1996, II, p. 347, n. 3; Marshall, 1961, vol. II, pp. 161-78). This is however rather more understandable than the omission of some of the *Correspondence* which looks tantalising (e.g. 1996, I, p. 109, n. 3)

Given Whitaker's unrivalled knowledge of Marshall and his background, it is rather disappointing to find this reflected rather sparsely in the editorial material. Instead of an introductory biographical survey cross-referenced to the contents of the volumes, we have a rather sketchy introduction originating in a piece which Whitaker wrote for another occasion, which is supplemented by appendix I. This latter contains remarkably little information about Marshall's family background; it does not mention the astonishing discovery by Ronald Coase that Marshall and Henry Thornton were related or that Marshall's mother's family had come down significantly in the world. The introductory essay also contains an instance of gratuitous belittlement of Marshall, who is described as 'prone to lead from the rear' (1996, I, p. xxiii). Yet in some respects Marshall was the archetype of the modern professor – attending conferences, raising money, introducing new degrees, seeking to raise the status of his subject. Cambridge economics owes this one man an incalculable debt. Nor is it particularly pleasant to read *Money, Credit and Commerce* described as a 'pastiche' (1996, I, p. xxii).

I sense some ambivalence in Whitaker's attitude towards Marshall. Perhaps this explains why one sometimes misses a sense of immersion in the *Correspondence.* Certainly Whitaker fails to note sub-texts in letters, such as when Marshall writes to Jevons about Cairnes (1996, I, p. 32) (the chapter Marshall referred to contained an unpleasant attack on Jevons), or when Nicholson, writing to Marshall about Ashley, makes an oblique reference to Ashley's 1891 attack on Marshall (1996, III, pp. 164-5). Whitaker also fails (and here the Biographical Register is no help) to pick up the point that when Marshall described Ingram as having a literary mind – the reference (1996, I, p. 209) was disdainful – he was apparently in ignorance of the fact that Ingram was an accomplished mathematician.

The references to the secondary literature are also somewhat uneven; it would take too long to document this in detail, but it is for instance rather surprising that, when Marshall is in dispute with Edgeworth over Giffen goods (1996, III, pp. 220-4), so little of the literature on Marshall and Giffen goods, from Stigler (1947, 1948) and Prest (1948) to Creedy (1990) is considered worthy of mention – perhaps there was simply too much of it.

In contrast to a number of other editions, but above all to Sraffa's Ricardo, both the lack of cross-referencing to other letters and a certain inconsistency in the use of such cross-references are also dispiriting. It would not have been too much to ask that if a letter is a reply to an earlier one, or is replied to, this could have been signalled. This is particularly unfortunate because sometimes it is later letters which have, in their attached notes, the information which the reader of an earlier letter immediately wants. It would be tiresome to give much chapter and verse for these reservations; but some small examples will suffice. A note (1996, II, p. 327, n. 1) tells the reader that Foxwell had decided to stand for a Chair at Birmingham and expected Marshall to write a testimonial. There is no cross-reference to the fact that Marshall did indeed write a testimonial and that it is printed a few pages later (1996, II, p. 331). Again, an isolated letter from Jowett (1996, I, p. 342) asks whether there was any candidate superior to Edgeworth for the Drummond Chair; but there is no cross reference to the point in the *Correspondence* explaining all this (1996, II, p. 7, n. 4) or to Marshall's letter of congratulation to Edgeworth (1996, II, pp. 7-8). We are told who Karl Marx was (1996, I, p. 303) but not whether Edgeworth got the Tooke Chair for which Marshall had written him a testimonial (1996, I, p. 328). When W.H. Dawson writes to Marshall to invite him to contribute to his book on post-war problems, Marshall wrote to decline (1996, III, p. 329). But in fact he did contribute to the volume, and this emerges a little later on, although there is no cross-reference to the later material (1996, III, pp. 336-8, 343). Although there is a certain amount of correspondence about the editorship of the newly founded *Economic Journal*, it is frustrating to read several letters before finally coming to a note (1996, I, p. 287, n. 4) which says Edgeworth was appointed. At one point we plough through six letters about possible republication of Marshall's *Memorandum* on trade policy (pp. 959-964) before coming to a footnote (1996, III, p. 247, n. 3) which explains what did happen. Again we plough through material about the Marshall portrait by Rothenstein, but it is only from the (admittedly excellent) index that we can trace the outcome of the attempt to raise funds and the commissioning of a portrait. Where there is discussion in the *Correspondence* about a German translation of the *Principles* we have to get to the third letter before we discover that the translation did appear in 1905 and the note does not give any bibliographical details, although later on details of a French edition *are* given (1996, III, pp. 8-12, 36). Eventually one finds – without the help of a cross-reference – the bibliographical details (1996, III, p. 114).

I mention these matters with regret. I know very well what goes into work of this sort (having had, indeed, no research assistance of any kind for *The Correspondence of Lord Overstone* – O'Brien, 1971). But we are not talking here about footnote chasing (where Whitaker has had not only the benefit of research assistance but also of the work done by Guillebaud previously) but about the general coherence of the edition, and in this respect I find the

Correspondence disappointing.

Of course there are strong points as well. Whitaker has taken considerable care over the accuracy of the transcriptions (and points to inaccuracies in other transcriptions), and at one point he even identifies a classics-loving headmaster referred to obliquely, and with opprobrium, by Marshall in *Industry and Trade* (1996, III, p. 279). But there are not enough of such flashes.

6.11.2 Official Papers Supplement

The odd typographical error apart (Groenewegen, 1995, p. 65) the presentation and editing of this volume are excellent. Notes are, for the most part, extremely informative even though, just occasionally, one felt that slightly fewer references to Groenewegen's recent (1995) biography of Marshall (tempting though this must have been, to avoid repeating information) would have been helpful. There is the occasional oddity; the coupling of Sidney Webb and the Marxist H.M. Hyndman as 'Social Theorists' resonates a little oddly (p. 89) and indeed Hyndman's Marxist economics was so primitive that, when he appeared before the Labour Commission, Marshall had difficulty in making sense of it (p. 271).

There are really only two editorial points on which it is worth commenting. Firstly, there is the piece critical of Nicholson which Groenewegen includes (pp. 70-77). Marshall had a low opinion of Nicholson, as is evident from the *Correspondence* (1996, III, p. 42). This no doubt explains his irritation at Nicholson's intervention. But Groenewegen seems to me to have completely misinterpreted the content of Marshall's piece. Marshall accepted classical monetary theory, and used it here expertly. Contrary to what Groenewegen believes, Marshall actually defends the quantity theory. He realised the possibility of changes in demand for balances (or velocity) and income but says explicitly (1995, p. 75) that these are stable and that changes are in the same direction. Marshall's main point is that a fall in the value of silver will not lower prices; despite the fact that Indian currency is now cheaper, the price level in India has risen in compensation – this is indeed his parting shot (1995, p. 77).

My other concern relates to the material included in the volume which is taken from the report of the Labour Commission (pp. 92-128). In interesting editorial material Groenewegen (1995, pp. 85-86) points out that Mrs Marshall had already drawn the attention of Keynes to sections of the report and suggested that these be included in the original volume of *Official Papers.* Keynes decided to ignore this recommendation; and it seems to me that his judgement was entirely correct. The report is written in a generalised Victorian prose, which bears no real resemblance to Marshall's own writings and indeed does not contain material which Marshall reused (as was his habit, as Groenewegen points out elsewhere – p. 307). Mrs Marshall, of course, had particular interests in labour economics; and she may have felt, therefore, a particular interest in the report of the Labour Commission. But there is really very little evidence that any of it was written by Marshall.

However the record of examinations of witnesses before the Commission, conducted by Marshall, is fascinating, and letters in volume II of Whitaker's *Correspondence* (1996, II, p. 350-94 *passim*) nicely complement the material provided by Groenewegen . In particular there is a letter to the American writer Benjamin Kidd (1996, II, pp. 384-6) in which Marshall recounts his clash with Sidney Webb over the latter's claim that the classical economists had opposed the Factory Acts.

Indeed this episode illustrates nicely the unreliability of Beatrice Webb's diary. As Groenewegen notes (without comment), Beatrice Webb claimed that it was the working class witnesses who suffered from being examined by Marshall (1995, p. 88, n. 30; Webb, 1983, pp. 25-6). Indeed she claimed that Marshall and others had 'puzzled the workmen with economic conundrums, balked inconvenient evidence by cross-questions, and delivered themselves of elaborate treatises on economics, history and philosophy' (Webb, 1983, pp. 25-6).

Yet if one looks at Marshall's examination of the dockers' leader Ben Tillet, one finds that it was courteous – on both sides – and fair. It was not, indeed, the working class witnesses with whom Marshall clashed. The exchanges with Giffen, who was aggressive, were extremely tense (see especially 1995, pp. 247, 250, 259-60). But it is the needling of Sidney Webb himself which is the most prominent characteristic of Marshall's examination. Webb was sufficiently rattled in one session that at his next appearance he felt compelled to start his evidence with an apology for his behaviour the previous day (p. 186). What Marshall was aiming to do was to destroy the credibility of Webb's account of the views of the classical economists, although there were also difficult exchanges over municipal enterprise, and some questions in which Marshall seems to have had a general equilibrium model in his mind (pp. 166-7, 197-8, 200-202).

6.12 Conclusions

Marshall did not have any great respect for Sidney Webb's intellectual powers. It is also clear that he had considerable reservations about those of a number of his professional colleagues, including, it must be said, his friend Foxwell. But with those he really respected – Edgeworth, Flux and Cannan (it was thus not completely necessary to be a mathematician to earn Marshall's respect) he remained on good terms.[10] This comes out in the *Correspondence* which, in its richness and complexity, nicely complements the richness and complexity that Whitaker correctly discerns (1996, I, p. xxi) in Marshall's masterpiece, the *Principles*. The Marshall that emerges is a fascinating and complex figure – hypersensitive in some respects (A. and

[10] See however Kadish (1983) on Cannan's sniping at Marshall (to which he did not respond).

E.M. Sidwick, 1906, p. 394), perhaps arrogant, occasionally perhaps devious – but from how many academics are these qualities absent? He pursued his mission to bring economic enlightenment to Cambridge and, through that, economic progress to a wider world; and Cambridge, and indeed economics in the English-speaking world, owes him a great debt. He pursued his research programme somewhat less successfully, partly because of the methodological tensions between the theoretical and the empirical and partly, as Keynes shrewdly observed, because he was not suited to the large multi-volume tasks which he set himself (1933, p. 197). But his achievements were still remarkable, and these volumes enable us to appreciate them.

Though I have been critical of some aspects of these volumes they constitute a major addition to the literature relating to Marshall, and indeed to that of the history of economic thought more generally. Work of this sort could not be done in Britain any longer in an Economics Department (under RAE), and we should be grateful that someone in an American university has managed to find sufficient flexibility in the system to produce the *Correspondence.* The volumes are well complemented by the *Supplement* to *Official Papers*, the editing of which (in an Australian university) is, for the most part, exemplary. Barring a fundamental change in the criteria which seem to be employed in peer appraisal, we shall not see the like of this work again and we should be very grateful for what we have got.

Chapter 7

Cannan: Theory and the History of Economic Thought

Edwin Cannan is chiefly remembered today as a historian of economic thought and, in particular, as an expert on the literature of classical economics. However his interests were much wider than this; essentially he treated the history of economic thought as a means of teaching economic theory. He was thus in the tradition of such writers as Taussig, Viner and Robbins. Indeed it was Robbins who, in reviewing Cannan's *A Review of Economic Theory*, pointed out that Cannan regarded this as the correct approach to the teaching of economic theory (Robbins, 1929). As Robbins noted in his *Autobiography*, while Pigou, unlike Marshall, 'had explicitly declared a lack of interest in the history of the subject', the situation at LSE was very different. 'Cannan's teaching... at the advanced level was largely based on the critical examination of the theories of others' (Robbins, 1971, p. 133; see also Postan in Robson 1972, p. 33). Robbins in turn also taught theory in this way (Coase, 1982, p. 33).

Such an approach has now been eliminated from the teaching of economics (though see Blaug, 1985), as a result of which both theorists and historians of economic thought have suffered. The former have lost that sense of perspective which offers some safeguard against uncritical adoption of whatever appears to be the 'novelle vague', while the latter have lost that sharp contact with theoretical standards which prevents retreat into a facile relativism.[1]

Cannan himself has now fallen into obscurity. It is noteworthy that the 18th volume of *International Encyclopaedia of the Social Sciences* (Sills, 1968) not only contains no article on Cannan; his name does not even appear in the index to the entire set. It is true that the earlier *Dictionary of National Biography 1931-40* (Legg, 1949) contains an article by Lionel Robbins (Robbins, 1970); and there is an entry by Murray Milgate in *The New Palgrave* (Milgate, 1987). But Cannan, once famous and widely respected,[2] is now almost forgotten, and in so far as he is remembered it is not always with clarity – a recent history of LSE claims that Cannan as an economist was 'largely orthodox' (Dahrendorf, 1995, p. 36), a claim which, as we shall see, is hard to reconcile with his writings. As is clear from Hayek's 1946 essay on the history of the London School of Economics, Cannan was 'orthodox' only by comparison with his colleagues. The aim in setting up LSE had been to recruit those opposed to orthodoxy.

> If Webb and Hewins were guided by any one conviction it was mainly that the theoretical and individualist economics of Ricardo and Mill had kept their dominant position far too long and that it was time to give other schools a chance. They therefore drew largely on all the different opposition movements, however these might differ amongst themselves (Hayek, 1946, p. 6).

Like these others, Cannan was an outsider, and his name is missing from those featuring in the authoritative account of the early years of the Royal

[1] By relativism I mean a concern with the historical circumstances of a theory's origin, leading in turn to neglect of its internal logic and a willingness to avoid judgement on its correctness.

[2] It is perhaps worth quoting the tribute of no less a critic than Schumpeter here. Schumpeter cites, with approval, Cannan's *Production and Distribution* (Cannan, 1893) at a number of points in his great *History of Economic Analysis*, and though he did not consider Cannan analytically refined, he wrote that 'nobody can peruse his lively short tracts on money and monetary policy without pleasure and profit. This of course entirely fails to do justice to the teacher and the man, his common sense, his loveable outspokenness, the strength of his convictions' (1954, p. 832n).

Economic Society (Coats, 1968b). Having succeeded in becoming, in the course of his career, a significant influence in British economics, Cannan has now become a forgotten figure, and his critical approach to the history of economics, as a method of teaching economic theory, has also largely disappeared. This paper seeks to reawaken some interest in the kind of approach epitomised by Cannan's work.

7.1 Biographia

Cannan was born in Madeira, 3 February 1861, and died in Bournemouth, 8 April 1935.[3] He was of Scottish descent and indeed T.E. Gregory found him 'very Scotch: "pawky" and angular, very exact and methodical, very shrewd and painstaking, and with certain practices of economy which in the course of time became part of the attraction of the man himself' (1935, p. 369). Be that as it may, Cannan's upbringing was entirely English, as is clear from the fragment of autobiography which he left (Cannan, 1935) and from other autobiographical material (1912, pp. 9-18). He married late, in 1907, and an only son died in 1918 (Gregory, 1935, p. 371; Bowley, 1935 p. 385; Fay, 1937, pp. 2, 3), an event which was described by Cannan as an 'almost overwhelming private sorrow' (1927, p. xi).

Cannan's education, as is clear from the autobiographical material, was severely affected by his poor health which made it necessary for him to break off his studies for an Oxford degree and to travel. He ultimately emerged with a pass degree (1912, p. 11; Bowley, 1935, p. 385).

In later life, however, Cannan showed extraordinary stamina and capacity for hard work. Indeed, despite the fact that he was of independent means and not dependent on an academic salary, his published output is extremely large, especially by the standard of academics of the time, and in later years

[3]A fascinating account of Cannan's family background can be found in Kadish (1982, pp. 5-11). Kadish's book is an excellent historical study of the period. Biographical data can also be found in Milgate (1987).

he described his recreation in *Who's Who* as simply 'work'.[4]

Cannan lectured at the London School of Economics from its foundation and was Professor of Political Economy from 1907 until his retirement in 1926. He was very active as a commentator on current economic problems, and collected together a volume of his contributions as *An Economist's Protest* (1927). He taught economic theory at LSE, approaching the subject through the history of economic thought, and it is in this field that his fame has survived.

7.2 Intellectual Equipment

There is no doubt that Cannan was intellectually agile to a remarkable degree. His pupil Lionel Robbins reports that Cannan had 'a strong dislike of the mathematical approach, and an almost passionate conviction that the important economic truths could be expressed, as he tried so hard to express them, in language which would be intelligible to laymen' (1970, p. 231). But the internal evidence from Cannan's writings indicates that this is not the whole story. For one thing it is clear that he was both able and prepared to use mathematics where this would clarify an issue, and a striking example is to be found in his treatment of rent which will be referred to below. But there is also evidence of a very good capacity to handle data, in his writings on population (1895, 1901, 1931), and a graphical device which he developed for presenting population data was thought so highly of by A.L. Bowley that he used it as an example in his lectures (Bowley, 1935, p. 388). It is true that he put into the mouth of Adam Smith some satirical comments about raising intellectual standing by using algebra in economics (1923, p. 93);[5]

[4]In earlier years his recreations were listed as cycling, demography and correspondence with government officials (Fay, 1937, pp. 1-2).

[5]'Adam Smith, who produced his great work at the very late age of fifty-three, did not grow old rapidly, but we can imagine that at two hundred he might have been a little stiff and unable to appreciate at their full value some of the later developments of economics. We can picture his somewhat contemptuous tolerance of 'the very ingenious speculations

and it is true also that he had an outstanding capacity for stating technical problems in plain English. But, despite an instinctive aversion to mystification, Cannan had considerable reserves of technical power, although these were rarely called upon.

Rather, the overwhelming impression which emerges from reading his work is one of scholarship rather than technicality. Admittedly he came from a more scholarly generation than our own – both Hawtrey and Foxwell pointed out to Cannan misprints in the version of the Bullion Report which even the eagle-eyed Cannan had missed in his first edition of it (Cannan, 1919/1925). His erudition strikes even those familiar with the classical literature as remarkable. In a bluff sort of way he sometimes gave the impression of insularity – as in his complaint about foreign economists which he made when reviewing Robbins's *Essay on the Nature and Significance of Economic Science* (Robbins, 1932; Cannan, 1932)[6] – but the internal evidence of his work belies this. He was clearly widely read in French and German, and although his delivery of French was apparently what is now described as 'Churchillian' (Robbins, 1935, p. 393),[7] he was sufficiently fluent in the reading of French to be able to pass stylistic comment on Cantillon (1929, p. 19).

But the bulk of his reading was certainly in the literature of economics written in English – in which Cannan did not cover a geographically wide area

of Mr. Jevons, Mr. Marshall, Mr. Edgeworth and others, who have introduced a sort of algebra or geometry into the science of political economy. The followers of that system are very numerous; and as men are fond of appearing to understand what surpasses the comprehension of ordinary people, the cypher, as it may be called, in which they have concealed, rather than exposed, their doctrine, has perhaps contributed not a little to increase the number of its admirers. While it has been of scarce any service to the statesman and has done little to provide either a plentiful subsistence for the people or a sufficient revenue for the sovereign, it has at least given rise to much thought and speculation among the youth at the universities, more especially at that of Cambridge, which in my time was sunk in a torpor, no less profound, I believe, than that of Oxford' (Cannan, 1923, p. 93).

[6]Cannan complained obliquely about references to 'dozens of foreign economists whom we shall never read' (1932, p. 426).

[7]See Churchill (1952, p. 401) for an amusing insight into the statesman's French. (I owe this reference to John Creedy.)

– and his valedictory work, the *Review of Economic Theory*, certainly reflects the geographically narrow area of literature, ignoring even most American work (Viner, 1930, p. 396; Robbins, 1971, p. 85)[8] and concentrates most of its attention on the English classical economists.

It should however be emphasised that Cannan was explicitly internationalist in outlook. He was opposed to economic nationalism (this is a recurrent theme of *An Economist's Protest*), and he held it against the classical economists that they looked to national than international welfare (1927, p. 67), though it has to be noted that he makes no mention of J.S. Mill (of whom this was not true) in this context. His own position was internationalist, and indeed he regarded internationalism as being a defence against war (1927, pp. 52, 69-70, 83-8). But the English focus of his critical writings is unmistakable, and nowhere more clearly than in his *Production and Distribution* which is explicitly devoted to the content of 'English Political Economy from 1776 to 1848'.

7.3 Production and Distribution

This book, *A History of the Theories of Production and Distribution in English Political Economy from 1776 to 1848*, which is undoubtedly Cannan's single most famous work, first appeared in 1893. The tangled history of its origins does not seem to be well known. Cannan had entered a work for the Cobden Prize competition, in which he was unsuccessful. The unsuccessful essay then formed the basis of his first book *Elementary Political Economy*, of 1888 (1912, p. 14; Bowley, 1935, p. 386). This book, which was adversely reviewed by L.L.F.R. Price (the book was, in his view, neither elementary nor accessible since it used existing terminology for different purposes – Price, 1889) was a failure (though a second edition did appear in 1897). According

[8] This was however a long standing problem in British economics – see the correspondence between Marshall and Ely in Coats (1961).

to Cannan's own account: 'I concluded that destruction of the old edifice must precede construction of the new, and after five years' work produced in 1893 [a book] . . . containing a vigorous and detailed attack on the slovenly way in which distribution had so far been treated' (1929, p. 301).

Whatever Cannan's intentions, however, the 1893 book *Production and Distribution* became established as a critique of classical economics, covering, as it did, the years 1776-1848. Though it did not cover money or trade, it covered wealth, land, labour, capital, production and distribution.

Cannan was also influenced in the writing of this book by the work of the now forgotten economist Adolf Held – indeed according to his own account 'I had been strongly influenced by Adolf Held's Zwei Bücher zur socialen Geschichte Englands' (1912, p. 17). It was the emphasis in this work on the historical circumstances under which classical economics developed which appealed to Cannan even though this did not make him a relativist – for him, an argument was right or wrong.

The 1893 book was not, at first, a success. Cannan later related that 'its sale was so small that it had to change its publisher when the first edition of only 502 copies was at last sold out in 1902' (1929, p. 301). But it probably helped to build up Cannan's connection with LSE, and the second edition of 1903, published once he had become established at LSE, was much more successful. A third edition appeared in 1917, and was reprinted three times subsequently (1920, 1924 and 1953).

7.4 Review of Economic Theory and The Paper Pound

Production and Distribution (1893) is much Cannan's most successful book. His *Review of Economic Theory*, covering much of the same ground as the earlier book, appeared after his retirement; it was published in 1929 and reprinted in 1930, but never enjoyed the same popularity as its predecessor.

The book was based upon Cannan's lectures, delivered in a two-year cycle at LSE. Over the two years he blended the teaching of economic theory with the history of economic thought, and the contents of the book demonstrate that for Cannan, history of economic thought was indeed the way to teach economic theory. Robbins, a former pupil, emphasised this when reviewing the volume (Robbins, 1929). As Viner commented, when reviewing the book, it must indeed have been 'rich fare' for undergraduates (Viner, 1930, p. 395). T.E. Gregory has confirmed that most of it went over the heads of the students (1935, p. 365), and the picture which Robbins has given of Cannan as a teacher (1935, p. 393-4) depicts a long lost world in which students expected to be challenged by the difficulties not merely of material but of delivery.[9]

For Cannan, history of economic thought had, however, wider aims than even the teaching of economic theory. His reprint of the *Bullion Report* as *The Paper Pound* was also designed as part of Cannan's vigorous contribution to the post-World War I debate on the restoration of the gold standard, and was intended to strengthen the case against an inconvertible paper currency. Cannan was explicit about this in his preface to the second edition (1925) and in his *An Economist's Protest* (1927, pp. xii, 187, 199-204). Indeed the *Bullion Report* stemmed from an era in which the Bank had behaved with greater responsibility than had been shown in monetary affairs during and immediately after World War I (1925, pp. xxxiv-xxxix).

[9]'Certainly he was not a good lecturer, at any rate in the ordinary sense of the term. He could deliver a very lucid and popular lecture when he set himself to do so, as his presidential addresses to the R.E.S. have demonstrated. But his normal lectures on Principles were not of this quality. It was not always possible to hear him. His delivery was never fluent and he had a habit of talking into his beard which made parts, and often the most important parts, of his lecture almost inaudible unless you were sitting in the first two rows. Moreover, they were not arranged with a view to the convenience of beginners. Cannan took great trouble preparing them, and when he came to write his *Review of Economic Theory* he was able to transcribe large chunks often without great alteration. But they went straight to the point whether simple or difficult. There was no preliminary statement of what he proposed to do. No summary of what he had done. He expected you to find that out for yourself' (Robbins, 1935, p. 393).

7.5 The Paradox of Cannanism

Cannan's approach, combining theory and the history of theory, resulted in a discussion of economic literature, which was abrasive. He favoured a style of economic reasoning which could be characterised as 'impatient common sense'. As Hugh Dalton put it:

> Economic science, in Professor Cannan's hands, is very conspicuously common sense. Nor does it err by being too highly or artificially organised. It is rather a bluff common sense, non-mathematical, without humbug or pretentiousness, and practising a strict economy of those technical terms which so easily degenerate into clumsy and aesthetically repulsive jargon. There is here no excessive abstraction, no pomposity of doctrine, but always a keen sense of reality (Dalton, 1927, p. 7).

Cannan coupled this with a relish for controversy which is very much in evidence in his collected volume An *Economist's Protest*, and indeed in other works, notably The *Economic Outlook* (1912) and *Economic Scares* (1933a). He was also an acid reviewer in the pages of professional journals.

Not surprisingly, his treatment did not find favour with his contemporaries. As Cunningham remarked, in reviewing the first edition of *Production and Distribution*: 'he is not a sympathetic critic; sometimes his remarks sound a little captious, and he does not seem in every case to have set himself to appreciate the strong points in the various writers whom he examines so carefully' (1893, p. 494).

Cannan remained unrepentant, as the preface to the second edition of this work makes clear: 'I have great hope that what appeared to be ill-tempered blasphemy in 1893 will now be seen to be the calm statement of undoubted fact' (1903, p. v). Not surprisingly, Cannan was disappointed in this hope. Edgeworth reviewed the second edition, commenting that 'we regret that the author has not taken the opportunity of recanting the acrimony which characterises his criticism of the older theorists' (1903, p. 625). Indeed Edgeworth's review was severe in its tone of reproof, as Viner's was later also to be concerning the *Review of Economic Theory* (Viner, 1930, pp. 396-7).

But this is hardly surprising. When we find Cannan claiming that 'it is not very easy to understand the admiration which was once felt for the progress made during that period [1776-1848]' (1893, p. 379) we may demur; and when we find J.S. Mill's treatment of capital dismissed as 'a most hopeless farrago of blunders' (p. 380) it is not difficult to sympathise with Cannan's critics. When we are told that 'Anything more unsatisfactory than this exposition [by Adam Smith, of distribution] itself would be difficult to conceive' (1893, p. 382), that Smith's treatment of wages was 'palpably absurd' (1893, p. 382) and his treatment of profits 'entirely baseless' (1893, p. 382) our sympathy with the critics is likely to increase, particularly as Cannan showed no hesitation in taking advantage of the easy targets offered by verbal confusions. Moreover his approach also tended to foster a disparaging attitude in those he taught (Robbins, 1971, pp. 85-6). Nonetheless many of Cannan's criticisms were of substance, and even Viner could not always offer convincing defences of the classical writers – notably of Malthus on population and food, of Ricardo on value theory and on rent, and of Mill's famous fourth proposition on capital (Viner, 1930).

Yet there is something of a paradox here. For although Robbins reported that Cannan had been, in his lectures, more tolerant of Smith than of Ricardo (or Marshall) (1935, p. 396), Cannan was quite capable of writing scathingly about Smith as he did at the end of his time at LSE (1926a, p. 123). But – and herein lies the paradox – he also recognised, and acknowledged, Smith's real achievements, while the son to whom he was devoted was named David Ricardo. He credited Smith with the substitution of national income per head for national income in total as a welfare standard, and as the father of an economics which understood the role of the market place and the entrepreneur; and he certainly thought Ricardo worthy of his critical attention. He misrepresented Smith as failing to recognise the need for a framework of restrictions on self-interest for a market system to operate (1926a, pp. 132-4; and see Robbins, 1952), but he did absolutely outstanding editorial work on Smith, making a major contribution to the appreciation of Smith and to standards in the history of economic thought. Though Cannan did not discover Smith's *Lectures* (1896, p. xv), he produced an exemplary edition with explanatory and historical notes, comparing the text with the *Wealth of Nations* to establish its accuracy, and demonstrated the debt which the lectures owed to Smith's teacher Francis Hutcheson (1896, pp. xxv-xxvi; 1904, pp. xxxvi-xli).

The quality of his editing of the *Wealth of Nations* is universally acknowledged. Indeed Viner believed that it set new standards for at least English-speaking economists (1965, p. 9; see also Fay, 1937, p. 7). With some help Cannan, who was critical of previous editions of the work (even that by McCulloch), collated the different editions of the work which had appeared during Smith's lifetime. He also added a second index to the work, giving the authorities on whom Smith relied, and made the splendid wry comment, which brings a smile to the face of any editor, that 'To discover a reference has often taken hours of labour: to fail to discover one has often taken days' (1904, p. vii). The end result was an edition so fine that the definitive modern Clarendon edition of the work, the product of a team, clearly owes a debt to Cannan.

Although he traced the *Wealth of Nations* to the lectures, he was not blind to the influence on Smith of French economic writing . He acknowledged what Smith had got from France, especially distribution (1896, p. xxvii; 1904, pp. xxx-xxxiii), and admitted the importance of the Physiocratic background (1893, pp. 67, 77) even though he believed that the Physiocrats had confused Smith (1933a, pp. 66-7).

The solution to the paradox that Cannan was deeply critical of classical economics and yet did remarkable work in bringing classical economic literature before the public is essentially that Cannan himself was a dissident classical economist. He was, as Robbins put it, 'deeply imbued with the spirit of the classical outlook' (Robbins, 1970, p. 231) and we have to remind ourselves that Cannan was close in time to classical economics – his undergraduate education at Oxford would have owed far more to classical economics than to the revolution in economics which Jevons, Marshall and their contemporaries were bringing about. In turn Cannan transmitted this classical spirit to Robbins, just as Taussig transmitted it to Jacob Viner – in some of their most important writings, both Robbins and Viner are essentially classical economists.[10]

It is the fact that Cannan was fundamentally a classical economist which explains the lack of clear impact of the Marginal Revolution on his writings.[11] He did recognise the importance of the concept of marginal utility, both dogmatically claiming it as an indisputable basis for income redistribution (1912, p. 61) and employing it in his discussion of value (1929, pp. 200-206). He was clearly aware, too, of the concept of marginal productivity, objecting strongly to this as an approach to the theory of distribution (1912, pp. 28-9, 247-8). But his resistance to this approach seems to have impeded his grasp of it; in particular, in discussing the origins of interest, he seems to confuse physical and value productivity (1893, p. 216; 1929, pp. 280-283),

[10]However it should be stressed that Robbins was a pupil, not a direct follower, of Cannan. His *Essay on the Nature and Significance of Economic Science* is indeed a critique of Cannan's exclusion of non-material sources of satisfaction from the area of economics; he was deeply interested in questions of equilibrium and disequilibrium; and he did not accept Cannan's 'cloakroom' theory of money (O'Brien, 1988b, pp. 8, 9, 15, 23-9, 42). Cannan for his part deplored, in his Presidential Address to the Royal Economic Society, the trend towards high theory set in train by Robbins at LSE (Cannan, 1933b, pp. 367-9, 378). Nonetheless Hicks, who experienced the early years of the Robbins era at LSE, believed that Robbins restored the Cannan approach after the Dalton-Allyn Young interregnum (Hicks, 1982, p. 4; see also Hicks, 1983, p. 344).

[11]On this neglect see also Milgate (1987).

and there are other points, notably in his discussion of West (1893, p. 279) where the reader feels that a clearer understanding of marginal productivity theory would have been of assistance to Cannan – impatient common sense was really not enough here.

His opposition to marginal productivity theory seems at times to have gone so far as to regard it as a smokescreen to avoid a proper discussion of the distribution of income (1912, pp. 219-229); Cannan favoured redistribution according to the Pigou criterion (Collard, 1981) – any redistribution from rich to poor which did not reduce output would increase welfare. In practice, as we shall see, Cannan was much more sceptical about redistribution than some of his more flamboyant statements might indicate, however.

7.6 Socialism

Cannan was not a socialist, even though Sidney Webb may have had hopes of him in this regard. Cannan (1912, pp. 15-17) recounted that while Webb regarded him with favour, 'Bernard Shaw and, I think, other speakers, repudiated me in more or less violent terms' when, in 1889, he addressed the Fabians, and he did not become a member of the Fabian Society. (His address to the Society is reprinted in Cannan, 1912, pp. 53-86). On the other hand, his position on redistribution meant that he was on Pigou's side when the latter's welfare economics was under attack by Robbins (Cannan, 1932), and the later developments of the 'New Welfare Economic' at LSE, under Robbins's inspiration and on Paretian foundations, was on lines entirely different from those congenial to Cannan. Cannan asserted – somewhat unfairly – that the classical economists had somehow muddied the question of distribution by using the term to denote the determinants of wages, profits and rent, rather than the division of net national income which he considered the prior question (1893, pp. 183-89, 339-78; 1912, pp. 226-30). It is important, however, to be clear that, despite his more extravagant criticisms of the existing distribution of wealth, Cannan was in no sense a socialist (1912, p. 81). He rejected explicitly socialist opposition to the profit motive (1912, pp. 21, 168), and stated emphatically that property was *not* theft (1927, p. 42). Private property did not cause poverty (1912, pp. 82-3) (which itself should bear no stigma – 1912, pp. 138-56) even though the justification for private property was purely utilitarian (1912, p. 191). He took the view that most inequality in the distribution of property was due to inheritance – but that most of that inequality had to be left undisturbed (1912, pp. 250-1). Indeed Cannan approved of inherited wealth (Gregory, 1935, p. 369), despite the effect of this on the distribution of income (Cannan, 1927, pp. 36-7).

He rejected the idea of public ownership (1912, p. 68) (and syndicalism – 1912, pp. 36-7), attacking both nationalisation of the railways (1912, p. 85) and council housing (1912, pp. 186-7). He ridiculed the idea of exploitation (1912, p. 82), was critical of mass trade union activity (1912, pp. 42-7), and even went so far as to express the view that means should be found to deprive the unemployed of sympathy (1912, p. 262) – unemployment was caused by wages being too high (1933a, pp. 37-8, 102, 104).

It is unfortunate that Cannan's fondness for striking attitudes should, on the one hand, have led some to detect socialist sympathies in his writings while, at the same time, he delivered himself of sentiments which were, in truth, far more reactionary than he was himself. But for all that he was clearly no believer in revolution (1912, p. 24), and, like Hayek, he had a deep appreciation of the way in which economic institutions evolved so as to produce harmony between public and private interest (1912, p. 25). He also had a deep appreciation of the extraordinary achievements of the market system which was distinctly unsocialist (1912, pp. 172-194). Indeed, according to Hicks, 'it was from Cannan that the LSE "free market" tradition descended' (Hicks, 1982, p. 4).

He did in fact explicitly state that he was not a socialist (Cannan, 1912, p. 281) and privately described Tawney as 'really a Bolshey' (Fay, 1937,

p. 10); and he took the view that socialism was muddled (1933a, p. 48). Socialism itself he blamed upon Malthus's pessimism and Ricardo's theory of subsistence wages (1912, pp. 69-77). As already noted, he read a paper to the Fabian Society in 1889, but it was undoubtedly an anti-socialist production, one which he was quite happy to reprint 23 years later (1912, pp. 53-86).

Socialism, though muddled, was not completely without merits in Cannan's opinion; the internationalist Cannan believed (wrongly, as history was to show) that socialism was an obstacle to the nationalism which he opposed (1912, p. 284). But he was praising its heart rather than its head.

7.7 Monetary Theory

Cannan's two great books, *Production and Distribution* and the *Review of Economic Theory*, both lack discussions of money. Indeed Bowley drew attention to the absence of money from Cannan's writings more generally (1935, p. 387). Yet in fact he wrote a good deal on money (Gregory, 1927, p. 39), and he was a keen collector of monetary literature. Apart, however, from one small book (1926b) (which had originally been intended as an extra chapter for his book *Wealth*, 1914), and the edition of the Bullion Report, most of Cannan's writings on money are short pieces of a controversial nature, gathered together in his *An Economist's Protest.*

The fact has to be faced, however, that, despite his self-confidence in controversy, monetary theory was an area in which Cannan was not at his best. He adhered – with quite extraordinary tenacity – to the 'cloakroom' theory of bank deposits (Cannan, 1921), under which a bank could only lend out what had been deposited with it, and was not in any position to multiply deposits through lending. Cannan provided a number of dogmatic statements of this primitive theory (e.g. Cannan, 1924a), and attacked, in particular, Hartley Withers, who understood the concept of a deposit multiplier perfectly well (Cannan, 1921, p. 33; Withers, 1909). He adhered to this position, as Gregory noted in his obituary, to the end (Gregory, 1935, p. 378; see also Gregory, 1927, pp. 54-60). In doing so, he displayed ignorance of the classical expositions of the deposit multiplier by Pennington and Torrens (O'Brien, 1975, p. 143), and, not surprisingly, clashed with the leading English monetary theorist of the time, J.M. Keynes (Cannan, 1924a, b; Keynes, 1924).[12]

One cannot even defend this position by arguing that it points towards monetary base control, citing Cannan's insistence that it was control of money, not of the rate of interest, which was of fundamental importance (1927, pp. 323-34). For by money, Cannan meant currency; bank deposits, he insisted firmly, were not money (1926b, pp. 81-3; 1927, p. 284).

It is perhaps hardly surprising that his history of economic thought work on money was not his best. In his preface to the second edition of his republication of the Bullion Report (Cannan, 1919/1925), he seemed to think that convertibility was its own safeguard (in apparent ignorance of the issues in the debate leading to the 1844 Bank Charter Act); his characterisation of the Real Bills Doctrine as relying on 'soundness' is hardly adequate (1919, p. xix); it was not always clear that he appreciated that over-issue of paper depreciated the whole of a mixed currency (1919, p. xiv) (he seemed to think that this was only true where gold export was forbidden – 1927, p. x); and in discussing the fall in the price of gold at the end of the Napoleonic wars, he makes no mention of the failures of the country banks (1919, pp. xxvii-xxix), even though the classical writers, notably McCulloch, had emphasised the importance of this in reducing the note issue (O'Brien, 1970, p. 153). Nor does he seem to have appreciated that Horner's monetary theory was simply taken from that of Henry Thornton.

[12]Cannan considered Keynes an unstable and dangerous individual, if his jocular comments as reported by Fay are to be taken at all seriously. Of the *Treatise on Money* he wrote privately 'Keynes will be in a mental asylum before he's done, if he goes on like this', and elsewhere he wrote 'I reckon J.M.K. the second most mischievous pseudo-economist, Marx being the first and the rest nowhere' (Fay, 1937, pp. 10, 16).

But this picture should be balanced by recognising some clear merits in Cannan's monetary work. His discussion of the elasticity of demand for balances is excellent (1926b, pp. 71-8), and in the sphere of policy he picked up an interesting retraction by the Bank of the Real Bills Doctrine.[13] He also offered plausible historical reasons why the Bank should have been so moderate in its over-issue of notes during the Napoleonic period – a moderation which he rightly compared favourably with that experienced during and after World War I (1919, pp. xxxiv-xxxix). Moreover, viewed from the perspective of almost a century after he was writing, it is now clear that his instinct concerning governments and inflation was sound. The twentieth century is unique in history in its experience of inflation. His warnings about over-issue of currency were prophetic; and, in a letter written to the Governor of the Bank of England in December 1919, he accurately forecast the hyperinflations which were to hit central and eastern Europe in the next decade (1927, p. 200).[14]

But, again viewed from a longer-term perspective, in other respects his judgement was sadly wanting. He was a strong supporter of a return not merely to the gold standard but to the gold standard at a pre-war parity (1927, pp. 200-202, 207), and indeed explicitly favoured deflation sufficient to bring this about (1927, p. 253). Unlike Wicksell, he does not seem to have recanted when he saw the damage that was done (Gårdlund, 1958, pp. 298-300; Uhr, 1962, pp. 9-13).[15]

[13]The doctrine that over-issue of notes was impossible if such issue was confined to discounting 'Real Bills' i.e. those originating in transactions in goods, as distinct from 'Accommodation Bills' which were, in effect, IOUs for loans.

[14]On these hyperinflations see Yeager (1976, pp. 312-15). The inflationary propensities of governments which Cannan foresaw may be illustrated by the fact that even British prices rose by a factor of about 20 between the late 1940s and the mid-1990s.

[15]On the subsequent change of mind on the character of the 1930s depression by Cannan's pupil Lionel Robbins; see O'Brien (1988, pp. 117-20).

7.8 Malthus and Population

At the time that Cannan was teaching, population was still a standard part of economics courses, and he lectured on the subject at LSE as Dalton did after him (Pimlott, 1985, p. 136). He published a number of papers on population (1895, 1901, 1931), and the ease with which he handled the data, referred to above, resulted in some extraordinarily accurate population projections, while his concept of an optimum population was, in turn, expounded by Lionel Robbins (1927). Cannan thus had an established position as a writer on population and, given his preference for approaching ideas through the history of ideas, it is hardly surprising that Malthus's treatment of population should have attracted Cannan's particular interest. In a merciless critique (1892a; 1893, pp. 123-147), Cannan was able to demonstrate that Malthus, who had started with borrowed ideas, had shifted his ground between the first and second editions of the *Essay*, that, although his celebrated ratios were meaningless, Malthus himself attached considerable importance to them (1929, pp. 72-3), and that (though Robbins was later to object to this – 1970, pp. 60,87) Malthus's theory relied upon the ratios not upon the concept of diminishing returns (1893, pp. 144-7). As Cannan put it:

> Deprived of the theory that the periodical additions to the average annual produce cannot possibly be increased, or, as Malthus preferred to put it, that subsistence can increase only in an arithmetical ratio, the *Essay on the Principle of Population* falls to the ground as an argument, and remains only a chaos of facts collected to illustrate the effect of laws which do not exist (1893, p. 144).[16]

[16] This verdict was endorsed by Schumpeter, who quoted it (Schumpeter 1954, p. 580).

7.9 Ricardo and Rent

Examined in detail, Cannan's critique of Malthus is indeed extremely damaging. But even more devastating was his critique of Ricardo. With sharp critical insights he showed the route by which Ricardo had arrived at his ideas (1892b; 1893, pp. 147-68). His explanation of Ricardo's arrival at 'his' rent theory is particularly impressive. Moreover he emphasises the very fundamental point, still not well appreciated, that to understand what Ricardo put forward in his *Principles* of 1817 it is essential to have read the preceding pamphlets (1893, p. 388). Cannan was a scholar, and he had read them. His criticisms of the basic model put forward by Ricardo in the *Essay on Profits* of 1815 pulled the rug from underneath the whole deterministic Ricardian model of profit decline by introducing the possibility of capital saving (1893, pp. 288-9).[17] He was scathing about Ricardo's attempt to prove that agricultural profit determined profit in the economy as a whole, so that lower agricultural profits meant an approach to the stationary state (1893, p. 284), and indeed he described Ricardo's theory of profit decline as 'grotesque' (1929, p. 260).

Consistently with his stance on distribution, Cannan argued that there was a perpetual confusion in the classical literature between long-run trends in relative shares and long-run trends in rewards per unit of input (e.g. 1893, pp. 70-1). This is less than fair to the classical writers. On the other hand Cannan's critique of the Ricardian doctrine on 'improvements' – advances in agricultural technology – was, despite the fact that he did not spot Ricardo's trick of treating the agricultural sector as one giant farm (McCulloch did so – 1849, p. 508), outstanding. (Without this trick it is clear that improvements are in the interests of *individual* landlords.) Cannan was able to show that Ricardo's conclusion that improvements would necessarily lower rents was

[17] The model set out by Ricardo produced profit decline as a result of declining marginal product, assuming a constant ratio of capital to labour for each increase in output, whereas Cannan raised the possibility of capital saving. See O'Brien (1975, p. 134).

simply mistaken (1893, pp. 323-31).[18] In view of the point made earlier about Cannan's ability to cope with technical matters, it is worth emphasising that he demonstrated this through the employment of some neat algebra – the algebra in itself is not in any sense advanced, but the way in which Cannan reduces the problem to simple algebra is elegant indeed. He was able to conclude that 'Ricardo's attempt to show that improvements must temporarily lower rent ... thus ends in complete and hopeless failure' (1893, p. 331).

So comprehensive was Cannan's critique of Ricardo that it is difficult to feel much sympathy for the modern Ricardo interpretation industry in all its many variants, from Ricardo as visionary proponent of general equilibrium analysis to Ricardo as a visionary proto-Marxist. But the truth of the matter is that Cannan's work is well known but not well read. Both Sraffa and Dobb in Cambridge in the late 1940s were apparently completely ignorant of this demonstration by Cannan. When Harry Johnson, encouraged by Schumpeter (who was also apparently in ignorance of the demonstration), produced an identical proof (itself an extraordinary intellectual coincidence), the reaction of Sraffa and Dobb was one of incredulity. Sraffa was indeed, so Johnson reports, on the point of publishing a reply when he found out that Cannan had pointed out the mistake 56 years before. Thus the two most important figures in the generation of a major branch of latter-day Ricardianism were ignorant, as Harry Johnson noted, of Cannan's devastating criticism (Johnson and Johnson, 1978, p. 94).

[18] For a discussion of these issues see O'Brien (1975, pp. 124-9). Ricardo had made the mistake of changing inputs by equal absolute (rather than by equal proportional) amounts, and Cannan was able to show that Ricardo's numerical example actually implied an increased corn rent, and a constant money rent. Ricardo had thought that he had demonstrated that corn rent would remain constant and money rent would fall.

7.10 J.S. Mill

Cannan's criticisms of Ricardo and of Malthus were major ones, and they should have been digested by later generations. In contrast, his treatment of J.S. Mill is very much less satisfactory. In a sense his criticisms seem almost personalised – he seems to have despised Mill because of the difficulty the latter had in extricating himself from the influence of his father (1893, pp. 175-82). Of course Mill's celebrated fourth proposition on capital – that demand for commodities is not demand for labour – has presented a soft target to critics both before and after Cannan (1929, p. 109)[19] – and Cannan himself recognised that some of Mill's contemporary critics (in particular Longe and W.T. Thornton) were weak analytically (1929, p. 355). But much else that Cannan has to say on Mill seems more characterised by rhetoric than by a penetrative discussion of the analysis, and it is unfortunate that Cannan apparently sought, for reasons to be found in the history of his own education in economics, even at school (1912, pp. 10-11),[20] to belittle Mill rather than recognise the substantial merits of his work.

Oddly enough, his attitude to Mill does not seem to have soured his relations with Marshall who had earlier taken exception to Jevons's treatment of Mill (Marshall, 1872). Indeed, despite the fact that his economic theory course contained, in Gregory's time as a student, 'a running commentary on Marshall's *Principles*' (Gregory, 1935, p. 367), and despite the sniping at Marshall to which Kadish has drawn attention (Kadish, 1983), the usually thin-skinned Marshall declined to be drawn into combat. Marshall respected Cannan (Whitaker, 1996, II, p. 379); and it is evident from Cannan's obituary of Marshall that the respect was mutual (Cannan, 1924c) even though,

[19]See in particular Pigou (1949) and the criticism of this in Johnson (1949).

[20]Cannan recalled in the introduction to *The Economic Outlook* how, in studying economics at his school, Clifton, he had rebelled against Fawcett's version of Mill's 'sophism' that demand for commodities is not demand for labour, and complained, after being given a copy of Mill's *Principles* as a prize, that 'J.S. Mill had doubtless confused my sixteen-year old intellect' (1912, p. 10).

as Fay has shown, Cannan was persistent in his needling of the older man (Fay, 1937, pp. 3-4).[21] The needling may, at least in part, have reflected Marshall's expression of worries about the development of economics teaching at LSE (Coats, 1967b; O'Brien, 1997a, p. 1878; and Chapter 6). This needling was, however, Cannan's privilege. As Lionel Robbins later testified, although Cannan 'sometimes made jokes at Marshall's expense when he was lecturing... his respect for Marshall was tremendous and woe betide the student who had not read the *Principles* and completely assimilated the main points' (private communication quoted in Coats, 1967a, p. 719). Moreover Cannan and Marshall were on the same side in, and cosignatories of the most famous document relating to, the great free trade controversy of 1903 (Coats, 1964, 1968a).

Yet there were undoubtedly areas where Cannan was vulnerable to attack. Despite the outstanding critiques of Malthus and Ricardo, there were aspects of his treatment of classical economics which were unsatisfactory. His treatment of rent exhibited the lack of clarity, prevalent amongst his contemporaries, concerning the 'extensive margin' and the 'intensive margin' (1929, pp. 230-37). Admittedly this was such a widespread confusion that Edgeworth felt it to be necessary to clarify it (Stigler, 1941, pp. 112-14); but somebody with the sharp edge of Cannan's mind should not have left the matter unclear. Again, like many of his contemporaries, he failed to make clear the fallacy involved in ignoring the transfer earnings of land in 'getting rid of rent' from value, though the issue was later explained by Buchanan (1929).[22] Perhaps most remarkably, Cannan failed to appreciate the role of

[21] His particular bête noir was the concept of consumer surplus.

[22] 'Getting rid of rent' involves disregarding it as a cost of production entering into supply price because it is, from an *aggregate* point of view, a price-determined surplus resulting from inelastic factor supply. This is a fallacious argument, since land has transfer earnings where it has more than one possible product, and to produce one product it is necessary to pay for the use of the land, such payment thus being a cost of production. Cannan seemed to sense that 'getting rid of rent' was wrong, but tried to attack the idea by positing varying factor proportions as the source of differences in cost (1929, pp. 177-80).

the invariable measure in Ricardo's value theory.

7.11 Smith and Turgot

Mention has already been made of the paradox that Cannan both recognised great merits in Smith's work, and did outstanding editorial work on his behalf while denouncing much of his treatment of economics. It has to be admitted, too, that he was quite needlessly critical of Smith, both in *Production and Distribution* and in the *Review of Economic Theory*, as well as in his 1926 article on Smith already referred to. In particular, Smith's treatment of capital attracted his ire (1929, pp. 147-50) and, as already noted, Cannan, unlike his pupil Robbins, failed to appreciate the fundamental importance for Smith of an institutional framework for the price system (Cannan, 1926a; Robbins, 1952). On the other hand Cannan was a very strong defender of Smith's own originality, and in particular in relation to the work of the French economists.

It was not that Cannan failed to appreciate the content of the Physiocratic literature. Indeed his knowledge of the French economic literature was remarkable, and he showed that Adam Smith's illustration of division of labour through pin manufacture came from the *Encyclopédie* (1929, pp. 94-5). He drew attention to an important statement by Turgot on diminishing returns (1929, pp. 74-5) although, both because of his resistance to marginal productivity theory and because of the problem over the intensive and extensive margin noted above, he failed to make clear that Turgot's statement related to the 'intensive margin'; and he showed considerable appreciation of the work of Cantillon. But he resolutely refused to accept the argument that the *Wealth of Nations* owed anything to Turgot's *Reflections*.

The case for such a debt had been argued by a number of authors, notably Thorold Rogers, and Cannan set about demolishing that case with relish (1896, pp. xxii-xxiv; 1904, p. xlvii). He probably went a little too far. Later scholars have been rather more cautious. In particular, Jacob Viner took the view that, 'Edwin Cannan, although he was generally an outstandingly careful and accurate scholar, did, I think, systematically put more weight than was warranted on absences from [Bonar's *Catalogue*] . . . of physiocratic items as negative evidence of what Smith at different periods had owned or read' (1965, p. 128).

Viner concluded that Smith probably did own the whole run of the *Éphémérides* containing the *Reflections.* Even granting the evidence of hindsight, Cannan 'took more seriously than was even then justified the evidence provided by Bonar's *Catalogue* as to what books Smith had *not* read or even seen' (1965, p. 132). Viner's view on this is endorsed by Groenewegen (1969) who, in a balanced account, nevertheless supports Cannan's demolition of claimed parallels between the text of the *Wealth of Nations* and the *Reflections.*

7.12 Mandeville and Longfield

Cannan was also, of course, well read in English economic literature outside the mainstream. In particular he emphasised the importance of Mandeville (1929, pp. 21, 94, 97), arguing (as Hayek was later to do) that Smith's perception of the beneficial effects of self-interest came from Mandeville (1904, p. xli). Another writer, one whose true importance has only become clear since 1945 (Black, 1945, 1971), to whom Cannan gave early recognition was Mountifort Longfield, before Longfield was hailed as a 'neglected British economist' by Seligman (Cannan 1893, p. 308; see also 1929, pp. 260-2; Seligman 1903). Despite the weaknesses in his appreciation of the monetary literature, he also pointed to the fact that Jevons's enumeration of the qualities of money had been anticipated long before by Pufendorf and Harris (Cannan, 1896, p. 186n).

7.13 Conclusions

Edwin Cannan was much more than a historian of economic thought. He ranged widely, and plunged with abandon into controversies, as his 1927 book *An Economist's Protest* shows clearly.[23] Robbins went so far as to claim Cannan as a philosopher in the mould of Smith and Hume (1935, p. 398). While that seems rather generous, there is no doubt that Cannan's range was wide, and there were few subjects, from local taxation (on which he was an authority) to labour economics and the foreign exchanges, on which he did not feel qualified to offer an opinion. But the stronghold from which he started was his tremendous knowledge of the history of economic thought.This was the basis for his teaching of economic theory – and it leads to an exhilaratingly incisive approach. It is impossible to read, in particular, *Production and Distribution* without learning; and the more the reader knows the classical literature, the more the reader learns. This is not in any sense to say that Cannan, opinionated and dogmatic as he was, was always right. But his opinions were never baseless, and even if the reader ends up disagreeing with him, the reader's own understanding of the classical literature is sharpened.

For Cannan, with his 'impatient common sense' approach, adopted what was essentially an absolutist perspective. Arguments were simply right or wrong. There was no taking refuge in watery generalisations about theories having been appropriate to particular historical circumstances. As Hayek (1946) and others have observed, he created an intellectual climate at LSE (even its motto) in which a *critical* approach was central and, as Dalton noted, Cannan believed in creating a deliberate variety of approaches. No one could have said, as they said of Cambridge economics, that it was 'all in Marshall', that it was 'all in Cannan' (see Dahrendorf, 1995, pp. 36, 148, 212-

[23]Fay gives an excellent picture of Cannan's robust love of dispute, recording that 'in all the arguments of his argument-loving life, no one ever counted ten over him' (Fay, 1937, p. 20).

13). As Hugh Dalton's biographer has written: 'Cannan was like Socrates, "skilled in promoting a clearance of traditional rubbish from the mind". He was not a systematiser and he was suspicious of orthodoxies' (Pimlott, 1985, p.83). It is true that Cannan, under the influence of Held, certainly took into account the historical circumstances (e.g. 1893, p. 221). He was not so unhistorical as to deny that Smith and Ricardo were affected by their environment (1912, p. 17). He wrote about Ricardo in Parliament in order to stress Ricardo's practical concerns, even where these practical concerns led Ricardo into ridiculous positions, as Cannan pointed out (1912, p. 137; Gordon, 1976, p. 67). But Cannan was not a relativist by instinct, as his unwavering adherence to the doctrine of free trade showed. As Mark Blaug has written, 'It is difficult nowadays to appreciate the freshness of Cannan's iconoclastic approach in his famous book ... *Production and Distribution* (1893) a veritable catalog of the elementary blunders of great economists – to a generation nurtured on the relativist texts of Blanqui, Roscher, Ingram, and Cossa' (1985, p. 4). This judgement seems correct; Cannan deserves not to be forgotten as he has been, for his strong critical attitude and wide scholarship are of great value to economists.

Chapter 8

Friedrich August von Hayek

Hayek was born in Vienna on 8 May 1899 and died in Freiburg in Breisgau, Germany on 23 March 1992. He came from that extraordinary background in educated Viennese society which has produced some of the greatest names in 20th century intellectual history including not only Hayek himself but also Popper, Wittgenstein and Mises. Indeed Hayek was related to Wittgenstein, and wrote some reminiscences of his dealings with him although, like some others, he seems to have had considerable doubts about the philosopher's mental stability (1992, pp. 176-81). Hayek's own family background was firmly academic – one brother became professor of anatomy at the University of Vienna, and another became professor of chemistry at the University of Innsbruck (Machlup, 1976, p. 13). Hayek's father taught botany at the University of Vienna; and after education at that institution Hayek entered the Austrian Civil Service in which he spent the years 1921-1926.

Hayek soon came under the influence of Ludwig von Mises and it was Mises who was to prove probably the most decisive single influence on Hayek's intellectual development. Hayek has left an account of this association (1992, pp. 25-30) which gives some insight into the extraordinary intellectual vitality of Mises, forever condemned to be an outsider yet of enormous influence. There were, it is true, significant differences of personality; Mises was much the more combative – even aggressive – and Hayek much the more scholarly and retiring. They shared an indomitable intellectual and moral courage; but Mises often showed little patience with opponents whereas Hayek went almost too far in the opposite direction in his tolerance of would-be petty totalitarians – this stands out particularly in his writings on legal philosophy.

One of Hayek's greatest contemporaries has paid tribute to this open-mindedness and patience. In his Memorial Address for Hayek at LSE in September 1992, Sir Karl Popper (1992b) said:

> Hayek's openmindedness was one of his most striking virtues. He was, as you know, an anti-socialist. But he took great trouble to convince communist and socialist students that they were welcome in his lectures and seminars; and they found, indeed, that he was ready to listen to them with sympathy. In this respect I had to learn a lot from Hayek, for I was far less ready to listen to ideological clichés than he was. Hayek's tolerance was indeed exemplary; and as far as students were concerned, he behaved with convincing tolerance, even to those who preached intolerance.

This patience was itself the result of a deliberate decision on Hayek's part to recognise that 'the foundations of totalitarian barbarism have been laid by honourable and well-meaning scholars' (1973-9, I, p. 70).

The slightly self-effacing aspect of Hayek's personality, which appears to have become more marked over the years, seems to have led to a measure of neglect of his work. There was indeed a time in the 1960s when Hayek's influence appeared to be retreating into the shadows. The painstakingly written work, patiently assembling a scholarly canvass, was not calculated to win converts. At the same time, in the chic leftishness of academic circles in the 1960s, the more juvenile seemed to think that they had established that Hayek was some kind of Nazi because of the 'von' in his name – thereby demonstrating not only an ignorance of the significance of this prefix but also of the Nazis themselves and, for good measure, of the fact that Hayek had been a naturalised Briton since 1938.

8.1 The Intellectual Canvas

Hayek's work spans both economics and philosophy (and even psychology) in a way totally outside the experience and training of modern economists.As Sir John Hicks wrote, perhaps rather teasingly, in the preface to his *Critical Essays in Monetary Theory*, 'Professor Hayek ... has turned from economics to social philosophy, but may sometimes be available for consultation' (1967, p. ix). It is however noteworthy that Hicks, in the 1960s when Hayek's star appeared to be in danger of eclipse, should have felt it worthwhile to try to disentangle Hayek's monetary model. For Hayek came to this country as an economist, and he participated vigorously in the economic controversies of the 1930s. His transmutation into an economist/philosopher, though perhaps immanent in the crucial Misean influences, has its roots in the key to his moral standard. This key was the emphasis upon freedom – not merely freedom for the individual, but freedom for society to respond to the needs of its individuals in such a way as to allocate resources optimally and, perhaps even more importantly, to evolve and to develop new social forms.

Another extremely important factor in Hayek's development was a passionate belief – shared with Keynes – in the importance of ideas per se. Though Hayek never held office, and never sought the ear of the powerful of the day, he believed that ideas had an enormous influence upon the conditions experienced by the individuals whose freedom constituted the ultimate moral standard. Frequently the effects of these ideas could be disastrous. It was because of this danger that Hayek became the most scholarly and outspoken opponent of 'scientism' (the naive belief, espoused by even distinguished scientists, that society could be operated like a factory) and was outspoken in his critical account of the force of ideas in German history which laid open the way for Hitler. Ideas influenced politicians and journalists, but their role within the educational establishment – especially in the promulgation of historical myths such as the conventional view of the Industrial Revolution – was particularly important.

8.2 The Scholarly Tradition

Hayek was extremely well fitted, both by temperament and background, for a scholarly life devoted to the examination of such ideas. Educated in the great Austro-German tradition of scholarship, he was able to compensate for the narrowness of his original education by the attention which he paid to a wide range of scholarly sources. This was very much a part of the Austrian tradition; Böhm-Bawerk's great work on capital (1884-9) is in fact two separate works, the first of which surveys, exhaustively, the previous literature on capital before Böhm-Bawerk, in the second volume, launches into the development of his 'Positive Theory'. Similarly when, in the late 1920s, Hayek began to write a major work on monetary theory (left incomplete because of the rise of the Nazis) he approached it via a study of the history of monetary thought, developing an extremely impressive knowledge of the literature in several languages. This work (though made available to other scholars in the interim) did not see the light of day for many years (1991, pp. 127-244). Like Menger, the founder of the Austrian school, Hayek lectured on the history of economic thought (in his case, for more than four decades) and, again like Menger, was a remarkable bibliophile who, as I can testify from my own experience, was extremely generous with his books even when he knew nothing of the potential user.

Hayek read widely, deeply and, it seems, continuously. Sir Karl Popper in his Memorial Address of September 1992 recounts how he delivered a copy of *Logik des Forschungs* (Popper, 1935) to Hayek at their first meeting in 1935. Hayek promised to read it and to be ready to discuss it at their next meeting in a week's time; and he was as good as his word. Popper said 'I know of no similar story, and it is characteristic of this man, of his intellectual honesty. Authors of non-fiction books will agree with me that this story is unique'.

Hayek's erudition was remarkable; as anyone dipping into his great *Law, Legislation and Liberty* (1973-9) quickly discovers, his citations range over centuries and countries in a way which has no parallel amongst modern economists. He seems to have had a detailed knowledge of economic literature in German and English – this perhaps to be expected – and a very considerable knowledge of Italian, French, and medieval Latin texts.

8.3 Economic Foundations

This scholarly tradition compensated, at least to some extent, for a training in economics which, as became apparent with the re-publication in 1984 of his early essays as *Money, Capital and Fluctuations*, was distinctly narrow. It seems to have been based very largely on the work of Menger, Wieser and Böhm-Bawerk, particularly that of Wieser, and later interpreters of this work within the narrowly Austrian tradition, notably Mayer and Strigl. It was really Mises – himself something of an outsider in Vienna because he managed to be both Jewish and non-socialist, and, as Hayek explained (1992, pp. 128n, 157), you could secure advancement if Jewish if you were at the same time left-wing – who substantially broadened Hayek's outlook, and introduced him to a much wider range of literature. Even more importantly, he seems to have alerted Hayek to the full possibilities of Austrian economics, and to the much wider considerations implied by Austrian subjectivism and the Austrian aversion to partial equilibrium analysis. When Hayek came under the influence of Mises he was, according to his own account, a mild socialist; it was Mises who opened his eyes to the fundamental and inherent contradictions in the pretensions of those who believed that man could plan and direct society (1992, pp. 133, 136). He did so by bringing home to

Hayek the full force and subtlety of the Austrian approach to subjectivist general equilibrium, an approach essentially originating with Wieser but one enormously expanded by the 1920s Austrian writers. Thus fired, and fired moreover by one whose own work showed very considerable knowledge of the British literature, Hayek broadened his reading. Ultimately he was to find in the work of Smith, Ferguson and Burke those ideas of spontaneous order, selective evolution, and unintended consequences (of human actions) which, in line with the inspiration he received from Mises, were to lie at the root of his rejection of the socialist and constructivist view of society.

It seems to have been this development in his outlook which caused a reappraisal on his part of the work of Menger. For his later references to Menger are overwhelmingly to the 1883 *Untersuchungen*. Indeed this is the single most important reference in Hayek's *Individualism and Economic Order* of 1949. Yet Hayek's early work, reprinted in 1984 as *Money, Capital and Fluctuations* (edited by Roy McCloughry), shows that while, at that date, Hayek was thoroughly immersed in the idea not merely of general equilibrium but of general equilibrium over time (this is particularly true of his 1928 essay 'Intertemporal Price Equilibrium and Movements in the Value of Money'), the evolutionism which was later to seem to him the most important legacy of Menger is absent. It is, instead, the subjectivism which is very much to the forefront in the earlier writings, while the problems of capital theory (which were ultimately fatal to Hayek's own programme in economics, narrowly defined) are central.

During the time that he produced these early essays, Hayek was already coming under the influence of Mises's work – the latter's *Gemeinwirtschaft* (1932) led directly to Hayek's abandonment of socialism – but Mises's work only took Hayek part of the way along the road towards his ultimate body of thought. For evolutionism is not a key matter in the work of Mises, whose central interest lay in subjectivism, the problem of knowledge, and the co-ordination of individual decisions.

Some clue to the various strands in Hayek's initial intellectual background can be gained from his discussions of the important members of the Austrian School. It was the subjectivism, above all, which he stressed – it was, he claimed in the early 1940s, 'probably no exaggeration to say that every important advance in economic theory during the last hundred years was a further step in the consistent application of subjectivism' (1942, p. 281). His main discussion of the work of Menger is particularly interesting because it was published in 1934, as the introduction to an LSE reprint of Menger's works. It thus predates his focus upon evolution and unintended consequences, and was also written at a time when, particularly at LSE, it was possible to feel that Austrian economics was a, if not the, dominant force in the subject. In introducing Menger's 1871 *Grundsätze* he emphasised the standard Mengerian themes – needs, the means of satisfying them, and the distinction between goods of first and higher order. He also argued – and this is relevant to Hayek's 1928 paper cited earlier – that Menger had given a prominent role to time in his analysis. But above all he emphasised the steady accumulation of the subjective basis of the analysis, starting with goods markets and extending the ideas to factor markets, while all the time concentrating upon individual decisions, and justifying assumptions through introspection.

It is noteworthy in all this that Menger's 1883 book already referred to was lightly emphasised by Hayek at this time, and indeed in his subsequent discussions of Menger's work, even though it was to be of such critical importance for parts of Hayek's own work in the later development of the latter.

Despite the importance which he attached to the work of Menger, as the founder of the Austrian school, it was however Wieser whom Hayek credited with introducing the majority of the concepts which were later to prove important in the development of Austrian economics. From his treatment of marginal utility, and of imputation (factor rewards), it was Wieser who laid down the path of development followed by Austrian economics from the 1880s through to the 1920s. Indeed it is clear that in Hayek's initial training, before he came under the influence of Mises, the single most important element was the work of Wieser, supplemented by the work of Wieser's later disciples.

In discussing a member of the next generation of Austrians, Joseph Schumpeter, Hayek's attitude was, it must be said, a good deal less than reverential. Though Schumpeter provided him with letters of introduction for his visit to the United States in the early 1920s – resulting from a conscious effort by Hayek to broaden his intellectual training – the latter poked gentle fun, in his account of this, at Schumpeter's bombast and self-importance (Hayek, 1992, pp. 34-5). He wryly observed that bank managers' offices got larger the further east one went in Europe and that Schumpeter's office really belonged in Bucharest, rather than in Vienna where the interview with Hayek took place. But he could write illuminatingly about Schumpeter as an economist (1992, pp. 160-165), pointing out that the later enthusiast for macroeconomics and econometrics had originally been a strict methodological individualist, but that he possessed an outstanding adaptability to intellectual fashions (ibid. p. 157).

8.4 Subjectivism, Historicism and Scientism

With this intellectual background, and above all with the key Austrian emphasis upon subjectivism combined with the decisive influence of Mises, Hayek was able to build up his own research programme, a central part of which involved a sustained, courageous, and at times brilliant critique of many of the fashionable intellectual ideas of his lifetime. Subjectivism was linked not only with an interest in psychology (which resulted in *The Sensory Order: An Inquiry into the Foundations of Theoretical Psychology*, 1952) but also with the key Austrian emphasis on introspection. Like Cairnes, Hayek felt able to argue not only that introspection was fundamental in separating social science from natural science but also that it provided the economist with a kind of knowledge denied to the natural scientist. The difficulties with an emphasis upon introspection are too well known to need emphasis here; but it could be argued that a sufficient agreement by the relevant 'scientific community' on assumptions derived from introspection is a satisfactory starting point for the development of theorems deduced from those assumptions. But at all events this approach gave Hayek the basis for his critique of important (and at times extremely fashionable) elements in the intellectual history of our time. He attacked Historicism as the product of a fundamentally fallacious attempt to apply to history the methods (or what were *believed* to be the methods) of natural science. The attempts to formulate historical 'laws', attempts stretching from Comte to Marx, were completely misconceived and the outcomes bogus. The way in which society developed was the result of an uncountable number of individual decisions; we could understand those decisions through a theory developed on the basis of introspection but we could certainly not predict future social and historical development.

Historicism involved aggregating social phenomena in a meaningless way. It was, in turn, the basis for 'Constructivism', the idea that well-informed (and even possibly well-meaning) intellectuals could somehow plan and direct society. In 'Constructivism', an a priori belief in the virtues of planning led in turn to the idea that unplanned institutions could not be satisfactory and, by a *non-sequitur*, to the idea that constructivist intellectuals could refashion institutions at will.

In attacking these ideas, Hayek produced distinguished work in intellectual history. Particularly noteworthy were his two series, of three articles each, appearing in *Economica* in 1941 ('The Counter Revolution of Science') and in 1942-44 ('Scientism and the Study of Society'). In his critique, meticulously documented, of the work of Saint Simon and Comte, Hayek traced not only the intellectual pretensions of these progenitors of both socialism and totalitarianism but also the series of intellectual fallacies upon which their position was grounded. Of these the most important was the naive belief – held particularly by dilettantes like Saint Simon – that the methods of natural science could be transferred to the much more complicated social and economic world. Following Mises, Hayek pointed out that social science had to cope with a world in which actions were based upon beliefs rather than upon objective facts, a world in which there could necessarily exist no detached body of fact on which the planner could operate, and a world in which order came about through the interaction between individuals, this interaction taking place by means of spontaneously evolved institutions – above all through markets. The attempt to import into the complex area of social and economic behaviour the attitudes and training of natural science led both to a primitive understanding of such complex matters as optimisation and to embarrassing naivety. Indeed Hayek seems to have taken a rather sardonic interest in the writings of scientists on matters of economics, up to and including Einstein, as well as in the writings of scientific popularisers. But he can hardly be blamed for failing to resist such a temptation when, as any reader of the correspondence columns in quality newspapers knows, natural scientists seem so anxious to give hostages to fortune.

The basis of Hayek's critique of 'scientism' in economics was fundamental. He remained completely unconvinced that the methods of natural science, whether in the form understood by Saint Simon and his followers, or in the similar form understood initially by Hayek himself, or, finally, in the form in which Sir Karl Popper persuaded Hayek that scientists really operated viz., hypothesis formation and testing, could be transferred to social science. Indeed he remained sceptical about the whole matter of testing, since facts in economics were not physical. They were, rather, the beliefs of market participants. While he did, as in his (1937a) article on 'Economics and Knowledge' in *Economica*, mention both verification and falsification, he was doing so in the context of the idea, stretching from Cairnes to Robbins, of checking that the *assumptions* on which the theory was based were met, rather than referring to the testing of the *predictions* of a theory.

The extent of Hayek's opposition to 'scientism', set out in his (1941b) 'Counter Revolution of Science' in *Economica*, is directly linked to his belief that the influence of the ideas of Saint Simon and his associates was far more widespread than had been appreciated (partly because many 'disciples' were reluctant to risk association with the ridicule attached to the name of Saint Simon) and that these ideas were linked, directly and indirectly, to the doctrines of both Hegel and Marx. Indeed Hayek was able to show that significant Marxist elements – notably the class struggle – originated with Saint Simon.

8.5 Socialism

In all this work Hayek was concerned to provide a serious, sustained, and scholarly critique, motivated not merely by his distaste for the principle participants, and for their totalitarian descendants who by 1941 had engulfed almost the whole of Continental Europe, but by a very real concern at the damage which attachment to such erstwhile chic ideas – not least at LSE during Hayek's time there as indeed Popper (1992a) has testified – could do to the development of a free society and its associated market economy. The three main planks of Hayek's critique were as follows. Firstly, he rejected the idea that society could be profitably studied as a whole without reference to the individuals constituting it and to their individual actions. The paradox of self-proclaimed 'positivists' postulating such metaphysical entities as 'society', 'the economy', 'capitalism' and 'the class struggle' demonstrated the basic intellectual weakness of scientism in its emphasis upon 'wholeism'. Secondly, Hayek attacked Comte's idea that it was possible to construct some kind of 'social physics' and to find laws governing society which would be as definite as those of (genuine) physics. The laws of real physics required a clear concept of what constituted an 'observed fact' but such clarity in the matter of 'social physics' was conspicuously absent from the work of Comte.

The third plank in Hayek's critique was the observation that Comte and his latter-day successors held, on the one hand, that the weakness of the human mind produced an unordered society while, on the other hand, they believed that the human mind was also capable of stretching to comprehend the problems of society as a whole and to plan that society.

Hayek was thus arguing, in his critique of scientism and constructivism, that a fundamental failure to understand the nature of human society – and above all a fundamental failure to understand the nature of markets and thus of resource allocation – lay at the basis of socialism. It is not entirely clear whether both Mises and Hayek considered socialism to be impossible or merely impossibly inefficient. In the last resort the arguments put forward by Hayek certainly point in the direction of impossibility – at least in the long run – and he lived long enough to see the breakdown of the eastern European régimes.The core problem which Hayek perceived was essentially that of knowledge.This initially involved a problem concerning goods markets; but the real problem lay in factor markets. It was this problem which showed that the idea of planning was fundamentally incoherent. For without a developed market system, in which unobservable preferences for factor uses could be registered through derived demand, there was no way that a planner could assign values to factor services.Thus 'cost' had no meaning outside a market system and a failure to recognise this was the central fallacy of the 'engineering of society' approach running from Saint Simon to Marx and Lenin (and their academic disciples). For without a competitive society there were no costs to be entered into calculations, and the parallel drawn by would-be planners between society and a single factory was shown to be fallacious.

Hayek did not stop at exposing the fallacies of totalitarian socialism; he must have derived a wry satisfaction from the failure of the 1960s' fashion for 'indicative planning' since he had, in the 1930s, foreseen the difficulties with this as well, as is shown by a 1936 lecture, reprinted in *Money Capital and Fluctuations* (1984a, pp. 176-7). He returned to the issue in 1976 (*New Studies*, 1978a, pp. 232-46), weary that the new chic advocates of indicative planning had apparently learned so little.

Most of Hayek's work is patiently – even exhaustively – argued. His 1935 review of the socialist calculation debate (reprinted in *Individualism and Economic Order*, 1949) is fair and temperate. He was occasionally prepared to be both more direct and more actively interventionist. His *The Road to Serfdom* (1944) was such a strong statement of the dangers inherent, as he believed, in state intervention that even Lionel Robbins distanced himself somewhat from the ideas in the work (*Political Economy Past and Present*, 1976, pp. 137-8). His foundation of the Mont Pelerin Society in 1947 (his opening address is reprinted in *Collected Works*, IV, 1992) was an active personal initiative to bring together those who, in Sir Karl Popper's words, were 'scholars and practical economists who were opposed to the fashionable socialist trend of the majority of intellectuals who believed in a socialist future' (Popper, 1992a). Hayek served for more than twelve years as the President of this organisation. He ultimately left after a disagreement, the nature of which has not been made public. But the initiative was a powerful one in an international context. In a more purely British context, though it has spawned imitations, Hayek's role in the foundation of the Institute of Economic Affairs (1992, pp. 192-3) was also an important and, in the long run, influential development.

Yet Hayek had to face the fact that, for long, academic conventional wisdom – and certainly the version of that wisdom conveyed to undergraduates – was that the contributions by Lange and Taylor had shown that socialism was, after all, plausible by employing Lausanne general equilibrium. As Hayek patiently pointed out, such writers had fundamentally failed to demonstrate how this could be done without markets (1949, pp. 148-80). Moreover, even if it were possible to accept the applicability of the Lausanne model to any real economic system, such a system would then be frozen at a particular stage of development, and would be incapable of the economic evolution which was essential to progress.

8.6 Evolution

Evolution – the evolution of economic and social institutions – was a central concern of Hayek, and a core element in his later writings. There seems little doubt that he came to stress this idea as part of his critique of socialism. Evolved institutions, the product of the unintended consequences, through their interaction, of decentralised decisions, reflected social preferences in a way that a planned system, even were it possible to have such a system in a workable form, never could. But the argument, particularly in his later work, went much further than this. According to Hayek, evolved social forms embodied knowledge, and transmitted socially beneficial values. A system evolved which compensated for the limited knowledge of each individual, and these individuals, acting with limited information, produced unintended consequences. These consequences were directed towards social good by the evolution of market institutions such as property and contracts, leading to the division of labour.

Hayek came ultimately to hold that the form of this evolution, and the role in it of unintended consequences, was the key question in economics from Hume and Smith onwards. But this evolutionary approach extended in his view beyond economic phenomena to religion and a moral code, and indeed to the whole structure of civilisation, which depended on the human co-operation associated with the market. The forms thus evolved incorporated the lessons which society had learnt in discovering ways to reconcile different objectives.

Hayek thus looked at earlier writers with this particular question very much in mind. It was this idea which led him to regard Mandeville as a particularly important writer (1978a, pp. 249-66; 1991, pp. 79-100), one who had advanced a pioneering statement of the doctrine of unintended consequences through his thesis that what are private vices are often public benefits. Mandeville had also argued that it was the growth of law which ensured that this transition came about – the law developed to ensure this. Law was thus an evolutionary product, as were morality, language and money.

8.7 Legal Institutions

It is in this context that Hayek's stress upon law (as distinct from discretionary government) has to be viewed. The law, as Locke, Hume, Smith and Kant had all argued, safeguarded the individual against discretionary government, while allowing society to develop. Hayek (1978a, p. 158) argued that the best form of this legal development was the Anglo-Saxon legal tradition, and he was a strong admirer of the great Common Lawyers such as Coke and Hale, whom he believed to have made the world safe from Hobbesian 'totalitarian-positivist conceptions'.

He drew a clear contrast between the British legal tradition, which he believed to have protected individual liberty, and the legal system ruling in Continental Europe. It was the British tradition of liberalism, as he saw it, which stressed the freedom of the individual under general law, that Hayek admired, contrasting it with the tradition of continental liberalism which he believed to have become corrupted, particularly in France, by the ambitions of the would-be planners. Hayek was particularly sad to see that this continental tradition had infected John Stuart Mill, an individual whom, without being blind to his personal weaknesses, he greatly admired and in the collection and publication of whose correspondence (notably that with Mrs Taylor) he had played a key role, demonstrating his usual impeccable scholarship (Hayek, 1951).

8.8 Monetary Economics

This scholarship was also very much to the fore when Hayek, under the influence of Mises and his seminal work on money *Theorie des Geldes und der Umlaufsmittel* (1912), began to work on monetary economics. From the belated publication in his *Collected Works* (1991, pp. 127-244) of work written many years earlier, it is apparent that Hayek had a remarkable knowledge not merely of English but also of French and Italian monetary literature, as well, of course, of work published in German. He also did much to establish the importance of Richard Cantillon as a monetary theorist (1991, pp. 245-94), and wrote illuminatingly about classical economics, perceiving the lack of originality in Ricardo's contributions to monetary debates (1991, pt. III) while, as the editor of a particularly fine edition of Thornton's *Paper Credit* (Hayek, 1939b), he was a witness to the very best and most original of nineteenth century monetary economics (1991, pp. 295-344). But though Hayek's approach to this material was scholarly, the background to his interpretations was undoubtedly the monetary theory of Mises. He became a distinguished exponent of Misean monetary theory in his own right and, together with Lionel Robbins, one of the two most important advocates of this neo-Wicksellian alternative to mainstream quantity theory and Keynesian analyses. Thus, in analysing the work of Cantillon, it was Cantillon's discussion of the effects of a change in *relative* prices which he stressed. He was also able to find much in the monetary theory of Thornton which could be related to the monetary theory which he and Mises put forward.

This monetary theory itself involved the idea that monetary expansion lowered the lending rate below the marginal rate of profit. This, an idea common to both Wicksell and Thornton, was the starting point. But for Mises, and for Hayek, the key element was not the fact that such monetary expansion raised the *general* price level; rather it was that monetary expansion altered the *relative* prices of consumption and investment goods.

This in turn distorted factor markets. The expansion of the investment good market resulting from cheap credit captured resources from the consumption good market, and the leftward shift in the supply schedules for consumption goods raised their prices and imposed forced saving on consumers. However the spending of the enhanced factor incomes, resulting from the bidding away of resources by the investment goods industries, restored the relative prices of consumer goods, and their outputs, through a rightward shift in the demand curves for consumer goods. A fresh bout of monetary expansion was thus necessary to enable the investment good industry to recapture resources to complete its projects. It is easy enough to see how this fits, as a disturbance, into a concept of general equilibrium in which, in equilibrium, the relative outputs of consumption goods and investment goods reflect consumer preferences for consumption goods and savings, the latter in turn reflecting social time preference.

It is also easy to see that a grounding in Böhm-Bawerk's capital theory could have led Hayek, in this context, to concern with the concept of the period of production, because this bore a key relationship to social time preference and also because the length of the production period determined the marginal profitability of investment. Such a concern was not strictly necessary. The Misean monetary theory can be put forward without this 'period of production'. Robbins's own version did not employ it; and it is absent from quite a lot of Hayek's own macroeconomic writings. However Hayek could not himself let go of the matter. Indeed, as will become clear, it was his unsuccessful grappling with capital theory which eventually brought an end to his purely economic writings, and which turned his interests towards the philosophy of the liberal market economic system.

We return to this issue below. It is however worth making the point at this stage that macroeconomic theory of this kind had important, and highly controversial, implications, during a world depression. For in the early 1930s Hayek, together with Robbins and a few others, resolutely opposed suggestions for increases in government expenditure and the use of an expansionary monetary policy, both designed by their advocates to raise the level of employment. His position was clear enough. Monetary expansion was itself the source of the depression since, the Misean analysis showed, it had distorted the relative prices of consumption goods and investment goods. The unemployment which existed was the result of difficulty in reabsorbing, into the consumer goods industries, labour which had initially been sucked from those industries into investment good industries and then released again as the initial promise of investment projects proved illusory. Further monetary expansion would simply delay the necessary readjustments in which a general equilibrium set of relative prices and interest rates was re-established, for it would enable investment projects which should never have been undertaken to be persevered with, as well as encouraging the undertaking of new sub-marginal projects. Public expenditure would not help either. It simply crowded out private expenditure and failed to produce a rise in aggregate demand – indeed all that resulted from it was a shortage of investment funds and even the failure to complete public investment projects.

Such a position was, hardly surprisingly, extremely controversial in the 1930s. It also seems to have involved, on the part of Hayek, Robbins and their allies, a fundamental error of fact: a failure to understand that the money supply of the United States had *fallen* sharply during the onset of the depression. Evidence for such a misapprehension on Hayek's part is provided by a 1932 article by him (republished in 1984a, pp. 118-35, especially p. 130). Robbins's *The Great Depression* (1934c pp. 73-5) also seems to have been written under the same misapprehension.

8.9 Hayek and Keynes

The Hayek-Robbins position naturally led to considerable difficulties in relations with Keynes. The relationship between Keynes and Hayek began badly in 1928 with 'strong disagreement' (1978a, p. 283); there followed an adverse review article by Hayek, considering Keynes's *Treatise*, which appeared in *Economica* in 1931 (Hayek, 1931b, c; 1932a, b). Part of his objection to this book can be traced to an aversion to the subjective originality of a work which was clearly Wicksellian, though with scant acknowledgement to Wicksell. A similar attitude can be discerned in Hayek's treatment of Keynes's *General Theory*, which he regarded as a 'tract for the times' (1978a, p. 284). At all events there is little doubt that during the 1930s Hayek, at least for a while, was Keynes's principal opponent. Hicks himself has recorded that:

> it is hardly remembered that there was a time when the new theories of Hayek were the principal rival of the new theories of Keynes. Which was right, Keynes or Hayek? There are many still living teachers of economics, and practical economists, who have passed through a time when they had to make up their minds on that question; and there are many of them (including the present writer) who took quite a time to make up their minds (1967, p. 203).

As a result of his difficulties with capital theory, Hayek withdrew from the controversy – though the primary reason which he gave for that withdrawal was that, having been assured by Keynes after the publication of the *Treatise* that he had already changed his mind, Hayek was reluctant to engage in a critique of the *General Theory* with the prospect of its author making the same response (1978a, p. 284; 1983b). At all events Keynes and Hayek became, at least on the surface, reconciled during World War II and Hayek has paid tribute both to Keynes's astuteness and intellectual grasp and also to their personal *rapprochement* (1984b; 1994, p. 91). But it seems reasonable to argue that this did not go very deep – perhaps on either side. On the one hand Hayek continued to hold that Keynes really knew no economics outside Cambridge economics, being particularly frank about this in an article written in 1966 for the *Oriental Economist* (reprinted in 1978a, pp. 283-9). He believed Keynes's knowledge both of trade and of capital theory to be seriously inadequate, and his lack of knowledge of German to be a significant handicap. He was opposed to Keynes's monetary nationalism (1937b; 1999b, pp. 37-105), and believed that the legacy of Keynesianism was inflation, although he seems disinclined to blame Keynes himself for this. On the Cambridge side there is no doubt that hard feelings remained; Lord Kahn, a leading member of the so-called 'circus', was still retailing what he clearly regarded as his definitive put-down of Hayek, dating apparently from 1931, as late as his 1978 Mattioli lectures (Kahn, 1984, p. 182).

In the end, Keynes – or rather, perhaps, the Keynesians and Keynesianism – triumphed. But the real story of Hayek's withdrawal from macroeconomic controversy has to be seen within the context of his struggles with the theory of capital. He clearly believed that this was the key to a satisfactory macroeconomic theory – and also, to the defeat of Keynes. Indeed one of his charges against Keynes was a lack of a knowledge of capital theory. When he failed to develop a capital theory which met his aims he, in effect, gave up the struggle.

Hayek's clearest account of what happened, and of the circumstances which led to his virtual abandonment of the main battleground in economics, and the switch of his concentration to the wider issues of the operation and evolution of a decentralised economy, coupled with a retreat into guerilla warfare on matters of macroeconomics, was given in an article in the *Economist* (11 June 1983, pp. 45-8). From this, and other briefer accounts, it is clear that he had reached the conclusion that he had to defeat the central Keynesian contention that increased aggregate demand resulted in increased investment, output and employment. His effort to establish this came in two stages. The first was his *Profits, Interest and Investment* (1939a) in which he used his celebrated 'Ricardo Effect' (which in truth does not derive from Ricardo) to explore the possibility that, with real wages in consumption goods industries falling in a boom, less capital intensive production processes might be substituted for more capital intensive production processes and that the net effect of this in the economy as a whole might actually be to lower overall investment. The next, and decisive, phase was the publication of his *Pure Theory of Capital* (1941a). This was the fruit of a sustained effort to develop Austrian capital theory to the point where it could be used as the basis for a decisive critique of the Keynesian multiplier. The book itself represented the first half of the enterprise; the second half of the enterprise was to be an application of the pure theory of capital to a critique of Keynesianism. But Hayek was intellectually exhausted at that point; and he also, he later wrote, was anxious not to undermine Keynes's position as a war-time adviser and, in particular, Keynes's opposition to war-time inflation.

Whether this is the whole story seems doubtful. While Hayek did not abandon his intellectual position on capital theory – indeed it is lucidly stated in the *Economist* article, and applied to Keynesianism – it seems reasonable to conclude both that he was too exhausted intellectually to work out fully the theoretical critique and to link it to the capital theory and – perhaps most importantly of all – that he had decided that aggregate demand management of a Keynesian variety constituted a much smaller threat to a free society than socialism and scientism in all their various forms. It was thus the latter on which he concentrated his efforts from 1940 onwards.

But the desire to find a theoretical basis for a fundamental critique of aggregate demand management – and for a revival of John Stuart Mill's dictum that 'Demand for Commodities is not Demand for Labour' – explains Hayek's constant return to the difficult matter of an average period of production for the economy. For the period of production in itself is not essential to the Mises-Hayek monetary theory of the cycle. The key factor in that is, as already noted, the proposition that the flows of consumption and investment goods should reflect the preferences of consumers as a whole for production today and production in the future. Early papers, reprinted in the 1984 volume on *Money, Capital and Fluctuations*, notably those on intertemporal equilibrium, on United States monetary policy, and on the theory of interest, do not in fact rely on the period of production concept. Moreover other 'Austrians' – Machlup and Robbins (the latter in his *The Great Depression* of 1934) – were able to explain the Mises-Hayek theory without reference to the period of production. Hayek's own *Monetary Theory and the Trade Cycle* (1929/1933) itself does not rely on this concept. But the key point seems to have been that Hayek felt that he had to use the period of production, not because it was central to his own macroeconomic model, but because he believed that it was the only way to defeat the aggregate demand model of Keynes. He failed.

In a sense the whole exercise was futile. Not only is it arguable – and has been argued, as Mark Blaug shows in his brilliant survey in *Economic Theory in Retrospect* (1985, pp. 498-564) that the whole Austrian theory of capital, and its central concept of the period of production, was so deeply flawed that the outcome could only be the dead end in which Hayek found himself; it is also true that the whole theoretical structure could be explained merely by reference to the marginal productivity of new investment without getting entangled in Austrian capital theory. It is perhaps a measure of the intellectual honesty of Hayek, however, that he was not prepared to leave the matter there but sought directly to confront the Keynesian contention that increased aggregate demand increased employment, braving the (ultimately fatal) quicksands of that capital theory.

Whether this was a sensible approach, methodologically speaking, is even more open to question. For one theoretical apparatus cannot invalidate, on a priori grounds, another theoretical apparatus. They should be tested by reference to the available data. Such a test would undoubtedly have supported the Keynesian position rather more strongly than the Hayek-Mises one, though Robbins's (1934c) gallant effort in *The Great Depression* to deploy the data to establish the opposite should not be overlooked. But at all events such a confrontation of theory with data was anathema to Hayek the a priorist.

8.10 Conclusions

But all this, though it goes a long way to explain Hayek's eclipse as a mainstream economist, should not blind us to his stature or his achievements. Mark Blaug has called him 'Böhm-Bawerk's last and greatest pupil' (1985, p. 541). But he was much much more than this. He was Mises's greatest pupil, the great voice of sanity countering the vain wishes of academics to plan society, the great inheritor and expositor of the Austrian understanding of the fundamental nature of markets, and perhaps the last great scholar-economist, roaming over the literature of centuries in an intimidating range of languages and patiently distilling his message of hope in an evolving free society under the rule of general law.

In considering Hayek's life there is, it is true, some sense of sadness at the intellectual isolation which he endured. On the one hand it is true that, in 1974, the Nobel Committee awarded him, jointly with Myrdal (in what many at the time saw as an ingenious balancing act), the Nobel Memorial Prize in Economics. The Committee indeed revealed that the names of both candidates had been amongst those proposed since the inception of the Prize. With considerable dexterity the Committee managed to pay tribute to *both* Myrdal and Hayek for their blending of political and economic considerations, while praising Hayek's individual achievements both in macroeconomics and in his critique of central planning. But even here there is some unease; for Hayek, it appears, did not believe that there should be a Nobel Prize for economists. Nonetheless, here was recognition. Again, it is true, that a limited number of writers of a different – and in one case, that of Lord Desai (1994; Desai and Redfern, 1994), it would perhaps be fair to say a *very* different – stamp to Hayek were prepared to treat his ideas – notably on the economics of information – seriously and with respect. These writers included R.C.O. Matthews (1981), and Lord Plant (1994).

But the broad picture is much more depressing. Hostility in Cambridge was perhaps to be expected – Kahn's jibe noted above pales into insignificance when compared with Joan Robinson's reminiscence of the same lecture, a reminiscence also dating from nearly half a century later (cited in Hayek, 1995, p. 25). But the hostility went wider than the Marxist left, as epitomised by the following reminiscence: 'One of us vividly remembers the difficulties he had when submitting a proposal for an MA thesis on Hayek's economics in the Netherlands at the end of the 1970s. It took quite some effort and persistence to get the subject accepted – grudgingly, because the only thing academics 'knew' about Hayek was that he was a reactionary' (Birner and Van Zijp, 1994, p. x).

As Jack Birner has noted, 'Until recently, F.A. Hayek was very much an intellectual outcast' (ibid., p. 1). Birner has explained the situation very well:

> To this very day, Hayek's economics is almost completely unknown to his fellow-economists, and Hayek the economist remains a lone-ranger. His social philosophy has fared only slightly better. Thus, most of Hayek's career is surrounded by a sense of tragedy. Personal tragedy in that he rarely found the recognition he deserves given the astounding width and depth of his thought which was so often so far ahead of developments in areas which he sometimes entered as a self-professed amateur. There was tragedy, too, for those fields of intellectual endeavour that, usually out of ignorance, failed to use Hayek's insights to their advantage (ibid., p. 2).

This theme could be illustrated at length. While Hayek received, particularly in *Politics and Economics* (1963) some limited recognition by Lionel

Robbins, his one-time close associate, it is quite extraordinary to record that a great figure like Michael Oakshott, with very much in common intellectually with Hayek, should so far have failed to appreciate Hayek's emphasis on evolutionism and unintended consequences, and his opposition – which went even further than Oakshott's – to a constructivist approach to political problems, that he could dismiss Hayek as a rationalist (1962, p. 21). Hayek for his part also failed to recognise a natural intellectual ally – his *Law, Legislation and Liberty* (1973-9) refers to Oakshott only twice, both of them distantly. This epitomises Hayek's isolation. Why and how it occurred is a considerable puzzle, though some may feel that it is one that does not reflect well on the academic profession, particularly in contrast with the deference accorded to the apologists for totalitarian regimes.

Yet somehow Hayek rose above the neglect of his work even by those who were his natural allies in the intellectual arguments against socialism, constructivism and totalitarianism. The valuable pluralism of American academic life – in his case, in Chicago – came to his aid, as it did to that of Mises. By patiently developing, refining, and expanding his exposition he ultimately succeeded – aided by that very evolutionary march of human affairs on which he laid so much stress – in bringing to the attention not merely of economists but of political writers and constitutional theorists the fundamental issues to which he had devoted his life's work.

Chapter 9

Hayek: The Union of Law and Economics

The interrelationship between economics and law is the background to Hayek's critique of 'scientism' and constructionism published in the early 1940s (Hayek, 1941b, 1942-44). (According to Hayek, in his preface to the republication of these articles, they formed 'part of a single comprehensive plan' (1955, p. 5)). However it is a central theme of Hayek's work from 1944 onwards when he published *The Road to Serfdom*. He devoted two major works to the subject; *The Constitution of Liberty* (1960) and his great three volume work, *Law, Legislation and Liberty* (1973-79). Although he had established a significant reputation as an economist in the 1930s – indeed as Keynes's most important opponent (O'Brien, 1994b: and Chapter 8) – his economics training was narrow and he qualified at Vienna in Law and Economics (though the latter degree was *doctor rerum politicarum*). His transmutation into a philosopher – and, in particular, into a philosopher of law – was thus relatively straightforward. It was aided by an extraordinary erudition, manifested in familiarity with a wide range of sources in a number of languages (O'Brien, 1994a, pp. 344-5).

In understanding Hayek, these are important factors. So also is one which has been relatively neglected, but which explains many of the implicit assumptions of his work, especially in *The Road to Serfdom*. This was his anglophilia. He became naturalised in 1938 (as 'von Hayek' because the British authorities naturally insisted on seeing his birth certificate, even though the title 'von' had been abolished when Austria became a Republic in 1918 (Hayek, 1994, p. 107)), and Hayek has acknowledged this anglophilia explicitly (1944, pp. 100, 159-60; 1994, pp. 98-101). It may also help to explain his remarkable tolerance, something which was commented on with surprise bordering on admiration by Popper, and which led Schumpeter to accuse him of politeness to a fault (O'Brien, 1994a, p. 370; 1994b, p. 348; and Chapter 8; Hayek, 1973-9, I, pp. 70, 161; Schumpeter, 1946).

Hayek's fundamental moral standard was freedom. It was necessary that this be acknowledged as an overriding principle (1973-9, I, p. 61). It was freedom which permitted the development of both social and economic organisation and of the individuals within a society, and protected those individuals from the threat of arbitrary – even horrible, as in an example Hayek gives (1944, p. 63n) – action by a government unconstrained by general rules.

It was the English Common lawyers whom Hayek believed to have been responsible, in the seventeenth century, for both articulating and developing this fundamental concept of freedom. They did so in the face of executive power and of its apologists, especially Thomas Hobbes (e.g. 1960, p. 181; 1973-9, I, pp. 9-11, 33, 91, 95; II, pp. 45, 58; 1978a, p. 158). This led Hayek to categorise writers as either heroes, who recognised the evolutionary nature of society and the freedoms which this brought, or 'constructivist' villains who sought to impose artificial arrangements on society (1973-9, I, pp. 52, 74). The first category included the seventeenth century Common Lawyers, notably Coke and Hale, as well as John Locke (1960, p. 58; 1967, pp. 107, 162; 1968, pp. 23, 25; 1973, pp. 10-11; 1973-9, I, pp. 22-4, 85), and the great names more familiar to economists – Adam Smith, Adam Ferguson, and Edmund Burke (1949, pp. 4, 7; 1960, pp. 172-4; 1967, pp. 77, 98-9; 1973-9, I, pp. 22-4; 1978a, pp. 124-5, 264). Hayek was particularly impressed not only with Smith's criticisms of the 'Man of System' (1973-9, I, pp. 35, 155) but with Ferguson's emphasis on social and economic phenomena which were the result of human action but not of human design (1973-9, I, pp. 20-1; 1978a, p. 264). However his real heroes in this connection were Mandeville and Hume. It was Mandeville who had developed the way in which the *unintended* consequences of individual actions under partial information interacted so as to produce social benefit (1968, p. 9; 1973-9, I, pp. 22-4, 29-31; 1978a, pp. 11, 73, 249-66; 1988, p. 71). It was Hume who had exposed the limits of human reason and the fallacies of 'constructivism' as embodied in the work of Bacon and Hobbes, and whose critique was applicable to the constructivist villains who followed, from Saint-Simon and Comte to Marx and, indeed, Galbraith (1960, p. 63; 1968, pp. 15,21; 1973-9, I, pp. 4, 6, 22-4, 29-31, 52, 67, 92, 113; II, pp. 1, 16, 17, 34, 62; III, p. 105). It was Hume, in particular, who was responsible for establishing the idea of the evolution of social and economic institutions, an idea which preceded the work of Charles Darwin who had indeed been influenced by it himself (1960, p. 59; 1973-9, I, pp. 23; III, p. 154). It was unfortunate that the 'Social Darwinists' who came after him neglected this heritage, and concentrated their attention on social evolution relating to individuals rather than to institutions.

Hayek himself was an agnostic (1994, p. 41). Yet in contrast to both Lionel Robbins and Jacob Viner, who were strongly opposed to religious beliefs (O'Brien, 1988, p. 7), Hayek showed some sympathy towards, and appreciation of, not merely individual Catholics – Lord Acton was one of the individuals whom Hayek admired most (1960, p. 177; 1973-9, I, pp. 8, 107) – or even the Catholic church as a whole (Hayek stressed the opposition which the Nazis had encountered from the Catholic church as then constituted in Germany (1967, p. 143)) but writers writing within the Thomistic tradition, notably Molina. Hayek emphasised that the Just Price for Molina was simply the price in a competitive market (1967, p. 170; 1973-9, I, pp. 20-1; 1978a, p. 255); noted that Molina appreciated the concept of orderliness which was not produced directly by human will (1967, p. 98); and pointed out that the

'Calvinist ethic' owed at least as much to strands in Catholic thinking and behaviour (1973-9, II, p. 145; III, p. 203).

Not surprisingly, Hayek also emphasised the evolutionary elements to be found in Menger's *Untersuchungen* (1883) even though he recognised that Menger himself had received the British evolutionary tradition through German sources (1967, pp. 99-103; 1973-9, I, pp. 22, 47; 1978a, p. 265). Hayek also showed appreciation of the work of Bastiat (1973-9, I, p. 57).

Many of these threads came together in Hayek's admiration for the English legal system. It was only England which had succeeded in building up the concept of liberty under the law, with the Common Law as a barrier to executive power (1973-9, I, p. 84). It was this, rather than any separation of powers, which had produced British liberty. The British tradition of liberalism was grounded on this, and on the writings of the common lawyers and of John Locke. It contrasted with Continental liberalism which was deeply infected with constructivism (1949, pp. 28-9, 110; 1960, pp. 55-7, 407; 1967, p. 160; 1978a, pp. 119-20). In his appreciation of the English Common Law, Hayek manifested a romanticism which made him vulnerable to criticism. Yet Hayek had a substantial point; even now, a public functionary defying a court order would run a serious risk of contempt of court whereas in France he would simply open negotiations with the judge (Lebrecht, 1996, p. 229). This remains true even though, as Hayek recognised, Britain has witnessed a remarkable development of that administrative law which had previously been thought to be a continental vice (1973-9, III, p. 29); and, especially under the auspices of EU directives, the bureaucracy in Britain has assumed quasi legislative powers far beyond those which alarmed Hayek when they were employed, in particular, during the era of the post-war Labour Government (1973-9, III, pp. 115, 144-5; Booker and North, 1994).

9.1 The Nature of Law

Hayek distinguished between law and legislation. Law was much older than legislation and became gradually articulated in words after being long established (1967, p. 102; 1973-9, I, pp. 72, 76-8, 95; III, pp. 33-4). The idea that society preceded law was a fallacy common to the constructivists and the legal positivists. The idea of a social contract was factually false (1967, p. 102; 1973-9, I, p. 11). The rules by which man lives 'have by a process of selection been evolved in the society in which he lives' (1973-9, I, p. 11) and groups which evolved good rules would themselves prosper (1967, pp. 67-81; 1973-9, I, p. 99; III, p. 166). The so-called 'Calvinist ethic' was an example of this (1973-9: II: 145). Hayek was able to find support for his view in the literature of ethology and cultural anthropology (1973-9, I, pp. 74-6). Some of the rules might well remain non-legal (1973-9, II, pp. 31, 34). But it was fundamentally necessary for people to follow rules of some sort, because everybody operated under limited information, and rules evolved in such a way as to enable society to cope with this problem (1978a, pp. 3-22, 59, 67-8, 71; 1988, p. 21). People did not need to understand the rules – indeed they usually did not – but the rules had evolved in such a way as to function precisely when people were in a state of ignorance (1960, p. 29; 1967, pp. 79-80, 115; 1973-9, I, pp. 11-15, 30; II, p. 8; III, p. 155). Without such rules, human action would have resulted in chaos. The actual rules for behaviour were 'genuine social growths' (1967, p. 243). But they were of fundamental importance: they were nothing less than the key to group survival (1973-9, I, p. 81). These rules resulted in strong moral beliefs (1967, pp. 229-36). Indeed 'a free society will work well only where free action is guided by strong moral beliefs' (1967, p. 230).

On this basis the articulation of the accepted rules of conduct as a legal system then proceeded. The example which, above all, Hayek had in mind was the English Common Law; but the early development of Roman Law also involved codification of accepted norms (1973-9, I, pp. 81-90). Of course in the development of all this there was a continuous process 'in which every step produces hitherto unforeseen consequences' (1973-9, I, p. 65), and the judiciary had to seek to produce an internally consistent system of rules in the course of dealing with particular problems (1973-9, II, pp. 25-9, 40). The role of the judiciary in all this was thus central; it had to select the good rules, ensure internal consistency, and apply the body of law to particular cases (1973-9, I, pp. 94-8, 118-20). This did not however mean the maintenance of the status quo; indeed legal evolution could sometimes lead to laws which favoured particular groups and this 'ought clearly to be corrected' (1973-9, II, p. 131). The development of law had, too, to take account of the factual setting (1973-9, I, pp. 105-6).

The rules which provided the framework in which society operated represented one kind of rule (1973-9, I, pp. 48-52). There were however two kinds. There were the general rules, of the kind discussed so far, which Hayek called *Nomos*; and there were rules which had a definite purpose, which Hayek called *Thesis.* The two categories of rule related to two different kinds of order; the first, Hayek called *Cosmos*, meaning a spontaneous order, and the second he called *Taxis*, meaning an organised system (1967, p. 163; 1968; 1973-9, I, pp. 35-54, 124-44; II, p. 15). The vast majority of legislation related to the rules of organisation (1973-9, I, pp. 127-40).

As Hayek noted at a number of points, these categories corresponded to ones used by Oakeshott, though with different terminology (Nomocracy for Cosmos and Teleocracy for Taxis (1967, p. 163; 1973-9, II, p. 15)). But, perhaps more fundamentally, the ideas also corresponded to a central element in classical economics, articulated in our own time by Lionel Robbins (1952) and by Warren Samuels (1966). This is the idea that all economic activity, and, in particular, the pursuit of self-interest, has to be limited by a framework of law, religion and custom.

The rules called Nomos governed just conduct. It was the essence of rules of just conduct that all power should be limited.

> The thesis of this book [*Law, Legislation and Liberty*] is that a condition of liberty in which all are allowed to use their knowledge for their purposes, restrained only by rules of just conduct of universal application, is likely to produce for them the best conditions for achieving their aims; and that such a system is likely to be achieved and maintained only if all authority, including that of the majority of the people, is limited in the exercise of coercive power by general principles to which the community has committed itself (Hayek, 1973-9, I, p. 55).

Government must thus come under the law (1973-9, I, pp. 130-1; III, p. 128; 1978a, pp. 65-6). The framework produced in this way resulted in expectations which could form the basis of action, and the reconciliation of different aims (which included the disappointment of some expectations through negative feedback to equilibrium) through the market (1973-9, I, p. 97; II, pp. 12, 124; 1978a, p. 184). When people pursued their own ends subject to such rules, a spontaneous order resulted (1973-9, I, pp. 38-46).

Following Hume, Hayek emphasised that the most fundamental rules related to property – stability of possession, and transference by consent. Equally important was the performance of promises. The market required the prevention of violence and fraud, the protection of property, the enforcement of contracts, and the recognition of the equal rights of all individuals to produce and sell in quantities and at prices they chose (1944, p. 78; 1949, pp. 110-11; 1960, pp. 140, 229; 1973-9, I, pp. 107-8; II, p. 40).

It was legitimate for the State to use coercion to enforce such general rules; but it was only such rules, which were end-independent (1960, pp. 148-61, 208; 1973-9, II, pp. 3, 20-1, 31, 123), which justified the coercive powers of the State (1960, p. 205; 1967, p. 165; 1973, p. 11; 1973-9, I, p. 141; III, pp. 5, 109, 139). End-independence was of the essence of such rules; they were designed to fit a range of situations and to limit conduct within those situations. Like J.S. Mill, Hayek did not believe that the coercive powers of the State should be employed to enforce moral standards which did not relate to the necessity of protecting the private domain of individuals (1973-9, II, p. 57).

As Lionel Robbins also emphasised in *The Economic Problem in Peace and War* (1947), Hayek insisted that a market economy did not involve a single social purpose or indeed an agreed set of social purposes. Rather the role of a market economy was to enable individuals to pursue their own ends, as a result of which resources would be used in a more efficient way than if common ends were imposed (1967, p. 163; 1973-9, II, pp. 1-2, 23). Individuals could do this by observing the rules of just conduct which were essentially prohibitions (1973-9, II, pp. 35-8), protecting the domain of fellow men (1967, p. 166). Laws had to lay down the boundaries of freedom of action – Hayek quoted Robert Frost's view that 'good fences make good neighbours' (1967, p. 167; 1973-9, I, p. 107). The rules of just conduct were not natural law 'in the sense that they are part of an external and eternal order of things' but they were rules, adherence to which efficient social function required (1973-9, II, pp. 59-60). They were essentially concerned with commutative justice (1967, p. 258; 1973-9, II, p. 87). The freedom which individuals enjoyed under them was productive of what Hayek called 'The Great Society' which 'arose through the discovery that men can live together in peace and mutually benefiting each other without agreeing on the particular aims which they severally pursue' (1973-9, II, p. 109; see also 1960, p. 35; 1967, pp. 163-4). Hayek referred to the resulting economic order as 'Catallaxy' (1967, p. 164; 1968; 1973-9; II, 107-32). 'A catallaxy is thus the special kind of spontaneous order produced by the market through people acting within the rules of the law of property, tort and contract' (1973-9, II, p. 109). The study of such a system was thus 'catallactics' (1973-9, III, p. 69). The resulting order did not amount to making 'economic ends' prevail for the simple reason that, as Robbins (1932) had pointed out, there was no such category of ends (1973-9, II, p. 113; III, p. 168). Rather it enabled individuals freely to pursue whatever ends they chose and to engage in the decisive step of exchange (1973-9, II, p. 109). Constrained by rules in this pursuit, they produced a complex order far more sophisticated than anything that the human mind could design (1973-9, I, pp. 110-14). Because they used their own knowledge they optimised the use of resources as a result of which society was able to afford more benefits for more people than under any other system (1973-9, II, pp. 106, 118).

The market processes generated knowledge, without any such aim on the part of participants (1973-9, II, pp. 111, 115). Prices transmitted unknown wants to potential producers (1973-9, II, p. 116; 1978a, p. 182). 'The manufacturer does not produce shoes because he knows that Jones needs them. He produces because he knows that dozens of traders will buy certain numbers at various prices because they ... know that thousands of Joneses, whom the manufacturer does not know, want to buy them.' (1973-9, II, p. 116). The information contained in prices resulted from competition (1973-9, II, p. 117). Competition is thus a discovery process (1973-9, II, p. 71; III, pp. 67-70, 75; 1978a, pp. 179-80). (Hayek's insight was vividly illustrated by experience with 1960s British attempts at governmental 'picking winners', the results of which indicated clearly that the market is far better fitted to perform this function than the State). Indeed economists were fundamentally misled by assuming that producers had certain knowledge – 'No theory can do justice to it [competition] which starts from the assumption that the facts to be discovered are already known' (1973-9, III, p. 68). Typically, of course, and indeed increasingly, economists have assumed perfect competition, with its ludicrous assumptions about perfect knowledge. Hayek was emphatic that the kind of competition about which he was talking was certainly not perfect competition (1949, pp. 92-106; 1967, p. 174; 1973-9, III, p. 65). Indeed the fixation of economists with perfect competition led them to misunderstand completely the magnitude of the achievement of a competitive system. Competition made it possible for resources to be used in the way which best reflected the wants of society, taking account of the alternative uses of those resources (1973-9, III, pp. 74-6; 1978a, p. 185). No central direction could accomplish such cost minimisation and consumer satisfaction. Where government did not interfere with it, the competitive system worked extremely well. The truth of this was demonstrated by the difficulty of finding unexploited profit opportunities. The market served minorities as well as majorities (1973-9, III, p. 49) and reconciled the desires of different consumers through price adjustment (1973-9, II, p. 112). It did not bestow power in the way that political action did; Hayek tellingly contrasted the power of men over men bestowed by socialism with the position of the mail-order company Sears Roebuck which could not be said to have power in that way (1973-9, III, pp. 80-1).

Because the market gave voice to both minorities and majorities, it was superior to a system which only served the majority (1960, pp. 110-11). But an increasing public sector share served only that majority (1973-9, III, p. 53). Hayek was understandably critical of writers like Galbraith and Downs who seriously maintained that the public sector was too small (1967, p. 317; 1973-9, III, p. 53). The converse was the case, because of the way in which democratic government operated, satisfying different groups at public expense in order to produce a political majority. Hayek was equally dismissive of the idea that the balance of power between such groups could produce anything other than a sub-optimal outcome (1973-9, III, p. 92).

9.2 Government

Hayek recognised a substantial legitimate role for government (1949, pp. 22-3, 110-15; 1960, p. 231; 1967, pp. 165-6; 1973-9, I, pp. 46-8; III, 41-64). This included such matters as 'Building regulations, pure food laws, the certification of certain professions, the restrictions on the sale of certain dangerous goods..., as well as some safety and health regulations for the processes of production' (1973-9, III, p. 62) and even compulsory purchase if general rules applied and were subject to court control. Hayek was not advocating a minimal state: government should provide a wide range of public goods. He discussed issues such as market failure, the standard characteristics of genuine public goods, and the issue of externalities. Government should also ensure that all were entitled to a minimum basic income (1944, pp. 89-90; 1949, p. 112; 1960, pp. 285-305; 1967, p. 175; 1968; 1973, p. 17; 1973-9, II, pp. 87, 136; III, pp. 55, 142). Unemployment relief was necessary (1960, p. 300).

The finance of government activities through taxation should not, however, involve progression (1949, p. 118; 1960, p. 307; 1967, p. 175; 1973-9, III, p. 127). Indeed Hayek's exposition reflected (and acknowledged) the writings of J.R. McCulloch who said that once the principal of proportionality was abandoned we were at sea without a rudder or a compass – a phrase which, indeed, Hayek quotes (1960, p. 308). However this did not rule out individual taxes, such as income tax, being progressive; it was the overall tax burden which Hayek looked at. Not only did progression involve legislatures voting for higher taxes when the legislators themselves would not have to pay them, as McCulloch had envisaged (1845b, p. 147), but it even encouraged government to pursue inflationary policies in order to benefit from fiscal drag (1960, p. 315).

Much of Hayek's approach here is not fully worked out. Although he appears to be taking a benefit approach to taxation (1960, pp. 315-6; 1973-9, III, pp. 52, 127), he does not make this explicit. Moreover, although he was concerned about the progressive increase in the size of government expenditure beyond that which voters would have preferred, he does not explore the issue of public debt, a prime tool for government in this context.

Although, armed with its revenue, government might finance a range of services, it did not necessarily follow that it had to provide them as well (1973-9, III, p. 46). In particular Hayek favoured Friedman's scheme for education vouchers. He emphasised, like John Stuart Mill, that where government provided it should not have a monopoly (1967, p. 175; 1973-9, III, p. 147). Like Marshall, he objected to the government monopoly of the postal service (1973-9, III, p. 57), and he objected strongly to the idea of a government monopoly of education (1960, pp. 376-94; 1973-9, III, pp. 60-1).

In approaching government regulation of private sector activities, Hayek was guided by the principle that such regulation should be according to rules and not a matter of discretion. Price controls, quite apart from their interference with markets, were to be rejected since they were necessarily discretionary (1960, pp. 227-8); by contrast, factory legislation was perfectly acceptable (1944, pp. 28, 60; 1960, pp. 224-5). Housing and town planning posed serious problems even though there was certainly a case for public involvement, if only because of the problem of externalities (1960, pp. 340-57; 1967, pp. 321-38). Agricultural policy was general counter productive (1960, pp. 358-75).

9.3 Government and Industry

Hayek made a number of suggestions for changes in the legal framework within which companies operated. In particular he objected to companies assuming to themselves a role as social benefit providers, using for this purpose funds which belonged to shareholders (1967, pp. 300-12; 1973-9, III, p. 82), and he proposed amending the law so that each individual shareholder could vote on the proportion of earnings per share which the company might retain (1967, p. 307). To prevent abuse of power through inter-locking share holdings, however, he proposed that companies with such share holdings should be barred from voting (1967, pp. 309-10).

He adopted a somewhat sceptical attitude towards competition policy

(1960, p. 136; 1967, pp. 176-7; 1973-9, III, pp. 66-7, 71-3, 78, 82-3, 86-7). This is important because when the opposition to that policy became fully articulated in Chicago in the 1970s, Hayek's position was influential, and indeed acknowledged to be such. In particular, the most important of such writers, Harold Demsetz, has acknowledged Hayek's contribution (Demsetz 1989, pp. 219, 223). Hayek believed that insofar as there was a monopoly problem, this stemmed very largely from government encouragement and re-enforcement of monopolies (1967, p. 176; 1973-9, III, p. 78). With the growth of large diversified firms the concept of industry, and thus of industrial concentration, had become virtually meaningless, and, like P.W.S. Andrews, Hayek believed that firms were under perpetual threat of competitive attack from other firms already established but active in different parts of the market system (1973-9, III, pp. 78-9; Andrews, 1964).

Hayek was insistent, in line with his general position, that competition policy, insofar as it was operated at all, must not be discretionary (1960, p. 265). He would thus have been dismayed by developments in Britain, in which the legal system established in the 1950s has been very largely superseded by administrative discretion (O'Brien 1982).

Competition policy was, in any case, seriously handicapped by the fact that costs were not in any sense given, but could be assumed to be minimised if there was entry into the industry. Size itself was of no significance – except where distorted by government, the choice of size was the result of the market process (1973-9, III, p. 78).

Interference based upon supposed knowledge of prices and costs was completely misguided. The idea of given cost curves was 'one of the chief sources of error in this field' (1973-9, III, p. 69). Indeed cost curves depended on the extent and nature of the competition (1973-9, III, p. 69) – a valid observation, but one destructive of whole areas of microeconomics. How people would behave under competition was unknown even to them, let alone anyone else. No outsider could know whether normal profits were being earned and firms could not be expected to take risks and then, if successful, be forced to equate price with marginal cost. It was part of the nature of competition that its pressure brought about a search for improvement which led to a divergence between price and marginal cost in the form of a temporary monopoly (1973-9, III, p. 71).

However Hayek had positive proposals for competition policy. The main harm which he believed to be done by monopoly occurred when a monopolist was in a position to exclude entrants into the industry (1973-9, III, pp. 72-3). Accordingly Hayek proposed to utilise the availability of private knowledge through prohibiting this exercise of market power via a civil claim using a multiple damages approach. Actions would be conducted on a contingency basis (1960, p. 136; 1973-9, III, pp. 85-7). (There was no recognition of the problem of moral hazard which has manifested itself in this area.) To avoid the use of a discretionary approach towards cartels, it was best to prohibit them, but to do so simply by making them unlawful (1967, pp. 176-7; 1973-9, III, p. 86), an approach which essentially relied upon the pressure to break ranks within such organisations.

9.4 Macroeconomic Policy

One area in which Hayek's views showed a sharp change in late life concerned government's monopoly of the monetary base. For a long while Hayek took the position that government should be prepared to seek stability in macroeconomic policy (1944, p. 90; 1960, pp. 223, 324-39) – and indeed, at least after the controversies of the 1930s, he was prepared to concede in principle, that public investment should be scheduled in a counter-cyclical manner (1944, pp. 90-1; 1973-9, III, p. 59). In *The Constitution of Liberty* (1960) he rejected the idea of removing money supply from the ambit of government, even though he recognised the propensity of government to inflate. To control this propensity, he suggested a commodity-based standard (since return to the Gold Standard was not practicable) (1949, pp. 209-219; 1960, p. 335). But in *Law, Legislation and Liberty* Hayek put forward proposals for 'denationalisation' of the money supply (1973-9, III, pp. 57-8, 148; 1976a, b; 1978a, pp. 224-8). Because government had 'shamelessly abused' (1973-9, III, p. 58) the money supply, in order to obtain command over resources, its control should be removed from the purview of government. Indeed he claimed that the market system would 'never again work satisfactorily' (1973-9, III, p. 148) until control was removed. In the 1990s this almost apocalyptic tone seems unwarranted; but viewed against the macroeconomic chaos of the 1970s, with broad money in the UK increasing by more than 60 per cent in two years, his tone is understandable.

The proposal was, however, remarkably short on detail – although Hayek made the point that Gresham's Law only operated with fixed ratios of exchange between competing money supplies so that his proposal was not vulnerable on that score (1967, pp. 318-20; 1976, p. 41). (In other contexts, however, he actually favoured fixed exchange rates as a monetary discipline (1978, pp. 201-2, 214)). Indeed his proposal was, as one critic complained, remarkably vague (Fischer, 1986, p. 433). But, when the details were worked out by others, it became clear that Hayek's proposal related essentially to the supply of bank notes (Dowd, 1988). The argument for freedom of issue turned out to depend on the ancient fallacy known in the mid-nineteenth century as the doctrine of 'Reflux', under which banks could not over-issue, as excess notes would be returned to them by their customers. Since the argument depended crucially upon the absolute price level being fixed in some other way, it could not be applied in a twentieth century context, even had it been applicable – which is doubtful – under the gold standard. In fact most of the issues had been comprehensively dealt with by Henry Thornton in his critique of the real bills doctrine in 1802, in a work subsequently reissued in a fine scholarly edition by Hayek himself (Thornton, 1802). But in any case, in a late twentieth century context, the proposals were massively irrelevant; competition already exists in the supply of bank deposits which is overwhelmingly the means of payment and government cannot help influence this supply as by far the largest borrower.

However, there are two points which may be made in Hayek's defence. Firstly, his proposal may have helped to strengthen the case of those who have argued for independence of central banks from government; and recent research has indeed demonstrated a negative association between the degree of independence and the propensity of government to debase the currency. Secondly, Hayek's proposal may well have lain behind the 1980s British case for currency competition rather than European monetary union and, in view of the subsequent debacle of British membership of the Exchange Rate Mechanism in Europe, there was much to be said for this.

The propensity of government to inflate the money supply was greatly strengthened by the privileged position of trade unions in Britain during much of Hayek's lifetime. Hayek regarded the Trade Disputes Act of 1906 as exemplifying a measure passed in the name of democratic control which was actually not desired by the vast majority of the population but which reflected the reality of assembling a political majority (1960, pp. 267-84; 1973-9, III, pp. 31-2). It bestowed upon trade unions a private power of coercion which should not have been available to them (1949, p. 117; 1967, pp. 281-93), and enabled them to interfere with the operation of the market, thus lowering national income (1967, p. 255). But most seriously it led government persistently to inflate the money supply to offset the unemployment-creating effects of trade union activity (1967, pp. 270-9; 1980). Ultimately inflation became the standard tool with which to counter unemployment (1978a, pp. 191-231). Unfortunately, money illusion was eroded, and thus it became progressively necessary to increase the rate of inflation (1967, pp. 282, 295-9). Hayek's exposition of this is based around the Austrian trade cycle theory, though without reference either explicitly to that or to the concept of the period of production. Without the privileged position enjoyed by trade unions,

Hayek believed that an important motive for debasing the money supply would have been removed.

9.5 The Myth of Social Justice

The privileged position enjoyed by the trade unions was defended – not least by the trade unions themselves – on the grounds of social justice. Hayek denounced the concept as simply meaningless (1973, p. 13; 1980, p. 44). In the face of his relentless critique – the title of the second volume of *Law, Legislation and Liberty* is *The Mirage of Social Justice* – it is indeed difficult to maintain the position that the phrase has any meaning. Hayek was scathing about it. Pursuit of this mirage was not merely pointless; it did positive harm (1973-9, II, p. 133) and, since it damaged the market system, it actually prolonged poverty (1973-9, II, p. 139). But it had become a new religion – one attractive to the purveyors of the older religions who were losing faith in them (1973-9, I, p. xvi; II, pp. 66-7, 80) – and a cloak for dishonesty.

> the phrase 'social justice' is not ... an innocent expression of good will towards the less fortunate, but .. a dishonest insinuation that one ought to agree to a demand of some special interest which can give no real reason for it ... the term is intellectually disreputable, the mark of demagogy or cheap journalism (1973-9, II, p. 97).

The word 'social' had simply become a replacement for 'moral' in the secular society even though it functioned as a cloak for envy (1967, pp. 239, 245).

The idea of imposing measures in the name of social justice was meaningless since, as David Hume had shown, there was no possibility of an agreed welfare standard (1973-9, II, pp. 1, 62, 80-4). As Hayek pointed out, the 'word "social" *presupposes* the existence of known and common aims behind the activities of a community, but does not *define* them' (1967, p. 242). The phrase 'value to society' was meaningless except in so far as such value was reflected in market valuation (1967, p. 172). But the market did not reflect, or require, agreed aims for society as a whole.

The more closely Hayek examined the concept 'social justice' the flimsier it seemed. At what point did one draw a frontier? Were we concerned with social justice for foreigners as well? (1973-9, II, pp. 88-91). But the essentially empty nature of the concept was brought out most clearly by pointing out that it was a slogan of totalitarian governments (1973-9, II, pp. 66, 78-80, 136).

Nonetheless, the pursuit of 'social justice' had led to a mass of legislation (1973, p. 12; 1973-9, I, pp. 141-3), resulting in the abandonment of the principle that coercion was only justified in relation to rules of just conduct. Social justice involved the use of coercion in a discriminatory rather than a uniform manner, and was linked to the development of the 'rights' culture (1973-9, II, pp. 101-106), commentary on which led Hayek to the sarcastic remark (concerning the United Nations Declaration) that 'The conception of a 'universal right' which assures to the peasant, to the Eskimo, and presumably to the Abominable Snowman, 'periodic holidays with pay' [article 24] shows the absurdity of the whole thing' (1973-9, II, pp. 105).

However, the supposed claims of 'social justice' had led to legislation to favour particular groups in society. In truth 'social justice' ultimately represented a struggle between groups (1973-9, II, p. 137, III, 9-11, 138). While selfish actions of individuals, constrained by law in the form of the rules of justice, produced benefit for all, the selfish actions of groups produced harm (1973-9, II, p. 138; III, p. 89). Ultimately indeed, egalitarianism could end cultural evolution (1973-9, III, pp. 172-3).

9.6 Distribution

Hayek's basic position on the question of distribution was that as long as the competitive system was fair – just – and applied the same rules to all, there were bound to be unequal outcomes (1960, p. 87) and that it was the operation of competition, not the outcome, with which we should be concerned (1972-3, II, pp. 38, 73). The market outcome might be regarded as unjust, but it emerged from a just system (1973-9, pp. 64, 73-4). We had a choice between maintaining the market system and destroying it by altering the outcomes through redistribution. Market clearing factor rewards had nothing to do with individual merit, but acted simply as resource allocation signals (1967, p. 233; 1973-9, II, p. 72). There was, if we accepted the benefits of the market system, an unavoidable discrepancy between moral merit and reward. Hayek pointed out in *The Road to Serfdom* that income differences in the Soviet Union were as great as in the United States (1944, p. 77).

The rules of justice determined the chances of economic actors not the outcomes. But the chances for any randomly selected person were maximised in a free society (1973-9, II, pp. 114, 126, 132; 1978a, p. 184). 'The Good Society is one in which the chances of anyone selected at random are likely to be as great as possible' (1973-9, II, p. 132). The matter of the relationship between Hayek's work and that of Rawls will be addressed below; but it is worth noting that this proposition is in Hayek's 1968 paper reprinted in *New Studies* (1978a, p. 184).

Hayek can hardly have been unaware of the qualifications to such a position, dating from the previous century, notably the Mill-Cairnes concept of non-competing groups. But he clearly took the view that the way to deal with this was through the removal of barriers to labour mobility (including education) rather than through redistribution. In any case, the plea for social justice in relation to some occupations simply amounted to a demand for the protection of entrenched interests (1973-9, II, pp. 93-6, 140).

Redistribution, as a form of socialist activity, was irreconcilable with the rule of law according to Hayek, because instead of everybody standing equally before the law it involved subordinates receiving and superiors allocating funds. The resulting interference was cumulative: the demand for equality was probably often based on a belief that existing inequalities were the result of somebody's decision rather than of market processes, and, once outcomes were altered through administrative decision, that belief had a firm foundation (1973-9, II, pp. 80-87). It thus led to demands for further intervention. The result was necessarily *ad hoc* (1960, p. 302). Indeed socialism itself was based on 'the atrocious idea that political power ought to determine the material position of the different individuals and groups' (1973-9, II, p. 99; see also II, p. 136 and III, p. 13) and this led him to interpret incomes policies – more often, in truth, the last resort of governments that had seriously mishandled macroeconomic management – entirely in such socialist terms, an interpretation which seems to have been influenced by his familiarity with the work of Barbara Wooton (1973-9, III, pp. 13, 95). But such interference in a 'catallaxy' could never be just because it replaced the spontaneous order, produced by the rules of justice, with disorder (1973-9, II, p. 128).

9.7 Democracy

Hayek, only too well aware of the nature of tyranny, regarded democracy as the only defence against oppression. He was thus alarmed by the evidence of disillusionment with democracy (1973-9, III, pp. 1-19, 98). The essential reason for this lay in the fact that democratic assemblies had assumed powers which were completely unlimited by general laws (1973-9, II, p. 61, III, 15, 33, 99, 128); they had then become the forum for the operation of pressure groups, and for the imposition of legislation to satisfy those pressure groups in order to be able to command a majority of the votes (1973-9, III, p. 99).

This assumption of power was buttressed by the writings of legal positivists on sovereignty which regarded such sovereignty, once vested in a democratic legislature, as unbounded (1973-9, II, p. 61). But the domination of government by coalitions of organised interests was 'the inescapable result of a system in which government has unlimited powers to take whatever measures are required to satisfy the wishes of those on whose support it relies' (1973-9, III, p. 15) and such coalitions could be assembled in the name of social justice dispensing 'gratuities at the expense of somebody else *who cannot be readily identified*' (1973-9, III, p. 103).

Because of the difficulties which democracy was encountering, and because of the abuse of the term democracy (both in such strange concepts as 'people's democracy' and in its use in demands by interest groups to gain control of a particular institution) Hayek preferred the term 'Demarchy' (1973-9, III, pp. 38-40, 1968). He put forward proposals for an ideal constitution (1973-9, III, pp. 35-8) with a three-tiered system of representative bodies, separating consideration of issues of government from rules of just conduct and the framework of the constitution. The separation of powers (1973-9, III, pp. 105-27) would make clear a distinction between rules of just conduct and the institutions of government, and establish the basic principle of such a constitution – that coercion was only for rules of just conduct. Historically the need to limit the powers of the executive had been recognised, and it was the doctrine of the Old Whigs. But sight of this had been lost with the increase in the franchise, so that even in Britain the executive was unconstrained and there were substantial areas of administrative law (1973, pp. 15-22; 1973-9, III, p. 20; 1978b, p. 66).

9.8 Constructivism

Hayek's whole thesis, as outlined so far, was developed in opposition to what he called constructivism – the belief that society could be designed by the efforts of the human mind (1973-9, I, pp. 10, 14-15, 24-6, 73; II, p. 59; III, pp. 155, 173). This supposedly positivist approach employed spurious aggregates such as 'society' and rested upon two related fallacies: that an unplanned system must necessarily be chaotic rather than coherent, and a belief that it could be replaced (1942-4, III, pp. 29-30; 1978a, pp. 3-22). Although Hayek recognised the origins of this in the writings of Saint Simon and his followers, especially Comte (1941b, III, pp. 307-12; 1942-4, II, pp. 50-63), Bentham and his followers attracted his particular ire (e.g. 1973-9, I, pp. 22, 128-9; II, pp. 17-23, 44-8), thus ensuring in turn the hostility of Lionel Robbins towards Hayek's position. Hayek believed that until Bentham, and James Mill, the idea of the separation of powers, and of government under the law, with government occupying a limited role, had been accepted. The fundamental fallacy of the pain/pleasure calculus was the assumption that *all* effects could be known. What Hayek called 'rule' utilitarianism, which he associated with Paley (1973-9, II, pp. 19-20), he regarded as less harmful although it too assumed that all the effects of rules could be known. In clear contrast, Hayek's position was that rules were needed precisely because of ignorance. The Benthamites aspired to build a society; but societies grew and were not built. 'From the insight that the benefits of civilization rest on the use of more knowledge than can be used in any deliberately concerted effort, it follows that it is not in our power to build a desirable society by simply putting together the particular elements that by themselves appear desirable' (1973-9, I, p. 56).

The efforts of the constructivists had been much encouraged by bad economic history, which continuously misrepresented the nineteenth century experience and concealed the enormous rise in real wages and general well-being that had occurred (1967, pp. 207-8; 1973-9, I, pp. 67-8; II, p. 131). In the edited volume *Capitalism and the Historians* (1954), Hayek attempted to assemble a counter-statement; but the process is a never-ending one, as even a cursory survey of more recent economic history literature makes clear.

Nonetheless, as he was able to point out, there was one inescapable piece of evidence; the huge rise in population had occurred simply because capitalism had made it possible for far more people to survive than had been possible ever before in history (1960, pp. 118-19). Economic historical work of the distorted kind had also led to bogus historical laws which had been employed by Comte and Marx (1973-9, I, pp. 23-4). Indeed the origins of totalitarianism could be found in the 'scientism' he associated with Comte – the misguided attempt to apply methods of natural science to the vastly more complex social world (1941b; 1942-4, I, p. 280; 1973-9, I, pp. 15-17, 64).

But the urge to plan society was flattering to the vanity of the would-be planners (1973-9, I, pp. 8-9; III, p. 130; 1988) and there was also, Hayek insisted, a persistent problem of reverting to pre-market, tribal, values in which individual welfare was the concern of group arrangements (1973-9, II, pp. 133-52, III, p. 165). This problem came about essentially because many people in modern society worked in large organisations and had no feel for the operation of the market. The academics were particularly to the fore; it should 'not surprise us that academic philosophers in their sheltered lives as members of organizations should have lost all understanding of the forces which hold the Great Society together and, imagining themselves to be Platonic philosopher-kings, should propose a re-organization of society on totalitarian lines.' (1973-9, II, p. 105). Socialism was thus a reactionary doctrine – a revival of tribal instincts (1973-9, III, p. 169). Ultimately, constructivism led not to the triumph of reason but to the 'enthronement of the will' (1973-9, I, p. 32) in an environment without rules.

The intellectual basis for this error was provided in part by legal positivists, who lacked any understanding of the true nature of law and of a spontaneous market order (1967, p. 101; 1973-9, I, pp. 66-7, 114; II, pp. 47-56). In his comments on the legal positivists, Hayek was no respecter of persons: Glanville Williams is equated with Humpty Dumpty (1973-9, II, p.

48). Hayek was particularly incensed, and on strong ground in his specialist knowledge, by the fact that the legal positivists had been defenceless before the Nazis (1973-9, II, pp. 55-6), since they had validated State action as law, and German legal theories for decades before Hitler had helped to prepare the way for totalitarianism (1960, pp. 234-9, 1967, p. 169).

The appearance of a regime like that of the Nazis might be an extreme case; but there was – or should be – a fundamental distinction between law and the activities of discretionary, interventionist, government (1949, p. 18; 1978, p. 134). Unless government were limited by law, recognition of principles was not enough; in a contest between principles and expediency, between long-term uncertain effects and short-term immediate benefits, expediency would always triumph (1973-9, I, pp. 55-93). But interference with the catallaxy always had unintended consequences which led to further interference (1967, pp. 264-5; 1973-9, III, p. 18). There was thus cumulative interference (1973-9, I, pp. 58-61, 63).

9.9 Socialism and Planning

Hayek, like his mentor Mises, was a sustained, and ultimately successful, critic of the concept of the planned economy, despite the myth, propagated even by those who were not Marxist, that Lange and Taylor had in some sense been able to meet the objections raised by Mises and Hayek. In fact as Hayek, for once relinquishing some of his habitual restraint, demonstrated in a biting deconstruction of Lange's claims about the information available in a planned economy, those claims are simply absurd (Hayek, 1982). It reflects ill on the academic profession that the Lange-Taylor claims should have been given such credence. In such an economy there can be no knowledge of individual preferences, and thus no market for factors in which factor prices embody information about the strength of competing claims on resources. Nor do the Lange-Taylor claims about knowledge of the 'production function' make any sense at an aggregate level. Lange for his part attempted to claim that the planning authorities would have knowledge of opportunity costs. Even were this true – and it is self-evidently impossible – it would provide no guide to choice amongst competing outputs, and thus to resource allocation.

However in the present context it is the introduction of planning into a basically market-orientated system which is more interesting. Hayek as early as 1944 pointed to the myth that economic planning was somehow 'inevitable' (1944, pp. 32-41). In fact 'in social evolution nothing is inevitable but thinking makes it so' (1944, p. 35). The whole idea was based upon a fundamental failure to understand the complexity of economic life (1973-9, III, p. 164). Once extended beyond the national frontier, its ludicrous nature became apparent (1944, pp. 164-6) as Robbins (1937) had pointed out in the 1930s. However the vanity of economists, in particular, caused the ideas involved in planning to resurface at regular intervals, even in the United States. Hayek was able to point to the failure of 'indicative planning' in France which had so attracted western intelligentsia and was highly critical of the proposal, involving Leontief, to employ input-output tables as a planning tool – he pointed out, with some justification, that these represented no more than economic history (because they have no prices) (1978a, pp. 232-46). Planning would indeed increase uncertainty and produce tension between conflicting ends which could only be solved by political means (1944, pp. 42-53, 66-75). Individual freedom was in any case incompatible with the imposition from above of social ends (1944, pp. 150-62). It was also incompatible with the replacement of known laws by the discretion necessarily employed under planning (1944, pp. 54-65).

Of course not all planning involved totalitarianism – and Hayek did not argue this in *The Road to Serfdom* (1944, pp. 100-123). He did however provide cogent reasons, based on the German experience, for believing that moral standards were impossible under totalitarianism and he entitled chapter X of *The Road to Serfdom* 'Why the Worst Get on Top'. But socialism, even in a dilute form, damaged individual moral responsibility – indeed he held that it 'must lead to the extinction of all moral responsibility of the individual' (1973-9, III, p. 129). Indeed he seems to have foreseen, in *The Constitution of Liberty* the present crisis in welfare provision, with the State assuming responsibility for so many decisions of the individual, that is now afflicting Western societies (1960, pp. 290-2).

But, though there was a clear distinction between socialist interventions in a market system and totalitarianism, Hayek did not believe that a so-called 'middle way' represented a viable long-term position (1973-9, III, p. 150). This was because of the activities of groups; group concessions bred further ones until socialism was significantly advanced. Socialism did not however simply represent different values; it was not that the socialist simply attached greater weight to equality (1988, pp. 66-88). By failing to understand the achievements of the market system, socialism was 'based on an intellectual error which makes its adherents blind to its consequences. This must be plainly said because the emphasis on the alleged difference of the ultimate values has become the common excuse of the socialists for shirking the real intellectual issue' (1973-9, II, p. 136).

Hayek lived throughout most of the century during which socialism, including Marxism, appeared to be an important intellectual force. Hayek did not share this view. Marxism he regarded as 'merely one among many characteristic 19th century products' of the 'theory of history' variety (1942-4, II, p. 59) and it was not even a particularly refined example – Marx even lacked an understanding of the price system (1973-9, III, p. 170). His contempt for Marx was coupled with that for Freud whose activities, he believed, had undermined the necessary human adherence to rules (1973-9, III, p. 174). As the end of the century approached, though writing before the collapse of the Berlin Wall, Hayek saw these twin currents drying up.

If our civilization survives, which it will do only if it renounces

> those errors, I believe men will look back on our age as an age of superstition, chiefly connected with the names of Karl Marx and Sigmund Freud. I believe people will discover that the most widely held ideas which dominated the 20th century, those of a planned economy with a just distribution, a freeing ourselves from repressions and conventional morals, of permissive education as a way to freedom, and the replacement of the market by a rational arrangement of a body with coercive powers, were all based on superstitions in the strict sense of the word (1973-9, III, pp. 175-176).

9.10 Preconceptions and Influence

Although Hayek's work has attracted a great deal of critical comment, even the best of it (e.g. Barry, 1979) does not bring out fully the twin foundations on which the vision sketched in this account rests. We have seen how Hayek envisaged law as a body of rules coming into existence spontaneously, and gradually being articulated so as to produce a society in which diffused information could be co-ordinated through a price system. In this system, economic maximisation by the individual was constrained by the legal system buttressed by religion and custom. Such a view is entirely consistent with the tradition stemming from Adam Smith. However in the case of Hayek there are two particular historical episodes, with the associated literature, which drove forward his statement of this vision, and which – and this is extremely important to emphasise – provided him with implicit assumptions which critics, especially in the United States, have not immediately sensed. The first of these eras was the period 1933-44 in Germany, in which an apparently civilised and highly developed country fell suddenly into the grip of an extreme totalitarian regime, the nature of which was hardly grasped by many people in Britain. The second was the period of the post-war Labour government in Britain, spanning the years 1944-51.

As someone with a first-hand knowledge not merely of Germany but of German socialist and anti-capitalist literature, and German legal writings, Hayek was almost uniquely qualified to appreciate the true roots of National Socialism. It was an appreciation of the intellectual roots of Nazism which led to comments such as the following, which infuriated his critics: 'It is indeed the concept of "social justice" which has been the Trojan Horse through which totalitarianism has entered' (1973-9, II, p. 136).

Viewed against the intellectual background of Nazism, and a century of German socialist writings, the background indeed of *The Road to Serfdom*, this is perfectly understandable: but it infuriated English critics both because of their lack of real appreciation of the nature and origins of Nazism and because they believed that Hayek's attitude was formed solely by the experience of Britain in the years 1944-51. Nor had they any appreciation of the true horrors of a totalitarian regime. As Hayek dryly remarked, it was those with some direct experience of a totalitarian regime who had 'a clearer conception of the conditions and value of a free society' (1967, p. 150).

At the time that he wrote *The Road to Serfdom*, Hayek clearly discerned amongst the intellectual classes strongly fashionable currents which mirrored those to be found in Germany 25 years before (1944, pp. 135-49). He cited in particular the Marxist work of E.H. Carr, which poured scorn on liberalism and put forward a collectivist view which was indistinguishable from that of the Nazis, including writings on 'The Moral Foundations of War' [sic] (1944, pp. 138-41). At the same time scientists, naive as ever about social matters, agitated for planning (1944, pp. 141-4); large firms looked to government to strengthen their market position (1944, pp. 144-7) (as had indeed happened during World War II (Swann, O'Brien *et al.*, 1974, p. 46)) and organised labour fell under the influence of people like Harold Laski who explicitly advocated the continuation of war-time controls after the end of the war (1944, p. 149). Hayek warned against this right at the beginning of *The*

Road to Serfdom (1944, p. 2).

But the actual experience of Britain in the years 1945-51, while it did not fulfil Hayek's worst nightmares, did provide for him a sort of mental conditioning which was at the back of his mind henceforth. *The Road to Serfdom* was published as it indeed became evident that war-time controls would be continued in the post-war period, and Hayek lived through the era of the post-war Labour government. This, because of the particular make-up of the commentating community, has had a much better press than it deserved, and only isolated exceptions – such as Jewkes (1948) – give any flavour of what it was like to live through that era, above all the winter of 1947. Indeed an apparently unimportant piece by Hayek on Town and Country Planning (1967, pp. 321-38), which is hardly referred to at all in the secondary literature (though see Barry, 1979, p. 121) is actually of key importance. For here we have all the concerns which lay behind much of his more elliptical writings: discretionary legislation, enabling acts, retrospective powers, confiscation of property (the Crichel Down affair eventually came to the public light, although not until after this era) and wide public disquiet. Lewis (later Lord) Silkin, the minister responsible for town and country planning, told the inhabitants of Stevenage, then a very small town north of London, which was at that time hardly more than a built-up section of the A1 road (there were only 4,810 on the electoral roll – *Times*, 20 May 1946, p. 2a), that they were going to have a new town. The residents demanded an enquiry; Mr Silkin made it clear that they were going to have a new town anyway. He referred arrogantly to the 'backward people of Stevenage' (*Times*, 12 July 1946, p. 6e). Protestors changed the railway station signs to 'Silkingrad' (*Times*, 21 December 1946, p. 2f). Viewed against the experience of that era by someone who lived through it, many of the paradoxes which American critics apparently see in Hayek's work are easily explained. One knows what he is getting at. But the existence of these implicit assumptions reduces the generality – hence the criticisms. Had this era not come to an end, many critics would have had much less difficulty in understanding what Hayek was driving at. As it was, even in post-war Germany under Allied control, the price controls were lifted – leading corporatist economists, as Hayek was later able to note sardonically, to tell anybody who would listen that the removal of these controls would wreck the German economy (1992, p. 194; cf. Galbraith, 1948, p. 95; Hutchison, 1981, pp. 155-75), a somewhat unfortunate prophecy at the start of a decade in which the German economy grew in real terms at the rate of 9 per cent per annum, an achievement unparalleled in the history of the developed world (Yeager, 1976, p. 485).

It was the experience of this period in Britain, which led to Hayek's later observation that there occurred an accelerated ending of the rule of law under the post-war Labour government (1967, pp. 224-7). But it was much more than this development which made an indelible impression on Hayek's outlook. As the study by Jewkes shows, the era was characterised by absurdly detailed regulations, massive incompetence, shoddy goods of the kind later familiar in Eastern Europe, and a rampant black market (Jewkes 1948, pp. 179-85, 212-13, 217-22, 224-5). Yet in the minds of many on the Left this era was – indeed continues to be – viewed with a roseate glow; a prominent Labour politician in the 1970s repeated the absurd claim made during this era (Jewkes, 1948, p. 205) that diet had improved during wartime food shortages, causing one to wonder what it was that politicians (as distinct from, say, nurses – Dickens, 1978, pp. 91, 98) were eating.

Hayek himself was well aware that the reception of *The Road to Serfdom*, by both critics and admirers, failed to take account of the English background.[1] As he observed in an interview in the posthumously published autobiographical volume *Hayek on Hayek* (1994), *The Road to Serfdom*, 'was written so definitely in an English frame of reference – and it was, of course,

[1] While paper shortages limited its circulation in England, the *Reader's Digest* condensed brought its message to a much wider audience in the United States and, in turn, more than a million reprints of this were distributed by the American Book-of-the-Month Club (Burton in Barry *et al.*, 1984, p. xi).

received in a completely different manner' (1994, p. 102). Hayek felt that, to some extent, British socialists had understood the background, even if they disagreed; but in the United States he 'was exposed to incredible abuse, something I never experienced in Britain at the time. It went so far as to completely discredit me professionally' (1994, pp. 102-103). The most extreme example of this, cited by Hayek himself (1967, p. 218) was Herman Finer (1945).

Later commentators, including those from the United States, have been able to see Hayek's message in a much better perspective (Barry *et al.*, 1984). This is only just. Many, including many sympathetic to Hayek's general position, have the impression that *The Road to Serfdom* is some kind of hysterical pamphlet, an impression which is a tribute to the success of the enemies of liberalism in implanting this idea. In truth, the work is the best compact statement of Hayek's views, one which is much easier to digest than the later more diffuse ones. It is true that Hayek's views developed further, and that, in particular, his seminal analysis of the central importance of uncertainty was still to be reflected fully in his treatment of markets, an achievement culminating in *Law, Legislation and Liberty* (1973-9). But *The Road to Serfdom* is an important and scholarly book. At the time of its publication, a number of reviewers appreciated this. Thus even Pigou, who might well have been unsympathetic, wrote that 'This is a scholarly and sincere book' (1944, p. 217). Jewkes explicitly linked his study of Britain under planning with Hayek's book (1948, p. ix).

Yet Hayek was aware that there was much hostility, even though not always publicly expressed, amongst his fellow economists, many of whom regarded planning as rather *chic* (Seldon in Barry *et al.*, 1984, p.xvi).

> I discredited myself with most of my fellow economists by writing *The Road to Serfdom*, which is disliked so much. So not only did my theoretical influence decline, most of the departments

> came to dislike me, so much that I can feel it to the present day. Economists very largely tend to treat me as an outsider, somebody who has discredited himself by writing a book like *The Road to Serfdom*, which has now become political science altogether (1994, p. 143).

Reviewing events after 12 years, Hayek (1967, pp. 216-217) wrote that the book was 'a warning to the socialist intelligentsia of England'; unfortunately it took until 1989 for many of them, unscathed by events in 1956 and 1968, to heed this warning.

Hayek's isolation – for that is what it became (O'Brien, 1994b, pp. 364-6; and Chapter 8) – was made easier by the fact that, like Lionel Robbins (O'Brien, 1988b, pp. 22, 71), he showed occasionally a tendency to alarm verging on panic (e.g. 1973-9, I, p. xx). There was at times almost an apocalyptic element in his work. As late as 1979 he was claiming that the only way to stop the ratio of government expenditure to GDP rising to 100 per cent was a complete reform of financial legislation (1973-9, III, p. 127), and that the role of trade unions in forcing government to inflate the money supply to accommodate wage inflation 'must before long destroy the whole market order, probably through the price controls which accelerating inflation will force governments to impose' (1973-9, III, p. 144). Similarly in 1976 he prophesied that 'Attempts to 'correct' the order of the market lead to its destruction' (1973-9, II, p. 142). But remarks like this have to be seen in context. Viewed against the history of the 1970s, the three-day week, and the experiences under the Heath government, this did not seem as far-fetched when published as it does now.

Hayek's scathing remarks about intellectuals also failed to endear him to the academic community (1944, p. 121; 1967, pp. 178-94, 201-5, 216-7; 1973-9, III, p. 130). He wrote about the Treason of the Intellectuals, castigated by Benda (1973-9, III, p. 136), and the support of intellectuals for the construction of society and the reductions of individual liberty in the name of 'positive liberty' and social justice, leading to the subsidisation of 'socialist experiments' in low income countries (1973-9, III, p. 133). 'Only fools believe that they know all, but there are many' (1973-9, III, p. 130). In an essay on 'The Intellectuals and Socialism' Hayek pointed out that socialism had never been a working class movement, and poured scorn on intellectuals as 'people who understand nothing in particular especially well, and whose judgement on matters they themselves understand shows little sign of special wisdom' (1967, pp. 178-94, at 182). The socialist interpretation of economic history was a prime example of what he was complaining about (1967, pp. 201-15). As a university teacher in England, Hayek was acutely sensitive, as World War II neared its end, to a contempt for individual liberty amongst a significant section of the intellectual classes and indeed to the anti-free enterprise teaching in universities (1944, pp. 97, 114-23). These people were, in his view, playing with fire; though he continued to insist that many of them meant well, he was acutely aware that Nazism was indeed National *Socialism* (1944, pp. 3-4) and that anti-capitalism and anti-semitism in Germany were from the same source (1944, p. 104). The roots of National Socialism went back 150 years and the movement gained intellectual dominance in the 1920s, producing a union of the anti-capitalist forces of the right and left, assisted by the destruction of the middle classes (by the 1923 inflation) (1944, pp. 124-134). Hayek was intensely aware of the way in which German socialist, and more general anti-free market, writings had prepared the way for the Nazis, who, of course, had a substantial, democratically elected, Parliamentary representation in 1933. But even today the origins of Nazism, and the mechanisms by which Hitler assumed power, are not well appreciated in western societies, partly because so many western intellectuals have been so anxious to differentiate the Nazis from the communist regimes in eastern Europe, and to depict communism as the opposite of Nazism instead of being, as Hayek (and indeed the journalist Malcom Muggeridge, who had observed matters at first hand) insisted, national variants of the same thing (Muggeridge, 1972, I, p. 268; see also Ingrams, 1995, pp. 50-76; Wolfe, 1995, pp. 98-124). (In this the intellectuals were only following the same line as the East German radio which, virtually until the day the Berlin Wall fell, seemed at times obsessed with detecting Nazis in other countries, 44 years after the end of the Nazi regime).

9.11 Conclusions

Partly through the activities of the Institute of Economic Affairs, in the foundation of which Hayek's advice had been influential (O'Brien, 1994b, p. 357; and Chapter 8), his own views seem to have enjoyed a resurgence of interest – with a nice irony, as the limitations of Keynesian policies became clear for all to see in the 1970s. His view that the mixed economy did not represent a stable long-run solution has received support (Littlechild, 1978); and even his scheme for privatisation of the money supply has been articulated and developed by Kevin Dowd (1988). His more general political programme has been articulated by a number of able writers notably Barry (1979, 1988) and Butler (1983), and his impact on the latter day Chicago School has also been acknowledged Demsetz (1988, 1989). This represents something of an advance from a situation in which even natural allies, such as Viner and Robbins, were critical of him. Viner (1961) did not believe that Hayek's positive proposals for government intervention were consistent with the rule of law as set out by Hayek, and this view was shared by Robbins (1961). Robbins also objected to Hayek's treatment of the Benthamites as 'constructivist', and he made the telling point that Hayek's view of the evolved body of Common Law was exceptionally romantic – a view which, as Robbins was able to point out, certainly contrasted with that of Acton whom Hayek so much admired. On this there is no doubt that Hayek was vulnerable; the evolved legal system, as criticised by Bentham and satirised by Charles Dickens, was characterised not only by significant anomalies but by a form of evolution which gave the maximum scope for producer (i.e. lawyer) power.

But subsequent developments have shown the way in which Hayek's insights could be developed. Thus the Virginia School has developed the concept of the maximising bureaucrat, one which is wholly consistent with Hayek's criticism of the 'Pigovian' vision of a benign omniscient government; and Olson has produced work on the group conflict which so worried Hayek in the context of democracy, which Hayek endorsed and indeed drew upon (1973-9, III, pp. 97, 143).

There remain however two major areas where the position bequeathed by Hayek is unclear and in which there are unresolved ambiguities. The first of these concerns the framework of evolved rules; the second relates to social justice.

With regard to evolved rules, Hayek insists that these predate legislation and that they emerge in such a way as to enable societies which adopt good rules to flourish. But any society is likely to contain different groups with different moral precepts, and essentially Hayek's position amounts to acceptance of majority values with some possible assimilation of minority insights. After all, different religious groupings have very different views on commutative justice (Wilson, 1996). It is even possible that tensions in this area may have made some contribution to the anti-semitism in Germany which, generalised to anti-capitalism, was viewed by Hayek as an important intellectual source of National Socialism.

The problem of social justice has two aspects. The first is the difficult question of the relationship between Hayek's position and that of Rawls. Some critics believed Hayek to be indebted to Rawls for the idea that under a just system the chances of the least advantaged would be maximised. In fact, however, the idea predates Rawls's 1972 book, being found in a 1966 paper by Hayek.

An optimal policy in a catallaxy may aim, and ought to aim, at increasing the chances of any member of society taken at random of having a high income, or, what amounts to the same thing, the chance that, whatever his share in total income may be, the real equivalent of this share will be as large as we know how to make it (1967, p. 173).

This explains why Hayek did not believe there were fundamental differences between himself and Rawls (1973-9, I, p. xvii; II, pp. 100, 114, 188-9). It is hardly necessary to emphasise that there are elements in Rawls's work which were not acceptable to Hayek (DiQuattro 1986; Barry, 1979, pp. 143-147). Rather the point is that some of Rawls's recommendations, notably his apparent enthusiasm for governmental redistribution, do not seem to follow from his basic starting point.

Yet the question of social justice, and the matter of redistribution, raise a final difficulty. For it is not clear why Hayek himself *necessarily* had to rule out redistribution, *so long as* this was according to known and clear rules. Thus, for instance, a negative income tax system, as endorsed by Milton Friedman, would indeed have avoided precisely that kind of *discretionary* intervention which Hayek regarded as unacceptable and subversive of law, while permitting a degree of redistribution which the majority of the population – and indeed a majority of not merely Hayek's fellow intellectuals but even Hayek's fellow economists – would find preferable to a system in which an unfortunate outcome in the 'game of catallaxy' (to use Hayek's own phrase) would (subject only to the minimum income qualification) have to be borne without amelioration.

Chapter 10

Hayek in the History of Economic Thought

In order to form a view on Hayek's place in the history of economic thought, it is necessary to look at his career, the impact of his ideas, their internal coherence, his relationships with his contemporaries and critics, and finally to consider the perspective a decade after his death. Each of these aspects of Hayek's life and work are considered in sections of this chapter. However it is first necessary to look at his intellectual background.

10.1 Hayek's background

Hayek was an Austrian economist, a product of the style of economics which developed under the leadership of Carl Menger in the four decades before 1914.[1] The Mengerian school developed a corpus of economic theory, and an approach to economic problems which was quite distinct from other forms of marginalism.[2] Yet within its ranks there are diverse elements.

As Hayek himself made clear when writing about Schumpeter (1967, pp. 339-41; 1992, pp. 160-5), members of the Austrian school themselves followed different paths in their development. Hayek made it possible to attempt some

[1]For a fascinating account of the Austrian background, see Caldwell (2004).

[2]It is now clear that Schumpeter's claim (1954, pp. 837, 918) that there was no fundamental difference between Menger, Walras and Jevons, was wrong (Jaffé, 1976).

evaluation of the importance of different members of the Austrian school, as seen from his own standpoint, through the series of essays he wrote on them (O'Brien, 1994a, pp. 366-7); and in this way he shed some light on their importance for him.

But the main sources for him are clear from the contents of, and acknowledgements in, his own economic writings. First comes Menger, whose emphasis on subjectivism proved a starting point, though Hayek later laid much more stress on the evolutionary elements in Menger's 1883 book. Second, from Böhm-Bawerk Hayek took – with highly adverse intellectual and professional consequences – a *non-subjective* theory of capital, one which he ultimately (but belatedly) abandoned. Third, the greatest influence on Hayek was neither of these. It was Ludwig von Mises (Hayek, 1992, pp. 25-30; 1984b).

Before Hayek came under the influence of Mises, his education in economics, was narrow, although he was familiar with the work of Wieser and of the later Austrians such as Mayer and Strigl. Under Mises's influence, he embarked upon a wide self-education in economics through scholarship (Rosner and Winckler, 1989; O'Brien, 1994a). Hayek read enormously widely, and was scrupulous in his acknowledgement of predecessors.[3] Indeed the first of the four lectures which make up his *Prices and Production* is essentially a lecture on the history of economic thought. For Hayek, scholarly study of the history of economics was inseparable from the development of the subject of economics itself (O'Brien, 1994a).

In addition it was Mises who brought home to Hayek the full implications of a subjectivist approach to general equilibrium; and it was Mises's *Gemeinwirtschaft* which led directly to Hayek's abandonment of socialism (Hayek, 1992, pp. 133, 136). It was Mises who found employment for Hayek, in the study of the trade cycle, and it was under the influence of Mises that Hayek

[3] I am quite unable to understand the implication in Streissler (1994, p. 48) that Hayek was grudging with acknowledgements.

was working in the 1920s.

10.2 The 1930s: An Outsider

As Hayek's Austrian colleague Ludwig Lachman has testified, Hayek 'made a triumphant entry into the University of London in 1931'; he 'had become a rather lonely figure by 1939' (Lachman, 1986, p. 225; see also Blaug, 1992, p. 31). In the intervening decade Hayek had been, as Hicks later remembered, a central figure in the intellectual dramas of the 1930s.

The story started with an invitation to Hayek from Lionel Robbins, newly established as professor of economics at LSE, to deliver a series of lectures, *Prices and Production*, which created a sensation (Schumpeter, 1954, p. 1120; Benassi, 1987, p. 263). Robbins read economic literature in German; something of an outsider himself, he sought to establish at LSE an alternative tradition to the Marshallian tradition embodied in the dominant Cambridge school of economics (Robbins, 1933, pp. xiv-xvi; 1930, 1934b, pp. xvii-xix). Menger's works were reprinted at LSE, with an introduction by Hayek; Mises's seminal book on money (1924/1934) (earlier reviewed by Keynes despite subsequently claiming that he could not read German – O'Brien, 1998a, p. 43; and Chapter 3) and his *Gemeinwirtschaft* (*Socialism*) (1932/1936) were translated under Robbins's auspices. Hayek, an outsider to the British system, and trained in a very different kind of economics, thus joined with Robbins in an attempt to alter fundamentally the centre of gravity of economics in Britain.

As if this were not enough, Hayek, like Robbins, was opposed to many of the fashionable academic nostrums of the day. His opposition to Marxism set him apart from a number of academics, notably at LSE itself, and his continuation of the criticisms of the idea of a planned socialist economy, following the work of Mises, ran entirely counter to the prevailing climate. His position was ultimately to be justified, but not before an academic myth had arisen (and been sedulously propagated) that Hayek had somehow been defeated on this issue by Lange who advocated such system; but the justification came long after the decade now being considered. Hayek was to continue this critique into the 1940s, and to live long long enough to see the breakdown of the east European Marxist regimes and the discoveries that followed – the Trabant plant in East Germany, supposedly the most efficient part of the old Soviet Empire, was described by one motoring journal as a 'toxic slag heap'. But such events were far in the future; in the 1930s Hayek's critical attitude won him few friends.

The perception, which Hayek derived from Mises, that there was a core problem stemming from factor valuation, and a fundamental failure to understand all that markets achieved, was not welcome.

But it was the success of Keynes's *General Theory*, and of the quite extraordinarily swift Keynesian Revolution, which did the most fundamental damage to Hayek's standing. It was not just a question of operating on aggregate demand, but a fundamental methodological opposition to the kind of aggregation embodied in the IS-LM Revolution which left Hayek such a lonely figure. In the view of Keynes's biographer, the impact of the *General Theory* was such that the Austrian outpost at LSE crumbled – Hayek and Robbins failed to reply, and Lerner, Kaldor and Hicks deserted to the Keynesian camp (Skidelsky, 1992, p. 573). The failure by Hayek to reply was probably a crucial blow to his reputation, and the reason that he later gave – that he thought that Keynes would change his mind yet again, as he had done between the *Treatise* and the *General Theory* – is unconvincing (O'Brien, 1994a, p. 362). It seems more likely that he had been worn down by the abuse directed at him by Cambridge writers early in the 1930s, a strategy on their part which thus proved successful.[4] At all events, as Lei-

[4]It is true that Pigou, himself the victim of such abuse, did courageously take up the challenge and review the *General Theory*, in the LSE journal *Economica* (Collard, 1981, pp. 125-6); but he did at least enjoy the status of an insider, unlike Hayek.

jonhufvud has observed, the Austrian approach to macroeconomics became of interest only to 'antiquarians' after 1936 – it was abandoned by monetary economists (Leijonhufvud, 1981, p. 133) and indeed Hayek acknowledged defeat in some comments delivered at the Royal Statistical Society in 1938. Critically he admitted that there might not be a regular periodicity of macroeconomic fluctuation and also rejected the idea of monocausal trade cycles (Hayek, 1938; Rühl, 1994, p. 190).

10.3 Hayek and Cambridge

The relationship between Hayek and Keynes got off to a bad start, with a 'strong disagreement' in 1928 (Hayek, 1978a, p. 283). But it was Hayek's review of Keynes's *Treatise on Money* (1930) in 1931 that proved the starting point for what was effectively a feud which lasted for the decade and was only stilled by a reconciliation during the war (Caldwell, 1995).

There was much in Keynes's *Treatise* that was irritating to someone familiar with the work of Wicksell and of Mises. It even made the outrageous claim, as Laidler has noted, that there was at the time of its publication no pre-existing body of monetary theory (Keynes, 1930, I, p. xviii; Laidler, 1999, p. 130). Moreover, Hayek's review made a number of good points. Keynes's curious treatment of profit as something distinct from other income, which could be explained by an inequality between savings and investment, the unsatisfactory treatment of investment and of the capital stock, the subjective originality of the book, the laborious equations, the tortured terminology – it was hardly surprising that Hayek found much that was unsatisfactory. Even later enthusiasts for Keynes's work, such as Patinkin (1976), have had strong reservations about the *Treatise*. Moreover, as Hayek continued his critique into a second part, he was able to quote a passage from the *Treatise* which could well have been written by Wicksell, only to find that the Wicksellian mechanism had been obscured by peculiar definitions of savings and investment so that 'the rate of interest which will equilibrate "savings" and "investment" in Mr. Keynes' sense is quite different from the rate which would keep them in equilibrium in the ordinary sense' (Hayek, 1932a, p. 66).

Nor was Hayek alone in his dismay at the *Treatise*. Robertson (1931) and Hawtrey were only two of those who were fundamentally unhappy about it. But Keynes's response to Hayek was abusive. He dragged into his response an attack upon Hayek's *Prices and Production*, which he described as 'one of the most frightful muddles I have ever read, with scarcely a sound proposition in it' (Keynes, 1931 pp. 55-6) and then, using his position as editor of the *Economic Journal*, he commissioned a review of Hayek's book by Sraffa. This managed to be both pompous and abusive. It was impossible from the content of Sraffa's review to see what Hayek's book actually said. The review began with the observation that 'all this in four lectures must have been a feat of endurance on the part of the audience as much as of the lecturer. For however peculiar, and probably unprecedented, the conclusions may be, there is one respect in which the lectures collected in this volume fully uphold the tradition which modern writers on money are rapidly establishing, that of unintelligibility' (Sraffa, 1932a, p. 86).

In the closed community of British academia, this abuse, delivered with the sanction of the editor of one of the leading journals in the world, did Hayek much harm, as Lachman subsequently testified. Elsewhere it was recognised that Hayek had been wronged; the American economist Howard Ellis referred to the 'astonishing misrepresentations' of Sraffa's attack (Ellis, 1934, p. 365n). But the biggest problem with the Sraffa review – and it reflects ill on the academic community that it should have done Hayek harm – was its own unintelligibility. Sraffa was clearly unwilling to reveal the theoretical standpoint from which he was arguing – as with his 1926 attack on Marshallian price theory, though it subsequently became clear in that case that the starting point was Marx and Ricardo (O'Brien, 1984, pp. 251-2). It was Ludwig Lachman who decoded Sraffa's review in the light of the latter's subsequent writings and pointed out that it marked the start of the neo-Ricardian counter-revolution, being, like Sraffa's 1926 article (though Lachman does not mention this) both anti-subjectivist and anti-neoclassical (Lachman, 1986, pp. 226-7).

But nobody appeared able or willing to sort this out at the time. Hayek challenged Sraffa to make explicit his theoretical starting point (Hayek, 1932b, p. 103) but Sraffa ducked the challenge (Sraffa, 1932b, p. 114).

It was thus impossible to have a dialogue with either Keynes or Sraffa. With Hayek's other critics it was possible. Thus Arthur Marget's (1932) review of *Prices and Production*, and that of Hansen and Tout (1933), both come like breaths of fresh air. The authors of both these articles were outside Britain; Hayek did indeed have a debate with Hansen and Tout, responding to their review in an article in *Econometrica* (Hayek, 1934a). Later critics within this country such as Tom Wilson (1939-40), and Nicholas Kaldor (1939, 1942), as well as Hawtrey (1932, 1933, 1940, 1941), may have disagreed strongly (in the case of Hawtrey in particular, very strongly indeed) with Hayek's analysis; and their criticisms were very far from groundless. But at least it was possible for Hayek to read the criticisms and to respond to them. With Cambridge, however, there seemed no possibility of dialogue.

10.4 Subjectivism

One of the bases of Sraffa's attack upon Hayek had been his aversion to subjectivism. Indeed a thorough-going subjectivism of the kind to be found in Austrian economics did not play well with a British audience. Yet employed as a critical tool – as in Hayek's later critique of 'scientism' – the idea drew attention to fundamental issues. Subjectivism was to play a central role in Hayek's sustained and brilliant critique of a set of ideas which many of his academic contemporaries found seductive – historicism, socialism and scientism. We could only understand the development of society resulting from countless individual decisions, he argued, on the basis of introspection as a key to subjectivism, not by misguidedly attempting to posit the existence of metaphysical entities such as 'society'. It was a fallacy that the methods of natural science could be transferred to the much more complicated social and economic world, because in the latter actions were based upon beliefs rather than upon objective facts, and there could not be an objective body of data on which a planner could operate (Hayek, 1941b, 1942-4).

To Anglo-Saxon tastes, Hayek was prone to overstate the claims for subjectivism, to claim indeed that it was the most important development in economics in the last hundred years (1942-4, I, p. 281), and even trying to find a subjective basis for the theory of rent (pp. 282-3). But the questions which subjectivism raised for such metaphysical entities as 'society', 'the economy', 'capitalism', and 'the class struggle', were real enough. If journalists and other political commentators seem unable to function without reference to such concepts in our own time, as well as the more recent, and even more nebulous, 'international community', Hayek's position has the merit of forcing recognition that such concepts are metaphysical and that statements such as 'society insists...' literally have no meaning, and are merely rhetorical flourishes. Moreover the reliance of scientism on such metaphysical concepts reveals the hollowness of its claims to be applying the methods of natural science to social phenomena.

Hayek's development of his critique of scientism was, for the most part, published in the early 1940s, by which time he had already become a lonely figure. But things did not improve much after World War II.

10.5 Hayek in the Post-war World

Hayek was to blame the 1944 publication of *The Road to Serfdom* – tremendous popular success though it was (Blundell, 2005, pp. 25-6) – for his becoming an outcast (Hayek, 1994, p. 103). Yet it is not clear that, at least as far as his fellow economists went, the reactions were extravagantly hostile. The review by Pigou expressed the opinion that 'Few who read through this earnest and admirably written plea will fail to be interested and stimulated by his treatment of it, and fewer still to close the book without a feeling of respect for and sympathy with the writer' (1944, p. 219). There were respectful reviews by Schumpeter (1946), Aaron Director (1945) and J.J. Spengler (1945). Even socialist writers such as Evan Durbin (1945) and Erich Roll (1945), however strongly they disagreed with Hayek, were prepared to debate the issues. The really vitriolic abuse came instead from those outside the ranks of economists.

But in 1950, on abruptly leaving LSE, Hayek was turned down by the Chicago economics department. This is unlikely to have been due, at least decisively, to *The Road to Serfdom*, though Hayek's book had been received with outrage by the American Left, and academics have an instinct to conform. It is also true that Hayek's opponent Oscar Lange had recently enjoyed a successful spell in a chair in the Chicago department, before becoming an ambassador (Backhouse, 2002b). But it would be hard to argue that the majority of the Chicago department, or the Chicago tradition, were instinctively opposed to the message of Hayek's book.[5] Rather the problem seems to have lain with Hayek's economics. Milton Friedman has testified that the problem was partly internal – the department's right to choose staff rather than accord with the wishes of the administrators – but particularly that the department did not like Hayek's capital theory and the analysis of *Prices and Production*. According to Friedman, 'if they had been looking around the world for an economist to add to their staff, their prescription would not have been the author of *Prices and Production*' (Ebenstein, 2001, p. 174). Moreover Friedman has expressed himself strongly about the monetary theory espoused by Hayek and Robbins at LSE in the 1930s, which he considered

[5] It is however surprising to learn that the Left was predominant amongst social scientists in Chicago in the 1930s (Caldwell, 2004, p. 233).

a disastrous version of the quantity theory. Hayek, through the intercession of John Neff, was given a position in the Committee on Social Thought, and he occupied this chair for about 15 years. But he was there in the role of a social philosopher rather than that of an economist more narrowly defined.

As Hayek's career as a social philosopher developed, those who might have been expected to provide some intellectual support could be seen distancing themselves from him. In particular Robbins, having already distanced himself from *The Road to Serfdom* (O'Brien, 1988b, p. 66), was unenthusiastic about Hayek's 1960 book *The Constitution of Liberty* (Robbins, 1961). The same was true of Viner's (1961) review of the book – this despite testifying that Hayek was an economist 'of the first rank'. There were, one suspects, particular causes for this. Hayek's hostility to Bentham, whom he regarded, with some justification (Rothbard, 1995, pp. 49-68), as a constructivist, would not have pleased Robbins (Hayek, 1960, pp. 55, 174, 435; cf. 1973-9, I, pp. 22, 128-9; II, pp. 17-23, 44-8). Hayek had indeed pointed to a fundamental fallacy of pain/pleasure evaluation – the assumption that all effects could be known at the outset when in truth there were always unintended consequences.

More troublingly, there is a suspicion raised by the reviews that the strongly anti-religious Robbins, Viner and (especially) Frank Knight (1967), who could all otherwise be expected to be sympathetic to Hayek, seemed to have found the agnostic Hayek insufficiently hostile to religion.

Hayek thus became successively more isolated, even from those who might have been expected to have much in common with him. His influence and standing clearly faded during the 1960s. Indeed one commentator has pointed to the fact that an acknowledgement by Malinvaud of Hayek's work on prices in intertemporal equilibrium was later dropped and replaced by a reference to Hicks (Milgate, 1979). Most startlingly of all, George Shackle, who had been a graduate student of Hayek in the 1930s, and who was later to write appreciatively about him (Shackle, 1981), omitted almost all mention of Hayek's economics from his 1967 book *The Years of High Theory*, which was supposed to be about economic theory in the 1930s (Böhm, 1992, p. 8).

In the Mont Pelerin Society and through the foundation of the Institute of Economic Affairs, Hayek managed to maintain some sort of contact with his contemporaries and some circulation for his ideas. But much of the 1960s was a bleak time for his reputation. It was with work by John Hicks from the mid-1960s that Hayek's reputation began to revive. Firstly, there was Hicks's pathbreaking *Capital and Growth* (1965), which undoubtedly helped to revive interest in the Austrian theory of capital. Secondly, there was the discussion in Hicks's *Critical Essays in Monetary Theory* (1967). This provided a serious re-evaluation of Hayek's macroeconomics. Then, with the growing awareness in the early 1970s that inflation throughout the western world was getting out of control, there was a reawakened interest in Hayek's approach to inflation (Spencer, 1975; Maling, 1975; Backhouse, 2002a). Moreover, as inflation was seen to distort economic signals in markets, there was renewed interest in Hayek's treatment of economics and knowledge.

The macroeconomic model, together with Hayek's work on the framework for economic activity, much of which dated from the 1960s, were identified by the Nobel Memorial Prize committee as his key contributions when the prize was awarded to Hayek (Royal Academy of Sciences, 1974). With the resurgence of interest, Fritz Machlup, in paying tribute to Hayek's contribution, was able to claim that 'The victory of Keynes' theory on the political scene and in the halls of the universities did not mean that all scholars turned their back to Hayek's hypotheses' (Machlup, 1974, p. 202).

The resurgence of interest in Hayek's work was to last well into the next decade. Since it was Hayek's trade cycle theory and his approach to inflation which reawakened interest, it seems best to examine this in more detail.

10.6 Trade Cycle Theory

Although Hayek had an extensive knowledge of the monetary literature in English, German, French and Italian, and had been working on monetary questions since the 1920s, the underlying mechanism for his analysis of the trade cycle was taken from Mises's reinterpretation of Wicksell's cumulative process. The idea was that, with a bank lending rate less than the marginal rate of profit, there would be a distortion of the relative prices of consumption and investment goods, compared with the relationship which would have existed in response solely to consumer preferences for present and future goods. Monetary expansion, which lay behind the lower bank lending rate, did not primarily affect the *general* price level but this *relative* price relationship, as both Mises and Hayek repeatedly emphasised. Then the expansion of the investment good market, resulting from the cheap credit, enabled producers of investment goods to capture resources from producers of consumption goods. This shifted leftwards the supply schedules for consumption goods. The resulting rises in their prices imposed forced savings on consumers. This was stage 1.

But an important – and often neglected – stage 2 followed. The enhanced factor incomes, resulting from factors being bid away from the production of consumption goods, shifted upwards the demand curves for consumption goods, restoring the pre-disturbance relative price ratio of consumption and investment goods, and the output of the former to their original levels. The increase in output involved the re-attraction of resources back into the consumption goods industries. This led the producers of investment goods to seek yet further loans from the banking system, in order once more to bid up the prices of factors, and to try to complete the investment projects upon which they had embarked as a result of the initial credit expansion. Thus monetary expansion disturbed a general equilibrium in which, prior to the disturbance, the relative outputs of consumption goods and investment goods reflected consumer preferences for consumption goods and savings, and the social rate of time preference.

As Kaldor (1942) was to argue persuasively (though Hayek, 1942, denied this) Hayek departed significantly from this model in his later writings on the trade cycle. The version put forward by Hayek in *Profits, Interest and Investment* (1939a) and in *The Pure Theory of Capital* (1941a) is different from the Mises-derived version described above, and which is to be found in *Prices and Production* (1931a) and *Monetary Theory and the Trade Cycle* (1929/1933). The later version is built around the (misnamed) Ricardo Effect. In this version, an increase in the demand for consumption goods, possibly because of a reduction in the rate of interest, raises profits in the consumption goods industries because real wages fall during a boom. Nominal wages are sticky, but the prices of consumption goods rise. The increased profitability leads to a demand for investment in capacity – but this is capital-widening, rather than the capital-deepening (more roundabout production processes) which was involved in the earlier model. However the fall in real wages reduces the equilibrium ratio of capital to labour – this is what Hayek called the Ricardo Effect. Hayek believed that this latter effect would be more powerful than the stimulating effect of demand for machinery for capital widening, so that there would be a slump in the capital goods industries as entrepreneurs substituted labour for capital. So, as Kaldor pointed out, the idea that production methods would become unduly roundabout was replaced in this later version by the idea that they might become unduly direct.

This later version was clearly not very satisfactory. As Wilson (1939-40) pointed out, the arithmetical examples in which Hayek showed a direct and dramatic effect of changes in real wages on profitability were highly sensitive to the unrealistically short turnover rates for capital which he posited.

By the time Hayek centred his trade cycle model around the so-called Ricardo Effect, he was engaged in what can be seen in retrospect to have been a defensive exercise – in Lakatosian terms, the scientific research programme of his trade cycle model was in a degenerating phase. But the earlier, Mises-derived, model is a much more impressive structure. It is true that the argument was developed within the context of a closed economy, a key assumption of which Hayek seems to have been scarcely conscious, though it was pointed out by Haberler (1937, pp. 32, 66) and by subsequent critics (Hummel, 1979, p. 134), and it was subject to sustained and accurate criticism. Dennis Robertson, who like Hayek attached importance to the phenomenon of forced saving, or 'induced lacking' as he called it (Presley, 1978, p. 115), found the Austrian model oversimplified (1940, pp. 184-88). He made the fundamental empirical criticism of the basic model that Hayek exaggerated the difficulty which a change in the interest rate, as the boom came to an end and banks moved to protect their reserves, would cause to those engaged in investment where this had been financed from retained profits or from long loans at lower rates of interest than those now prevailing (1940, p. 100). Robertson believed that Hayek exaggerated the sensitivity of investment to small changes in the interest rate.

More damagingly still Hawtrey, the still largely unsung hero of inter-war British macroeconomics, made two fundamental criticisms of the Mises model. Firstly – and this criticism was primarily directed at Keynes's *Treatise* – Hawtrey argued that changes in the bank lending rate did not have a significant effect upon the long-run rate of interest (Hawtrey, 1938, pp. 184-95). Secondly, Hawtrey (1941) argued that Hayek had fundamentally misunderstood how investment worked. Capital could not be viewed apart from the enterprise, and within the enterprise the costs and returns associated with investment were only part of a much wider picture involving marginal costs and returns. The aim of the enterprise was to maximise the net return, not to maximise the return per unit of capital, a point made also by Kaldor (1942). Moreover, increased investment could take the form of widening rather than deepening capital. Which of the two was more important was essentially an empirical question, but capital deepening was forced upon Hayek by the assumption that the cycle started from a position of general equilibrium with full employment.

But the assumption by Hayek was not arbitrary. All the factor price effects of the model would not work if there were unemployed resources on which the capital goods industries could draw without bidding factors away from the consumption goods industries.

There were other difficulties. Hayek believed that the end of a boom involved uncompleted investment projects (1931a, p. 139). Like much else in the theory this was an empirical question, though the belief seems to have been grounded on central European experience around 1930. But, in the logic of the theory, investment projects *must* be incomplete, as Neisser pointed out (Haberler, 1937, pp. 49-50). Otherwise the whole resource-recapture cycle would not be necessary because the extra investment, as it came on stream, should be able to provide the required consumer goods (as consumers ceased to suffer forced saving) without competition for resources.

The original version of Hayek's trade cycle theory was thus distinctly shaky, and this was apparent to his contemporary critics. But the Ricardo Effect was even less convincing. Firstly, it relies upon a stylised fact (which, like other stylised facts, turns out not to be a fact) that real wages fall during a boom. (It was however implied by the forced saving argument of the earlier trade cycle theory.) Put forward by Hayek on a number of occasions, the Effect was criticised by Kaldor (1942) and by Tom Wilson (1939-40). It seems to be quite clear, despite attempts to defend it (O'Driscoll, 1975), that it is not even in Ricardo – and certainly not in the passages cited by Hayek in support of this origin (Kaldor, 1942; Ferguson, 1973; O'Brien, 1994a, p. 368). But, most damagingly of all, as Kaldor showed in a series of articles, the Effect did not provide a satisfactory theory of a trade cycle; in particular, as Wilson pointed out (1939-40, p. 234), the change in real wages would not necessarily influence the choice of method – it would raise profits on both capital-widening *and* capital deepening.

10.7 The Quantity Theory of Money

Hayek's theory of the trade cycle, at least in the version in *Monetary Theory and the Trade Cycle (MTTC)*, was a monetary theory. This was clear enough to Hayek's contemporaries. Ellis (1934, pp. 162-5) saw the Mises theory as part of the cash balance approach. Haberler (1937, pp. 31ff.), surveying trade cycle theories, classified Hayek as offering a monetary over-investment theory. Friedman (1974, p. 158) identified the LSE theory in the 1930s as a distorted version of the quantity theory.

There are dissenters from this last view. Hicks (1977, p. 63) has denied the quantity theory classification, on the surprising ground that a direct link between the money supply and the price level is broken by the possibility of holding balances, where credit supply is unconstrained by bank liquidity. O'Driscoll and Rizzo have argued that the theory differs from the quantity theory because of the microeconomic focus of the argument (O'Driscoll, 1977, pp. 135-42; O'Driscoll and Rizzo, 1985, pp. 188-228). But there is no genuine microeconomics in Hayek's trade cycle theory, because the myriad of prices somehow become aggregated into representative consumer and producer goods prices and factor rewards.

As has been pointed out by Hagemann (1994), Hayek was actually trying in 1929 to reintroduce money into the dominant German trade cycle theory. His treatment of historical figures such as Thornton, and above all of Cantillon, shows causality as running from money supply changes to prices (O'Brien, 1994a, p. 360). Fundamentally all that is different from the quantity theory is that one price level is replaced by two – representing the prices of consumer and investment goods respectively. Hayek says explicitly that a change in the money supply is central to the argument (1929/1933, pp. 101-2, 107). Indeed several writers (Humphrey, 1993, pp. 280-6; Bellante and Garrison, 1988; Seccareccia, 1994) have noted parallels with Fisher's treatment of the quantity theory. Undoubtedly Hayek (1929/1933, pp. 106-7) confused the issue because, following Mises's own emphasis, and in common with Haberler (1927), and later Robbins, he dismissed the concept of a general price level as without significance.

Hayek, like Mises, maintained that changes in the general price level could not *cause* a trade cycle (1929/1933, p. 13), but the way in which he presented this has caused confusion. It has been suggested that he did not believe that changes in the money supply caused cyclical fluctuations at all (Rühl, 1994, p. 195) and he has even been hailed as an opponent of the quantity theory (Aréna, 2002). But the inescapable fact is that the price level *must* rise in Hayek's model. Firstly, the price of investment goods rises and, secondly, that of consumption goods rises, restoring the original relative price ratio. Furthermore since, as we shall see, Hayek envisaged the acceleration of inflation, he must indeed have had some concept of the general price level.

Hayek's exposition caused further confusion because some believed – even so perceptive a critic as Hicks (1967, p. 208) – that the secondary recovery in the consumption goods industries had been left out of *Prices and Production*. Even an acute critic like Marget (1932) believed that Hayek's theory was compatible with a stable overall price level. This was something that Hayek asserted, but overall price stability could only be explained by productivity rising so fast that without the trade cycle-induced changes the general price level would have fallen. But were productivity rising that fast, it is by no means obvious that a restoration of expenditure on consumer goods would have caused their prices to rise.

In summary, Friedman's perception of the fundamental similarity of Hayek's approach with the quantity theory was not misplaced. Rather it was Hayek's exposition which has misled later commentators. Indeed it has been plausibly argued by Bellante and Garrison (1988; Garrison, 1989; Bellante, 1994) that Hayek's and Friedman's two versions of monetary disequilibrium can be regarded as complementary; Friedman focuses upon labour market disequilibrium, Hayek upon capital market disequilibrium.

10.8 Capital Theory

Perhaps the major problem raised by Hayek's treatment of macroeconomic fluctuations is to be found in capital theory. Hayek started from the position that the period of production – Böhm-Bawerk's concept – was related to the preferences of individuals for present and future goods, and its length determined marginal investment and profitability. Hayek refers to Böhm-Bawek in an essay on factor rewards dating from 1926, a 1927 essay on interest theory, and in the essay on intertemporal equilibrium of 1928 (McCloughry, 1984, pp. 33-54, 55-70, 71-117); and the period of production features in *Prices and Production (P&P)* (1931a, ch. 2).

It was an unfortunate theoretical path to follow. Hawtrey took the trouble to understand as fully as was possible the model underlying *P&P*, unlike those in Cambridge who simply abused Hayek. He also reviewed the English version of *MTTC*, and was scathing about the capital theory. Of that in *P&P* he wrote:

> I feel bound to say that Dr. Hayek has spoiled an original piece of work which might have been an important contribution to monetary theory, by entangling his argument with the intolerably cumbersome theory of capital derived from Jevons and Böhm-Bawerk. This theory, when it was enunciated, was a noteworthy new departure in the metaphysics of political economy. But it is singularly ill-adapted for use in monetary theory, or indeed in any practical treatment of the capital market.
>
> The result has been to make Dr. Hayek's work so difficult and obscure that it is impossible to understand his little book of 112 pages except at the cost of many hours of hard work. And at the end we are left with the impression, not only that this is not a necessary consequence of the difficulty of the subject, but that

> he himself has been led by so ill-chosen a method of analysis to conclusions which he would hardly have accepted if given a more straightforward form of expression (Hawtrey, 1932, p. 125).

Indeed it was apparently the capital theory which had led Hayek to the belief that an extension of credit would necessarily be spent in lengthening the period of production. But, as Hawtrey pointed out, not only was extra credit used to hold increased stocks, but Hayek's view did not of itself produce a trade cycle. It was apparently necessary, Hawtrey (1933, pp. 185-7) argued in his review of *MTTC*, to introduce non-monetary causes to do this. As we shall see, in the discussion of a falling price level, this was not necessarily the case; but even Hawtrey missed that.

It was clear to Hayek's colleagues that the period of production was an encumbrance. Lionel Robbins omitted it from his Hayekian *The Great Depression* of 1934 (O'Brien, 1988b, pp. 106-7), and Kaldor, one of the two translators of *MTTC*, attacked the concept (Kaldor, 1939).

It is easy to show that it is impossible to arrive at a scalar measure of capital stock (Laidler, 1999, pp. 33-4). But in truth nothing hinges on a scalar measure of this kind. Though Hayek talked about shortening or lengthening of the production *process*, he frequently avoided reference to a *period* of production (e.g. Hayek, 1934a; O'Brien, 1994a, p. 359). The period of production was essentially an irrelevance, a fifth wheel to which Occam's Razor must necessarily apply. It has no empirical counterpart, and nothing in the theory stands by its presence, as Hayek (1936, pp. 206-7) admitted in controversy with Frank Knight. If removed, we are simply left with the proposition that investment may become greater than voluntary saving. This can be clearly seen if we look at John Presley's (1978) illuminating discussion of Dennis Robertson. The crucial indication for both Hayek and Robertson that something was wrong was not a lengthening of the immeasurable – the period of production – but the occurrence of forced saving (Robertson's induced lacking). The policy implication is clear enough – an increase in the rate of interest. But it only differs in detail from Wicksell, whose policy prescription, as Tom Humphrey (1992) has shown, requires both an inflation and a price *level* target for stability. What Hayek required for his model was a relative price target. There is no role for the metaphysical idea of a period of production.

Hayek could have seen clearly enough from Robbins's 1934 book that it was possible to give a clear exposition of his theory without the period of production. Perhaps the book did help to turn Hayek away from the concept. It had already received little emphasis in *MTTC*, dating originally from 1929, though it was prominent in *P&P* of 1931. But that book was designed to impress a London audience with the difficult novelty of an alternative tradition. Later Hayek rejected the period of production concept outright, as in his *The Pure Theory of Capital* (1941a). The last link with Böhm-Bawerk had gone (Blaug, 1992, p. 32).

In some ways it is puzzling that Hayek stuck with the concept for as long as he did. In so doing he left himself open to Cambridge critics, who, even now, focus upon the concept (e.g. de Vivo, 1994). Yet Mises himself was to reject the period of production as an 'empty concept' (1949, p. 489; Moss, 1976, p. 54).

There were, I think, three reasons why Hayek persevered with this unfortunate concept. Firstly, it was part of the programme to establish the legitimacy of an Austrian alternative to Anglo-Saxon economics. For this, a lineage was necessary, and Böhm-Bawerk was a founding father of the line. Never mind that the period of production in the latter's work is crude. This can be put down to inferior technique. Secondly, the period of production was part of Hayek's ill-judged product differentiation – distinguishing his trade cycle theory from that of Fisher. This was a mistake. It had the unfortunate effect of alienating a potential source of support in the Chicago department; and it later enabled those who wished to dismiss Hayek's work to point to his ill-advised use of the period of production concept. Thirdly, the sad truth is that, in his review of Keynes's *Treatise*, Hayek had painted himself into a corner. He made great play with the absence of capital theory from the *Treatise*, and with Keynes's failure to acquaint himself with Böhm-Bawerk's work (Hayek, 1931b, pp. 7-8; 1931c, p. 63; 1932a, pp. 81-3). He thus placed himself in the position of having to show why capital theory was of central importance.

The triangles through which Hayek sought to explain his theory of capital, and which involve a scalar quantity, one which is thus vulnerable to the standard criticism that its value will change with a change in relative prices, really make no sense, and there is ample testimony that they confused contemporaries (e.g. Robinson, 1972). Jevons, whose priority Hayek scrupulously acknowledged (1931a, p. 38), had a clear understanding of such triangles with time on the horizontal axis and investment on the vertical one. But Hayek attempted to use the vertical axis both for inputs – 'intermediate products', the Austrian 'higher-order' goods – and outputs of consumer goods. Howard Ellis, in his book on German monetary theory, saw clearly enough that the triangles were meaningless (1934, pp. 353-4); but others persevered in an attempt to make sense of them. One of the particular difficulties which they encountered was the problem of fixed capital (Hicks and Weber, 1973, p. 192; Steedman, 1994, p. 14). There was no correspondence between inputs and outputs where capital lasted a long time. Even Lutz (1943, p. 304), who tried to solve the dimensionality problem of the triangles by arguing that they could only be interpreted by measuring inputs in terms of the output to which they gave rise, had to accept that with fixed capital there was an insoluble problem.

Modern Austrians – with some exceptions (Steele, 1993) – have understandably distanced themselves from this part of Hayek's work. He has been criticised for the abandonment of subjectivism in *P&P* (O'Driscoll and Rizzo, 1985); and most recent Austrian writers, from Lachman (1956) onwards, employ a thoroughgoing subjective treatment of capital as a structure of plans (e.g. Horwitz, 1996), without any idea of a scalar.

10.9 The Inflation-Acceleration Issue

Hayek undoubtedly expected that, if inflationary bank lending were allowed to occur, inflation itself would accelerate unless the banks were constrained by reserve considerations (1934a, pp. 155-7). For this he has been criticised. Yet it would be surprising if Hayek had not given some thought to the matter, given that he had witnessed the hyper-inflation in continental countries after World War I (Rosner and Winckler, 1989), and given that he was to maintain this theme in his later work, though without reliance upon his trade cycle model, relying subsequently on the erosion of money illusion (1967, pp. 282, 295-9).

The acceleration mechanism in the trade cycle model is however perfectly comprehensible in terms of the model. Starting from full employment, resources have to be bid away from the production of consumer goods, and they are then recaptured by the consumer goods industries once factors with enhanced incomes spend those incomes. We thus have a sequence involving a rise in the price of producer goods, a rise in the price of labour, a rise in the price of consumer goods, another rise in the price of labour, and so on. Assuming for simplicity that all the price rises are at an equal percentage rate r, we have a series of the form $(1+r)^n$. If the money supply increases to finance these price increases is proportionate to the price increases, and if we assume that the proportion is unity for simplicity, the money supply increases will be of the form (with the first term set to unity) $1+(1+r)+(1+r)^2+\ldots+(1+r)^n$. Over any finite period of time the series will produce a finite sum, and that sum will provide the starting value for the next run of the series. Thus the money supply is growing at an increasing rate.

This was recognised by contemporaries, even Haberler (1937, pp. 44, 46,

51) despite his resistance (1927) to the idea of a general price level. For the mechanism to work it is necessary that the initial monetary expansion should occur in an economy at full employment general equilibrium. While this was understood, it was not fully appreciated that the resource recapture played a central role. As already noted, Hicks mistakenly believed it to be absent from *P&P*, even though it is present in both that book (Hayek, 1931a, pp. 57, 89) and in *MTTC* (1929/1933, p. 217). It was clearly recognised by Haberler who cited it in his *Prosperity and Depression* (1937, pp. 45-6).

The fear of an acceleration of inflation undoubtedly underlay the opposition of Hayek to monetary and fiscal expansion in the 1930s. Hayek consistently maintained this position (Skidelsky, 1992, p. 469; O'Brien, 1994b, p. 360; and Chapter 8), arguing in his 1934 reply to Hansen and Tout (1933) that boosting demand was mistaken, thus ensuring that the 'LSE Austrians' repelled their potential allies in Chicago as Friedman (1974, pp. 162-3) has subsequently testified. Hayek later softened his opposition to government macroeconomic policy (1960, pp. 223, 324-39); but not very much.

10.10 The Falling Price Level

In controversy with Wicksell, the Swedish economist Davidson had pointed out that equality of the bank lending rate with the marginal rate of profit would not produce a stable price level (Hayek, 1929/1933, pp. 113-15; 1932c, pp. 122-4, 129; Uhr, 1960, pp. 279-92; 1975, pp. 21-2). With a trend growth in productivity, the price level would fall unless the money supply were steadily increased, for which it would be necessary to have the bank lending rate below the 'natural rate'. Mises and Hayek, as Wicksell's successors, were then faced with the realisation that in this dilemma lay the key to a periodic cycle. For if the bank lending rate were kept below the 'natural rate', the whole process of expansion which they envisaged would be set in motion; and it would only be checked, after successive rounds of price increases, when banks became concerned about their liquidity positions. Thus to aim for a stable price level involved commitment to a trade cycle (Hayek, 1929/1933, p. 119).

Faced with this difficulty, Hayek, Haberler and Robbins were prepared instead to envisage a price level falling in line with the secular increase in productivity. But such a policy raised a host of difficulties – not merely the distributive implication of increasing rentier income, which was hardly likely to be popular in the 1930s, but, as Hummel (1979) has pointed out, a falling price level would have the effect of raising the value of the deflated rate of interest (where inflation was now negative), which could thus rise above the marginal rate of profit and produce a depression without a preceding boom. As subsequent controversy has shown (Dowd, 1995; Selgin, 1995a, b) there exist many difficulties with the falling price level policy prescription.[6] But it was a logical outcome of the Mises-Hayek model, as is indeed clear from Hayek's paper on intertemporal equilibrium, where it is argued that if future prices are not expected to fall (in line with productivity) then more investment than warranted will take place (1928, pp. 92-3).

10.11 The Role of General Equilibrium

Perhaps the difficulties concerning the future price level may explain why Hayek showed some signs of moving away from equilibrium theorising from 1937, as Bruce Caldwell (1988) has argued. Others believe that his commitment to at least Lausanne general equilibrium was rather superficial in the first place. Aréna (1994, p. 211) has pointed out that the passage frequently cited as evidence of Hayek's commitment to general equilibrium (1929/1933, pp. 42-3) is normally curtailed before the point at which it goes on to refer not merely to Lausanne but also to James Mill and to Say. There is also a

[6] As Howard (1977) has pointed out, Hayek later settled for a stable price level. Haberler (1986) also came to recognise problems with a falling price level.

discernable change in Hayek's work from about 1937, in a much increased emphasis on evolutionary forms, linking this with the same element in Menger's work (O'Brien, 1994b, pp. 351-2, 357, and chapter 8 above). Moreover, as Lachman (1940) pointed out, general equilibrium involves reversibility, whereas Hayek's apparatus does not.

But, all that conceded, it is still true, as Smithies (1941) pointed out in his perceptive review of Hayek's *Pure Theory of Capital*, that the later book is still about equilibrium, albeit a moving equilibrium in which all plans are fully realised. This is a matter of some importance in relation to modern developments in economics which cite Hayek as a forerunner, as we shall see.

10.12 Methodology

There is considerable controversy about Hayek's methodological position. By many commentators, including the present writer (O'Brien, 1994b, p. 364; and Chapter 8), he has been seen as an *a priorist* in the Misean mould. Bruce Caldwell (1994) has maintained that Hayek never was an *a priorist.* Terence Hutchison, as a middle way, has argued that Hayek, having read the original German version of Popper's *Logik des Forschungs*, changed his approach in 1937 (1981, p. 125; Hamouda and Rowley, 1994, p. 186).

But the weight of the evidence from Hayek's writings seems clear enough. He was, and he remained, an *a priorist*, and somebody who was led seriously astray by this methodological stance. In this methodological position, which dates at least back to J.E. Cairnes, and which was espoused also by Robbins (O'Brien, 1988b, ch. 3), reasoning to a necessary conclusion proceeds on the basis of assumptions. Any contact with reality takes the form of 'verification' – checking the validity of the assumptions in order to be satisfied that the theoretical approach used was appropriate for the particular conditions to which it was applied. This still seems a reasonable reading of Hayek's 1937 paper which is sometimes taken as evidence of his change of view. Of course if introspection is regarded as a source of assumptions – and it certainly was by Hayek (O'Brien, 1994b, pp. 351-3; and Chapter 8) – verification becomes very tricky. There can be no assurance of uniformity of psychological response, as Robbins himself emphasised strongly when attacking attempts to justify progressive taxation by reference to diminishing marginal utility (O'Brien, 1988b, pp. 23-5, 39).

But it is even doubtful whether Hayek took very seriously the idea of verification. After all it was *assumed* in his writing, and in that of his allies, that the US money supply had increased, and that this has produced a boom followed by a depression (e.g. 1934a, p. 161). But this was an assumption which was eminently subject to verification, and it was simply wrong (O'Brien, 1998a, pp. 33-5; and Chapter 3). Hayek's position here led him seriously astray and damaged his standing for ever – indeed the Austrians have been charged, however unfairly, with facilitating the rise of Hitler by opposing reflationary measures (Hutchison, 1992, pp. 110-12).

Latterly Austrian writers have accepted that the US money supply had actually fallen – Haberler (1986) is an example. But the whole of Hayek's trade cycle theory suffered from a fundamental empirical weakness. For Hayek, like Keynes in the *Treatise*, believed that Bank Rate influenced short-term rates of interest, and that these in turn affected long-term rates, which influenced investment in fixed capital. In fairness to Keynes, he did attempt to justify this on the basis of what was, it later emerged, an unsatisfactory run of data. Ralph Hawtrey, who was very much better at this kind of work than Keynes, denied all these connections, and showed in *A Century of Bank Rate* (1938, pp. 184-95) that Keynes was mistaken. Reviewing the evidence, Hicks (1940) in turn accepted the argument. Hawtrey established that the short term rate had very little influence on capital outlay. This result was fundamentally damaging to Hayek – far more damaging than to Keynes, who had moved on from the apparatus of the *Treatise*. Yet Hayek appears to have been unmoved, and to have regarded the empirical results as irrelevant.

After shifting the balance of his argument concerning the trade cycle towards the Ricardo Effect, he supervised the doctoral research of Tsiang (1947). The latter, though phrasing his findings very cautiously, did not find empirical support for either the Ricardo Effect or for the idea that real wages fell in the upswing of the cycle, which underpinned the Effect. Tsiang's (1947, pp. 2-3) result here confirmed earlier work concerning the behaviour of real wages in the cycle. Yet there is no sign that Hayek responded to these findings. In his comments at the Royal Statistical Society in 1938 Hayek had remained sceptical about empirical work, despite his putative change of heart in 1937, and he does not seem to have altered his view, leaving a legacy of suspicion of empirical work in the later Austrian literature (Dolan, 1976, pp. 6-7; Spadaro, 1978, p. 212).

10.13 Hayek and New Classicism

In 1977 Robert Lucas, the leading figure in New Classicism, explicitly linked his work to Hayek's *MTTC* (1929/1933). In particular he argued that the book accepted the need, recognised until Keynes's *General Theory*, to incorporate trade cycle theory into Lausanne general equilibrium. He made the point that Keynes had redirected professional effort towards 'the apparently simpler question of the determination of output at a point in time, taking history as given' (Lucas, 1977, p. 7). He went on to argue that the trade cycle literature 'had been directed at identifying institutional sources of instability, with the hope that, once understood, these sources could be removed or their influence mitigated by appropriate institutional change' (p. 8). By contrast Keynes offered a way of rectifying the economy *however* the position in which it found itself had been arrived at.

It is true that Lucas rejected Hayek's reliance upon the interest mechanism, as requiring interest-elasticities of investment which were far too high to be plausible. But there was clearly a link in Lucas's mind between what he was trying to do, as signalled in particular by his 1975 paper, and Hayek.

Subsequently a number of writers have argued that any similarity between Hayek's work and New Classicism is superficial. Thus some (Butos, 1985; Cochran and Glahe, 1999) have argued that the New Classical models require markets to clear continuously, which was not true of Hayek, and that the new models are equilibrium models, whereas in Hayek the economy is out of equilibrium. Rühl (1994) has concluded that Hayek's analysis has little in common with the New Classical one, even though the question of a trade cycle within an equilibrium model remains a concern because the problem has not been solved. Aréna (1994) has argued that the New Classical approach is very much closer to Walras than Hayek was, and Hamouda and Rowley (1994) have rejected the New Classical parallel on the grounds that such an approach involves a closed probability distribution, as distinct from something like Shackle's 'possibility' (1972, pp. 364-404).

The most fundamental criticisms have come from Kevin Hoover (1988, 1994). He argues that the New Classicals ask how a Walrasian economy adapts, with given tastes, endowments and production possibilities, to exogenous or policy-generated fluctuations; the Austrians ask much broader questions with the evolution of tastes, expectations and technology involved. Secondly, the New Classicals want a predictive model, and they use mathematics and econometrics. The Austrians do not use these tools, and want understanding rather than prediction. Thirdly, the latter take the dispersal of information as fundamental; for the former it is limited to the degree necessary to produce fluctuations. Fourthly, Lucas *et al.* duck out of real disaggregation of macroeconomics by the use of Representative Agent models. Finally, equilibrium of New Classicals is market clearing, while for Austrians it is plans becoming compatible – a distinction short-circuited by New Classicals using tâtonnement to achieve market clearing (Hoover, 1994, p. 579).

Hoover has also pointed out that the use of rational expectations, which puts the economy close to, if not at, equilibrium, poses a real problem for Austrians and that the New Classicals have incorporated a cycle into general equilibrium via stochastic elements. However such stochastic differential equations are still deterministic. The New Classical model assumes that plans are already in existence whereas for the Austrians they are part of a continual learning process operating through the market mechanisms (1988, pp. 235-6, 247).

Rational expectations blur the distinction between risk and uncertainty (Hoover, 1988, p. 239); and Hayek's work provides a good basis for criticising rational expectations in whichever of the competing definitions one accepts (O'Driscoll and Rizzo, 1985, pp. 214ff). Furthermore Hayek's doctrine of unintended consequences sits very ill with the rational expectations concept. The idea of some physics-type model, as constructed by the New Classicals, being in any way acceptable to Hayek, is clearly strained (Hoover, 1988, p. 240).

While there is substantial weight in all these points, there is more to be said. It is true that the attempt to use representative agents as a micro reduction of macroeconomics is regarded as at best a failure and at worst as bogus (Hoover, 1988, pp. 243-4; Hausman, 2003). But it has been persuasively argued that an individualist reduction of macroeconomics is probably impossible (Levy, 1985); and in any case, Austrian trade cycle theory itself involves aggregation. We have production goods lumped together as one category, and consumption goods in another category. The trade cycle hinges on a change in the relative prices of these two aggregated sectors.

In summary, New Classical economics has encountered some of the same problems which Hayek and his successors encountered. The New Classicists have, with technical apparatus, attempted to deal with what Hayek regarded as an important question – a trade cycle in the context of general equilibrium. While, viewing Hayek's work as a whole, it is possible to argue that he was concerned with the broad range of issues which critics of the New

Classical parallel have cited, there are important parts of Hayek's later theoretical work, including *The Pure Theory of Capital* (1941a), which did indeed involve an equilibrium trade cycle. The links between Hayek's trade cycle writings and those of the New Classicists are perhaps rather greater than the assembled critics have allowed.[7]

10.14 Overview

Hayek's career fits into a recognisable pattern. Firstly, there is the late 1920s and the 1930s, when Hayek rose to considerable prominence as a theorist and was, up to 1936, the main intellectual opponent of Keynes. But the victory of Keynes's *General Theory* undoubtedly led to a significant reduction in Hayek's personal standing, and it did not recover as a result of his later theoretical work which culminated in *The Pure Theory of Capital.*

What brought Hayek to a new peak was his critique of scientism and of the roots of totalitarianism. This encompassed his continuation of Mises's exposition of the impossibility of central planning, his withering examination of the work of Saint Simon and Comte (1941b, 1942-4), and his brave (and possibly personally disastrous) attack upon the direction in which he saw western society going after World War II, which found expression most notably in *The Road to Serfdom* (1944); see O'Brien (1994a, pp. 351-9). The third and most sustained peak was that in which he worked out, with great care and scholarship, a vision of economic activity based upon a legal framework, which was essentially developing Smith's vision of the constraint of economic activity by law, religion and custom (O'Brien, 1998c; and Chapter 9). This found its expression in two great works, *The Constitution of Liberty* of 1960, and *Law, Legislation and Liberty*, the three volumes of which appeared over the years 1973-9. It was in the 1970s also that he received the

[7]It seems that Lucas himself has accepted Hoover's view (Snowdon and Vane, 1998, p. 121).

Table 10.1: Hayek Citations

Period	Citations	Period	Citations
1926-30	7	1960-70	228
1931-36	32	1971-80	291
1937-43	26	1981-90	104
1944-45	751	1991-03	17
1946-59	116		

Nobel Prize, when his earlier work on the trade cycle and his most recent on a free society were cited as particular achievements.

The pattern of citations shown in Table 10.1 corresponds to this outline of his career. Only in the 1990s did the citations almost cease. Furthermore, from analysis of relative citations by Deutscher (1990, pp. 189-202), it is evident that Hayek was amongst the most cited authors in the great theoretical controversies of the 1930s.[8]

Yet Hayek's work remains largely unread today. As Dostaler (1994, p. 148) has emphasised, it is important to read what Hayek actually wrote. Like Adam Smith, he is cited but unread (Hamouda and Rowley, 1994, p. 178), which leads to inaccuracy and distortion. Yet even in his Teutonic-professor style, his work has much greater immediacy than the secondary literature. Return to this work is both necessary and profitable. Hayek quite clearly anticipated Rawls's principle by suggesting maximising the income potential of the least well off (1967, p. 173)[9] – yet it is possible for the secondary literature to contest this because few readers will be familiar with the original.

There is also a quite extraordinary mainstream hostility to Austrian economics in general and to Hayek in particular. Some of the latter seems

[8] In the period 1931-5, Hayek was third in the list of most cited macroeconomists (behind Keynes and Robertson), and for 1936-9 he was seventh. The data on citations come from Deutscher (1990).

[9] Rawls, it is true, focuses on the distributive outcome. But experience shows that, precisely because of unintended consequences, we have limited control over that. Hayek instead looked to the creation of conditions for the attainment of such equality.

visceral.[10]

Despite this hostility, there are still those who attempt to carry the Austrian flag. There are different kinds of Austrians – but the gaps between them are much smaller than the gulf between all of them and mainstream economics; and the heritage which the Austrians share, as Backhouse (1985, p. 378) has pointed out, is not Böhm-Bawerk or Schumpeter, it is Menger, Mises and Hayek. The main Austrian centres seem to be New York and Auburn universities, though the list of contributors to volumes on Hayek reveals a much wider constituency. Particular Hayekian themes are also being developed, such as the sustained work by Roger Garrison (1985, 1989, 2001) on Hayek's trade cycle model.

Moreover an Austrian approach to economics provides a good basis for criticising the mainstream literature. Although Spadaro (1978, pp. 206-7) has suggested that such an approach, at least if primarily defensive, is a misallocation of resources, it is apparent from the Austrian literature that criticism can be a good method of developing an alternative research programme.[11] The intellectual descendants of Hayek have been good at asking awkward questions (e.g. Lachman, 1978). The vulnerable areas of mainstream economics are many, and Hicks himself has testified to the inadequacy of so central a part as the Paretian system (1967, p. 138). Hayek and other Austrians asked the awkward questions that mainstream theory sidesteps. Such questions include economic actors taking decisions on the basis of a constantly changing supply of knowledge, which causes in turn constant revision of plans. This difficulty extends to the problem of intertemporal co-ordination and the revision of plans across time (Garrison,

[10] Thus Fischer (1986, p. 433), in a very hostile article, accuses Hayek (1976a) of ignorance of Klein (1974) – yet Hayek (1976a, p. 37) explicitly cites Klein's article. See also the comments by Ackley quoted by Bellante and Garrison (1988, pp. 335-6) and Solow's description of Hayek's trade cycle model as 'completely incomprehensible' cited by Garrison (2001, p. 4).

[11] O'Driscoll and Rizzo (1985) provide a good example of this.

1985). More generally, what meaning has the concept of rational behaviour with time-dependent knowledge? (Boland, 1978; Langlois, 1985). Again, the Hayekian treatment of expectations is much less constrained than the mechanistic treatment of rational expectations, and far more suggestive than the arbitrary changes in expectations which Keynes employed in the *General Theory*. The questions raised by Hayek's treatment of knowledge[12] are fundamental to an understanding of how a real economy works, as Leijonhufvud has argued (1968, p. 401). Yet the mainstream is averse to even acknowledging the existence of such questions.[13] Indeed, the Keynesian mainstream for long largely ignored the time dimension of investment (Tsiang, 1949).[14]

But Hayek bequeathed more than awkward questions. There are possibilities of developing his understanding of markets through experimental economics (Smith, 1982) and game theory (Schmidt, 2002), though the closed probability distributions would not have appealed to Hayek (cf. Shackle, 1972, pp. 24, 161, 422). Even the capital theory may not be a dead end; following the pioneering work of Hicks, writers such as Desai and Redfern (1994) and Zamagni (1984, 1987) have produced highly mathematical interpretations of 'traverses' between equilibria.

Less promising is Hayek's work on the denationalisation of money. While the free banking literature has taken its inspiration from Hayek (Dowd, 1994), there has been serious criticism of the idea of competition in currencies (King, 1983; Summers, 1983). The transactions costs of multiple issues (Edwards, 1980), and the possibility of moral hazard, are so serious that it is unlikely that any unitary state would follow this path although, as Hayek himself pointed out, in border areas, especially in Europe, competing currencies have in the past operated in parallel. But they are currencies originating with

[12] Or Hayek's and Morgenstern's – see Caldwell (1994) and Foss (1995).

[13] Hutt, whose work on search was belatedly acknowledged by Leijonhufvud (1969, p. 31), with chagrin, was simply pushed out of mainstream consciousness.

[14] In Leijonhufvud's view (1981, p. 173), Keynes gave little thought to capital or economic growth.

national issuers, not commercial organisations. Of course, as Hayek stressed, states have abused their powers of issue; but currency competition has to be considered as a remedy for this not in isolation but in comparison with other possible remedies such as inflation targeting (Howard, 1977).

On the other hand Hayek's treatment of competition in the markets for goods and services has proved important. He insisted on analysing the way in which competition works, as distinct from the sterile definitional approach of Lausanne general equilibrium. The fixation of economists with perfect competition led them grossly to underestimate the achievements of the competitive system (1949, pp. 102-6; 1967, p. 174; 1973-9, III, pp. 65-8). As Backhouse (2002a, pp. 278-9) has emphasised, Hayek focused on rivalry, new products and new processes; to put it another way, Hayek addressed not maximisation subject to constraints but the much more fundamental issue of moving the constraints. Competition should be viewed as a continuous discovery process, as Smith understood, not a set of conditions like perfect competition. Such a view has lasting validity.[15] Moreover it has had an important policy impact. For competition policy illustrates perfectly why Austrian, and specifically Hayekian, economics lacks fashionable appeal. It undermines the idea of an active competition policy (in which many economists have found highly remunerative employment) and thus accords with the devastatingly successful Chicago anti-Anti-Trust school[16] (O'Brien, 1998a, p. 29; and Chapter 3). Indeed a key member of that school cites Hayek (Demsetz, 1988, 1989, pp. 219, 223; 1995, p. 171; DiLorenzo, 1994).

[15]It is thus capable of further development. It has been argued that Kirzner's theory of entrepreneurship derives from Hayek (Kirzner, 1997; Palermo, 1999, pp. 104-5). The suggestion (Hamouda and Rowley, 1994, pp. 191-2) that the Japanese keiretsu system might render Hayek's vision of competition irrelevant now seems, a decade later, rather quaint.

[16]In destroying anti-trust policy, the Chicago economists destroyed industrial economics, creating a desert in which game theory took root.

10.15 Conclusions

Hayek came into the English speaking world as an economist, not as a philosopher. But his work broadened out to embrace philosophical considerations relating to the framework of economic activity, which linked with his overriding concern with freedom and responsibility. He thus found a key role in the development of British liberalism, as Cockett (1995) has shown at length. The influence of Mises led Hayek on to Smith, Burke, Ferguson and Hume, and to the concept of spontaneous order, and ultimately to some of the most important writing that economists have produced about the framework of economic activity (O'Brien, 1998c; and Chapter 9). The Austrian understanding of the operation of markets, with which this is associated, has been of great importance, notably at those times when fashionable opinion has favoured planning, whether indicative (as in the 1960s) or directive (Lavoie, 1986; O'Brien, 1998b, p. 115).

The line of development goes from Menger to Mises to Hayek. The combined direct influence of the last two continues, and historians of economic thought cannot neglect the importance of Hayek in the story of the development of the subject. Hayek has been called Böhm-Bawerk's greatest pupil (Blaug, 1985, p. 541). The link is unfortunate; it has been argued above that Hayek would have done well to steer clear of Böhm-Bawerk's capital theory. He was Mises's greatest pupil far more, and he managed, starting from that base, to counter the vanity of academics who wished to plan society, to explain the fundamental nature of markets, and also – and this is worth emphasising in an academic climate in which scholarship is at a discount – he was one of the last of the great scholar economists. The questions which he asked were not trivial, and they do not permit of easy answers. They are thus not attractive to the economist-as-technician school of thought. To be blunt, Austrian economics is not good for outside career opportunities and, because of the ruling mainstream, it is not good for academic career opportunities either.[17] But of its importance as one of the strands in the development of our subject there can be no doubt.

[17] For exploration of possible links with another 'outside' branch of economics – institutionalism – see Boettke (1989), Caldwell (1989), Samuels (1989), Rutherford (1989, 1994).

Chapter 11

McCulloch and the Literature of Economics

John Ramsay McCulloch was born on 1 March 1789 in the South West of Scotland at Whithorn and died in London at the Stationery Office, of which he was Comptroller, on 11 November 1864. He was editor of the *Scotsman* newspaper 1817-21, Professor of Political Economy at London University 1828-37, and Comptroller of the Stationery Office from 1838 to his death.[1]

The bare facts do not begin to do justice to the variety and interest of McCulloch's career. A pioneer of economic journalism, who thought nothing of devoting the front page of the *Scotsman* to abstruse discussions of abstract subjects, he became the most prolific of all the classical economists, producing large numbers of books, many articles (including 78 for the *Edinburgh Review*) and large 'statistical' works containing pioneer compilations of economic data. Although he was an active, and effective, Comptroller of the Stationery Office, he still managed to continue his literary activities; indeed it was after he had assumed the Comptrollership that he produced the major

[1] O'Brien (1970, chs 2-6) contains biographical material relating to McCulloch. Of McCulloch's Comptrollership of the Stationery Office, his friend the book dealer Quaritch claimed that, 'in that capacity he not only did his routine duties faithfully, but by rigorous insistence on small economies was able to save from the general funds of the office enough to found the libraries of the House of Commons and the Board of Trade, as well as greatly to improve the library of the Patent Office' (Quaritch, 1895, p. 1).

classical economic work on public finance, his *Treatise on Taxation.*

At his death he left the substantial sum – for one who had started with very little – of £16,000 which, at today's prices might represent a sum of approximately £640,000.

Of that £16,000, the assessment for probate of the value of McCulloch's book collection was more than £3,000 (the library, together with furniture and prints, was valued at £3,504 19s.). McCulloch was a pioneer amongst economists as a historian of economic thought, and as a book collector he is surpassed only by Foxwell (who built up the two great collections of the Kress and Goldsmith libraries).[2]

McCulloch's collecting interests extended far beyond the literature of economics, in something of a contrast to Foxwell whose interest was much more narrowly focused. But the six volumes discussed here represent a knowledge and appreciation of rare and significant economic literature which is indeed remarkable. The volumes are not merely, as McCulloch himself wrote modestly, a means of 'preserving some valuable and little known works; and ... a desirable addition to the historical and political literature of the empire' (1859b, p. xxii); they were also a celebration of McCulloch as both book collector and historian of economics.

11.1 McCulloch as a Collector

McCulloch did not inherit any of the books collected by a maternal great grandfather whose activities apparently provided him with some inspiration.[3]

[2]Canney *et al.* (1970-75); Kress Library (1940). On Foxwell as a collector see Keynes (1936, pp. 283-92). However, if Keynes's recollection is to be trusted, Foxwell did McCulloch an injustice, claiming that he 'excluded with rare exceptions all books which did not come up to his standard of orthodoxy' (p. 283). Although Keynes himself put the quoted passage in quotes, it seems doubtful whether it is an accurate representation of Foxwell's view, since some of the latter's marginalia in the Goldsmiths' Library collection indicate admiration for McCulloch's balance. At all events it is certainly not a just accusation to level at McCulloch, as will become clear in the course of this chapter.

[3]It is perhaps surprising that it should have done so since McCulloch was apparently badly treated by this (maternal) grandfather (O'Brien, 1970, pp. 17-18).

Yet he built up a library of about 8,000 books, concentrating on economics, but covering an enormous range.[4] The width of McCulloch's reading, something which he was able to turn to his advantage when dealing with questions of uncertain authorship, was truly impressive. His collection contained a very wide selection of works in English and French on literary, philosophical, and even mathematical topics; there were works by Italian and Spanish authors (though McCulloch appears not to have read German) and a substantial number of works in Latin.

French literature seems to have attracted him particularly. According to Quaritch, 'He loved French books, and gave more serious attention (more than enough perhaps) to historical essays in that language than in any other' (Quaritch 1895, p. 5). Rather like Smith's library (though on a much bigger scale) it reflected, in its very broad base, the essential width of the Scottish approach to learning.[5] This approach, combined with a classical bias in McCulloch's elementary education, and a passion for book collecting, produced an exceptional collection.[6]

---

[4]There are roughly 8,000 books in the Overstone Library at Reading; some however were not McCulloch's and others which did belong to him 'leaked' from the collection before its presentation to Reading University. Overstone believed that he was buying 10,000 books (letter to George Warde Norman, 18 January 1865 in O'Brien (1971, III, p. 1065). The overall size of McCulloch's own collection may reasonably be put at 8,000, but, as he emphasised in the introduction to his *Catalogue*, this was built up by selective purchase. 'I have endeavoured to find out the books that bore the highest character in the different departments of literature and science; and of these, when I bought any, I endeavoured to select the best or most useful editions. It appears to me to be bad husbandry to purchase whole sacks of chaff for the sake of the few grains of wheat they may chance to contain. The extraction of the latter costs more than they are worth. I have not aimed at the collection of a large, but rather of a choice library' (McCulloch, 1862, p. viii). Foxwell, by contrast, was a much more wholesale buyer. According to Keynes: 'In course of time he became ever more insatiable, sometimes buying whole collections, and not merely single volumes. He came to regard it almost as a moral fault to miss a desireable purchase' (1936a, p. 284).

[5]Smith's library was probably of about 3000 volumes (Viner 1965, pp. 121, 127-8). McCulloch however estimated its size at 5000 books (1863, p. xvii).

[6]See Murray (1911, pp. 74-5) for McCulloch's curious early education at the hands of a refugee from Ireland who was apparently a classical scholar. See also O'Brien (1970, pp. 69-70).

When McCulloch's friend Lord Overstone, himself an eminent writer on monetary economics, paid £5,000 for the library, he was rather exceeding the probate value but he acquired a very fine library.[7] It was also a fine working library. McCulloch says in the preface to the second of his *Catalogues* of the library that it had enabled him 'to finish works of much research and labour without either resorting to public libraries, or borrowing books' (McCulloch, 1862, p. v). Considering the scope and volume of McCulloch's own writing on economics, this is indeed a striking testimony to the value of the library.

McCulloch had been a diligent collector of books, especially of economic material, since his early years in Edinburgh. On visits to London, he added to his collection and indeed obtained an advance of funds from one of the proprietors of the *Scotsman* for this purpose.[8] As early as 1820 he seems to have had a considerable collection, and this early collecting marked the beginning of a lifetime devoted to the creation of his library.[9] This activity gave him the opportunity to acquire a knowledge of foreign writers, and of earlier British writers, which far outshines that of any other classical economist except perhaps Smith, writing much earlier, whom, indeed, McCulloch (1862, p. vi; 1863, p. xvii) took as his model.

McCulloch clearly became well known to book dealers. Indeed the famous dealer Bernard Quaritch claimed that McCulloch virtually discovered him. His account of his relationship with McCulloch is so interesting that it is worth quoting at length. He wrote:

---

[7]On Overstone's purchase see A. Black to Overstone 21 December 1864, in O'Brien (1971, III, p. 1063).

[8]He requested '£20 or £30' from William Ritchie, proprietor of the *Scotsman*, to enable him to buy books in London (*Scotsman* Mss., n.d.). This may have been in connection with his visit to London in 1823 – he wrote to Francis Place about his wish to buy economic pamphlets while there (BL Add. Mss. 37949 f.127, letter of 4 March 1823).

[9]A Polish student, Karol Sienkiewicz recorded, in his diary for 26 December 1820, being received by McCulloch 'in a room full of books'. On Sienkiewicz and his diary see O'Brien (1970, pp. 27-8). There were amongst the Overstone papers at Wantage in Berkshire a number of pamphlets marked 'J.R. McCulloch, 1821' in McCulloch's own hand. These are now in the Overstone Library at Reading.

As might be expected McCulloch had many friends among the booksellers. He may be said to have discovered Mr. Quaritch. Mr. Quaritch came to England as a lad of twenty to serve in Bohn's shop, but made good use of his spare time and was soon noted for his knowledge of English politics and his general information, acting in 1842 as English correspondent to the *Rheinische Zeitung* of Marx and Engels. In 1847, he started business for himself at 16 Castle Street, Leicester Square, now in Charing Cross Road, and to this day he uses the old place under his name, though only as a warehouse. At that time Mr. Quaritch was, like McCulloch, a keen Radical and political economist. He knew McCulloch's books well, and when McCulloch visited his shop they soon became friends. McCulloch recognized Quaritch's first classified catalogue (1860) as 'one of the best published in England for many years' (*Catalogue* [McCulloch, 1862], page 31, under Bibliography), and pressed its compiler to move to a more important locality. His advice was taken in that very year. Mr. Quaritch remembers a dialogue between himself and the economist in the year 1861, when the latter refused to allow that the gold discoveries were lowering the purchasing power of money. Gladstone happened to join the party and sided with McCulloch. In a note on Chevalier's book on gold (*Catalogue* [McCulloch, 1862], page 62), McCulloch persists in his contention. But it is now acknowledged that Mr. Quaritch was right and these eminent authorities in error. Another incident of those years may be mentioned. McCulloch entered the new shop one day, and its master said to him, 'Here is a book you would like to read.' The other bent over him and said with great emphasis, 'Do you think I am one of those low fellows who buy books for the sake of reading them?' The remark was not quite serious ...

> The friendship continued to the end. Mr. Quaritch remembers his last drive with McCulloch a few weeks before the death of the latter. They went from Reigate by Dorking, and McCulloch remarked, when they passed a group of agricultural labourers, 'It is astonishing how few of these men ever rise' (Quaritch, 1895, p. 4).

McCulloch assembled a library which was, as he said, 'the result of a pursuit which I have followed with uninterrupted ardour for more than half a century' (McCulloch, 1862, p. v). After admitting that he had perhaps devoted rather more of his income than was proper to the purchase of books, he then went on: 'Their acquisition has been a business in which I have always taken the greatest interest; it has not palled upon me for a single moment'.

McCulloch (1862, p. vi) was prepared to 'confess to the folly, if such it be, of being no less an admirer of well-bound than of well-printed books'. This 'folly' is confirmed by others, Overstone's comment will be noted below, and Quaritch the book dealer recorded that, 'he bought books for the purpose of reading them only, and not, like the ordinary book-collector, for the purpose of preserving rarities. The volumes in his library were all useful for study or reference; but he liked, nevertheless, to possess fine copies in fine old bindings. The bindings which are usually attributed to Derome, were those which pleased his taste beyond all others, and my ear has not yet forgotten the unctuous emphasis with which he would speak about 'auld red morocco' (Quaritch, 1895, p. 5).

But as Quaritch indicates, McCulloch bought books primarily to read – indeed in one letter to Quaritch he regrets returning a book to Quaritch because the contents (on the art of war) did not interest him though the binding was admirable (letter of 15 October 1859, facsimile in Quaritch, 1895). Nor did McCulloch acquire books simply because they were scarce.

It was content, not rarity on its own, which he sought.

> The collection of books on Political Economy, the study of which has been the principal business of my life, comprises most part of the works of any value in that science. But neither in that nor in any other department have I bought books because they happened to be scarce. Unless they had something else than rarity to recommend them, they have not been inquired for by me (McCulloch, 1862, p. vi).[10]

McCulloch's aim therefore was to build a choice library. He was keenly interested in assembling the key references on particular topics, something which is highly relevant to the six collected volumes here under consideration.

Bibliography itself seems to have been something which attracted McCulloch. While at the newly-formed London University he prepared a 'Catalogue Raisonèe' of books on economics. Although he claimed, in a letter to his friend MacVey Napier, that he had done this to please the Council of the University, it seems highly likely that it was also for his own satisfaction.[11] It very probably formed the basis for *The Literature of Political Economy*, which he published in 1845 and which was essentially a subject bibliography of economics. It was itself the fruit of McCulloch's tenacious collection of a library which, amongst its other merits, mirrored the development of economics. 'For many years past we have taken every means in our power, by collecting books and otherwise, to become acquainted with the history of the science, and with the leading publications in its different departments.' (1845, p. viii). Quaritch described *The Literature of Political Economy* as 'like the best of its kind, a catalogue raisonné,' adding that 'if it has defects,

[10]See also McCulloch (1845, p. viii): 'Neither have we referred to any work merely because it happened to be scarce: it must have had something else than rarity to recommend it to a place in our pages'.

[11]On this see O'Brien (1970, p. 80, n. 6). The letter to MacVey Napier, of 25 June 1829, is BL Add. Mss. 34614 f. 99.

they were such as no others of his countrymen could remedy or even perceive' (Quaritch, 1895, p. 1).

The Literature of Political Economy was followed, in 1856 and 1862, by the two editions of the *Catalogue* of McCulloch's own library. These were not published, but privately printed. However they again display McCulloch's interest in bibliography, for though not sectioned like the *Literature of Political Economy* they do contain a number of separate sub-sections dealing with matters as diverse as classics, commerce, finance, money and coins, and bibliography itself.

Given McCulloch's status as a bibliophile and book collector, it was hardly surprising that when two of his friends, Lord Overstone and Walter Coulson were nominated by the Political Economy Club to consider use of its surplus funds, they should have financed the printing of the first two of the collected volumes considered in this chapter, particularly as McCulloch had been planning such an exercise for a long time.[12]

McCulloch then wrote to Overstone a letter which included the following:

> I wish much to print three or four more volumes of tracts – One on Trade, one on Paper money, one on Population, and one on the Public Debt, sinking Fund, &ca. – I venture to flatter myself with the idea that you will probably authorize me to print one or more of these volumes. – The last mentioned Volume might I think be made an excellent one.[13]

Overstone obviously volunteered to pay for these volumes out of his own pocket. A few days later McCulloch responded as follows: 'I am delighted by what you say about the tracts – if I had 4 Volumes more to add to the

[12] Political Economy Club (1882, p. 183, minutes of 1 March 1855). In the introduction to McCulloch (1845a, p. x) he referred to plans to publish 'in 3 or 4 vols. 8 vo., a Collection of some of the most important and curious Tracts referred to in this work, including, also, a few not noticed'.

[13] McCulloch to Overstone, 24 November 1856, in O'Brien (1971, II, pp. 684-5).

two volumes already printed, it would be, out of all sight, the best collection of Economical tracts in Christendom'.[14]

At the end of the preface to the last volume of the set, that of 'Economical Tracts' which appeared in 1859, McCulloch expressed his thanks to his benefactor.

> This terminates the collection of Tracts, reprinted by Lord Overstone. It will, perhaps, be generally admitted, that the volumes are both interesting and valuable. But the defects of the collection, whatever they may be, are entirely to be set down to the account of the Editor, and not of the Noble Lord who has defrayed the expense of the publication. He made no stipulations of any kind. I ventured to suggest to his Lordship that the reprinting of a selection of the rarest and best tracts connected with our trade, finance, paper currency, &c., would be desirable; and having approved of the suggestion, he left me to carry it out as I thought best. But for this munificence on the part of my noble friend, not one of these volumes would have appeared (O'Brien, 1971, p. xxii).

The contents of the volumes display McCulloch's extraordinarily wide range of knowledge; indeed they even include items which are not possessed by the Goldsmiths' library (Canney *et al.*, 1970-75). Where the works are anonymous, McCulloch's attributions have stood the test of time pretty well. He was well aware that, to appreciate fully the significance of a work, one should know not only the author's name but something about the author. The preface to his *Literature of Political Economy* indeed contains a French quotation to this effect. But McCulloch did not accept that a work should be excluded from consideration simply because such information was lacking: 'the authors of many valuable treatises in this science are wholly unknown;

[14]McCulloch to Overstone, 2 December 1856, in O'Brien (1971, II, pp. 688-9)

and it is often all but impossible to learn anything respecting others, with whose names only we are acquainted. We have, however, endeavoured to supply the information on which so high a value has been set, whenever it can be had, or appeared to be of consequence' (McCulloch, 1845a, p. ix). Later research has added a little information to McCulloch's attributions; but not a great deal.

The copies of the volumes which resulted from Overstone's sponsorship, both via the Political Economy Club and from his own pocket, were deliberately limited in number, in accordance with McCulloch's philosophy that such limitation was desirable even though the marginal cost of extra copies was 'nothing or not worth a thought'.[15] This gives the volumes a rarity in their own right – Durham University possesses the copies of the four volumes financed by Overstone which were presented to his close friend and associate Charles Wood, Viscount Halifax.

Overstone himself acquired the original works reprinted in the volumes when, after McCulloch's death, he bought his friend's library from the estate. He explained his motives to his close friend and confidant George Warde Norman in a letter of 18 January 1865, the arrangements having been made just before the preceding Christmas:

> I likewise have taken a bold step – in purchasing the library of our old friend McCulloch – He was a great Book-worm – careful in selecting best Editions – finest paper – and a perfect Martinet about binding – The Library consists of Ten thousand Volumes – which are all to go down to Overstone [Park]. ... I have made this purchase principally from respect to McCulloch, and because I knew that he entertained a latent wish that the Library, which it had been the pleasure of his life to collect – should not be dispersed.[16]

[15]McCulloch to Overstone, 8 December 1856, in O'Brien (1971, II, p. 690)

[16]Overstone to Norman 18 January, 1865, in O'Brien (1971, III, p. 1065).

The library did indeed go to Overstone's seat, Overstone Park, Northamptonshire. There the vast majority of the books and pamphlets remained until the library was presented to Reading University in 1920 under the provisions of the will of Lady Wantage, Overstone's daughter and only child. The facilities at Overstone Park, though considerably larger than at Overstone's other – and preferred – residence, Lockinge, at Wantage in Berkshire, were inadequate for such a large collection, and the books seem to have been housed not merely in the library at Overstone but at a number of other locations around the house.[17] How much contact Overstone himself had with them after his purchase is unclear. In the years before her death in November 1864, Lady Overstone had persuaded him to sanction the rebuilding of the house at Overstone.[18] After her death Overstone came to find the house very depressing. On the one hand he greatly missed his wife there; on the other, as he wrote to Norman he was appalled by the efforts of the architect – 'We have fallen into the hands of an architect, in whom incapacity is his smallest fault'.[19] The majority of Overstone's letters after this date are written either from Lockinge or from his London house, 2 Carlton Gardens. But he did visit Overstone Park and so he certainly had some contact with the books during his lifetime.

Overstone had acquired a great collection. This collection was however made in the course of McCulloch's self-education as a pioneer of the study of the history of economic thought. It is worth paying some attention to this.

[17] I am indebted to David Knott, the Rare Books Librarian at the University of Reading, for information about the library at Overstone Park and the transfer of the books to Reading. When the present writer visited Overstone Park in the late 1970s, at the end of the house's life as a boarding school, the library room was in a deplorable condition but it was evident that it would never have been large enough to house McCulloch's library, even had it been empty before the arrival of his books which, clearly, it would not have been.

[18] Overstone to Norman, 12 March 1861, in O'Brien (1971, II, pp. 950-1); Overstone to Norman, 14 September 1863 ('The park remains as it was, growing in beauty every year - but in the midst of it is being erected an edifice – ambitious, pretentious – and with little promise of domestic comfort'), in O'Brien (1971, III, pp. 1007-8).

[19] Overstone to Norman, 8 April 1865, in O'Brien (1971, III, pp. 1071-2)

11.2 The History of Economics

McCulloch seems to have become interested in the history of economics almost as soon as he became interested in economics itself. By 1822 he had already published a 'Sketch of the Progress of Commercial Science in England in the Seventeenth Century' in the *Scotsman* (19 January 1822) and he informed Ricardo that, 'The history of the different theories and opinions entertained respecting commerce has long been a favourite subject with me; and if I had got rid of some of my heavier tasks I should like to bestow a little attention on it'.[20]

It probably would not be going too far to say that McCulloch was the first historian of economic thought. There are no obvious predecessors for his work in this field in which he published from the 1820s onwards. It is true that J.B. Say included a *Preliminary Discourse* in his *Traité*; but this was a modest effort compared with McCulloch's *Discourse on the Rise of Political Economy* which will be discussed below.[21] Dugald Stewart also included material in his lectures on political economy at Edinburgh on the 'Rise and Progress of this Branch of the Science', and he appended notes to his Account of the Life and Writings of Adam Smith.[22] McCulloch did indeed refer to the latter in his *Discourse*; but there is no indication that he attended Stewart's lectures while at Edinburgh, and these were not published.[23]

However, McCulloch's early interest in the history of economic thought, referred to in the letter to Ricardo quoted above, began more narrowly as

[20] McCulloch to Ricardo, 17 April 1822, in Sraffa (1951-5, IX, pp. 186-7).

[21] Say (1803, pp. 1-54). See also Say (1817, pp. xv-lx). In truth, McCulloch's *Discourse* seems to owe nothing obvious to Say, even though the latter unjustly accused McCulloch of plagiarism (Say, 1825, pp. 263-4). However, Say (1828-9, pp. 562, 564, 568) later praised the work.

[22] Stewart (1854-60, VIII, p. xvii; X, pp. 88-95, n.1). McCulloch refers to this source in his *Discourse* (McCulloch, 1824, p. 114) and in his Introduction to the *Wealth of Nations* (McCulloch, 1863, p. xlii, n).

[23] McCulloch studied mathematics, agriculture and ethics, under Professors John Leslie, Andrew Coventry and Thomas Brown. This information has been supplied from the records of Edinburgh University, for whose help I am grateful.

an interest in the history of thought concerning commerce, and here there is earlier work, of a somewhat sketchy nature, which would at least have directed McCulloch's attention to the names of earlier writers, by MacPherson, and Grant.[24] Nonetheless none of these writers could be said to have done anything more than provide a starting point for McCulloch.

Consistently with his initial interest in the history of ideas on commerce, he was naturally interested in an early Edinburgh reprint of Dudley North's *Discourses upon Trade* (a work also reprinted by McCulloch). It looks as if John Archibald Murray was the prime mover in this enterprise, since it was from him that McCulloch obtained a copy of the pamphlet which he sent to Ricardo in January 1822.[25]

Later generations have sometimes regarded McCulloch as exhibiting an excessive Whiggishness in his approach to the history of economics. Since no economist writing on the history of economics can do so independently of the particular 'paradigm' currently ruling, as a glance at modern histories of economic of thought shows instantly, this accusation seems less than fair. Some have gone further and accused McCulloch of berating all previous writers who did not conform with 'Ricardianism'. Such accusations reveal only, however, a significant ignorance both of the content of what McCulloch wrote on the history of economic thought and of Ricardo's own writings. For not only is it the case that McCulloch was no slavish follower of Ricardo, and that Ricardo was not (as these critics imply) a doctrinaire free trader, but McCulloch's approach to the previous writers whom he discussed was, by and large, temperate and concerned to find what was good in the earlier writings. It certainly was not the kind of work that Mark Blaug (1985, p. 1) has very aptly characterised as a 'boring exercise in omniscience'. As will

[24] MacPherson (1805, especially pp. 297-300, 316, 511). This makes particular reference to Munn and Misselden. See also MacPherson (1812) and pp. 103-4 concerning Munn and Grant (1813) pp. i-liii (especially pp. xix-xxii and xxvi-xxvii) and pp. 45-62.

[25] McCulloch to Ricardo, 13 January 1822, in Sraffa (1951-5, IX, pp. 150-151). North's work is reprinted in McCulloch (1856a, pp. 505-40).

be clear to the reader of his introductions to the volumes of tracts included in this set, McCulloch looks for the good in writers with whom he disagrees. His selection of authors is judicious and his erudition is considerable. Of course he was not infallible; while recognising Henry Thornton's greatness he confused him with Samuel Thornton, and thus credited him with being a Director of the Bank of England, which he never was.[26] He also credited Ricardo, and in particular the latter's *High Price of Bullion*, with an influence over the Bullion Report which it never had.[27] Indeed, although he certainly did not interpret all previous writers in Ricardo's terms, it is true to say that his praise of Ricardo himself was out of all proportion to Ricardo's influence either on him or on other writers. This is partly because, following what an earlier Edinburgh adversary had called his 'Principles of Political Economy' he reused, again and again, material which he had written about Ricardo for an obituary published in 1823.[28] Even though his own intellectual position moved steadily away from that of Ricardo, he kept pressing this old material into service.[29]

He believed that the history of economic thought was of importance for a number of reasons. Firstly, valid and invalid ideas continued to coexist in economics. Secondly, economic arguments were likely to be distorted by party or other special interests, so it was important to have some knowledge of the kind and range of arguments deployed in relation to a particular problem. Thirdly, there was a continual risk of what Schumpeter was later to call 'subjective originality' on the part of those ignorant – as, indeed, he recognised Ricardo had been when writing about rent – of the work of predecessors.

[26] McCulloch (1857b, pp. xi-xii). On the confusion see Hayek (1939b, pp. 14-15).

[27] McCulloch (1857b, pp. xiv-xv). Ricardo's *High Price of Bullion* is reprinted at pp. 361-401 of this volume. On the question of Ricardo's influence see Fetter (1953).

[28] The adversary was John Wilson and his work appeared under the pen name 'Mordecai Mullion'; see Wilson (1826). On the episode see O'Brien (1970, pp. 26-7, 31, 73-5, 85).

[29] It appeared in McCulloch (1824a, 1842a, 1846, 1853, 1859c).

> Whether a writer ... undertakes to unfold principles, to set them in a novel and more striking light, or to recommend their application, he should know what has been already undertaken, what has been accomplished, and what remains for discovery and elucidation. The following work gives sundry examples of the inconveniences resulting from the want of this information, by exhibiting able men engaged in the investigation of principles and the development of laws which had been previously established and traced, and putting forward speculations as original which had been long before the public (McCulloch, 1845a, pp. vi-vii).[30]

Numerous examples of McCulloch's judicious approach to previous writers can be found in the prefaces that he wrote to the volumes he reprinted. Thus for the 1859 volume on Commerce, he insists that while the first item in the volume exaggerated considerably the size of the Dutch fleet, 'it would not be fair to judge the tract by this single specimen' (p. vi). We also find him writing in friendly terms about Josiah Tucker, who was indubitably a mercantilist. Again, in the 1856 volume on Commerce we find that the work of Lewes Roberts on the benefits of trade is not criticised in Ricardian terms, a tolerant attitude is displayed towards the author of 'Britannia Languens', despite the fundamental error of assuming a decline in national income, and even that leading mercantilist Sir Josiah Child is praised – and, be it noted, there was no obvious occasion for this since no tract of his is included in the volume.

McCulloch's discerning approach to the history of economic thought is also demonstrated in some of his editorial work. While his editing of Ricardo's works was perfunctory, and simply utilised the by then 23 year old obituary of Ricardo to serve as an introduction with only minor modifica-

[30]The preface to this work contains a good statement of McCulloch's views on the importance of the study of the history of economic thought.

tions, an obituary which itself incorporated an article from the *Scotsman*,[31] his editing of the *Wealth of Nations* was a considerable achievement. His additions to the work lengthened it by a third; they included introductory material, footnotes and supplementary notes. Of course not all of the material first saw publication in this form. Several notes (those on tithes, and on taxes on profits, rent and wages) had first appeared in the *Scotsman*;[32] and the *Introductory Discourse* was not new. Moreover the note on rent was substantially provided by J.S. Mill, though McCulloch may have edited it; (see MacMinn *et al.*, 1945, p. 9). Nonetheless the end result was a significant labour of love, and without doubt the best edition of Smith prior to that of Edwin Cannan.[33]

The *Discourse on the Rise of Political Economy* was included in all of McCulloch's editions of the *Wealth of Nations*, from 1828 to 1863. Since this work is McCulloch's longest and most thoroughly considered essay on the history of economics, it is perhaps worth saying a little about it. It first appeared in Edinburgh in 1824, and its origins lie in the *Scotsman* article on the history of commerce referred to above, and in McCulloch's lecturing.[34]

[31]The obituary appeared in the *Edinburgh Annual Register (EAR)* for 1823 (Part II, pp. 392-403) and incorporated 'Works and Character of Mr. Ricardo', *Scotsman*, 6 December 1823, p. 777. Of the 35 paragraphs of the *Edinburgh Annual Register* obituary, twelve and a half (and a fragment of another) are from the *Scotsman* article. The longevity of the material was known to contemporaries; reviewing McCulloch (1846), Hodgskin regretted that he had not taken advantage of the lapse of time to produce a more balanced appraisal (*Economist*, 28 November 1846, pp. 1556-8). There are small changes to the old material; a reference to James Mill's 'clear and discriminating judgement' is removed (*EAR*, p. 396; McCulloch, 1846, p. xxi); comments on the Bullion Report are modified (*EAR*, pp. 396-7; McCulloch, 1846, pp. xxii-xxiii); material endorsing the Ricardian stagnation thesis is removed (*EAR*, pp. 398-9) and a paragraph added criticising that idea (McCulloch 1846 pp. xxv-xxvi); and endorsement of Ricardo's capital levy scheme and plan for a national bank is now retracted (*EAR*, pp. 400, 402; McCulloch, 1846, pp. xxviii, xxxi). But these are very minimal changes in the context of the essay as a whole.

[32]*Scotsman*, 27 September 1823, p. 618 (taxes on rent); ibid., 18 October 1823, p. 665 (taxes on profits); ibid., 1 November 1826, p. 689 (tithes). The corresponding pages are in McCulloch (1828, IV, pp. 535-53, notes XXII-XXV).

[33]This was the view of Jacob Viner (1965, p. 9).

[34]A three paragraph article 'Sketch of the Progress of Commercial Science in England in the Seventeenth Century, Part I', *Scotsman*, 19 January 1822, p. 22, is incorporated.

McCulloch commenced his activities as a teacher of economics in Edinburgh in 1820. He made a start with private classes, but in the winter of 1822-3 he began to deliver public lectures. These public lectures provided the foundation for McCulloch's appointment as Ricardo Memorial lecturer in London in 1824, and the first of the lectures was one on the history of economics.[35] It seems highly likely that the Edinburgh lectures had begun in the same way.

In 1825 a second edition of the *Discourse* appeared, and it was well received, notably by J.S. Mill (1825).[36] McCulloch (1825) incorporated it into the first edition of his *Principles of Political Economy* of that year, and the following year it appeared under a different title, as an *Historical Sketch of the Rise of Political Economy.*

It was clearly a work to which McCulloch, understandably, attached considerable importance. From the present point of view it is significant as establishing without question his credentials as a pioneer of writing on the history of economics.

11.3 McCulloch's Collections

11.3.1 Tracts on Commerce, 1856

This is one of the two volumes financed by the Political Economy Club and it is interesting to note that, when it was reprinted in 1952, the copy used was the one belonging to George Warde Norman, a stalwart of the Club since its earliest days as well as a very close friend of Overstone.[37] McCulloch

There is also a passage in the original version of the *Discourse* (McCulloch, 1824a, pp. 10-19), omitted from the version in the *Wealth of Nations*, which comes from another *Scotsman* article 'Nature of the Evidence from which Conclusions in Political Economy ought to be deduced – Mr Owen's Pretended Experiment shown to be no Experiment at all', (12 May 1821, p. 145).

[35] On McCulloch as a teacher see O'Brien (1970, ch. IV).

[36] However it seems that the review was partly by William Ellis – see the editorial note in Mill (1967, II, p. 757).

[37] The correspondence between Overstone and Norman forms the continuing thread in the three volumes of O'Brien (1971).

begins by explaining his motives in assembling the collection, including that of providing an accessible picture of the predominant seventeenth century mercantilist approach to trade. Items I and III are by Thomas Mun, famous as a defender of the foreign exchange transactions of the East India Company. McCulloch also has something to say about the work of Misselden, the spokesman for the Merchant Adventurers, though he does not include the latter's *Circle of Commerce*; see Viner (1937, p. 114). McCulloch explains the role of the balance of trade doctrine and makes the fair point that there were State resources involved in attempting to obtain a balance of payments surplus.

Between the Mun pamphlets comes one by Lewes Roberts, which McCulloch valued as displaying a remarkable depth of commercial knowledge. The fourth tract is by Samuel Fortrey. McCulloch rightly included this, since it was a source for other, and more important, writers especially Petty, but equally correctly, he is highly sceptical of the value of the contents of the work on other grounds.

The fifth tract, *England's Greatest Happiness*, published in 1677, has no known author – modern scholarship does not seem to have provided any enlightenment here. But McCulloch understandably admired the work and noted that, with the possible exception of its style, it would not have needed re-writing in the nineteenth century (p. x).[38] The pamphlet *Britannia Languens* is also anonymous. McCulloch, aware of the attribution to William Petyt, was doubtful about the authorship although that attribution is confirmed by the catalogue of the Goldsmiths' Library (Canney *et al.*, 1970-1975). Here, as elsewhere, we find McCulloch insisting that while there is much that is erroneous in the work it still contains much else that is of considerable interest.

The seventh tract is one of McCulloch's favourites, the *Discourses upon*

[38] In the remainder of this chapter, the page numbers (in lower case Roman letters) refer to the book edited by McCulloch given in the relevant subsubsection title.

Trade of 1691 by Dudley North. In fact the first part of this, upon which McCulloch drew for material in his *Discourse*, may actually have been written by Roger rather than Dudley North. But this is a finding of recent scholarship; see Letwin (1963, pp. 189-91).

The last tract in the volume, *Considerations on the East India Trade* did not carry the name of an author; but McCulloch's speculation that its author was Henry Martyn is endorsed by both the Goldsmiths' and Kress Library catalogues (Canney *et al.*,1970-75; Kress Library, 1940).

11.3.2 Tracts on Money, 1856

If the history of economic thought on commerce was the first to engage McCulloch's attention, that of economic thought on money seems to have followed very closely behind. The erudition which McCulloch had displayed in his *Encyclopaedia Britannica* article on money, in successive editions of that publication, bears witness to long immersion in the literature of the subject and a detailed knowledge of monetary history.[39]

The first tract is by Rice Vaughan. Despite Vaughan's error in believing that the value of metallic money depended on the official stamp, McCulloch finds much that has merit in the work. The next contribution is the speech of Sir Robert Cotton, apparently delivered in 1626 although not published until about 1679. McCulloch had drawn attention to this speech in his edition of the *Wealth of Nations*. No alternative author has subsequently been accepted although Sir John Hicks, who considered it a very fine speech, privately queried the attribution in correspondence with the present author.[40] At all events the speech contains a powerful argument against monetary inflation through a reduction in the value of the metallic standard, and McCulloch's judgement that 'we do not know that the arguments against such a proceed-

[39] McCulloch (1824b, 1842b, 1858)

[40] See for example McCulloch (1839, p. xxxvii). Cotton was not the author originally credited with the speech; McCulloch records that it was initially attributed to Sir Thomas Rowe.

ing have ever been stated more briefly or with greater force' (p. viii) is still valid. The next tract is an official report of the Council of Trade which, in an enlightened manner, recommended lifting the prohibition on the exportation of bullion and foreign coin. This is followed by Petty's *Quantulumcunque Concerning Money.* McCulloch considered Petty to be an important writer, and devoted some attention to him in his Historical Sketch and his *Literature of Political Economy.*[41] As he notes here, this particular work was more rare than others by Petty. McCulloch considered it well argued, both in relation to its opposition to depreciation of the currency and to the usury laws.

The next tract, by Lowndes, proposed precisely such a degradation. But McCulloch believed that it was still valuable for the information which it contained on the history of the silver coinage. Indeed the historical material undoubtedly influenced McCulloch himself in his own writings. McCulloch sketches the history of the controversy in which the proposal for depreciation was defeated. Locke and Newton both played an important part in the controversy. Though McCulloch does not reprint Locke, he does, with evident respect, reprint Newton's contribution.

The next tract was by Prior, who was the author of work on absenteeism which McCulloch, a participant in the nineteenth century controversy on this matter, judged to be factually valuable and theoretically mistaken.[42] The tract reprinted here dealt with coinage and it was judged by McCulloch to be with one exception 'the most valuable work on the coins of Ireland that had appeared down to a recent period' (p. xii).

The next, and very substantial, contribution is the *Essay on Money and Coins* by Joseph Harris. McCulloch praised the monetary understanding of this work, which opposed inflation, and went on to deal with the risks posed by an inconvertible paper currency. McCulloch was himself mildly supportive of a measure of inflation; but only where this was brought about by precious

[41] McCulloch (1826b, pp. 29-31; 1845a, pp. 155, 210, 211-12, 318).
[42] McCulloch (1825); see also O'Brien (1970, pp. 26, 41).

metal discoveries rather than by the creation of paper money.

The next tract, for which McCulloch gives no author, although modern scholarship believes it to have been by one G. Whatley, contained a discussion of Gresham's Law – which in this context meant that it was impossible to have a bi-metallic standard. This was something widely understood by the classical economists.

The final tract in the volume, by Matthew Raper, had previously been buried, as McCulloch notes, in Royal Society papers and only recently brought to light by other authors. It deals with Greek and Roman money.

McCulloch's interest in monetary history also led him to append to the volume a note on the recoinage of 1696-9 (which draws upon Gresham's Law and explains that it was precisely because of this that England, by chance, accepted a de facto gold standard from the beginning of the eighteenth century), tables showing changes in the standard and weight of English money, and, from a *Dictionary of Antiquities*, a table of Greek and Roman Coinage.

11.3.3 Tracts on Paper Currency and Banking, 1857

This volume really constitutes a complementary one to the 1856 volume on money. The first part of the introduction deals with the status of bank notes as money substitutes almost indistinguishable from money itself which, when convertible into gold, would normally circulate at their par value. As such, their status was relatively uncontroversial, though Hume opposed them. As McCulloch noted, the monetary literature only really began to develop when notes became inconvertible in 1797. Nonetheless the first pamphlet which he chose for inclusion is one of 1740, on paper currency in North America. McCulloch considered this an excellent exposition of the dangers of over-issue of paper money (in this case of bills). Modern research gives the name of the author, which was unknown to McCulloch, as one William Douglass (Kress Library, 1940).

This is followed by two short extracts from Hume's *Essays* of 1752, one from the essay on Money, and one from the essay on the Balance of Trade. McCulloch makes the perfectly valid point that, in his opposition to paper money, Hume failed to distinguish between convertible and inconvertible notes, but pays tribute to Hume's 'ingenuity and unrivalled felicity of illustration' (p. viii). These two extracts are followed by a paper by Patrick, Lord Elibank for which McCulloch had little respect. He merely included it as an example of literature opposed to paper currency.

It was followed by an extract from a work by the Scottish clergyman and economic writer Robert Wallace who is also famous for his writings on population. Wallace provided an analysis of paper currency which was a distinct advance, in some respects, on that in the previous two tracts.

McCulloch followed this work with one of his useful historical notes, on the 1797 suspension of convertibility of the note issue into gold. This note is itself followed by an anonymous essay on the usefulness of country banks. McCulloch (1836), who had advocated the establishment of banking in India with an argument along similar lines, approved the thesis put forward in this work that country banks improve the allocation of capital and enable savings to find outlets as investment. He took the opportunity however to say that it was quite unnecessary for such banks to issue notes – as indeed was the case. This relatively minor work is followed by one of the greatest documents in the history of monetary economics, Henry Thornton's *Paper Credit of Great Britain*, dating from 1802. McCulloch using, as Hayek (1939b, p. 58) was later to note, the American edition of 1807, reprinted the entire work. Although he believed Thornton mistaken on some matters, and attributed this to his supposed connection with the Bank of England, he endorsed the work as 'a most valuable contribution to our commercial literature' (p. xiii).

This is followed by another contribution by McCulloch, a note on the exchange between London and Dublin, which certainly provides clear evidence of the effects of over-issue of inconvertible notes.

The seventh tract is an extract from Lord Liverpool's work on coinage, the part dealing with the paper currency. McCulloch valued it both for the historical information it contained and for its forebodings about the effects of the suspension of convertibility.

This is followed by a reprint of Ricardo's *High Price of Bullion*. Reproducing, yet again, material from that 1823 obituary of Ricardo referred to earlier, McCulloch praises this publication while failing to note its lack of originality. Ricardo is followed in the volume by the Bullion Report which, despite its 'divided paternity' was still 'one of the most valuable papers that has ever proceeded from a Committee of the Legislature' (p. xvi). The following tract, that by William Blake, on exchange, receives high praise – McCulloch himself had certainly profited from it, not least in his own *Encyclopaedia Britannica* article 'Exchange' which followed Blake (with somewhat incomplete acknowledgement) in his distinction between the Real, Nominal, and Computed exchange.[43]

The last tract in the volume is William Huskisson's highly successful defense of the Bullion Report, of which he was indeed one of the authors. Huskisson is perhaps underrated as a monetary writer and this is a particularly fortunate inclusion in the volume.

McCulloch's collection is of considerable value. Indeed a better collection of works on paper currency, for the period covered by this volume – essentially that of the Suspension of Cash Payments – it would be hard to imagine, with the qualification that Lord King (1804) and Walter Boyd (1801) are both omitted from the volume.

[43]McCulloch provided an article on this subject to all three of the editions of the *Encyclopaedia* to which he contributed, the 6th, 7th, and 8th. For the last see McCulloch (1855).

11.3.4 Tracts on the National Debt, 1857

McCulloch was the author of the major work on public finance written by a classical economist, his *Treatise on the Principles and Practical Influence of Taxation and the Funding System*, editions of which appeared in 1845, 1852, and 1863.[44] The third part of this substantial work was devoted to the Funding System, that is to government borrowing. The volume of tracts on the National Debt provides a good selection of the important works on this topic, many of which were very scarce.

McCulloch considered government borrowing to be justified only under very limited circumstances – although, as he points out in the introduction, these certainly included the dangers faced by the new government after the Revolution of 1688.[45] But even justifiable borrowing left government with a problem – that of debt service. The problem of service was partially solved by borrowing on perpetuities, but high interest had to be paid at first. Government then proposed to deal with this by levying a special tax on the holders of government securities. The proposal was defeated, according to McCulloch, by the first two tracts in the volume. The first of them was believed, by McCulloch, to be the production of the Earl of Oxford. Modern scholarship attributes it, however, to Daniel Defoe (Kress Library 1940). The second tract, which McCulloch considered to be 'the more able of the two' (p. vii) was of unknown authorship although the Goldsmiths' Library Catalogue gives the author as A. Sykes (Canney *et al*, 1970-75).

The government then attempted to deal with the problem by the seductive idea of a Sinking Fund. A Sinking Fund was introduced in 1716 and it was supposed to buy back debt in the hands of the public. Ten years later Sir Nathanial Gould introduced the idea of compound interest into the argument. His proposition was that a Sinking Fund could accumulate at compound

[44] See O'Brien (1975) for details of the editions.
[45] See O'Brien (1975, pp. lv-lxiv, 401-63; 1992, pp. 263-9).

interest and thus wipe out the debt.

McCulloch reprints the tract by Gould, an attack on it by Pulteney, and a reply by Gould. But the controversy came to focus on a question of fact – whether the Fund had actually reduced the size of the debt between 1716 and 1726 – and the compound interest issue dropped out of sight until later in the century.

The sixth tract is Hume's attack upon public debt and the growth of a rentier class, together with his discussion of the possibilities of public bankruptcy. Hume's trenchant denunciation is followed by an extract from Blackstone's *Commentaries* which criticises the idea that the National Debt adds to wealth.

With the next tract, that of Richard Price, the subject of compound interest returns to the centre of the stage. Neither Hume nor Blackstone had referred to this issue, and the stage was thus left free for Price whose views were no more advanced than those of Gould but, as McCulloch notes, were stated 'with incomparably greater force and earnestness' (p. xii). Though Price was answered by other authors, including one Wimpey, whose work is included here as Tract X, these replies 'appear to have fallen still-born from the press. They attracted no attention and had no effect.' (p. xii). McCulloch, whose mathematical training was undoubtedly at its best in matters of compound interest and present values, was sufficiently in command of the mathematical argument to see that it was beside the point.[46] He explained in his introduction the fallacy of the sinking fund. The delusion put forward by writers like Price was reinforced by their mathematical competence; but, as McCulloch pointed out, the mathematics of compound interest were really irrelevant to the main issue. There was no source of revenue to be compounded, apart from taxation. If a penny compounded at 5 per cent at the time of the birth of Christ would have amounted in 1770 to an immense

[46] On McCulloch's mathematical training see O'Brien (1970, p. 70).

fortune, as Price had argued, such a fortune would all have been compounded tax revenue!

Unfortunately a belief in the power of the Sinking Fund actually encouraged governments to borrow, as McCulloch noted. The eleventh tract in the volume, that by Robert Hamilton, one which greatly influenced McCulloch's own work, exposed the fallacy of the whole operation and showed that the Sinking Fund had resulted in an increase in the size of the public debt.[47] Indeed, since the yield on the debt purchased by the Sinking Fund was less than the cost of the debt incurred to keep up the fund, borrowing for the purposes of maintaining a Sinking Fund actually increased public expenditure.

The Sinking Fund was abolished in 1829, but government began borrowing again in the early 1840s and the Sinking Fund returned to the political agenda in 1855. As McCulloch pointed out, unless government had a sufficient budget surplus to maintain payments into the fund it would indeed find itself engaged in additional borrowings to maintain such payments; in the last resort, the only effectual way to reduce public debt was to budget for a surplus.

11.3.5 Tracts on Commerce, 1859

Given McCulloch's life-long interest in the history of economic thought on commerce, it is perhaps appropriate that there should be a second volume of tracts on this topic, in addition to that of 1856 discussed above. He was indeed one of the foremost nineteenth century writers on commerce, and included amongst his publications a *Treatise on Commerce* (McCulloch, 1832a), written for the Society for the Diffusion of Useful Knowledge, and the hugely successful *Dictionary of Commerce* (McCulloch, 1832b) which first appeared in 1832, had 10 editions in McCulloch's lifetime, and continued to appear after his death.

---

[47] See O'Brien (1975, ed., pp. lxiii-lxiv, 452-9; 1992, pp. 268-9).

The first work in this volume is one on trade with the Dutch. McCulloch doubted that the author was Sir Walter Raleigh, and noted the suggestion that it was the work of one John Keymore (spelt 'Kymer' by McCulloch), an attribution which now seems to be accepted (Canney *et al.*, 1970-75). While the work exaggerated the strength of the Dutch, it had been influential in its lifetime and had useful observations concerning the circumstances which had produced Dutch prosperity.

The second tract was the production of John Evelyn. McCulloch's motive in reprinting this, which he knew to be a self-promoting work, was simply to demonstrate the kind of arguments used to support British claims to domination.

The third tract in this volume is the work of Daniel Defoe. McCulloch contrasts the failure of this excellent exposition of the benefits of trade and industry with the success enjoyed by another author, Gee, with an inferior work.

Gee had maintained, falsely, that trade was declining, leading McCulloch to the shrewd observation that 'when conscious of the contrary, people are rather well pleased to be reckoned unprosperous' (p. viii). But the supposed decline in foreign trade is the subject of the next pamphlet by Decker – an attribution made by Adam Smith which McCulloch rather doubted though Decker is still given as the author by both the Kress and Goldsmiths Library catalogues. McCulloch valued the work because although it started from a mistaken supposition, the remedies proposed – including the removal of protection – were sensible.

The fifth tract is by Josiah Tucker, Dean of Gloucester, of whom it was said, as McCulloch notes, that 'trade was his religion, and religion his trade' (p. x, n). The work was, in McCulloch's view, well written and interesting concerning the state of the country, and it offered sensible proposals even if it was too sanguine about the effects of State intervention. At the end of this tract McCulloch, who had a very marked interest in French history, as his *Catalogues* show, inserted a letter of Smollett dated 1765, which clearly foretold the revolution which was to follow in France 24 years later.

The sixth tract, an official document from Holland, on the rise and decline of Dutch trade, was of particular interest to McCulloch since it seems to have provided the basis for his *Edinburgh Review* article 'Rise, Progress, and Decline of Commerce in Holland' (McCulloch, 1830). It is followed by the seventh tract, which McCulloch was able to trace to a Mr William Temple, on the basis of a letter by Dean Tucker, published in a life of Lord Kames. The tract was itself a reply to a work which McCulloch regarded as inferior to it and as only having attracted attention because it had been published by the University of Cambridge. The Cambridge tract had been a romantic exposition of the simple life and an attack on trade, and it was forcefully repudiated by the work of Temple.

The last tract in the volume, comparing Smith's advocacy of freedom of trade with a restrictive system, McCulloch considered to be a fair and satisfactory exposition. He does not give an author for this but the Kress Library catalogue records that the copy in the Library of Congress gives the author as one William Vaughan (Kress Library, 1940).

11.3.6 Miscellaneous Economical Tracts, 1859

The first tract in this volume, which McCulloch praises as 'well-written and well-reasoned' (p. vi) was anonymous and McCulloch offers no view on possible authorship. It is now however believed to be by the celebrated Nicholas Barbon (son of the Puritan Divine, Praise-God Barebones).[48] This work explains the advantages of cities as centres of economic growth, in opposition to those who see them as a source of social corruption. McCulloch however takes issue with Barbon over the latter's belief that people in cities are more easily governed; McCulloch believes that this is not the case but that it is

[48] Kress Library (1940); Canney *et al.*, (1970-75). On Barbon's father see Hutchison (1988, p. 73).

not is, indeed, a further advantage of cities because the concentration of population increases democratic resistance to misgovernment.

The second tract is another one by Daniel Defoe. Indeed, without McCulloch's reprinting, it is doubtful whether Defoe would have been recognised as a writer on economics, at least until the exhaustive scholarly efforts of the present century. Defoe had attacked the idea of giving people in workhouses useful jobs to do, on the grounds that this displaced the demand for the output of normal market activity. McCulloch opposed this, invoking what is now known as Say's Law and extending it, possibly unwisely, to include public sector activities. Nonetheless, though he believed Defoe wrong on this matter, he found other material of value in the pamphlet, especially the material about pauperism.

The third tract is on Greenland and Whale Fishery. It is an interesting reminder of the fact that overfishing was a problem long before the fleets of the European Union and, a bit earlier, the Soviet Union. The author was one Henry Elking (Kress Library, 1940).

McCulloch's inclusion of the next tract, on pawnbroking, exemplifies both the width of his reading and the inaccuracy of the caricature of him, and indeed of other classical economists, as a laissez-faire dogmatist. For McCulloch believed in the desirability of the regulation of pawnbroking because of the inequality of bargaining between borrower and lender, and also because of the problem that the existence of pawnbrokers provided the opportunity for disposal of stolen goods. But he believed pawnbrokers provided a valuable service, and indeed that they helped to keep down crime, to which those in need would otherwise have to turn. The subject was one which interested McCulloch and he included quite a lengthy entry on the matter in his *Commercial Dictionary* (McCulloch, 1832b, pp. 819-23). McCulloch does not give an author for the tract; both the Goldsmiths' and Kress Library catalogues cautiously report Thomas Wise as the 'supposed author' (Kress Library, 1940; Canney *et al.*, 1970-75).

The inclusion of the next work again indicates the width of McCulloch's reading and the breadth of his sympathies. It is a reprint of the 1793 English translation of Turgot's great *Reflections.* As McCulloch rightly emphasises, the work was little known in England, even though Turgot was a major writer who influenced Smith (indeed McCulloch attributes Smith's overemphasis on the importance of agriculture to Turgot's influence) and who performed a valuable role as a public servant before his dismissal. McCulloch speculates that had Louis XVI supported Turgot, rather than dismissing him in the face of criticism, the Revolution might have been prevented.

The next tract illustrates a further aspect of McCulloch's work – his discovery, because of his interest in the history of economics, that the so-called 'Ricardian' theory of rent (which would be in any case, in the light of the work of Malthus, West and Torrens, an inaccurate label) originated not in 1815 but in 1777 in the work of the Scottish writer James Anderson. McCulloch refers also to the work of Malthus and West although there is no mention of Torrens, with whom he seems to have developed personal differences.[49] McCulloch points out that Anderson's theory was well based but was ignored; amongst those ignoring it was Adam Smith who could have learned from it – indeed McCulloch says that to Smith it 'might have been of infinite service' (pp. xvii-xviii).

We next come to a tract by Schomberg on the maritime laws of Rhodes. McCulloch had a considerable interest not merely in the literature of the classics but in Ancient History. Indeed his *Treatises and Essays* of 1853 contained both a Sketch of the Progress of Maritime Law and an Essay on the Colonial System of the Ancients (McCulloch, 1853, pp. 391-427). The practice of averaging losses amongst those with interests in a particular cargo passed from the law of Rhodes to that of Rome, and thus became the basis of the modern commercial legislation (pp. xviii-xix). This legal topic was a

[49]On the genesis of the rent theory see Robbins (1958, pp. 41-7). On the estrangement of McCulloch and Torrens, see O'Brien (1971, II, pp. 867-77, 921-2).

matter about which McCulloch (1842c) contributed an article to the seventh edition of *Encyclopaedia Britannica.*

The next tract, which McCulloch correctly identified as the work of Townsend, was an attack upon the whole idea of public provision for the poor. McCulloch disagreed – he favoured the Poor Law – but he still accepted that this was a very good statement of the opposing case.[50] He also commended the tract because of what Townsend wrote about population – 'not so much a foreshadowing of Malthus' theory, as the theory itself' (p. xx). Here, as in the case of the Anderson tract, we see McCulloch concerned with the scholarly attribution of priorities – an interest which may, one has to concede, have been intensified in this particular case (as it was not in the case of the 'Ricardian' theory of rent) by a personal antipathy to Malthus.

The ninth pamphlet is a reprint of Edmund Burke's *Thoughts and Details on Scarcity,* which was apparently written in 1795 though not published until 1800. Although the work had been reprinted in editions of Burke's works, McCulloch defended its inclusion here both on account of its being 'so brilliant a gem' (p. xxi) and on account of its being 'detached from the mass of other matters in which it is usually buried' .

One of the issues with which Burke had dealt in his tract was the prohibition of the use of corn for making spirits, at a time of harvest failure. This matter is the topic of the last tract in the volume, written by Archibald Bell, which appeared in 1808. McCulloch included it not only because of the, perhaps remote, chance that such a measure might be proposed in future, but also as 'an able and energetic protest against those ill-advised and quackish measures, by which it is attempted to stave off some immediate evil, or to gain some temporary advantage by trenching on those great principles, all tampering with which is sure to be productive of ruinous results' (pp. xxi-xxii).

[50] On McCulloch and the Poor Law see O'Brien (1970, ch. XIII).

11.4 Conclusions

Though McCulloch's trenchant style, so different from the measured and apparently judicious approach of Ricardo and other English writers, has frequently led later commentators to undervalue his work, he was a considerable scholar. The set of six volumes of tracts discussed in this chapter illustrates that scholarship, which has had much more influence on later historians of economic thought than they have admitted or, in all probability, been conscious of. He was genuinely interested in the history of his subject and was a major book collector as well. This set bears witness to both aspects of McCulloch's life and career and provides, at the same time, an excellent collection of economic literature from three centuries, much of it otherwise inaccessible.

Chapter 12

Samuelson: The Theorist as Historian of Economic Thought

Paul Samuelson enjoys a unique standing amongst twentieth century economic theorists. According to Kenneth Arrow (1967, p. 735), 'Samuelson is one of the greatest economic theorists of all time'. Frank Hahn recalls visiting MIT in 1956, and encountering Samuelson. Three and a half decades later he recalled the effect: 'Not only was Samuelson by far the cleverest and most versatile economist I had ever met, but he disposed of a wide and vast intellectual capital' (in Szenberg, 1992, p. 163).

But the vast intellectual capital to which Hahn refers has been productive of a large volume of work – a much larger volume than Samuelson himself seems to recognise, as we shall see – in which he has, like great theorists before him, especially Jacob Viner, approached theoretical problems through the history of economic thought, and the history of economic thought through modern theory. In this he is almost alone amongst leading theorists of recent decades, and his work has run counter to the steady narrowing of outlook amongst professional economists of all kinds.

This is all the more remarkable because Samuelson is above all a mathematical economic theorist. It has been said that he flaunts his mathematics (Fischer, 1987, p. 235), and although he declared in his pathbreaking *Foun-*

dations (1947) that mathematics is a language (and see 1952, II, p. 1751),[1] and was prepared to maintain as late as 1960 that it was not necessary to be a mathematician to be a theorist (1952, II, p. 1760; 1962, II, p. 1652), there is no mistaking either the mathematical character of the work or the lack of concession to readers (Fischer, 1987, p. 235) (though this is true also of some of his verbal expositions – e.g. 1967, III, pp. 644-5). Yet he clearly has not merely an interest in the history of economics, but a love for its literature, and has even (like another great theorist, Arrow – see Breit and Spencer, 1990, p. 44) lectured on the history of economic thought (1982, V, p. 633).

12.1 Samuelson's Historical Output

Paul Samuelson has described himself as the last generalist amongst economists, and explicitly listed the history of economics as one of his interests (1986, V, p. 800). But his work in this field has been neglected by others. In particular it is not discussed in Fischer's exemplary essay on Samuelson in *The New Palgrave* (Fischer, 1987).[2] But this is not surprising; not only are the majority of those who have written about Samuelson specialists, but the comment made by Bliss when reviewing Samuelson's *Collected Scientific Papers (CSP)* – that it needed a Samuelson to review them (Bliss, 1967, p. 338) – applies even to the subset covering the history of economic thought, even when the historical content of other papers is not taken into account.

Samuelson's own estimate is that around 5 per cent of his output is history of economic thought (1991, p. 3). Given the huge output – the *CSP* contain 388 articles, and the flow has continued unabated since their publication – this would represent a sizeable absolute amount. But in truth his figure involves a significant underestimate. Including a small number of papers on

[1] References to the *Collected Scientific Papers* (Samuelson, 1966-86) are of the form: date of first appearance of statement, followed by volume number and pages in the *Collected Scientific Papers*.

[2] But see Niehans (1990, pp. 170-1).

methodology, no less than 25 per cent of the papers in the *CSP* are concerned with economists and the history of economic thought, reasonably defined, and 22 per cent of the pages.

His Presidential address to the American Economic Association in 1961 was on 'Economists and the History of Ideas' (1961, II, pp. 1499-1516), and his 1969 Presidential Address to the International Economic Association was again concerned with the history of ideas (1969, III, pp. 675-85).

Amongst those who have specialised in the history of economic thought, Samuelson is taken seriously as a commentator (e.g. Hollander, 1980; see also Niehans, 1990, p. 425), and although his work has often been designedly provocative and controversial, he is generally good tempered as a controversialist (1960, I, pp. 370-2; 1972, IV, p. 227-83; 1973, IV, p. 284-8; 1974, IV, p. 298-97; 1980, V, p. 618-21). He clearly regards the issues as important – too important to be dismissed lightly – and regrets the decline in interest in the subject (1987a, pp. 181-2).

For Samuelson, history is an important subject (1969, III, p. 694), and there are lessons to be learned from economic history and from the history of economics (1999, p. 53). (Even detours may provide useful lessons in retrospect – 1974, IV, p. 296). Both analytical history – Samuelson's forte – and the kind of broader account of opinions to be found in texts like that of Gide and Rist are of value (1969, III, p. 676). Reference to the original texts is also important (1978, V, p. 598), though Samuelson is not a devotee of the textual analysis school.

History of economic thought is an important part of that essential intellectual pursuit, the history of ideas (1963, II, p. 1729). There is, in Samuelson's view, much to be learned about the creative process from the study of scientific biography (1969, III, pp. 676-7; 1983, V, pp. 846-8; 1998 p.1379).

Reading Samuelson's writings on the history of economics, one is struck by the importance which he attaches to scholarship – not something which can, any longer, be taken for granted amongst economists. This is part of what might be called 'scholarly hygene'; he believes that it is important to read what others have written on a subject before tackling it (1988c, p. 325), and is firmly convinced of the need to avoid subjective originality (1967, III, p. 688). This reflects an older, and truer, scholarly tradition; the modern practice of relying on citation indexes is no substitute for scholarship, as Samuelson implicitly notes in deploring 'the 365-day wonders that sweep and resweep our science' (1963, II, p. 527).

12.2 Background

12.2.1 Education

It seems that Samuelson attended a large number of schools (Fischer, 1987, p. 324),[3] and was, by his own account, an underachiever in high school (1985, V, pp. 844-5; 1986, V, p. 801). This is important when considering his achievments in the history of economic thought. For Samuelson did not arrive at economics after mathematics – unlike Friedman in his own generation (Breit and Spencer, 1990, pp. 81-2), and many modern American economists. He was thus exposed to economics first, and learned his mathematics as he went along, initially working, as he has revealed, with little mathematical equipment (1954, II, p. 1764n; 1986, V, p. 802).

His initial exposure to economics came at the University of Chicago, where his teachers included many famous names, but above all Jacob Viner. He then progressed as a graduate student to Harvard where he was again taught by teachers who combined a deep concern with economic theory with a great regard for its history, notably Schumpeter and Haberler. Along the way he managed to take two courses in economic history (1998a, p. 1379); but, more importantly, he came under the influence, at Harvard, of the mathematician

[3] Samuelson has however said that they (or some of them – he is not explicit) were good schools (1998, p. 1375).

E.B. Wilson who clearly recognised the extent of the talent in the graduate student (1969, III, p. 683; 1998, p. 1376; Fischer 1987, p. 234).

But perhaps above all, while absorbing these influences, Samuelson read voraciously (1967, III, p. 687-8). In dramatic contrast to the modern graduate student, whose command of the wider literature of economics is typically minimal, Samuelson considered it 'a matter of pride to do justice to the literature' (1967, III, p. 688) and he still reads exceptionally widely (1992b, p. 10).

12.2.2 Teachers

Viner

The importance of the influence of Jacob Viner on Samuelson's intellectual development cannot be overrated. Viner's teaching methods were notoriously ferocious, as Samuelson has confirmed; but the latter seems to have thrived in an environment which others found really unpleasant (1959, I, pp. 381, 391; 1963, II, p. 1738; 1972, IV, pp. 887, 908-14; 1980, V, p. 397). He developed enormous respect for Viner's intellectual powers, and has expressed the view that there has never been a greater neo-classical economist (1972, IV, p. 912).[4]

Viner approached the study of economic theory through the historical literature of the subject, and this approach was thus Samuelson's first exposure to graduate work. It has left him with a deep appreciation of Viner's achievments in the field, paying particular tribute to the great *Studies in the Theory of International Trade* (1988c, p. 322; Viner, 1937). Indeed he has said that he regards Viner's approach to the history of economic thought as the model one. The discussion should be both critical and constructive,

[4] Samuelson relates that Viner taught his students to replace 'Nihil nisi bonum' (Nothing unless good) as the motto of the obituarist with 'Nihil nisi verum' (Nothing unless true), thus making the task of writing Viner's obituaries particularly challenging (private correspondence).

making the best and worst cases of the historical material. But both parts are necessary; a scathingly critical approach, like that of Edwin Cannan, was not the right one (1987a, pp. 183-4; 1991a, p. 8).

Schumpeter

If Samuelson admires Viner unreservedly, his attitude to his Harvard teacher Schumpeter is much more complicated. Indeed, after referring to him as a 'brilliant economist and social prophet', the compliment is qualified by the description 'Half mountebank, half sage' (1971, III, p. 710).

On the one hand, Samuelson has expressed the view that Schumpeter was a good economist (1965, III, p. 774) – even that he is now undervalued (1983, V, pp. 270-1). He had his good points, notably his work on innovation and the business cycle, and his scholarship, and especially his great *History of Economic Analysis* (Schumpeter, 1954), is praised (1983, V, p. 279; 1987a, p. 186). But there is scorn for his reading of the depression of the 1930s in cyclical terms (1971, IV, p. 867; 1983, V, pp. 270-1), and his attitude to Keynes is obviously deeply resented (1983, V, pp. 272-3). But there is much more to the matter than intellectual differences. There are a number of cutting asides about Schumpeter in Samuelson's work, and a particular condescension towards the gap between Schumpeter's mathematical aspirations and his achievments and even – surprisingly – a questioning of his linguistic attainments (1963, II, pp. 1551-6; 1983, V, p. 793; 1994a, pp. 623n, 624).

There is no doubt that Schumpeter succeeded in interesting the Harvard students in the history of economic thought; Harry Johnson, another Schumpeter student at Harvard, published his first three articles in the field, as Samuelson noted (1977, V, p. 683). But Samuelson himself, unlike for instance George Stigler under Frank Knight (Breit and Spencer, 1990, pp. 97-8), did not choose a history of thought subject for his Ph.D; as all the world knows, he chose what is in the *Foundations*. It is clear that he found Schumpeter's personality and indeed his behaviour – inflation of grades for female students is mentioned (1976, IV, p. 905) – deeply irritating (1982, V, p. 302-3).

But in this he was not alone. The late George Shackle, a retiring personality of a completely different kind from that of Samuelson, was repelled by what he described as Schumpeter's 'bombast' when the latter visited LSE in the 1930s,[5] and undoubtedly there was much about personal contact with Schumpeter which tended to impede appreciation of his very real merits.

Haberler

It does not, however, appear to have been Schumpeter's Viennese affectations (1989b, p. 127) which upset Samuelson; his attitude to Gottried Haberler, another of his Harvard teachers, is far more positive. In an appreciative obituary, Samuelson recalled how Schumpeter would write flowery praise on his essays, but Haberler questioned every paragraph and really made him think (1995, p. 410). The latter's 1927 work on index numbers (Haberler, 1927) – a work so scholarly that it contains an allusion to the medieaval concepts of *lucrum cessans* and *damnum emergens* – may also have played some part in leading Samuelson towards his path-breaking Revealed Preference work.

12.3 Review of the Troops

As befits someone taught by Viner and Schumpeter, and himself enormously widely read, Samuelson has developed over the years a ranking of his great predecessors (e.g. 1946a, II, p. 152; 1991, p. 4; 1998, p. 1381). His greatest heroes are Smith, Walras and Keynes (1976, IV, p. 926; 1982, V, p. 870; 1983, V, p. 275; 1983, V, p. 262), though Cournot is sometimes admitted to this select gathering (e.g. 1946, II, p. 152; 1969, III, p. 679-80). These he awards alpha plus. The alpha team comprises Hume, Ricardo, J. S. Mill, Jevons, Pareto, Wicksell, and – surprisingly, in view of the number of

[5] Described in conversation with the author.

hostile comments about him to be found in Samuelson's writings – Marshall (1982, V, p. 870). Samuelson has a particular affection for Wicksell whose combination of scholarship and analytical powers he clearly finds appealing (1962, II, p. 1682).

The influence of Schumpeter is apparent in the evaluation of Walras; indeed Schumpeter's exaltation of Walras as the greatest of all economists, as far as pure theory is concerned, is explicitly endorsed by Samuelson (1952, II, p. 1756; 1981, V, p. 343).

Samuelson's consistently negative attitude to Marshall[6] is also consistent with Schumpeter's (cf. 1982, V, pp. 307-8; 1983, V, pp. 573-6), though the former avoids any direct acknowledgment, most of the time, and it seems likely that some of Samuelson's hostility was absorbed in a visit to Cambridge in the 1930s (1998, p. 1382). Yet it is not clear what the source of the hostility is, for the criticisms are asides in the context of other discussions, rather than a developed critique of Marshall himself (1961, II, pp. 1513-15; 1969, III, pp. 680-1; 1976, IV, p. 922; 1989b, p. 125; 1991a, p. 4). Partly, at least, the explanation may lie in resentment at what Samuelson regards as Marshall's negative influence on the mathematisation of economics, and some support for this can be found in his obituary of Hotelling where a suitably enthusiastic account of Hotelling's work is juxtaposed with negative comment about Marshall (1960, II, p. 1588). Further support can be found in an article on monopolistic competition (1967, III, pp. 18-51) where Marshall's ingenious hyperbolas for the analysis of monopoly are described as silly, even though it turns out that, by using them, Marshall side-stepped a problem which has been overlooked in the monopolistic competition literature (Creedy and O'Brien, 1990).

To the admirer of Alfred Marshall, it is rather sad to see the number of

[6]This dates from some of his earliest work; the *Foundations* contains 18 references to Marshall, almost all of them negative. Marshall's failure, as Samuelson sees it, to develop his system analytically after 1890 is also a source of regret (private correspondence).

instances in which Samuelson seeks to belittle Marshall. Indeed Samuelson goes so far as to describe himself as a 'debunker of Marshall' (1963, II, p. 1612).

In contrast, Pigou is venerated (e.g. 1941, II, pp. 1183-90;[7] 1947 p.207; 1954, II, p. 1763; 1958, II, p. 1233), despite acknowledgement of a key mistake in his welfare economics which had been pointed out by Allyn Young and others (1967, II, p. 26). Given Samuelson's enthusiasm for Keynes, this may seem rather surprising; but his view of Pigou is unorthodox, for he describes Pigou as a 'neo-Keynesian' (1950, II, p. 1759; 1963, II, p. 1596).

Samuelson is also very appreciative of the quality of Irving Fisher's work (1967, III, pp. 653-73) – again no doubt independently, though Fisher was also admired by Schumpeter. Indeed he is prepared to go so far as to defend Fisher's health faddism, if not his enthusiasm for Prohibition. He has argued that Fisher's *The Theory of Interest* (1930) anticipates the core of the micro analysis in Hicks's *Value and Capital*, and writes appreciatively of Fisher's pure theory work and his monetary theory, though he is less appreciative of the work on index numbers.

Samuelson is particularly impressed by Fisher's approach to the rate of interest. He agrees with Schumpeter's judgement that Böhm-Bawerk's and Fisher's theories of the rate of interest are fundamentally compatible (1967, III, pp. 661,673; 1994c, p. 204) – though some may feel that Samuelson's account of Böhm-Bawerk is too kind (1994c, p. 207) in that it does not bring out the fact that time preference disappears when Böhm-Bawerk explains market clearing for both labour and capital supplies in his *Positive Theory*, with the optimal period of production dependent on productivity. (It is also true that time preference is absent from the Wicksell-Dorfman mathematisation of Böhm-Bawerk).

Samuelson appreciated the quality of Hayek (1988c, p. 324), and recog-

[7] This is particularly remarkable for its date, for at that time Pigou was regarded with extreme disfavour by the Cambridge Keynesians.

nised – unlike many – that Hayek was the true victor in the Mises-Lange debate on socialist pricing (1971, IV, p. 876n; 1975, IV, p. 943; 1982, V, p. 315; 1983, V, p. 271), having focused on the problem of information (generated by market systems but unobtainable by planners) – though this is perhaps a little hard on Mises, in whose work this issue is present. Moreover Samuelson shows familiarity with Hayek's *Prices and Production* (1994c, p. 215; Hayek, 1931a), though he believes the work to be fundamentally faulty.

However, in common with many American authors, Samuelson misrepresents *The Road to Serfdom* (Hayek, 1944). It simply is not true that in that work Hayek 'warned that partial reform was the sure path to total tyranny' (1983, V, p. 791; see also 1975, IV, p. 942; O'Brien, 1998c, p. 226; and Chapter 9). In that connection it is interesting that even Hahn now believes the work to contain much good sense; see Szenberg (1992, p. 162).

Cassel is another economist who attracts Samuelson's unlikely sympathy. As a person, Samuelson seems to have found Cassel eminently dislikeable. According to Samuelson, 'Cassel made many claims to originality – indeed more than can be substantiated.' (1993, p. 518).But he conceded that the latter's reputation had fallen too far (1959, II, p. 1614; 1962, II, pp. 1686-7; 1982, V, p. 303).

In general, Samuelson's attitude to Cassel is similar to that of Schumpeter, but he believes that 'Cassel was an important theorist' (1993, p. 521), and criticised the *New Palgrave* article on the economist as patronising. It is important to get the history of economic thought right, and Cassel can be credited with important innovations. These include life cycle factors in the rate of interest, anticipation of Hotelling's economics of exhaustible resources, and, as early as 1918, an exponential growth model which anticipated Harrod-Domar (though the scholarly Samuelson points out that Hawtrey had got to this even earlier) (1993, pp. 521-4). Moreover his discussion of countercyclical monetary policy, and the role of the rate of interest in a socialist society, were meritorious, and Cassel can be defended over the dichotomisation of relative prices and the absolute price level.

While Samuelson's reference to Hicks, in a history of economic thought context, are limited (e.g. 1972, IV, p. 933-8), there is no doubt that he appreciated the importance of *Value and Capital*, a work which appeared while he was engaged in the research leading to his *Foundations* (1947, p. vii) and which must have presented a considerable challenge to Samuelson at the time.

Finally, mention should be made of Frank Knight. Knight made no secret of his dislike of both mathematical economists and Keynesians, a description which, as Samuelson wryly observed, fitted him perfectly (1972, IV, p. 886). But he recognised that 'It was the priceless contribution of Frank Knight and the Chicago School to remind us of the market's merits. This is a message that falls on deaf ears in the common rooms of Britain's ancient universities. But it is one whose relevance a Russian, Yugoslav or Czech can understand' (1972, IV, p. 886).

12.4 Samuelson's Approach: Whig History

Samuelson has noted that according to 'Voltaire (and Horace Walpole and Napoleon) ... history is a fable agreed upon. The history of economic thought is a series of fables not agreed upon' (1997, p. 179). The reasons for this are many. Firstly, there is the division between mainstream economists and Marxists, a group disproportionately represented in the study of the history of economic thought, for fairly obvious reasons. But more fundamentally there is no agreement on the correct way to write the history of economic thought.

Samuelson has however boldly proclaimed that there is one correct way – Whig History. He has proclaimed 'A Program for the Whig History of Economic Science' (1987a; 1991a, p. 3). The case for such an approach is that the insights of older writers may be better than their terminology (1998a,

p. 203). 'Modern analysis shows how Böhm-Bawerk can drop over-strong conditions and still retain much of his vision. Much but not all. The historian of doctrine cannot fully tell how it was without also telling how it can and cannot be' (1994c, p. 217). 'This is not "Whig History" with a complacent capital W. It is sympathetic elucidation of antiquarian fundamentals utilizing the latest knowledge.'(1994c, p. 219). Such an approach is kinder to previous economists, for instance the Physiocrats, than the alternative, which Samuelson unkindly calls the Antiquarian view (1998a, p. 205).

Of course such an approach is wide open to criticism, as imposing the structures of mathematical neo-Classicism – and one particular and disputable structure at that (Patinkin, pp. 145-6 in Samuelson *et al.*, 1991) – on economists who would have been bewildered by them. (Samuelson admits to detecting primitive neo-Classicism in earlier writers – 1992a, pp. 5-6). But Samuelson can reply that history of economic thought is impossible without the use of some theoretical structure; indeed Marxist interpretations are as vulnerable as Samuelson's to the above criticism. Moreover the customers appear to vote strongly in favour of a Whig approach, as exemplified by Mark Blaug's *Economic Theory in Retrospect* (1987a, p. 186; 1997, p. 180).

Another work applauded by Samuelson as an example of Whig history of economics is Schumpeter's *History* (1987a, p. 186; Schumpeter, 1954).

However it is Samuelson's own Whig history choices (1987a, pp. 186-7) which illustrate his position most clearly. They are his article 'Thünen at 200' (1983, V, pp. 575-97), his 'Canonical Classical Model' (1978, V, pp. 598-617) (discussed further below), his interpretation of Quesnay's *Tableau* as an anticipation of Input-Output analysis (1982, V, pp. 630-3), and his defence of Ricardo's chapter on machinery (1988b, 1989a). This is also discussed further below.

The key point which emerges from these examples is that – in the style of Jacob Viner – the key question to be addressed is whether an argument is right or wrong, or, perhaps more widely, under what interpretation of its logical structure can it be right, and how might it be wrong. The basic approach is thus wholly consistent with that of Viner to which Samuelson was exposed as a (very) young graduate student. What makes it different, however, is that Samuelson is able to draw upon a battery of mathematical techniques, which were not available to Viner, in order to elucidate the logical structure. (It may also be the case that, as in his endorsement of Collery's criticism of Hume – and of Viner (1980, V, pp. 397-414) – Samuelson is willing to impose upon a historical author a structure which that author would have rejected – O'Brien, 1995c, p. 59).

What emerges with crystal clarity from this is that Whig history is incompatible with a relativist approach to the history of economic thought (1974, IV, p. 298). Thus, despite a long flirtation with the ideas of Thomas Kuhn (1973, IV, p. 285; 1983, V, p. 277; 1985, V, p. 285), Samuelson has ultimately expressed the view that there is 'the Whig (anti-Kuhn) lesson: Even in ideological revolts, later does tend to be better in scholarly terms' (1997, p. 186).

Perhaps most fundamentally, Samuelson rejects the Kuhnian notion of incommensurability of paradigms (1983, V, p. 793). Rather he takes the Popperian view that knowledge is additive (1991a, p. 6) – in terms of Venn diagrams, the set of problems which the old paradigm addressed is a subset of the set addressed by the new paradigm (O'Brien, 1983b, p. 54). 'I believe that knowledge is additive and that the history of economic doctrine suggests that progress comes from unpredictable and varied sources' (1954, II, p. 1765). We see more than our predecessors; but we stand on their shoulders (1969, III, p. 693-4).

12.5 Samuelson and Classical Economics

Samuelson has displayed a life-long interest in Classical economics, which is hardly surprising in one deeply influenced by Jacob Viner. The Classical economists themselves were 'great scholars' and 'we stand on their shoulders' (1994a, pp. 630-1). But Classical economics is part of the unfinished business of economics; and Samuelson has attempted to take the agenda forward.

12.5.1 Adam Smith

Samuelson has made a major effort to revive the reputation of Adam Smith as a theorist, attempting to reverse the damage done by Ricardo (whose logical skills have been overrated, while those of Smith have been underrated) and then Schumpeter, whose opinion was not properly challenged because history of economic thought studies declined (1959, I, p. 421; 1961, II, pp. 505, 507; 1976, IV, pp. 862-4; 1977, V, pp. 622-9; 1992a). Samuelson has argued, rightly, that the charge that Smith determined rent and profit as residuals is false (1992a, pp. 3-4).

The reading of Smith is deliberately Whiggish (1977, V, pp. 622-9; 1978, V, pp. 598-617); Smith is credited with anticipating Leontief, and general equilibrium (even to equating price with marginal cost – 1976, IV, p. 683) and providing a model of economic growth with recurrent inventions. Moreover, in his analysis of economic growth, Smith 'envisioned so much more clearly than Ricardo... that the real wage is higher in the transient state of progressive growth' (1978, V, p. 600).

Smith, unlike Ricardo, was alive to the acute limitations of a labour theory of value – it could only be used where there was no land and no capital, and thus it could not explain exploitation (1990, p. 272). Conversely, land might well not be the only scarce factor, and profits could decline in ways ruled out by Ricardo but not by Smith – such as capital accumulation proceeding faster than the growth of the labour force (1988a, p. 203). Smith's model was both more general and more realistic than Ricardo's.

12.5.2 Ricardo

Samuelson considers Ricardo's *Principles* to be an 'overpraised work' (1988b, p. 274; see also 1991a, p. 8). 'One must never go overboard in praising the uneven Ricardo... Ricardo was away from school the day they taught the difference between necessary and sufficient conditions' (1988b, p. 278).

But Samuelson has provided a lengthy two-part article described as 'A Modern Treatment of the Ricardian Economy' (1959, I, pp. 373-407). This is essentially an interpretation of the (or perhaps 'a') Ricardian economy in terms of the apparatus set out in the classic text on linear programming of which Samuelson was co-author (Dorfman *et al.*, 1958).

The model deals with the pricing of labour and land services, and of goods, in terms of the linear programming apparatus, as well as with capital and interest. A key conclusion of the article is that we cannot 'get rid of rent' by going to the margin of cultivation once commodity substitution is allowed for, a conclusion which – though even the scholarly Samuelson was evidently unaware of this (1959, I, p. 379) – had been established thirty years earlier by D.H. Buchanan (1929).

However Samuelson is concerned to establish the more general point that exactly where the margin of cultivation falls depends on demand – the marginal employment of all factors depends on the composition of demand (1989b, p. 126; 1990, p. 272; 1992a, p. 7), so it is futile to seek a 'no-rent' margin and then attempt to explain the earnings of labour and capital. (This insight Samuelson has later (1999) extended illuminatingly to the vexed question of commodity money, reinforcing the conclusion (O'Brien, 1975, p. 146) that the mining margin is endogenous too).

Samuelson is thus led to be critical of the editorial introduction to the Sraffa edition of Ricardo, which should, he feels, have pointed this out – editors should be critical (1987a, p. 183; 1988a, p. 204; 1991a, p. 11). Ricardo was simply wrong to claim that only land shortage could cause profits to decline. (Samuelson also made some unsuccessful attempts to dispel the cloud of mystery concerning whether Sraffa or Dobb was responsible for the introduction – 1987a, pp. 184-5). While the Ricardo edition was superb from an 'antiquarian point of view', it was sadly lacking a critical editorial spirit – something which in truth is hardly suprising given Sraffa's resistance to the Harry Johnson demonstration of an error in Ricardo's rent theory, a demonstration which had, in any case, been completely anticipated by Cannan half a century earlier (1977, V, p. 684; O'Brien, 1999a, pp. 12-13; and Chapter 7).

12.5.3 Thünen

Samuelson's treatment of Thünen has been hailed as having 'shown brilliantly how a better mathematician might have extended the model to a general equilibrium system' (Niehans, 1990, p. 170). Certainly the treatment is impressive, and deeply appreciative of Thünen's achievment, crediting him with creating marginalism, managerial economics and general equilibrium (1983, V, pp. 575-97). The article makes strong claims for Thünen – his model is said to include comparative advantage, the so-called Ricardian theory of rent (correctly identified by Samuelson as the Malthus-West-Ricardo theory – only the name of James Anderson is missing),[8] Heckscher-Ohlin and Stolper-Samuelson theories of goods and factor pricing, and input-output (1983, V, p. 588). Moreover Samuelson manages to defend Thünen against earlier critics who had interpreted him in terms of a one-sector model, making the case for an interpretation on the basis of a two-sector model. It is perhaps not surprising that, as noted earlier, Samuelson selected this article as an exemplar of his Whig approach.

[8] However, see (1998b, p. 28).

12.5.4 The Canonical Model

Perhaps Samuelson's most controversial selection as an exemplar is his 'Canonical Classical Model' (1978, V, pp. 598-617). He set out to provide one model which would embrace the work of Smith, Ricardo, Malthus and J.S. Mill – even, with adjustments, Marx. His starting point was indeed Whiggish; he proclaimed the view that within every classical economist there was a modern one trying to be born (1978, V, p. 598). The model used is a one sector one, with output divided between consumption and investment, competitive determination of rewards to factors, a production function with land and combined labour and capital inputs, and equilibrium values for wages and profits where the long run supply of labour and capital is perfectly elastic at those values. The model exhibits a stable long-run equilibrium.

There are clearly some short cuts. Samuelson acknowledges that fixed combinations of labour and capital as inputs is 'a caricature' (1978, V, p. 606) and that a single-sector model hardly does justice to the classical vision (1978, V, p. 612), while the bold ascription to Adam Smith of concern with diminishing returns provided ammunition for his critics.

His critics focused on two main issues. Firstly, there was the historical evidence. Hollander (1980) had no difficulty in demonstrating that Ricardo and his contemporaries did not see in Smith what Samuelson maintains is there (and for which, indeed, Hollander, 1980, p. 559, conceded that textual support can be found) and thus they developed a model which was, as they saw it, truly distinct, in which diminishing returns played a central role. Secondly, there is the fact, pointed out by Kurdas (1988), that the first three chapters of the *Wealth of Nations* are concerned not with diminishing returns but with technical progress, with the technical change being clearly endogenous.

Samuelson, for his part, remains unrepentant (1991a, 1992b). In particular, he reiterates the point that Smith's model is more general, and can encompass the Ricardian one; profits can fall without land shortage, a matter on which Ricardo was simply wrong (1991, pp. 9-10).

12.5.5 Machinery

In two emphatic articles (1988b, 1989a) Samuelson, not otherwise an uncritical admirer of Ricardo as noted above, has come to the defence of Ricardo's chapter on machinery against the criticisms made by Wicksell, which have seemed cogent to almost all other commentators, as Samuelson noted. Wicksell's case, which was correctly restated by Jonung (1981), involved the following proposition: mechanisation will not create unemployment, as the fall in wages caused by initial displacement of labour following the introduction of machinery will render previous techniques again profitable and thus output will increase. Samuelson's model, however, involved only one technique. This result was achieved by setting wages at their long-run subsistence level in the model (see also Samuelson, 1992b). There was thus no scope for wages to fall any further as a result of mechanisation, and thus no scope for rendering old techniques profitable again. Samuelson had elsewhere remarked on Ricardo's tendency to telescope the long run and short run together (1959, I, pp. 414); here he turned this tendency to his (and Ricardo's) advantage.

12.5.6 The Classical 'Fallacy'

In an article published in 1994, Samuelson (1994a) displaying that impressive command of a literature ranging from Tugot through the Classical economists (including Thünen) to Böhm-Bawerk and Wicksell, charged the Classical writers with maintaining a persistent fallacy – that an increase in fixed capital lowered wages, while an increase in variable capital raised them. There were two essential parts to the prosecution case; firstly, circulating capital paid not only wages, but the cost of raw materials and extra spending on these would not raise wages. Secondly, there were various possible patterns of complementarity and competition between factors employed by different kinds of capital, and the existence of such possibilities ruled out simple conclusions of the kind that Samuelson accused the Classical writers of accepting. For instance 'a newly invented machine could... be *rival* to land and *complementary* to labour' (1994a, p. 621). In addition, 'fixed capital [should be] ...understood to be as capable of being rival to land as rival to labor'. Thus 'the psychological temptations to fall into the classical fallacy are neutralised' (1994a, pp. 629-30).

While the article can be seen as a valuable piece of ground clearing, it is only fair to point out that the Classical writers were hardly unaware of such possibilities, as may be seen from Torrens's *Wages and Combination* (1834); but faced with the world as it was, they were more exercised by the problem of the hand loom weavers than by land saving inventions, and in any case the Classical analysis of 'improvements' (technical advance in agriculture) recognised at least implicitly (in the work of Senior and McCulloch) that land saving inventions could raise wages.

12.6 Marx

To the reader of Samuelson's huge output, there is one persistent puzzle; his interest in, almost amounting to an obsession with, Marx. His knowledge of not merely the original texts but even the vast – and to most non-Marxists unattractive – secondary literature is astonishing, despite recognising clearly, as early as 1971, that Marxist economics had been decaying for 40 years (1971, IV, p. 878). At times he seems to be endlessly working out the curious mathematical conditions under which it could possibly be true that some theorem of Marx could be valid (e.g. 1971, III, pp. 276-308). At other times he seems to be trying to reclaim Marx from the Marxists and to make him into a mainstream economist (1974, IV, pp. 231-69) – he confessed to having leaned over backwards to make the best sense that he could of such peculiarly

Marxist concepts as value, 'explicitly passing up a few opportunities to expose confusions and logical contradictions' (1972, IV, p. 278).

According to Samuelson, 'I take Marx seriously' (1982, V, p. 869). In 1991 he claimed that he 'took Marx seriously because one out of four billion used to do so' (1991, pp. 4-5) – a claim rather undermined by the recollections of those who have lived under Marxist regimes. Yet he himself admits to being puzzled by the addiction of Japanese economists to Marx (1982, V, pp. 872-3), and the detached outsider instinctively searches for some explanation for Samuelson's own interest. One possibility is personal – his early association with the American Marxist Paul Sweezy (1976, IV, p. 901). Another is the repeated expressions of admiration for Marx delivered by Samuelson's teacher Schumpeter. Yet this seems unlikely. Samuelson regarded this admiration as a bit of a pose; Schumpeter's work had nothing in common with that of Marx (1976, V, pp. 349-50; 1981, V, p. 344; 1983, V, p. 272).

Perhaps the most important essay on Marxian economics which Samuelson has written is the 1957 'Wages and Interest. A Modern Dissection of Marxian Economic Models' (1957, I, pp. 341-69). This was guaranteed to upset the Marxists; not only was it the first appearance of Samuelson's description of Marx as 'A minor Post-Ricardian' (1957, I, pp. 368), but the author also endorsed long-standing criticisms of Marx by Böhm-Bawerk, Wicksteed and Pareto. Nevertheless, it was a serious discussion grounded, like the 1959 discussion of Ricardo, in the Dorfman, Samuelson and Solow work on linear programming, an approach which seemed the one most likely to be able to provide a basis for a constructive interpretation of Marx. Samuelson quickly got to the heart of the so-called Transformation Problem: 'a model based on equal rates of surplus value is like a made-up nursery tale of no particular relevance to the ascertainable facts of the simple competitive model' (1957, I, p. 347). But he managed to model Marx's 'Expanded Reproduction', producing a determinate solution consistent with technology and competitive markets

(1957, I, pp. 352-5), while noting the extraordinary difficulties created for capital accumulation by the Marxian fixed coefficients. 'The fixed-coefficient Marxian model makes all "real" accumulation impossible; there can be no technical "deepening of capital" in it.' (1957, I, p. 359). The equilibrium time path requires variations in technique in response to variations in the rate of profit (1957, I, p. 363).

From this it should be clear that Samuelson is no dewey-eyed admirer of the secular prophet Karl. Indeed he is regarded as an incisive critic (Blaug, 1985, pp. 290-3). His view of Marx is at most ambivalent and, as he acknowledges, his views are unpopular on the left (1998a, p. 1385). His classification of Marx as a minor post-Ricardian has already been noted; although he appeared to recant this description, which he has used more than once (1957, I, p. 368; 1961, II, p. 1510), in 1983 (1983, V, p. 263), he has since reused it (1991, pp. 4-5).

He holds that there are no insights into distribution (or indeed any real problem) to be gained from Marx (1982, V, pp. 873-4; 1991, p. 5), that Marx was wrong about immiserisation, monopolisation, and the increasing business cycle (1967, III, p. 274), and even, horror of horrors, accepts that Böhm-Bawerk's critique of Marx was 'essentially cogent and not captiously partisan' (1994c, p. 208).

He is dismissive of the surplus value concept – 'there is never macroeconomic or microeconomic advantage in rate-of-surplus-value analysis' (1975, IV, p. 304), and surplus value is simply a detour (1974, IV, pp. 289-97). It tells us nothing about capitalism, exploitation and distribution (1983, V, p. 359). 'To remedy Marx's Mehrwert paradigm is to reject it; even in the singular case where the paradigm is not numerically wrong, it contributes zero of extra understanding concerning distribution or exploitation or dynamic laws of capitalist development' (1997, p. 181). The idea that profit is the ratio of surplus value to capital and that this leads to a necessary decline in the rate of profit is dismissed (1990, pp. 274-5).

It is thus hardly suprising that Samuelson is also dismissive of the so-called Transformation Problem (1971, III, pp. 276-308) – the 'transformation' of Marxist 'values' into prices. According to Samuelson, this amounts to no more than erasing one set of figures and replacing it with another. Wittily verbalising the algebra of Seton's well-known article, with its price-value coefficients, Samuelson writes: 'The well-known transformation procedure... is... logically of the form: "Anything" equals "anything else" multiplied by "anything/anything else"' (1970, III, p. 309).

In this connection Samuelson hardly mentions the so-called Invariance Postulates (1973, IV, p. 286 touches on it) – total price equal to total value and total profit equal to total (imputed) surplus – over which Marxist writers have toiled; he clearly considers the issue to be of no importance.

Ricardo's labour theory of value is dismissed – changes in consumer demand must still alter wage and profit shares, without any change in the rate of profit while changes in profit rates generally alter relative prices (1971, III, p. 282; 1987a, p. 187); 'As soon as changed composition of demand for goods alters *endogenously marginal* labour embodiments, nothing substantive is left of the labour theory of value' (1992a, p. 8). But Marx had attempted to go down the same road (1971, III, p. 282). Price ratios are invariant to interest rate changes if and only if all industries have the same capital-labour ratios (1983, V, pp. 375-8).

Given the strength of these sustained criticisms, the reader naturally wonders where Samuelson sees merit in Marx's writings. It turns out that it is the scheme of steady and expanded reproduction – the circular flow – in Marx's neglected second volume of *Kapital* which attracts Samuelson's admiration (1974, IV, pp. 323-54; 1976, IV, p. 863; 1988a, p. 206; 1990, p. 266; 1991a, pp. 4-5). 'Marx's own finest *analytical* work came in this area of circular interdependence' (1982, V, p. 631).

But there was nothing original in this. It can be traced back to Quesnay whose *Tableau* Marx revered. (Schumpeter's influence in this judgement is apparent – 1982, V, p. 630). Moreover, there is nothing inconsistent with mainstream economics – even with Hayek – in Marx's treatment of this material (1974, IV, p. 242). 'What is valid in this seminal contribution is in no sense contrary to mainstream economics of predecessors, contemporaries, or successors' (1974, IV, p. 254).

Not unnaturally such an evaluation led to some disagreements not merely with avowed Marxists but also with those, especially in Cambridge, who sought to build on the Marxist analysis and what they regarded as the Ricardo-Marx alternative (alternative, that is, to mainstream economics) tradition. Samuelson's attitude towards Joan Robinson (despite her admiration for Stalin, Castro, Mao, Kim il Sung) and Sraffa seems, despite their disagreements, to have been generous (Samuelson, 1988c, 1989b), though it would seem that this generosity was not entirely reciprocated (Feiwel, 1982, p. 25, n. 12). In particular, it is clear that Samuelson genuinely admired Sraffa (1987a, pp. 184-5), despite seeing clearly that the latter's famous 1926 *Economic Journal* article was neither particularly original nor without error (1989b, p. 125; 1990, p. 269); and it is clear that Sraffa's work exercised a considerable influence on Samuelson's own writings on Marx, an influence explicitly acknowledged (1973, IV, p. 284; 1982, V, p. 632; 1983, V, pp. 385-6). Samuelson was, too, happy to acknowledge the worth of Joan Robinson as an adversary (1989b) despite some caustic – and merited – comments about the intellectual struggles in which it had apparently been necessary for the Cambridge economists to engage in order to discover (subjectively) the first derivative of total revenue (1967, III, p. 23; 1972, IV, p. 895n).

12.7 Keynes

That Samuelson placed Keynes in the Pantheon – his select group of the three greatest economists of all time – has already been noted. Samuelson mentions Keynes in the same breath as Newton and Einstein (1971, IV, p. 874) and has described him as 'the greatest economist since Adam Smith and Leon Walras' (1976, IV, p. 926). It is true that in 1946 Samuelson wrote that he did not understand the *General Theory* until the mathematical formulations by Hicks and others (1946, II, pp. 1517-33); and both then and later he expressed the belief that the author of the work did not understand it either (1951, II, p. 1578). But his admiration for the work is clearly profound (1971, IV, p. 874; 1976, IV, p. 926); indeed 'the *General Theory* provided the tools of analysis for classical writers to understand and defend their own views. If only Say, James Mill and Ricardo had lived after 1936, think of what sense they might have made of Say's Law!' (1963, II, p. 1537).

So powerful was the Keynesian message that Samuelson , who had a good knowledge of the business cycle literature (1975, IV, pp. 854-7), at one stage believed the business cycle to have been abolished – a pull on a Keynesian lever here, an adjustment of a valve there, and activity could be stabilised so that the idea of a cycle was no longer appropriate (1959, II, pp. 1619-20, 645-7; 1963, II, pp. 1537-8).

Samuelson's Keynesianism has however to be distinguished from the British variety with its endogenous money supply. 'How is it' he asked 'that some Keynesians should ever have become identified with the doctrine that money doesn't matter? ... for a quarter of a century before 1936, Keynes was the principal exponent on monetary theory. The *General Theory* represented a continuation of culmination of many of his monetary doctrines' (1971, IV, p. 769). Though Samuelson was sharply critical of Friedman, and of monetarism in general, he applauded the emphasis on money in the writings of those he called 'eclectic post-Keynesians', and in 1983 confessed to having been 'sharply critical of the Neanderthal Keynesian that still dominated British economics as recently as 20 years ago' – a dating which is actually very kind to the British economic establishment which showed signs of being 'Neanderthal' long after 1963 (Eltis, 1993, p. xxi). As Samuelson observed 'The Radcliffe committee testimony testifies to the moribund state of the subject in the home counties' (1983, V, p. 277).

Yet there is a puzzle in this which deserves attention. Samuelson identifies the core of the Keynesian message, correctly in my view, as instability of the investment function. Yet this is not picked up by the mathematical models which he believes made sense – both for him and for Keynes – of the *General Theory*. It is Shackle, and even Leijonhufvud – whose interpretation Samuelson explicitly rejects, on the grounds that Keynes had plenty of opportunity to disagree with Hicks and others, and did not (1982, V, p. 859) – who are much closer to the message on this reading.

12.8 Short Essays

Samuelson excels at the short essay on a distinguished economist. His portraits of Nobel Prize winners in economics are models of their kind, providing excellent examples of the skills of the accomplished historian of economic thought – stating issues compactly, clearly and fairly. The exposition is helped by the fact that Samuelson is really interested in economists as people (1988c). Even where he has had sharp public differences with a subject, he is still capable of a fair and affectionate appraisal, most notably in his portrait of Milton Friedman (1976, IV, pp. 944-5). He has produced generous and perceptive tributes to, amongst others, Seymour Harris (1975, IV, pp. 917-20), Alvin Hansen (1976, IV, pp. 921-8), Wassily Leontief (1973, IV, pp. 939-40) and Franco Modigliani (1987b).

Samuelson paid particular tribute to Hansen's influence in the development of the concept of the Balanced Budget Multiplier (1976, IV, p. 928), a topic on which he has himself published a separate essay (1975, IV, pp. 841-53) – history of economic thought from the inside, so to speak.

He has provided essays on Kahn (1994b) (raising the apparently taboo subject of how far Kahn was responsible for solving technical problems faced by Joan Robinson in her *Imperfect Competition*), Meade (1977, V, pp. 831-

2), Stone (1984, V, pp. 841-3), Debreu (1983, V, pp. 838-40), Tobin (1981, V, pp. 834-7), Okun (1980, V, p. 826), Lloyd Metzler (1980, V, pp. 827-30), and Ohlin (1977, V, pp. 831-2; 1981, V, pp. 809-25). While appreciative of the latter's scholarly, and indeed personal, qualities, Samuelson however adheres to the Patinkin view that the Stockholm School in the 1930s were more concerned with the price level than the income level. This is reasonable, given that they were essentially developing the macroeconomics of Wicksell, and Samuelson does accept that there were implied changes in income involved in the analysis.

12.9 *Foundations* and *Economics*

The vast majority of Samuelson's output has been in the form of articles – indeed he seems to believe, in the conventional American manner, that books are not read (1987a, p. 186). But he has published two very different books, both of them in their own way highly inflential, and both testify to the scholarship standards that he sets himself.

In 1947 Samuelson published his *Foundations*, a work which, amongst its other achievments, effectively rewrote the required technical standard for professional economists. However there was another characteristic of the book which has attracted much less attention, even though Samuelson alludes to it in his 1998 essay on the origins of the book. This is its scholarship (Fischer, 1987, p. 236). It may have been less remarkable in the context of the 1940s, but in the days when 'provincialism in time' has become elevated to the level of a professional virtue, it is salutary to see the huge range of the historical literature of economics on which the author of this pathbreaking theoretical work drew. From Bentham to Wicksell, from Dupuit via Launhardt, Senior, and Thünen to Walras, the book is a monument to the scholarship, as well as the theoretical virtuosity, of its young author.

The following year Samuelson published the single most influential introductory textbook of all times, simply called *Economics*. The witty George Stigler, as Samuelson has noted, remarked that the author, having achieved fame (with the *Foundations*) was now seeking fortune (Samuelson, 1986, V, p. 803). In that he was not disappointed. But there is much more to be said.

For *Economics* stresses the historical literature of the subject. Later editions have even contained a genealogical diagram, showing the lines of development from the Schoolmen and the Greeks; and throughout the text there are references to the great names of the subject.

But perhaps most striking of all, the history of economic thought content of the book has actually increased in successive editions, defiantly swimming against the tide. While a modern competitor, the text by Begg *et al.* (1987), mentions Smith four times, Ricardo once (in a note), and no other great figure of the previous centuries, a comparison of Samuelson's first (1948) and eleventh (1980) editions reveals the history of economic thought content to have *increased* sharply. There are no fewer than 23 extra historical figures mentioned in the text – even Thomas More and Copernicus make an appearance. Moreover the number of references to the great figures has increased sharply. Those to Ricardo (and Schumpeter) have increased about fivefold; those to Smith sixfold. Those to Marx have increased by a factor of eight.

12.10 Conclusions

Paul Samuelson has his foibles as a historian of economic thought. He sometimes seems unable to spell the name of McCulloch (who often appears as 'McCullough', though even 'McCullouch' is not unknown – e.g. 1977, V, p. 688; 1983, V, p. 270; 1989a, p. 49; 1991a, p. 5). More seriously, he seems to have a blindspot about Dennis Robertson (1941, II, p. 1185; 1963, II, pp. 1593-1612; 1964, III, pp. 640-2). While it is not hard to sympathise with the view that Robertson's *Banking Policy and the Price Level* is unreadable (1963, II, p. 1594) (which would hardly make it unique amongst economic literature), there is much more to Robertson's work than that, as John Presley's full length study (Presley, 1978) has made clear; and it is unfortunate that Samuelson's obituary article on Robertson was so negative[9] that it brought forth a reply (Wright, 1964). It seems, moreover, that the nub of the matter was not scientific; Samuelson made clear in the obituary that the award of an honorary degree to Robertson by Harvard in 1936 (a year of such deep significance to Keynesians) rankled deeply (1963, II, pp. 520-1). Given the range and subtlety of Robertson's work, it is a disappointment that it did not stimulate Samuelson to apply his analytical powers to disentangling the threads.

Set against Samuelson's erudition and achievement in the history of economic thought, and remembering that this is only a minority – though a much bigger minority than its author seems to appreciate – of his output, the foibles are mostly minor matters. They are far outweighed by many positive factors. These include the erudition which recognises that Bagehot advanced a multiplier-like concept (1985, V, p. 288), that knew of Cairnes's challenge to Jevons (to tell the world what new and undiscovered truths had been laid bare by the employment of mathematics; see 1952, II, pp. 1755-6), that had encountered rare work by Cliffe Leslie (1963, II, pp. 1733), and that could produce interesting and scholarly reflections even when merely ruminating on a subject (1963, II, pp. 1738-47).

In addition to this Samuelson, who prizes good judgement in others (1980, V, p. 826), can lay claim to good judgement, based on the intellectual capital referred to at the beginning of this paper, on a number of issues in the history of economic thought. These include the 'discovery' of marginal revenue (1961, II, p. 1502), the limited nature of Ricardo's influence on the free trade movement and the repeal of the Corn Laws (1961, II, pp. 1507-8), his early questioning (though later revised) of the substance of Keynes's admiration for

[9] Though its author feels that it was written with laudatory intent (private correspondence).

Ramsey's work on saving (1946, II, p. 1528), the recognition of the probable priority of Torrens over Ricardo in the formulation of comparative advantage (1969, III, p. 678), and of the worth of J.S. Mill (1961, II, pp. 1508-10), and his appreciation of the much greater width of Smith's vision compared with that of Ricardo (1978, V, p. 600).

Samuelson is in the line of the great theorists in economics who have also been scholars – men like Edgeworth, Jevons and Wicksell, and his own teacher Jacob Viner. Given the development of the profession in the last few decades, the reader cannot but fear that he may be one of the last, so that the profession will be condemned to go round in circles rediscovering things. Let us hope that his example may help to keep scholarship alive.

Bibliography

[1] Allen, W.R. (1965) Discussion. *American Economic Review*, 55 (Supplement), pp. 143-5.

[2] Anderson, G.M. and Tollison, R.D. (1986) Dead men tell no tales. *History of Economics Society Bulletin*, 8, pp. 59-68.

[3] Andrews, P.W.S. (1949) *Manufacturing Business*. London: Macmillan.

[4] Andrews, P.W.S. (1964) *On Competition in Economic Theory*. London: Macmillan.

[5] Aréna, R. (1994) Hayek and modern business cycle theory. In *Money and Business Cycles: The Economics of F.A. Hayek, vol. II* (ed. by M. Colonna and H. Hagemann), pp. 203-17. Aldershot: Edward Elgar.

[6] Aréna, R. (2002) Monetary policy and business cycles: Hayek as an opponent of the quantity theory tradition. In *F.A. Hayek as a Political Economist* (ed. by J. Birner, T. Garrouste and T. Aimar), pp. 64-78. London: Routledge.

[7] Arrow, K.J. (1962) Economic welfare and the allocation of resources for invention. In *The Rate and Direction of Inventive Activity: Economic and Social Factors* (ed. by R. Nelson), pp. 609-28. Princeton: Princeton University Press.

[8] Arrow, K.J. (1967) Samuelson collected. *Journal of Political Economy*, 75, pp. 730-37.

[9] Arrow, K.J. and Hahn, F. (1971) *General Competitive Analysis*. Edinburgh: Oliver and Boyd.

[10] Ashley, W.J. (1891) The rehabilitation of Ricardo. *Economic Journal*, 1, pp. 474-89.

[11] Attwood, T. (1816-43) *Selected Economic Writings* (ed. by F.W. Fetter). London: London School of Economics.

[12] Babbage, C. (1832) *On the Economy of Machinery and Manufactures*. London: Knight.

[13] Backhaus, J. (1986) History of economic thought - what for? Empirical observations from German universities. *History of Economics Society Bulletin*, 8 (Winter), pp. 60-66.

[14] Backhouse, R.E. (1985) *A History of Modern Economic Analysis*. Oxford: Blackwell.

[15] Backhouse, R.E. (1992) Should we ignore methodology? *Royal Economic Society Newsletter*, 78, pp. 4-5.

[16] Backhouse, R.E. (1995) *Interpreting Macroeconomics*. London: Routledge.

[17] Backhouse, R.E. (1996) Economics is a historical process. In *Foundations of Research in Economics: How Do Economists Do Economics?* (ed. by S. Medema and W. Samuels), pp. 7-17. Cheltenham: Edward Elgar.

[18] Backhouse, R.E. (1997) *Truth and Progress in Economic Knowledge*. Aldershot: Edward Elgar.

[19] Backhouse, R.E. (1998) *Explorations in Economic Methodology: From Lakatos to Empirical Philosophy of Science*. London: Routledge.

[20] Backhouse, R.E. (2002a) *The Penguin History of Economics*. London: Penguin.

[21] Backhouse, R.E. (2002b) Don Patinkin: interpreter of the Keynesian revolution. *European Journal of the History of Economic Thought*, 9, pp. 186-204.

[22] Bailey, S. (1825) *A Critical Dissertation on the Nature, Measure and Causes of Value*. Reprinted (1931), London: London School of Economics.

[23] Barber, W.J. (1998) Not so dismal a science: reflections. *Journal of the History of Economic Thought*, 20, pp. 177-89.

[24] Baring, F. (1797) *Observations on the Establishment of the Bank of England & the Paper Circulation of the Country*. Reprinted (1967), New York: A.M. Kelley.

[25] Barkai, H. (1967) The empirical assumptions of Ricardo's '93 per cent' labour theory of value. *Economica*, 34, pp. 418-23.

[26] Barry, N. (1979) *Hayek's Social and Economic Philosophy*. London: Macmillan.

[27] Barry, N. (1988) *The Invisible Hand in Economics and Politics: Hobart Paper No. 111*. London: Institute of Economic Affairs.

[28] Barry, N., Burton, J., Gissurarson, H., Gray, J., Shearmur, J., Vaughn, K. and Seldon, A. (1984) *Hayek's 'Serfdom' Revisited.* Hobart Paperback 18, London: Institute of Economic Affairs.

[29] Barton, J. (1817) *Observations on the Circumstances which Influence the Condition of the Labouring Classes.* London: J. and A. Arch.

[30] Barucci, P. (1983) Pantaleoni, Einaudi, and the history of economic 'dogma'. *Research in the History of Economic Thought and Methodology*, 1, pp. 79-92.

[31] Begg, D., Fischer, S. and Dornbusch, R. (1987) *Economics*, 2nd ed. London: McGraw Hill.

[32] Behe, M. (1996) *Darwin's Black Box: The Biochemical Challenge to Evolution.* New York: Free Press.

[33] Bellante, D. (1994) The Phillips curve. In *The Elgar Companion to Austrian Economics* (ed. by P. Boettke), pp. 372-7. Aldershot: Edward Elgar.

[34] Bellante, D. and Garrison, R.W. (1988) Phillips curves and Hayekian triangles: two perspectives on monetary dynamics. *History of Political Economy*, 20, pp. 207-34.

[35] Benassi, C. (1987) An input-output formulation of the 'coefficient of money transactions': a note on Hayek's trade cycle theory. *Economica Internazionale*, 1, pp. 1-19. Reprinted in *Friedrich A. Hayek: Critical Assessments, vol. 4* (ed. by J.C. Wood and R.N. Woods), pp. 263-79 (1991), London: Routledge.

[36] Bhaskar, V. and Machin, S. (1993) Pricing asymmetries. In *Small Business Enterprise: An Economic Analysis* (ed. by G. Reid), pp. 172-186. London: Routledge.

[37] Bhaskar, V., Machin, S. and Reid, G. (1991) Testing a model of the kinked demand curve. *Journal of Industrial Economics*, 39, pp. 241-54.

[38] Bhaskar, V., Machin, S. and Reid, G. (1993) Price and quantity adjustment over the business cycle. *Oxford Economic Papers*, 45, pp. 257-68.

[39] Birner, J. and van Zijp, R. (eds.) (1994) *Hayek, Co-ordination and Evolution.* London: Routledge.

[40] Black, R.D.C. (1945) Trinity College, Dublin, and the theory of value, 1832-1863. *Economica*, 12, pp. 140-48.

[41] Black, R.D.C. (1947) Economic studies at Trinity College, Dublin - I. *Hermathena*, 70, pp. 65-80.

[42] Black, R.D.C. (1948) Economic studies at Trinity College, Dublin - II. *Hermathena*, 71, pp. 52-63.

[43] Black, R.D.C. (1960a) *Economic Thought and the Irish Question 1817-1870.* Cambridge: Cambridge University Press.

[44] Black, R.D.C. (1960b) Jevons and Cairnes. *Economica*, 27, pp. 214-32.

[45] Black, R.D.C. (1962) W.S. Jevons and the economists of his time. *Manchester School*, 30, pp. 203-21.

[46] Black, R.D.C. (1965) Review of A.B. Cramp, *Opinion on Bank Rate. Victorian Studies*, 9, pp. 60-62.

[47] Black, R.D.C. (1967) Parson Malthus, the general and the captain. *Economic Journal*, 77, pp. 59-74.

[48] Black, R.D.C. (1968) Economic policy in Ireland and India in the time of J.S. Mill. *Economic History Review*, 2nd series, 21, pp. 321-36.

[49] Black, R.D.C. (1970) Introduction to W.S. Jevons *The Theory of Political Economy*, pp. 7-40. Harmondsworth: Penguin.

[50] Black, R.D.C. (ed.) (1971) *The Economic Writings of Mountifort Longfield.* New York: A.M. Kelley.

[51] Black, R.D.C. (1972a) Jevons, Bentham and De Morgan. *Economica*, 39, pp. 119-34.

[52] Black, R.D.C. (1972b) Jevons, marginalism and Manchester. *Manchester School*, 40, pp. 2-8.

[53] Black, R.D.C. (1972c) W.S. Jevons and the foundation of modern economics. *History of Political Economy*, 4, pp. 364-78.

[54] Black, R.D.C. (ed.) (1973-1981) *Papers and Correspondence of William Stanley Jevons, vol. 7.* London: Macmillan.

[55] Black, R.D.C. (1976) Smith's contribution in historical perspective. In *The Market and the State: Essays in Honour of Adam Smith* (ed. by T. Wilson and A.S. Skinner), pp. 42-63. Oxford: Oxford University Press.

[56] Black, R.D.C. (1982) Political economy and the Irish. *History of Economics Society Bulletin*, 4, pp. 33-47.

[57] Black, R.D.C. (1983) The Irish dissenters and nineteenth-century political economy. *Hermathena*, 135, pp. 120-37.

[58] Black, R.D.C. (1988a) Bentham and the political economists of the nineteenth century. *Bentham Newsletter*, 12, pp. 24-36.

[59] Black, R.D.C. (1988b) Editing the papers of W.S. Jevons. In *Editing Modern Economists* (ed. by D. Moggridge), pp. 19-42. New York: AMS Press.

[60] Black, R.D.C. (1992) Dr. Kondratieff and Mr. Hyde Clarke. *Research in the History of Economic Thought and Methodology*, 9, pp. 35-58.

[61] Black, R.D.C. and Könekamp, R. (eds.) (1972) *Papers and Correspondence of William Stanley Jevons. Vol. I. Biography and Personal Journal.* London: Macmillan with the Royal Economic Society.

[62] Blaug, M. (1956) The empirical content of Ricardian economics. *Journal of Political Economy*, 64, pp. 41-58.

[63] Blaug, M. (1980) *The Methodology of Economics.* Reprinted (1982), Cambridge: Cambridge University Press.

[64] Blaug, M. (1985) *Economic Theory in Retrospect,* 4th ed. Cambridge: Cambridge University Press.

[65] Blaug, M. (1987) Classical economics. In *The New Palgrave: A Dictionary of Economics* (ed. by J. Eatwell, M. Milgate and P. Newman), vol. I, pp. 434-45. London: Macmillan.

[66] Blaug, M. (1988) Commentary. In *Classical Political Economy* (ed. by W.O. Thweatt), pp. 132-36. Boston: Kluwer.

[67] Blaug, M. (1992) Commentary. In *Austrian Economics: Tensions and New Directions* (ed. by B. Caldwell, and S. Böhm), pp. 31-4. Boston: Kluwer.

[68] Blaug, M. (1994) Why I am not a constructivist: confessions of an unrepentant popperian. In *New Directions in Economic Methodology* (ed. by R.E. Backhouse), pp. 109-136. London: Routledge.

[69] Blaug, M. (1999) Misunderstanding classical economics: The Sraffian interpretation of the surplus approach. *History of Political Economy*, 31, pp. 213-36.

[70] Blinder, A. (1991) Why are prices sticky? Preliminary results from an interview study. *American Economic Review Papers and Proceedings*, 81, pp. 89-96.

[71] Bliss, C.J. (1967) Review of collected scientific papers of Paul A. Samuelson. *Economic Journal*, 77, pp. 338-45.

[72] Blundell, J. (2005) Hayek, Fisher and *The Road to Serfdom.* In F.A. Hayek *The Road to Serfdom* (new edition). pp. 22-33. London: Institute of Economic Affairs.

[73] Boethke, P. (1989) Evolution and economics: Austrians as institutionalists. *Review of the History of Economic Thought and Methodology*, 6, pp. 73-89.

[74] Boettke, P.J. (ed.) (1994) *The Elgar Companion to Austrian Economics.* Aldershot: Edward Elgar.

[75] Böhm, S. (1992) Austrian economics between the wars: some historiographical problems. In *Austrian Economics: Tensions and New Directions* (ed. by B. Caldwell and S. Böhm). Boston: Kluwer.

[76] Böhm, S. (1994) Hayek and knowledge: some question marks. In *Money and Business Cycles. The Economics of F.A. Hayek, vol. II* (ed. by M. Colonna, H. Hagemann and O. Hamouda) pp. 160-77 (1994). Aldershot: Edward Elgar.

[77] Böhm-Bawerk, E.v. (1884-9) *Kapital und Kapitalzins*, 2 vols. Innsbruck: Wagner.

[78] Boland, L.A. (1978) Time in economics vs. economics in time: the Hayek problem. *Canadian Journal of Economics*, 11, pp. 240-62.

[79] Bonn, M.J. (1906) *Modern Ireland and her Agrarian Problems.* Translated by T.W. Rolleston. Dublin: Hodges Figgis.

[80] Booker, C. and North, R. (1994) *The Mad Officials.* London: Constable.

[81] Bork, R.H. (1978) *The Antitrust Paradox.* New York: Basic Books.

[82] Bowley, A.L. (1935) Obituary: Edwin Cannan. *Economic Journal*, 45, pp. 385-92.

[83] Boyd, W. (1801) *A Letter to the Right Hon. William Pitt on the Influence of the Stoppage of Issues in Specie at the Bank of England on the Prices of Provisions and other Commodities.* London: Wright.

[84] Breit, W. and Spencer, R. (eds.) (1990) *Lives of the Laureates*, 2nd ed. Cambridge, Massachusetts: MIT Press.

[85] Buchanan, D.H. (1929) The historical approach to rent and price theory. *Economica*, 9, pp. 123-55.

[86] Butler, E. (1983) *Hayek: His Contribution to the Political and Economic Thought of our Time.* London: Temple Smith.

[87] Butos, W.N. (1985) Hayek and general equilibrium analysis. *Southern Economic Journal*, 52, pp. 332-43.

[88] Butos, W.N. (1994) The Hayek-Keynes macro debate. In *The Elgar Companion to Austrian Economics* (ed. by P. Boettke), pp. 471-7. Aldershot: Edward Elgar.

[89] Cairnes, J.E. (1874) *Some Leading Principles of Political Economy Newly Expounded.* London: Macmillan.

[90] Caldwell, B. (1988) Hayek's transformation. *History of Political Economy*, 20, pp. 513-41.

[91] Caldwell, B. (1989) Austrians and institutionalists: the historical origins of their shared characteristics. *Review of the History of Economic Thought and Methodology*, 6, pp. 91-100.

[92] Caldwell, B. (1994) Four theses on Hayek. In M. Colonna, H. Hagemann and O. Hamouda (eds.) (1994b), pp. 117-30. Aldershot: Edward Elgar.

[93] Caldwell, B. (2004) *Hayek's Challenge: An Intellectual Biography of F.A. Hayek*. Chicago: University of Chicago Press.

[94] Caldwell, B. (ed.) (1995) *Contra Keynes and Cambridge: The Collected Works of F.A. Hayek, vol. 9*. London: Routledge.

[95] Caldwell, B. and Böhm, S. (eds.) (1992) *Austrian Economics: Tensions and New Directions*. Boston: Kluwer.

[96] Cannan, E. (1888) *Elementary Political Economy*. Oxford: Oxford University Press.

[97] Cannan, E. (1892a) The Malthusian anti-socialist argument. *Economic Review*, Jan, pp. 71-87.

[98] Cannan, E. (1892b) The origins of the law of diminishing returns, 1813-1815. *Economic Journal*, 2, pp. 53-69.

[99] Cannan, E. (1893) *A History of the Theories of Production and Distribution in English Political Economy from 1776 to 1848*, 2nd ed. (1903). London: P.S. King.

[100] Cannan, E. (1895) The probability of a cessation of the growth of population in England and Wales during the next century. *Economic Journal*, 5, pp. 505-15.

[101] Cannan, E. (1896) (ed.) *Lectures on Justice, Police, Revenue and Arms, Delivered in the University of Glasgow by Adam Smith*. Oxford: Clarendon.

[102] Cannan, E. (1901) The recent decline in natality in Great Britain. *Fortnightly Review*. Reprinted as 'Forecast of natality made in 1901', in *Economic Scares*, pp. 125-35 (1933). London: P.S. King.

[103] Cannan, E. (ed.) (1904) *Adam Smith: An Enquiry into the Nature and Causes of the Wealth of Nations*. London: Methuen.

[104] Cannan, E. (1912) *The Economic Outlook*. London: P.S. King.

[105] Cannan, E. (1914) *Wealth: A Brief Examination of the Causes of Economic Welfare*, 3rd ed. (1928). London: P.S. King.

[106] Cannan, E. (1919/1925) *The Paper Pound of 1797-1821*, 2nd ed. (1925). London: P.S. King. Reprinted (1969), London: Frank Cass.

[107] Cannan, E. (1921) The meaning of bank deposits. *Economica*, 1, pp. 28-36.

[108] Cannan, E. (1923) Adam Smith on twentieth century finance. *Economica*, 3, pp. 93-97.

[109] Cannan, E. (1924a) Limitation of currency or limitation of credit? *Economic Journal*, 34, pp. 52-68.

[110] Cannan, E. (1924b) Discussion on monetary reform. *Economic Journal*, 34, pp. 155-162.

[111] Cannan, E. (1924c) Alfred Marshall 1842-1924. *Economica*, 4, pp. 257-61.

[112] Cannan, E. (1926a) Adam Smith as an economist. *Economica*, 6, pp. 123-34.

[113] Cannan, E. (1926b) *Money: Its Connexion with Rising and Falling Prices*, 5th ed. London: P.S. King.

[114] Cannan, E. (1927) *An Economist's Protest*. London: P.S. King.

[115] Cannan, E. (1929) *A Review of Economic Theory*. London: P.S. King.

[116] Cannan, E. (1931) The changed outlook in regard to population, 1831-1931. *Economic Journal*, 41, pp. 519-533.

[117] Cannan, E. (1932) Review of Robbins, *An Essay on the Nature and Significance of Economic Science*. *Economic Journal*, 42, pp. 424-7.

[118] Cannan, E. (1933a) *Economic Scares*. London: P.S. King.

[119] Cannan, E. (1933b) The need for simpler economics. *Economic Journal*, 43, pp. 367-78.

[120] Cannan, E. (1935) Pages from an Autobiography. *Clare Market Review*, Michaelmas, pp. 16-17.

[121] Canney, M., Knott, D. and Gibbs, J. (1970-1975) *Catalogue of the Goldsmiths' Library of Economic Literature, 2 vols.* Cambridge: Cambridge University Press.

[122] Cantillon, R. (1730). *Essai sur la Nature du Commerce en Général.* Translated by H. Higgs. Reprinted (1964), New York: A.M.Kelley.

[123] Chacholiades, M. (1986) *Microeconomics*. London: Collier Macmillan.

[124] Chamberlin, E.H. (1933) *The Theory of Monopolistic Competition*. 2nd ed. (1936). Cambridge, Massachusetts: Harvard University Press.

[125] Chamberlin, E.H. (1948) An experimental imperfect market. *Journal of Political Economy*, 56, pp. 95-108.

[126] Cheung, S.N. (1973) The fable of the bees: an economic investigation. *Journal of Law and Economics*, 16, pp. 11-33.

[127] Churchill, W.S. (1952) *The Second World War, vol. V. Closing the Ring*. London: Cassel.

[128] Clapham, J.H. (1922) Of empty economic boxes. *Economic Journal*, 32, pp. 305-14.

[129] Clarke, A. (1993) *Diaries*. London: Weidenfeld and Nicholson. Reprinted (1994), Phoenix.

[130] Coase, R.H. (1937) The nature of the firm. *Economica*, 4, pp. 386-405.

[131] Coase, R.H. (1960) The problem of social cost. *Journal of Law and Economics*, 3, pp. 1-44.

[132] Coase, R.H. (1972) The appointment of Pigou as Marshall's successor. *Journal of Law and Economics*, 15, pp. 473-85.

[133] Coase, R.H. (1974) The lighthouse in economics. *Journal of Law and Economics*, 17, pp. 357-376.

[134] Coase, R.H. (1975) Marshall on method. *Journal of Law and Economics*, 18, pp. 25-31.

[135] Coase, R.H. (1982) Economics at LSE in the 1930s: a personal view. *Atlantic Economic Journal*, 10, pp. 31-4.

[136] Coase, R.H. (1984) Alfred Marshall's mother and father. *History of Political Economy*, 16, pp. 519-27.

[137] Coase, R.H. (1990) Alfred Marshall's family and ancestry. In *Alfred Marshall in Retrospect* (ed. by R. McWilliams Tullberg), pp. 9-27. Aldershot: Edward Elgar.

[138] Coats, A.W. (1961) Alfred Marshall and Richard T. Ely: some unpublished letters. *Economica*, 28, pp. 191-4.

[139] Coats, A.W. (1964) The role of authority in the development of British economics. *Journal of Law and Economics*, 7, pp. 85-106.

[140] Coats, A.W. (1967a) Sociological aspects of British economic thought (ca. 1880-1930). *Journal of Political Economy*, 75, pp. 706-29.

[141] Coats, A.W. (1967b) Alfred Marshall and the early development of the London School of Economics: some unpublished letters. *Economica*, 34, pp. 408-17.

[142] Coats, A.W. (1968a) Political economy and the tariff reform campaign of 1903. *Journal of Law and Economics*, 11, pp. 181-219.

[143] Coats, A.W. (1968b) The origins and early development of the Royal Economic Society. *Economic Journal*, 78, pp. 349-71.

[144] Coats, A.W. (1972) Comment. *Journal of Law and Economics*, 15, pp. 487-95.

[145] Coats, A.W. (1973) The economic and social context of the marginal revolution of the 1870s. In *The Marginal Revolution in Economics* (ed. by R.D.C. Black, A.W. Coats, C.D. Goodwin), pp. 37-58. Durham, NC: Duke University Press.

[146] Coats, A.W. (1983a) John R. Commons as a historian of economics: the quest for the antecedents of collective action. *Research in the History of Economic Thought and Methodology*, 1, pp. 147-61.

[147] Coats, A.W. (1983b) T.W. Hutchison as a historian of economics. *Research in the History of Economic Thought and Methodology*, 1, pp. 187-207.

[148] Coats, A.W. (1983c) The first decade of HOPE. *History of Political Economy*, 15, pp. 303-19.

[149] Coats, A.W. (1987) Economics, history and hope. *History of Economics Society Bulletin*, 8(2), pp. 1-20.

[150] Coats, A.W. (1996) Memoirs of an economist watcher. *Journal of the History of Economic Thought*, 18, pp. 250-70.

[151] Cochran, J. and Glahe, F. (1999) *The Hayek-Keynes Debate – Lessons for Current Business Cycle Research*. Lampeter: Edwin Mellen.

[152] Cockett, R. (1995) *Thinking the Unthinkable*. London: Fontana.

[153] Coddington, A. (1975) The rationale of general equilibrium theory. *Economic Inquiry*, 13, pp. 539-58.

[154] Collard, D. (1981) A. C. Pigou, 1877-1959. In *Pioneers of Modern Economics in Britain* (ed. by D.P. O'Brien and J.R. Presley), pp. 105-39. London: Macmillan.

[155] Collard, D. (1992) Review of J. Creedy, *Demand and Exchange in Economic Analysis: A History from Cournot to Marshall*. *Manchester School*, 60, pp. 333-4.

[156] Colonna, M. (1994) Hayek's trade cycle theory and its contemporary critics. In *Money and Business Cycles: The Economics of F.A. Hayek, vol. II* (ed. by M. Colonna and H. Hagemann), pp. 27-52. Aldershot: Edward Elgar.

[157] Colonna, M. and Hagemann, H. (eds.) (1994a) *Money and Business Cycles: The Economics of F.A. Hayek, vol. I*. Aldershot: Edward Elgar.

[158] Colonna, M., Hagemann, H., Hamouda, O. (eds.) (1994b) *Capitalism, Socialism and Knowledge: The Economics of F.A. Hayek, vol. II.* Aldershot: Edward Elgar.

[159] Cosimano, T.F. (1981) The incentive to adopt cost reducing innovation in the presence of a non-linear demand curve. *Southern Economic Journal*, 48, pp. 97-104.

[160] Cossa, L. (1893) *An Introduction to the Study of Political Economy.* Translated by L. Dyer. London: Macmillan.

[161] Creedy, J. (1986) *Edgeworth and the Development of Neoclassical Economics.* Oxford: Blackwell.

[162] Creedy, J. (1989) Whewell's 'Translation' of J.S. Mill. Reprinted in *The History of Economic Analysis* (1998). Cheltenham: Edward Elgar.

[163] Creedy, J. (1990) Marshall and Edgeworth. *Scottish Journal of Political Economy*, 37, pp. 18-39.

[164] Creedy, J. (1992) *Demand and Exchange in Economic Analysis.* Aldershot: Edward Elgar.

[165] Creedy, J. and O'Brien, D.P. (1990) Marshall, monopoly and rectangular hyperbolas. *Australian Economic Papers*, 29, pp. 141-53.

[166] Cunningham, A. (1950) *William Cunningham, Teacher and Priest.* London: SPCK.

[167] Cunningham, W. (1892) The perversion of economic history. *Economic Journal*, 2, pp. 491-506.

[168] Cunningham, W. (1893) Review of E. Cannan, *A History of the Theories of Production and Distribution. Economic Journal*, 3, pp. 493-4.

[169] Dahrendorf, R. (1995) *LSE: A History of the London School of Economics and Political Science.* Oxford: Oxford University Press.

[170] Dalton, H. (1927) Professor Cannan's general contribution. In *London Essays in Economics: In Honour of Edwin Cannan* (ed. by T.E. Gregory and H. Dalton), pp. 3-27. London: Routledge.

[171] De Marchi, N. (1970) The empirical content and longevity of Ricardian economics. *Economica*, 37, pp. 257-76.

[172] De Marchi, N. and Lodewijks, J. (1983) HOPE and the journal literature in the history of economic thought. *History of Political Economy*, 15, pp. 321-43.

[173] De Vivo, G. (1994) Comment. In *Money and Business Cycles: The Economics of F.A. Hayek, vol. I* (ed. by M. Colonna and H. Hagemann), pp. 94-7. Aldershot: Edward Elgar.

[174] DeLamarter, R.T. (1986) *Big Blue: IBM's Use and Abuse of Power.* New York: Dodd Mead.

[175] Demsetz, H. (1969) Information and efficiency: another viewpoint. *Journal of Law and Economics*, 11, pp. 1-22.

[176] Demsetz, H. (1988) *Ownership, Control, and the Firm.* Oxford: Blackwell.

[177] Demsetz, H. (1989) *Efficiency, Competition and Policy.* Oxford: Blackwell.

[178] Demsetz, H. (1995) *The Economics of the Business Firm.* Cambridge: Cambridge University Press.

[179] Desai, M. and Redfern, P. (1994) Trade cycle as a frustrated traverse: an analytical reconstruction of Hayek's model. In *Money and Business Cycles: The Economics of F.A. Hayek, vol. II* (ed. by M. Colonna and H. Hagemann), pp. 121-43. Aldershot: Edward Elgar.

[180] Deutscher, P. (1990) *R.G. Hawtrey and the Development of Macroeconomics.* London: Macmillan.

[181] Desai, M. (1994) Equilibrium, expectations and knowledge. In *Hayek, Co-ordination and Evolution* (ed. by J. Birner and R. van Zijp), pp. 25-50. London: Routledge.

[182] De Vivo (1994) Comment. In *Money and Business Cycles: The Economics of F.A. Hayek, vol. II* (ed. by M. Colonna and H. Hagemann), pp. 94-7. Aldershot: Edward Elgar.

[183] Dickens, M. (1978). *An Open Book.* London: Heinemann.

[184] DiLorenzo, T. (1994) Industrial organisation and the Austrian school. In *The Elgar Companion to Austrian Economics* (ed. by P. Boettke), pp. 382-8. Aldershot: Edward Elgar.

[185] DiQuattro, A. (1986). Rawls versus Hayek. *Political Theory*, 14, pp. 307-10.

[186] Director, A. (1945) Review of F.A. Hayek, *The Road to Serfdom. American Economic Review*, 35, pp. 173-5.

[187] Dolan, E.G. (ed.) (1976) *The Foundations of Modern Austrian Economics.* Kansas: Sheed and Ward.

[188] Dorfman, R., Samuelson, P.A. and Solow, R. (1958) *Linear Programming and Economic Analysis.* New York: McGraw Hill.

[189] Dornbusch, R. (1976) Expectations and exchange rate dynamics. *Journal of Political Economy*, 84, pp. 1161-76.

[190] Dostaler, G. (1994) The formation and evolution of Hayek's trade cycle theory. In *Money and Business Cycles: The Economics of F.A. Hayek, vol. II* (ed. by M. Colonna and H. Hagemann), pp. 147-67. Aldershot: Edward Elgar.

[191] Dowd, K. (1988). *Private Money: Hobart Paper No. 112.* London: Institute of Economic Affairs.

[192] Dowd, K. (1994) Free banking. In *The Elgar Companion to Austrian Economics* (ed. by P. Boettke), pp. 408-13. Aldershot: Edward Elgar.

[193] Dowd, K. (1995) Deflating the productivity norm. *Journal of Macroeconomics*, 17, pp. 717-32.

[194] Durbin, E. (1945) Professor Hayek on economic planning and political liberty. *Economic Journal*, 55, pp. 357-70.

[195] Eatwell, J. (1975) The interpretation of Ricardo's essay on profits. *Economica*, 42, pp. 182-7.

[196] Ebenstein, A. (2001) *Friedrich Hayek.* Basingstoke: Palgrave.

[197] Edgeworth, F.Y. (1881) *Mathematical Psychics.* London: Keegan Paul.

[198] Edgeworth, F.Y. (1891) The objects and methods of political economy. Reprinted in *Papers Relating to Political Economy, vol. I*, pp. 3-12 (1925), London: Macmillan.

[199] Edgeworth, F.Y. (1903) Review of E. Cannan, *A History of the Theories of Production and Distribution*, 2nd ed. *Economic Journal*, 13, pp. 624-27.

[200] Edwards, J.R. (1980) Monopoly and competition in money. *Journal of Libertarian Studies*, 4, pp. 107-17. Reprinted in *Friedrich A. Hayek: Critical Assessments, vol. 3* (ed. by J.C. Wood and R.N. Woods), pp. 145-55 (1991), London: Routledge.

[201] Eisner, M.A. (1991) *Antitrust and the Triumph of Economics.* N. Carolina: University of North Carolina Press.

[202] Ellis, H.S. (1934) *German Monetary Theory 1905-1933.* Cambridge, Massachusetts: Harvard University Press.

[203] Ellis, H.S. and Fellner, W. (1943) External economies and diseconomies. *American Economic Review*, 33, pp. 493-511.

[204] Eltis, W. (1984) *The Classical Theory of Economic Growth.* London: Macmillan.

[205] Eltis, W. (1993) *Classical Economics, Public Expenditure and Growth.* Aldershot: Edward Elgar.

[206] Fay, C.R. (1937) Edwin Cannan: the tribute of a friend. *Economic Record*, 13, pp. 1-21.

[207] Feiwel, G. (1982) Samuelson and contemporary economics: an introduction. In *Samuelson and Neoclassical Economics* (ed. by G. Feiwel), pp. 1-28. Boston: Kluwer-Nijhof.

[208] Feiwel, G. (1987) *Arrow and the Ascent of Modern Economic Theory*. London: Macmillan.

[209] Ferguson, C.E. (1973) The specialisation gap: Barton, Ricardo, and Hollander. *History of Political Economy*, 5, pp. 1-13.

[210] Fetter, F.W. (1953) The bullion report re-examined. In *Papers in English Monetary History* (ed. by T.S. Ashton and R.S. Sayers), pp. 66-75. Oxford: Clarendon.

[211] Fetter, F.W. (1969) The rise and decline of Ricardian economics. *History of Political Economy*, 1, pp. 67-84.

[212] Finer, H. (1945) *Road to Reaction*. Boston: Little Brown.

[213] Fischer, S. (1986) Friedman versus Hayek on private money. *Journal of Monetary Economics*, 17, pp. 433-9.

[214] Fischer, S. (1987) Samuelson, Paul Anthony. In *The New Palgrave: A Dictionary of Economics, vol. 4* (ed. by J. Eatwell, M. Milgate, P. Newman), pp. 234-41. London: Macmillan.

[215] Fisher, F.M. (1989) Games economists play: a noncooperative view. *Rand Journal of Economics*, 20, pp. 113-24.

[216] Fisher, F.M., McGowan, J.J. and Greenwood, J.E. (1983) *Folded, Spindled, and Mutilated: Economic Analysis and U.S. v. IBM*. Cambridge, Massachusetts: MIT Press.

[217] Fisher, I. (1930) *The Theory of Interest*. New York: Macmillan.

[218] Flam, H. and Flanders, M.J. (ed. and translated) (1991) *Heckscher-Ohlin Trade Theory*. Cambridge, Massachusetts: MIT Press.

[219] Foss, N.J. (1995) More on Hayek's transformation. *History of Poltiical Economy*, 27, pp. 345-64.

[220] Friedman, M. (1974) Comments on the critics. In *Milton Friedman's Monetary Framework: A Debate with his Critics* (ed. by R.J. Gordon). Chicago: University of Chicago Press.

[221] Friedman, M. and Schwartz, A.J. (1963) *A Monetary History of the United States: 1867-1960*. Princeton, NJ: Princeton University Press.

[222] Galbraith, J.K. (1948) The German economy. In *Foreign Economic Policy for the United States* (ed. by S.E. Harris), pp. 91-103. Cambridge Massachusetts: Harvard University Press.

[223] Gårdlund, T. (1958) *The Life of Knut Wicksell.* Stockholm: Almqvist & Wiksell.

[224] Garrison, R.W. (1985) Intertemporal coordination and the invisible hand: an Austrian perspective on the Keynesian vision. *History of Political Economy,* 17, pp. 309-21.

[225] Garrison, R.W. (1989) The Austrian theory of the business cycle, in the light of modern macroeconomics. *The Review of Austrian Economics,* 3, pp. 3-29.

[226] Garrison, R.W. (2001) *Time and Money: The Macroeconomics of Capital Structure.* London: Routledge.

[227] Gissurarson, H. *et al.* (1984) *Hayek's 'Serfdom' Revisited: Hobart Paperback No. 18.* London: Institute of Economic Affairs.

[228] Goldschmid, H.J., Mann, H.M. and Weston, J.F. (1974) *Industrial Concentration: the New Learning.* Boston: Little Brown.

[229] Goodwin, C.D. (1980) Towards a theory of the history of economics. *History of Political Economy,* 12, pp. 610-19.

[230] Gordon, B. (1976) *Political Economy in Parliament 1819-1823.* London: Macmillan.

[231] Gordon, B. (1989) *The Economic Problem in Biblical and Patristic Thought.* Leiden: E.J. Brill.

[232] Gordon, D.G. (1965) The role of the history of economic thought in the understanding of modern economic theory. *American Economic Review,* 55 (Supplement), pp. 119-27.

[233] Grampp, W.D. (1965) On the history of economic thought and policy. *American Economic Review,* 55 (Supplement), pp. 128-35.

[234] Grant, R. (1813) *A Sketch of the History of the East India Company.* London: Black, Parry.

[235] Gregory, T.E. (1927) Professor Cannan and contemporary monetary theory. In *London Essays in Economics: in Honour of Edwin Cannan* (ed. by T.E. Gregory and H. Dalton), pp. 31-65. London: Routledge.

[236] Gregory, T.E. (1935) Edwin Cannan: a personal impression. *Economica,* 2, pp. 365-79.

[237] Griliches, Z. (1986) Productivity, R&D and basic research at the firm level in the 1970s. *American Economic Review,* 76, pp. 141-54.

[238] Groenewegen, P.D. (1969) Turgot and Adam Smith. *Scottish Journal of Political Economy*, 16, pp. 271-287.

[239] Groenewegen, P. (1995) *A Soaring Eagle: Alfred Marshall 1842-1924*. Aldershot: Edward Elgar.

[240] Guillebaud, C.W. (1965) The Marshall-Macmillan correspondence over the net book agreement. *Economic Journal*, 75, pp. 518-38.

[241] Haberler, G. (1927) *Der Sinn der Indexzahlen*. Tübingen: Mohr.

[242] Haberler, G. (1937) *Prosperity and Depression*. Geneva: League of Nations.

[243] Haberler, G. (1986) Reflections on Hayek's business cycle theory. *Cato Journal*, 6, pp. 421-35. Reprinted in *Friedrich A. Hayek: Critical Assessments, vol. 4* (ed. by J.C. Wood and R.N. Woods), pp. 249-62 (1991), London: Routledge.

[244] Haberler, G. (1995) Reviewing a book without reading it. *Austrian Economics Newsletter*, Winter, p. 9.

[245] Hageman, H. (1994) Hayek and the Kiel school: some reflections on the German debate on business cycles in the late 1920s and early 1930s. In *Money and Business Cycles: The Economics of F.A. Hayek, vol. II* (ed. by M. Colonna and H. Hagemann), pp. 101-20. Aldershot: Edward Elgar.

[246] Hall, R.L. and Hitch, C.J. (1939) Price theory and business behaviour. *Oxford Economic Papers*, 2, pp. 12-45. Reprinted in *Oxford Studies in the Price Mechanism* (ed. by T. Wilson and P.W.S. Andrews), pp. 107-38 (1951). Oxford: Clarendon.

[247] Hamouda, O. and Rowley, R. (1994) Rational processes: markets, knowledge and uncertainty. In *Capitalism, Socialism and Knowledge: The Economics of F.A. Hayek, vol. II* (ed. by M. Colonna, H. Hagemann and O. Hamouda), pp. 178-94. Aldershot: Edward Elgar.

[248] Hands, D.W. (1993) *Testing, Rationality and Progress: Essays on the Popperian Tradition in Economic Methodology*. Lanham, MD: Rowman & Littlefield.

[249] Hansen, A.H. and Tout, H. (1933) Investment and saving in business cycle theory. *Econometrica*, 1, pp. 119-47.

[250] Harcourt, G.C. (1984) Reflections on the development of economics as a discipline. *History of Political Economy*, 16, pp. 489-517.

[251] Hausman, D. (2003) Taking causal questions seriously. *Journal of Economic Methodology*, 10, pp. 259-69.

[252] Hawtrey, R.G. (1932) Review of F.A. Hayek, *Prices and Production. Economica*, 12, pp. 119-25.

[253] Hawtrey, R.G. (1933) Review of F.A. Hayek, *Monetary Theory and the Trade Cycle. Economic Journal*, 43, pp. 669-72.

[254] Hawtrey, R.G (1938) *A Century of Bank Rate*. Reprinted (1962), London: Frank Cass.

[255] Hawtrey, R.G. (1940) The trade cycle and capital intensity. *Economica*, 7, pp. 1-15.

[256] Hawtrey, R.G. (1941) Professor Hayek's pure theory of capital. *Economic Journal*, 51, pp. 281-90.

[257] Hayek, F.A. (1928) Intertemporal price equilibrium and movements in the value of money. Translated and reprinted in *Money, Capital and Fluctuations: Early Essays* (ed. by R. McCloughry) (1984). London: Routledge and Kegan Paul.

[258] Hayek, F.A. (1929/1933) *Monetary Theory and the Trade Cycle*. Translated by N. Kaldor and H. Croome. London: Cape.

[259] Hayek, F.A. (1931a) *Prices and Production*, 2nd ed. (1935). London: Routledge and Kegan Paul.

[260] Hayek, F.A. (1931b) Reflections on the pure theory of money of Mr. J.M. Keynes (I). *Economica*, 11, pp. 270-95. Reprinted in *Friedrich A. Hayek: Critical Assessments, vol. 1* (ed. by J.C. Wood and R.N. Woods), pp. 1-23 (1991), London: Routledge.

[261] Hayek, F.A. (1931c) A rejoinder to Mr. Keynes. *Economica*, 11, pp. 398-403. Reprinted in *Friedrich A. Hayek: Critical Assessments, vol. 1* (ed. by J.C. Wood and R.N. Woods), pp. 60-4 (1991), London: Routledge.

[262] Hayek, F.A. (1932a) Reflections on the pure theory of money of Mr. J.M. Keynes (II). *Economica*, 12, pp. 22-44. Reprinted in *Friedrich A. Hayek: Critical Assessments, vol. 1* (ed. by J.C. Wood and R.N. Woods), pp. 65-85 (1991), London: Routledge.

[263] Hayek, F.A. (1932b) Money and capital: a reply. *Economic Journal*, 42, pp. 237-49. Reprinted in *Friedrich A. Hayek: Critical Assessments, vol. 1* (ed. by J.C. Wood and R.N. Woods), pp. 102-12 (1991), London: Routledge.

[264] Hayek, F.A. (1932c) The fate of the gold standard. Translated in *Money, Capital and Fluctuations: Early Essays by F.A. Hayek* (ed. by R. McCloughry), pp. 118-35 (1984). London: Routledge and Kegan Paul.

[265] Hayek, F.A. (1934a) Capital and industrial fluctuations. *Econometrica*, 2, pp. 152-67. Reprinted in *Friedrich A. Hayek: Critical Assessments, vol. 1* (ed. by J.C. Wood and R.N. Woods), pp. 148-63 (1991), London: Routledge.

[266] Hayek, F.A. (1934b) Carl Menger. *Economica*, NS, 1, pp. 393-420. Also reprinted as the Introduction to the LSE reprint of Menger's *Grundsätze der Volkswirtschaftslehre.*

[267] Hayek, F.A. (1936) The mythology of capital. *Quarterly Journal of Economics*, 50, pp. 199-228.

[268] Hayek, F.A. (1937a) Economics and knowledge. *Economica*, 4, pp. 33-54.

[269] Hayek, F.A. (1937b) *Monetary Nationalism and International Stability.* London: Longman.

[270] Hayek, F.A. (1938) Discussion on the trade cycle. *Journal of the Royal Statistical Society*, 101, Part III, pp. 578-80.

[271] Hayek, F.A. (1939a) *Profits, Interest and Investment.* London: Routledge.

[272] Hayek, F.A. (1939b) Introduction. In *Henry Thornton: An Enquiry into the Nature and Effects of the Paper Credit of Great Britain*, pp. 11-63 (1802). London: Allen & Unwin.

[273] Hayek, F.A. (1941a) *The Pure Theory of Capital.* London: Routledge.

[274] Hayek, F.A. (1941b) The counter-revolution of science. *Economica*, 8, Part I, pp. 9-36, Part II, pp. 119-50, Part III, pp. 281-320.

[275] Hayek, F.A. (1942) A Comment. *Economica*, 9, pp. 383-5.

[276] Hayek, F.A. (1942-4) Scientism and the study of society. *Economica*, 9, pp. 267-91; 10, pp. 34-63; 11, pp. 27-39.

[277] Hayek, F.A. (1944) *The Road to Serfdom.* London: Routledge.

[278] Hayek, F.A. (1946) The London School of Economics 1895-1945. *Economica*, 13, pp. 1-31.

[279] Hayek, F.A. (1949) *Individualism and Economic Order.* London: Routledge.

[280] Hayek, F.A. (1951) *John Stuart Mill and Harriet Taylor: Their Correspondence and Subsequent Marriage.* London: Routledge.

[281] Hayek, F.A. (1952) *The Sensory Order: An Inquiry into the Foundations of Theoretical Psychology.* London: Routledge and Kegan Paul.

[282] Hayek, F.A. (ed.) (1954) *Capitalism and the Historians.* London: Routledge.

[283] Hayek, F.A. (1960) *The Constitution of Liberty.* London: Routledge and Kegan Paul.

[284] Hayek, F.A. (1967) *Studies in Philosophy, Politics, and Economics.* London: Routledge.

[285] Hayek, F.A. (1968) *The Confusion of Language in Political Thought.* Occasional Paper No. 20. London: Institute of Economic Affairs.

[286] Hayek, F.A. (1972) *A Tiger by the Tail* (ed. by S. R. Shenoy). London: Institute of Economic Affairs.

[287] Hayek, F.A. (1973) *Economic Freedom and Representative Government.* Occasional Paper No. 39. London: Institute of Economic Affairs.

[288] Hayek, F.A. (1973-9) *Law, Legislation and Liberty*, vol. I *Rules and Order* (1973); vol. II *The Mirage of Social Justice* (1976); vol. III *The Political Order of a Free People* (1979). London: Routledge and Kegan Paul.

[289] Hayek, F.A. (1976a) *Denationalisation of Money*, 2nd edition (1978). London: Institute of Economic Affairs.

[290] Hayek, F.A. (1976b) *Choice in Currency.* Occasional Paper No. 48. London: Institute of Economic Affairs.

[291] Hayek, F.A. (1978a) *New Studies in Philosophy, Politics, Economics and the History of Ideas.* London: Routledge.

[292] Hayek, F.A. (1978b) Will the democratic ideal prevail? In Chaloner, W., Fletcher, R., Gash, N., Grimmond, J., Hayek, F.A., Lawson, N., Gould, J., the Duke of Edinburgh, Pearce, I., Harris, R., Hartwell, M. and Seldon, A. *Confrontation: Will the Open Society Survive to 1989?.* London: Institute of Economic Affairs.

[293] Hayek, F.A. (1980) *Unemployment and the Unions.* Hobart Paper No. 87, 2nd ed. (1984). London: Institute of Economic Affairs.

[294] Hayek, F.A. (1982) Two pages of fiction: the impossibility of socialist calculation. *Economic Affairs*, April, pp. 135-142.

[295] Hayek, F.A. (1983a) The Austrian critique. *Economist*, 11 June, pp. 45-8.

[296] Hayek F.A., (1983b) An interview with F.A. Hayek. *Cato Policy Report*, 5, February, p. 4.

[297] Hayek, F.A. (1984a) *Money, Capital and Fluctuations: Early Essays* (ed. by R. McCloughry). London: Routledge.

[298] Hayek, F.A. (1984b) Exclusive interview with F.A. Hayek. *Cato Policy Report*, 6, May/June, pp. 1-3.

[299] Hayek, F.A. (1988) *The Fatal Conceit: The Errors of Socialism.* London: Routledge.

[300] Hayek, F.A. (1991) *The Trend of Economic Thinking: The Collected Works of F.A. Hayek, vol. 3* (ed. by W.W. Bartley and S. Kresge). London: Routledge.

[301] Hayek, F.A. (1992) *The Fortunes of Liberalism: The Collected Works of F.A. Hayek, vol. 4* (ed. by P.G. Klein). London: Routledge.

[302] Hayek, F.A. (1994) *Hayek on Hayek* (ed. by S. Kresge and L. Wenar). London: Routledge.

[303] Hayek, F.A. (1995) *Contra Keynes and Cambridge. Essays and Correspondence: The Collected Works of F.A. Hayek, vol. 9* (ed. by B. Caldwell). London: Routledge.

[304] Hayek, F.A. (1999a) *Good Money Part I. The New World: The Collected Works of F.A. Hayek, vol. 5* (ed. by S. Kresge). Chicago: University of Chicago Press.

[305] Hayek, F.A. (1999b) *Good Money Part II. The Standard: The Collected Works of F.A. Hayek, vol. 6* (ed. by S. Kresge). Chicago: University of Chicago Press.

[306] Held, A. (1881) *Zwei Bücher zur Socialen Geschichte Englands.* Leipzig: Altenburg.

[307] Hetzel, R.L. (1998) Arthur Burns and inflation. *Federal Reserve Bank of Richmond Economic Quarterly*, 84, pp. 21-44.

[308] Hicks, J.R. (1940) Mr. Hawtrey on bank rate and the long term rate of interest. *Manchester School*, 10, pp. 21-37.

[309] Hicks, J.R. (1965) *Capital and Growth.* Oxford: Clarendon.

[310] Hicks, J.R. (1967) *Critical Essays in Monetary Theory.* Oxford: Clarendon.

[311] Hicks, J.R. (1977) *Economic Perspectives.* Oxford: Clarendon.

[312] Hicks, J.R. (1982) *Money, Interest and Wages: Collected Essays on Economic Theory, vol. II.* Oxford: Blackwell.

[313] Hicks, J.R. (1983) *Classics and Moderns: Collected Essays on Economic Theory, vol. III.* Oxford: Blackwell.

[314] Hicks, J.R. and Weber, W. (eds.) (1973) *Carl Menger and the Austrian School of Economics.* Oxford: Clarendon.

[315] Hirsch, A. (1983) Wesley Clair Mitchell's approach to the history of economics. *Research in the History of Economic Thought and Methodology*, 1, pp. 93-112.

[316] Hogben, L. (1936) *Mathematics for the Million.* London: Allen & Unwin.

[317] Hollander, S. (1973) Ricardo's analysis of the profit rate. *Economica*, 40, pp. 260-82.

[318] Hollander, S. (1975) Ricardo and the corn profit model: reply to Eatwell. *Economica*, 42, pp. 188-202.

[319] Hollander, S. (1979) *The Economics of David Ricardo.* Toronto: University of Toronto Press.

[320] Hollander, S. (1980) On Professor Samuelson's canonical classical model of political economy. *Journal of Economic Literature*, 18, pp. 559-74.

[321] Hollander, S. (1995) It's an ill wind... : a memoir. *Journal of the History of Economic Thought*, 17, pp. 285-306.

[322] Hoover, K.D. (1988) *The New Classical Macroeconomics: A Sceptical Enquiry.* Oxford: Blackwell.

[323] Hoover, K.D. (1994) The new classical economics. In *The Elgar Companion to Austrian Economics* (ed. by P. Boettke), pp. 576-81. Aldershot: Edward Elgar.

[324] Hope Jones, A. (1939) *Income Tax in the Napoleonic Wars.* Cambridge: Cambridge University Press.

[325] Horwitz, S. (1996) Capital theory, inflation and deflation: the Austrian and monetary disequilibrium theory compared. *Journal of the History of Economic Thought*, 18, pp. 287-308.

[326] Horwitz, S. (2000) *Microfoundations and Macroeconomics.* London: Routledge.

[327] Howard, D.H. (1977) Review of F.A. Hayek, *Denationalisation of Money. Journal of Monetary Economics*, 8, pp. 483-5.

[328] Howey, R.S. (1983) Frank Hyneman Knight and the history of economic thought. *Research in the History of Economic Thought and Methodology*, 1, pp. 163-86.

[329] Hume, D. (1752) *Writings on Economics* (ed. by E. Rotwein) (1955). Edinburgh: Nelson.

[330] Hummel, J.R. (1979) Problems with the Austrian business cycle theory. *Reason Papers*, 5, pp. 41-53. Reprinted in *Friedrich A. Hayek: Critical Assessments* (ed. by J.C. Wood and R.N. Woods), pp. 124-36 (1991), London: Routledge.

[331] Humphrey, T.M. (1992) Price-level stabilisation rules in a Wicksellian model of the cumulative process. *Scandinavian Journal of Economics*, 94, pp. 509-18.

[332] Humphrey, T.M. (1993) *Money, Banking and Inflation*. Aldershot: Edward Elgar.

[333] Humphrey, T.M. (1997) Fisher and Wicksell on the quantity theory. *Federal Reserve Bank of Richmond Economic Quarterly*, 83, pp. 71-90.

[334] Hutcheson, A. (1714) *A Proposal for Payment of the Public Debts.* Published with *Some Considerations Relating to the Payment of the Public Debts. By a Member of the House of Commons* (1717), London: Henry Clements.

[335] Hutchison, T.W. (1951) Review of W.C. Mitchell, *Lecture Notes on Types of Economic Theory. Economic Journal*, 61, pp. 123-30.

[336] Hutchison, T.W. (1952) Some questions about Ricardo. *Economica*, 19, pp. 415-32.

[337] Hutchison, T.W. (1968) *Economics and Economic Policy in Britain, 1946-1966*. London: Allen & Unwin. Reprinted (1992), Aldershot: Gregg.

[338] Hutchison, T.W. (1977) *Knowledge and Ignorance in Economics*. Oxford: Blackwell.

[339] Hutchison, T.W. (1978) *On Revolutions and Progress in Economic Knowledge*. Cambridge: Cambridge University Press.

[340] Hutchison, T.W. (1981) *The Politics and Philosophy of Economics: Marxians Keynesians and Austrians*. Oxford: Blackwell.

[341] Hutchison, T.W. (1988) *Before Adam Smith*. Oxford: Blackwell.

[342] Hutchison, T.W. (1992) *Changing Aims in Economics*. Oxford: Blackwell..

[343] Hutchison, T.W. (1994) *The Uses and Abuses of Economics*. London: Routledge.

[344] Ingrams, R. (1995) *Muggeridge*. London: Harper Collins.

[345] Jaffé, W. (ed.) (1965a) *Correspondence of Léon Walras and Related Papers*, 3 vols. Amsterdam: North Holland.

[346] Jaffé, W. (1965b) Biography and economic analysis. *Western Economic Journal*, 3, pp. 223-32.

[347] Jaffé, W. (1976) Menger, Jevons and Walras de-homogenised. *Economic Inquiry*, 14, pp. 511-24.

[348] Jevons, W.S. (1884) *Investigations in Currency and Finance* (ed. by H.S. Foxwell). London: Macmillan.

[349] Jewkes, J. (1948) *Ordeal by Planning*. London: Macmillan.

[350] Johnson, E.S. and Johnson, H.G. (1978) *The Shadow of Keynes*. Oxford: Blackwell.

[351] Johnson, H.G. (1949) Demand for commodities is not demand for labour. *Economic Journal*, 59, pp. 531-36.

[352] Johnson, H.G and Carter, C.F (1950) Unrequited imports and the terms of trade; a note. *Economic Journal*, 60, pp. 837-39.

[353] Jones, T.W. (1978) The appointment of Pigou as Marshall's successor: the other side of the coin. *Journal of Law and Economics*, 21, pp. 235-43.

[354] Jonung, L. (1981) Ricardo on machinery and present unemployment: an unpublished manuscript by Knut Wicksell. *Economic Journal*, 91, pp. 195-205.

[355] Joplin, T. (1828) *Views on the Corn Bill of 1827, and Other Measures of Government*. London: Ridgway.

[356] Kadish, A. (1982) *The Oxford Economists in the Late Nineteenth Century*. Oxford: Clarendon.

[357] Kadish, A. (1983) Cannan vs. Marshall and the history of economic thought. *Research in the History of Economic Thought and Methodology*, 1, pp. 61-77.

[358] Kadish, A. (1989) *Historians, Economists, and Economic History*. London: Routledge.

[359] Kadish, A. and Tribe, K. (eds.) (1993) *The Market for Political Economy*. London: Routledge.

[360] Kahn, R.F. (1984) *The Making of Keynes' General Theory*. Cambridge: Cambridge University Press.

[361] Kaldor, N. (1939) Capital intensity and the trade cycle. *Economica*, 9, pp. 359-82.

[362] Kaldor, N. (1942) Professor Hayek and the concertina-effect. *Economica*, 9, pp. 359-82.

[363] Kaysen, C. and Turner, D.F. (1959) *Antitrust Policy: An Economic and Legal Analysis.* Harvard: Harvard University Press.

[364] Kealey, T. (1996) *The Economic Laws of Scientific Research.* London: Macmillan.

[365] Keynes, J.M. (1914) Review of L.V. Mises, *Theorie des Geldes und der Umlaufsmittel. Economic Journal*, 24, pp. 417-419.

[366] Keynes, J.M. (1923) *A Tract on Monetary Reform.* Reprinted in *The Collected Writings of John Maynard Keynes, vol. IV* (1971), London: Macmillan.

[367] Keynes, J.M. (1924) A comment on Professor Cannan's article. *Economic Journal*, 34, pp. 65-68.

[368] Keynes, J.M. (ed.) (1926) *Official Papers by Alfred Marshall.* London: Macmillan.

[369] Keynes, J.M. (1930) *A Treatise on Money*, vol. 1 *The Pure Theory of Money*; vol. 2 *The Applied Theory of Money.* Reprinted as vols. V and VI of *The Collected Writings of John Maynard Keynes* (1971), London: Macmillan for the Royal Economic Society.

[370] Keynes, J.M. (1931) The pure theory of money: a reply to Dr. Hayek. *Economica*, 2, pp. 387-97. Reprinted in *Friedrich A. Hayek: Critical Assessments, vol. 1* (ed. by J.C. Wood and R.N. Woods), pp. 50-9 (1991), London: Routledge.

[371] Keynes, J.M. (1933) *Essays in Biography.* London: Macmillan. Reprinted (1972), London: Macmillan.

[372] Keynes, J.M. (1936a) Herbert Somerton Foxwell. *Economic Journal*, 46, pp. 589-614. Reprinted in *Essays in Biography, Collected Works, vol. X* (1972), London: Macmillan.

[373] Keynes, J.M. (1936b) *The General Theory of Employment, Interest and Money.* Reprinted as Vol. VII of The Collected Writings of John Maynard Keynes, London: Macmillan for the Royal Economic Society.

[374] King, Lord (1804) *Thoughts on the Effects of the Bank Restrictions*, 2nd ed. London: Cadell and Davies, and J. Debrett.

[375] King, R.G. (1983) On the economics of private money. *Journal of Monetary Economics*, 12, pp. 127-58.

[376] Kirzner, I.M. (1973) *Competition and Entrepreneurship.* Chicago: University of Chicago Press.

[377] Kirzner, I.M. (1997) Entrepreneurial discovery and the competitive market process: an Austrian approach. *Journal of Economic Literature*, 35, pp. 60-85.

[378] Klamer, A. (1984) *The New Classical Macroeconomics: Conversations with New Classical Economists and their Opponents.* Brighton: Wheatsheaf.

[379] Klein, B. (1974) The competitive supply of money. *Journal of Money, Credit and Banking*, 6, pp. 423-54.

[380] Knight, F.H. (1921) *Risk, Uncertainty and Profit.* Boston: Houghton Mifflin.

[381] Knight, F.H. (1924) Some fallacies in the interpretation of social cost. *Quarterly Journal of Economics*, 38, pp. 582-606.

[382] Knight, F.H. (1935) The Ricardian theory of production and distribution. *Canadian Journal of Economics and Political Science*, 1, pp. 3-25, 171-96.

[383] Knight, F.H. (1955) Schumpeter's history of economics. *Southern Economic Journal*, 21, pp. 261-72.

[384] Knight, F.H. (1967) Laissez faire: pro and con. *Journal of Political Economy*, 75, pp. 782-95.

[385] Koopmans, T.C. (1947) Measurement without theory. *Review of Economics and Statistics*, 29, pp. 161-72.

[386] Kress Library (1940) *The Kress Library of Business and Economics Catalogue, Baker Library, Harvard University.* Reprinted (1964), New York: Kelley.

[387] Kuhn, T.S. (1962) *The Structure of Scientific Revolutions*, 2nd ed. (1970). Chicago: University of Chicago Press.

[388] Kurdas, C. (1988) The Whig historian on Adam Smith: Paul Samuelson's canonical classical model. *History of Economics Society Bulletin*, 10, pp. 13-23.

[389] Lachman, L.M. (1940) A reconsideration of the Austrian theory of industrial fluctuations. *Economica*, 7, pp. 179-96.

[390] Lachman, L.M. (1956) *Capital and its Structure.* Reprinted (1978), Kansas: Sheed Andrews and McMeel.

[391] Lachman, L.M. (1978) The Austrian stocktaking: unsettled questions and tentative answers. In *New Directions in Austrian Economics* (ed. by L.M. Spadaro), pp. 1-18. Kansas City: Sheed Andrews and McMeel.

[392] Lachman, L.M. (1986) Austrian economics under fire: the Hayek-Sraffra duel in retrospect. In *Austrian Economics. Historical and Philosophical Background* (ed. by W. Grassl and B. Smith), pp. 225-342. New York: New York University Press.

[393] Laidler, D. (1990) *Taking Money Seriously.* London: Philip Allan.

[394] Laidler, D. (1999) *Fabricating the Keynesian Revolution.* Cambridge: Cambridge University Press.

[395] Lancaster, K. (1960) A new approach to consumer theory. *Journal of Political Economy*, 68, pp. 132-57.

[396] Lancaster, K. (1972) Review of K. Arrow and F. Hahn, *General Competitive Analysis* (1971). *Journal of Economic Literature*, 10, pp. 1202-4.

[397] Langlois, R.N. (1985) Knowledge and rationality in the Austrian school: an analytical survey. *Eastern Economic Journal*, 9, pp. 309-30. Reprinted in *Friedrich A. Hayek: Critical Assessments, vol. 4* (ed. by J.C. Wood and R.N. Woods), pp. 118-40 (1991), London: Routledge.

[398] Lavoie, D. (1986) The market as a procedure for discovery and conveyance of inarticulate knowledge. *Comparative Economic Studies*, 28, pp. 1-19. Reprinted in *Friedrich A. Hayek: Critical Assessments, vol. 4* (ed. by J.C. Wood and R.N. Woods), pp. 213-33 (1991), London: Routledge.

[399] Lebrecht, N. (1996) *When the Music Stops.* London: Simon and Schuster.

[400] Legg, L.G.W. (ed.) (1949) *The Dictionary of National Biography 1931-1940.* London: Oxford University Press.

[401] Leijonhufvud, A. (1968) *On Keynesian Economics and the Economics of Keynes.* Oxford: Oxford University Press.

[402] Leijonhufvud, A. (1969) *Keynes and the Classics.* London: Institute of Economic Affairs.

[403] Leijonhufvud, A. (1981) *Information and Coordination.* Oxford: Oxford University Press.

[404] Leontief, W. (1933) The use of indifference curves in the analysis of foreign trade. *Quarterly Journal of Economics*, 47, pp. 493-503.

[405] Leontief, W. (1937) Implicit theorising: a methodological criticism of the neo-Cambridge school. *Quarterly Journal of Economics*, 51, pp. 337-51.

[406] Lerner, A.P. (1933-4) The concept of monopoly and the measurement of monopoly power. *Review of Economic Studies*, 1, pp. 157-175.

[407] Letwin, W.O. (1963) *The Origins of Scientific Economics: English Economic Thought 1660-1776.* London: Methuen.

[408] Levy, D. (1985) The impossibility of a complete methological individualist reduction when knowledge is imperfect. *Economics and Philosophy*, 1, pp. 101-8.

[409] Lieberman, M. and Montgomery, D. (1988) First mover advantage. *Strategic Management Journal*, 9, pp. 41-58.

[410] Lindbeck, A. (1972) Paul Anthony Samuelson's contribution to economics. *Swedish Journal of Economics*, 72, pp. 342-54.

[411] Little, I.M.D. (1955) History of economic analysis. *Economic History Review*, 8 (2nd series), pp. 91-98.

[412] Littlechild, S.C. (1978) *The Fallacy of the Mixed Economy: Hobart Paper No. 80.* London: Institute of Economic Affairs.

[413] Lloyd, W.F. (1833) A lecture on the notion of value. Reprinted in *Economic History*, 1, pp. 168-83.

[414] Loasby, B.J. (1978) Whatever happened to Marshall's theory of value? *Scottish Journal of Political Economy*, 25, pp. 1-12.

[415] Loasby, B.J. (1991) *Equilibrium and Evolution.* Manchester: Manchester University Press.

[416] Longfield, M. (1834) Lectures on political economy. In *The Economic Writings of Mountifort Longfield* (ed. by R.D.C. Black), pp. 1-267 (1971). New York: A.M. Kelley.

[417] Lucas, R.E. (1975) An equilibrium model of the business cycle. *Journal of Political Economy*, 83, pp. 1113-44.

[418] Lucas, R.E. (1977) Understanding business cycles. In *Stability of the Domestic and International Economy* (ed. by K. Brunner and A.H. Meltzer), pp. 7-30. Amsterdam: North Holland.

[419] Lutz, F.A. (1943) Professor Hayek's theory of interest. *Economica*, 10, pp. 302-10.

[420] MacDonald, R. and Taylor, M.P. (1992) Exchange rate economics: a survey. *International Monetary Fund Staff Papers*, 39, pp. 1-57.

[421] Machlup, F. (1974) Friedrich von Hayek's contribution to economics. *Swedish Journal of Economics*, 76, pp. 498-531. Reprinted in *Friedrich A. Hayek: Critical Assessments, vol. 2* (ed. by J.C. Wood and R.N. Woods), pp. 193-229 (1991), London: Routledge.

[422] Machlup, F. (ed.) (1976) *Essays on Hayek.* New York: New York University Press.

[423] Macmillan, D. (1942) The Principles of Economics – a bibliographic note. *Economic Journal*, 52, pp. 290-93.

[424] MacMinn, N., Hainds, J.R. and McCrimmon, J. (1945) *Bibliography of the Published Writings of John Stuart Mill.* Evanston, Illinois: Northwestern University.

[425] MacPherson, D. (1805) *Annals of Commerce, Manufactures, Fisheries, and Navigation, with Brief Notices of the Arts and Sciences Connected with Them.* London and Edinburgh: Nichols.

[426] MacPherson, D. (1812) *The History of the European Commerce with India.* London: Longman.

[427] Maling, C. (1975) The Austrian business cycle theory and its implications for economic stability under laissez faire. *Reason Papers*, 2, pp. 65-90. Reprinted in *Friedrich A. Hayek: Critical Assessments, vol. 2* (ed. by J.C. Wood and R.N. Woods), pp. 248-68 (1991), London: Routledge.

[428] Maling, C. (1980) Hicks' neo-Austrian capital theory. *Atlantic Economic Journal*, 8, pp. 20-32. Reprinted in *Friedrich A. Hayek: Critical Assessments, vol. 3* (ed. by J.C. Wood and R.N. Woods), pp. 187-205 (1991), London: Routledge.

[429] Maloney, J. (1985) *Marshall, Orthodoxy and the Professionalisation of Economics.* Cambridge: Cambridge University Press.

[430] Malthus, T.R. (1803) *An Essay on the Principle of Population*, 2nd ed. London: Johnson.

[431] Malthus, T.R. (1815) *An Inquiry into the Nature and Progress of Rent, and the Principles by which it is Regulated.* London: Murray.

[432] Mandeville, B. (1714-29) *The Fable of the Bees* (ed. by F.B. Kaye). Reprinted (1988), Indianapolis: Liberty Press.

[433] Mansfield, E. (1980) Basic research and productivity increase in manufacturing. *American Economic Review*, 70, pp. 863-73.

[434] Marget, A.W. (1932) Review of F.A. Hayek, *Prices and Production. Journal of Political Economy*, 40, pp. 261-6.

[435] Marshall, A. (1872) Mr Jevons' theory of political economy. *Academy*, 1 April 1872. Reprinted in *Memorials of Alfred Marshall* (with comment by Marshall) (ed. by A.C. Pigou), pp. 93-100 (1925), London: Macmillan.

[436] Marshall, A. (1879) *The Pure Theory of Foreign Trade: The Pure Theory of Domestic Values.* Reprinted (1949), London: London School of Economics.

[437] Marshall, A. (1919) *Industry and Trade*, 3rd edition (1920). Reprinted (1929), London: Macmillan.

[438] Marshall, A. (1920) *Principles of Economics*, 8th ed. Reprinted (ed. by C.W. Guillebaud) (1961), London: Macmillan.

[439] Marshall, A. (1923) *Money, Credit and Commerce.* Reprinted (1929), London: Macmillan.

[440] Marshall, M.P. (1947) *What I Remember.* Cambridge: Cambridge University Press.

[441] Matthews, R.C.O. (1981) Morality, competition and efficiency. *Manchester School*, 49, pp. 289-309.

[442] Mayer, T. (1995) *Doing Economic Research.* Aldershot: Edward Elgar.

[443] McCloughry, R. (ed.) (1984) *Money, Capital and Fluctuations: Early Essays by F.A. Hayek.* London: Routledge and Kegan Paul.

[444] McCulloch, J.R. (1823) David Ricardo. *Edinburgh Annual Register*, Part II, pp. 392-403.

[445] McCulloch, J.R. (1824a) *A Discourse on the Rise, Progress, Peculiar Objects and Importance of Political Economy.* Edinburgh: Constable.

[446] McCulloch, J.R. (1824b) Money. In *Encyclopaedia Britannica*, 6th ed., V (Supplement), pp. 491-536. Edinburgh: Constable.

[447] McCulloch, J.R. (1825) Absenteeism. *Edinburgh Review*, 43, pp. 54-76.

[448] McCulloch, J.R. (1826a) Commercial revulsions. *Edinburgh Review*, 44, pp. 70-93.

[449] McCulloch, J.R. (1826b) *Historical Sketch of the Rise and Progress of the Science of Political Economy.* Edinburgh: Balfour.

[450] McCulloch, J.R. (ed.) (1828) *Adam Smith: An Inquiry into the Nature and Causes of the Wealth of Nations.* Edinburgh: Tait.

[451] McCulloch, J.R. (1830) Rise, progress, and decline of commerce in Holland. *Edinburgh Review*, 51, pp. 418-43.

[452] McCulloch, J.R. (1832a) *Principles, Practice, and History of Commerce.* London: Society for the Diffusion of Useful Knowledge.

[453] McCulloch, J.R. (1832b) *A Dictionary of Commerce and Commercial Navigation.* London: Longman.

[454] McCulloch, J.R. (1836) *Reasons for the Establishment of a New Bank in India.* London: Longman.

[455] McCulloch, J.R. (1839) Introductory discourse. In *Adam Smith: An Inquiry into the Nature and Causes of the Wealth of Nations*, pp. xv-lv. Edinburgh and London: Black and Tait, and Longman.

[456] McCulloch, J.R. (1842a) Ricardo, David. In *Encyclopaedia Britannica*, 7th ed., XIX, pp. 229-35. Edinburgh: Black.

[457] McCulloch, J.R. (1842b) Money. In *Encyclopaedia Britannica*, 7th ed., XV, pp. 383-413. Edinburgh: Black.

[458] McCulloch, J.R. (1842c) Average. In *Encyclopaedia Britannica*, 7th ed., IV, pp. 250-4. Edinburgh: Black.

[459] McCulloch, J.R. (1845a) *The Literature of Political Economy: A Classified Catalogue*. London: Longman.

[460] McCulloch, J.R. (1845b) *A Treatise on the Principles and Practical Influence of Taxation and the Funding System* (ed. by D.P. O'Brien) (1975). Edinburgh: Scottish Academic Press.

[461] McCulloch, J.R. (ed.) (1846) *The Works of David Ricardo, Esq. M.P., with a Notice of the Life and Writings of the Author*. London: Murray.

[462] McCulloch, J.R. (1849) *The Principles of Political Economy*, 4th ed. Edinburgh: A. & C. Black and London: Longmans. Reprinted (1995), London: Routledge/Thoemmes.

[463] McCulloch, J.R. (1853) *Treatises and Essays on Subjects Connected with Economical Policy, with Biographical Sketches of Quesnay, Adam Smith, and Ricardo*. Edinburgh: Black.

[464] McCulloch, J.R. (1855) Exchange. In *Encyclopaedia Britannica*, 8th ed., IX, pp. 428-47. Edinburgh: Black.

[465] McCulloch, J.R. (ed.) (1856a) *A Select Collection of Early English Tracts on Commerce, from the Originals of Mun, Roberts, North, and Others*. Printed for the Political Economy Club.

[466] McCulloch, J.R. (ed.) (1856b) *A Select Collection of Scarce and Valuable Tracts on Money, from the Originals of Vaughan, Cotton, Petty, Lowndes, Newton, Prior, Harris, and Others*. Printed for the Political Economy Club.

[467] McCulloch, J.R. (1856c) *A Catalogue of Books, the Property of the Author of the Commercial Dictionary*. London: privately printed.

[468] McCulloch, J.R. (ed.) (1857a) *A Select Collection of Scarce and Valuable Tracts and other Publications on the National Debt and the Sinking Fund, from the originals of Harley, Gould, Pulteney, Walpole, Hume, Price, Hamilton, and Others*. Printed for Lord Overstone.

[469] McCulloch, J.R. (ed.) (1857b) *A Select Collection of Scarce and Valuable Tracts and Other Publications, on Paper Currency and Banking, from the originals of Hume, Wallace, Thornton, Ricardo, Blake, Huskisson, and Others*. Printed for Lord Overstone.

[470] McCulloch, J.R. (1858) Money. In *Encyclopaedia Britannica*, 8th ed., XV, pp. 416-94. Edinburgh: Black.

[471] McCulloch, J.R. (ed.) (1859a) *A Select Collection of Scarce and Valuable Tracts on Commerce, from the Originals of Evelyn, Defoe, Richardson, Tucker, Temple, and Others.* Printed for Lord Overstone.

[472] McCulloch, J.R. (ed.) (1859b) *A Select Collection of Scarce and Valuable Economical Tracts, from the Originals of Defoe, Elking, Franklin, Turgot, Anderson, Schomberg, Townsend, Burke, Bell, and Others.* Printed for Lord Overstone.

[473] McCulloch, J.R. (1859c) Ricardo, David. In *Encyclopaedia Britannica*, 8th ed., XIX, pp. 152-6. Edinburgh: Black.

[474] McCulloch, J.R. (1859d) *Treatises and Essays on Money, Exchange, Interest, the Letting of Land, Absenteeism, the History of Commerce, Manufactures, etc.* Edinburgh: A. & C. Black. Reprinted (1995), Bristol: Routledge Thoemmes.

[475] McCulloch, J.R. (1862) *A Catalogue of Books, the Property of a Political Economist.* London: Privately printed.

[476] McCulloch, J.R. (1863) Sketch of the life and writings of Adam Smith. In *Adam Smith: An Inquiry into the Nature and Causes of the Wealth of Nations*, pp. i-xxiii. Edinburgh: Black.

[477] McGee, J.S. (1958) Predatory price cutting: the standard oil (N.J.) case. *Journal of Law and Economics*, 1, pp. 137-169.

[478] McGee, J.S. (1974) Efficiency and economies of size. In *Industrial Concentration: The New Learning* (ed. by H.J. Goldschmid, H.M. Mann and J.F. Weston), pp. 55-97, 101-104. Boston: Little Brown.

[479] McWilliams-Tullberg, R. (1975) *Women at Cambridge.* London: Gollancz

[480] Meade, J.E. (1952) External economies and diseconomies in a competitive situation. *Economic Journal*, 62, pp. 54-67.

[481] Meek, R.L. (1957) Is economics biased? *Scottish Journal of Political Economy*, 4, pp. 1-17.

[482] Meese, R.A. and Rogoff, K. (1983) Empirical exchange rate models of the seventies: do they fit out of sample? *Journal of International Economics*, 14, pp. 3-24.

[483] Meltzer, A.H. (1988) *Keynes's Monetary Theory: A different interpretation.* Cambridge: Cambridge University Press.

[484] Menger, C. (1871) *Gründsatze der Volkswirthschaftslehre.* Wien: Braumüller. Reprinted (1934), London: LSE.

[485] Menger, C. (1883) *Untersuchungen über die Methoden der Socialwissenschaften und der Politischen Oekonomie Insbesondere.* Translated by F. J. Nock and ed. by L. Schneider as *Problems of Economics and Sociology* (1963). Urbana: University of Illinois Press.

[486] Metzler, L. (1949) Tariffs, the terms of trade, and the distribution of national income. *Journal of Political Economy*, 57, pp. 1-29.

[487] Milgate, M. (1979) On the origin of the notion of intertemporal equilibrium. *Economica*, 46, pp. 1-10.

[488] Milgate, M. (1987) Cannan, Edwin. In *The New Palgrave Dictionary of Economics* (ed. by J. Eatwell, M. Milgate, P. Newman) vol. I, pp. 315-16. London: Macmillan.

[489] Mill, J.S. (1825) McCulloch's discourse on political economy. *Westminster Review*, IV, pp. 88-92.

[490] Mill, J.S. (1844). Unsettled questions of political economy. In *Collected Works. vol. IV* (ed. by J.M. Robson), pp. 229-339. Toronto: University of Toronto Press.

[491] Mill, J.S. (1848) *Principles of Political Economy* (ed. by W.J. Ashley) (1923). London: Longman.

[492] Mill, J.S. (1967) *Essays on Economics and Society* (ed. by J.M. Robson). Toronto: University of Toronto Press.

[493] Mincer, J. (1983) George Stigler's contributions to economics. *Scandinavian Journal of Economics*, 85, pp. 65-75.

[494] Mineka, F. (ed.) (1963) *The Earlier Letters of John Stuart Mill.* Toronto: University of Toronto Press.

[495] Mises, L. (1912) *Theorie des Geldes und der Umlaufsmittel.* Munich: Duncker & Humblott.

[496] Mises, L. (1924) *The Theory of Money and Credit*, 2nd ed. Translated by H. E. Batson (1934). London: Cape.

[497] Mises, L. (1932) *Gemeinwirtschaft*, 2nd ed. Jena: Fischer. Translated by J. Kahane as *Socialism.* Reprinted (1979), Indianapolis: Liberty Classics.

[498] Mises, L. (1949) *Human Action*, 3rd ed. (1966). Chicago: Regneri.

[499] Mitchell, B.R. and Deane, P. (1962) *Abstract of British Historical Statistics.* Cambridge: Cambridge University Press.

[500] Moggridge. D.E. (ed.) (1983) *The Collected Writings of John Maynard Keynes, vol XI. Economic Articles and Correspondence: Academic.* London: Macmillan .

[501] Moggridge, D.E. (1997) Among the most fascinating of scholarly objects: a memoir. *Journal of the History of Economic Thought*, 19, pp. 24-48.

[502] Moss, L.S. (ed.) (1976) *The Economics of Ludwig von Mises.* Kansas: Sheed and Ward.

[503] Muggeridge, M. (1972) *Chronicles of Wasted Time,* 2 vols. London: Collins.

[504] Murray, T. (1911) *Autobiographical Notes, also Reminiscences of a Journey to London in 1840.* Dumfries: Printed at the Standard Office.

[505] Musgrave, A. (1981) 'Unreal assumptions' in economic theory: the f-twist untwisted. *Kyklos*, 34, pp. 377-87.

[506] Mussa, M. (1976) The exchange rate, the balance of payments, and monetary and fiscal policy under a regime of controlled floating. *Scandinavian Journal of Economics*, 78, pp. 229-48.

[507] Mussa, M. (1979) Empirical regularities in the behavior of exchange rates and theories of the foreign exchange market. *Journal of Monetary Economics*, 11 (Supplement), pp. 9-57.

[508] Neale, A.D. and Goyder, D.G. (1980) *The Antitrust Laws of the United States of America*, 3rd ed. Cambridge: Cambridge University Press.

[509] Neumann, J.V. and Morgenstern, O. (1944) *Theory of Games and Economic Behaviour.* Princeton, N.J: Princeton University Press.

[510] Newman, J.H. (1970) *The Letters and Diaries of John Henry Newman vol. XX* (ed. by C.S. Dessain). London: Nelson.

[511] Newman, P. (1990) Reviews by Edgeworth. In *A Century of Economics* (ed. by J.D. Hey and D. Winch), pp. 109-42. Oxford: Blackwell.

[512] Nicholson, J.S. (1883) *Tenant's Gain Not Landlord's Loss.* Edinburgh: Douglas.

[513] Nicholson, J.S. (1902) *Principles of Political Economy, vol. I.* London: A. & C. Black.

[514] Niehans, J. (1990) *A History of Economic Theory: Classic Contributions, 1720-1980.* Baltimore: John Hopkins University Press.

[515] Norman, G.W. (1860) *Remarks on the Incidence of Import Duties.* Privately printed.

[516] Oakeshott, M. (1962) *Rationalism in Politics and Other Essays.* London: Methuen.

[517] O'Brien, D.P. (1970) *J.R. McCulloch: A Study in Classical Economics.* London: Allen and Unwin. Reprinted (1992), Aldershot: Gregg; (2003), London: Routledge.

[518] O'Brien, D.P. (ed.) (1971) *The Correspondence of Lord Overstone*, 3 vols. Cambridge: Cambridge University Press.

[519] O'Brien, D.P. (1973) *Whither Economics.* Reprinted in *Methodology, Money and the Firm, vol. I*, pp. 3-32 (1994), Aldershot: Edward Elgar.

[520] O'Brien, D.P. (1975) *The Classical Economists.* Oxford: Clarendon.

[521] O'Brien, D.P. (ed.) (1975) *J.R. McCulloch: A Treatise on the Principles and Practical Influence of Taxation and the Funding System.* Edinburgh: Scottish Academic Press.

[522] O'Brien, D.P. (1977) Torrens, McCulloch and Disraeli. *Scottish Journal of Political Economy*, 24, pp. 1-8.

[523] O'Brien, D.P. (1981) Ricardian economics and the economics of David Ricardo. *Oxford Economic Papers*, 33, pp. 352-86.

[524] O'Brien, D.P. (1982) Competition policy in Britain: the silent revolution. *Antitrust Bulletin*, 27, pp. 217-39. Reprinted in *Methodology, Money and the Firm*, vol. I (1994), pp. 151-73, Aldershot: Edward Elgar.

[525] O'Brien, D.P. (1983a) Research programmes in competitive structure. Reprinted in *Methodology, Money and the Firm, vol. I*, pp. 277-99 (1994), Aldershot: Edward Elgar.

[526] O'Brien, D.P. (1983b) Theories of the history of science: a test case. Reprinted in *Methodology, Money and the Firm, vol. I*, pp. 33-68 (1994), Aldershot: Edward Elgar.

[527] O'Brien, D.P. (1984) The evolution of the theory of the firm. Reprinted in *Methodology, Money and the Firm, vol. I*, pp. 247-276 (1994), Aldershot: Edward Elgar.

[528] O'Brien, D.P. (1986) Divestiture: the case of AT&T. Reprinted in *Methodology, Money and the Firm, vol. I*, pp. 174-209 (1994), Aldershot: Edward Elgar.

[529] O'Brien, D.P. (1988a) Classical reassessments. In *Classical Political Economy* (ed. by W.O. Thweatt), pp. 179-220. Boston: Kluwer.

[530] O'Brien, D.P. (1988b) *Lionel Robbins.* London: Macmillan.

[531] O'Brien, D.P. (1990a) Lionel Robbins and the Austrian connection. *History of Political Economy*, 22 (Supplement), pp. 155-84.

[532] O'Brien D.P. (1990b) Marshall's work in relation to classical economics. In *Centenary Essays on Alfred Marshall* (ed. by J.K. Whitaker), pp. 127-63. Cambridge: Cambridge University Press.

[533] O'Brien, D.P. (1993) *Thomas Joplin and Classical Macroeconomics.* Aldershot: Edward Elgar.

[534] O'Brien, D.P. (1994a) Hayek as an intellectual historian. In *Hayek, Co-ordination and Evolution* (ed. by J. Birner and R. van Zijp), pp. 343-74. London: Routledge.

[535] O'Brien, D.P. (1994b) Friedrich August von Hayek 1899-1992. *Proceedings of the British Academy*, 84, pp. 347-66.

[536] O'Brien, D.P. (1994c) Introduction. In *A. and M.P. Marshall The Economics of Industry* (1879). Bristol: Thoemmes Press.

[537] O'Brien, D.P. (1995a) Introduction. *In The Collected Works of J.R. McCulloch*, 3, pp. v-xlix. London: Routledge/Thoemmes.

[538] O'Brien, D.P. (1995b) Introduction: McCulloch and the literature of economics. In *Classical Writings on Economics as Selected by J.R. McCulloch*, pp. vii-xxxviii. London: Pickering and Chatto.

[539] O'Brien, D.P. (1995c) Long-run equilibrium and cyclical disturbances: the currency and banking controversy over monetary control. In *The Quantity Theory of Money* (by M. Blaug, W. Eltis, D.P. O'Brien, D. Patinkin, R. Skidelsky and G. Wood), pp. 50-79. Aldershot: Edward Elgar.

[540] O'Brien, D.P. (1997a) Marshall and his correspondence. *Economic Journal*, 107, pp. 1859-1885.

[541] O'Brien, D.P. (1997b) *The Foundations of Business Cycle Theory*, 3 vols. Cheltenham: Edward Elgar.

[542] O'Brien, D.P. (1998a) Four detours. *The Journal of Economic Methodology*, 5, pp. 23-42.

[543] O'Brien, D.P. (1998b) Information and investment in a wider context. In *Economic Organisation, Capabilities and Co-ordination* (ed. by N.J. Foss and B.J. Loasby), pp. 104-20. London: Routledge.

[544] O'Brien, D.P. (1998c) Hayek, Friedrich August von. In *The Palgrave Dictionary of Economics and the Law* (ed. by P. Newman), 2, pp. 217-28. London: Macmillan.

[545] O'Brien, D.P. (1999a) Edwin Cannan: economic theory and the history of economic thought. *Research in the History of Economic Thought and Methodology*, 17, pp. 1-21.

[546] O'Brien, D.P. (ed.) (1999b) *The History of Taxation,* 8 vols. London: Pickering and Chatto.

[547] O'Brien, D.P. (2004) *The Classical Economists Revisited.* Princeton: Princeton University Press.

[548] O'Brien, D.P. and Swann, D. (1966) Information agreements - a problem in search of a policy. *Manchester School,* 24, pp. 285-306.

[549] O'Brien, D.P. and Swann, D. (1968) *Information Agreements, Competition and Efficiency.* London: Macmillan.

[550] O'Brien, D.P., Howe, W.S. and Wright, D.M., with O'Brien, R.J (1979) *Competition Policy, Profitability and Growth.* London: Macmillan.

[551] O'Driscoll, G.P. (1975) The specialisation gap and the Ricardo effect: comment on Ferguson. *History of Political Economy,* 7, pp. 261-9.

[552] O'Driscoll, G.P. (1977) *Economics as a Coordination Problem: the Contributions of Friedrich A. Hayek.* Kansas City: Sheed, Andrews and McMeel.

[553] O'Driscoll, G.P. and Rizzo, M.J. (1985) *The Economics of Time and Ignorance.* Oxford: Blackwell.

[554] Odagiri, H. and Murakami, N. (1992) Private and quasi-social rates of return on pharmaceutical R&D in Japan. *Research Policy,* 21, pp. 335-345.

[555] Ohrenstein, R.A. and Gordon, B. (1992) *Economic Analysis in Talmudic Literature: Rabbinic Thought in the Light of Modern Economics.* Leiden: E.J. Brill.

[556] Opie, R. (1931) Marshall's time analysis. *Economic Journal,* 41, pp. 199-215.

[557] Palermo, S. (1999) *The Evolution of Austrian Economics.* London: Routledge.

[558] Patinkin, D. (1976) Keynes' monetary thought: a study of its development. *History of Political Economy,* 8, pp. 7-150.

[559] Patinkin, D. (1991) Comment. In *The Stockholm School of Economics Revisited* (ed. by L. Jonung), pp. 407-10. Cambridge: Cambridge University Press.

[560] Peach, T. (1988) David Ricardo: a review of some interpretative issues. In *Classical Political Economy* (ed. by W.O. Thweatt), pp. 103-31. Boston: Kluwer.

[561] Peach, T. (1999) Surplus to requirements: Kurz and Salvadori's the Elgar companion to classical economics. *Journal of the History of Economic Thought*, 21, pp. 449-62.

[562] Pennington, J. (1826-40) *Economic Writings* (ed. by R.S. Sayers) (1963). London: London School of Economics.

[563] Perlman, M. (1983) Schumpeter as a historian of economic thought. *Research in the History of Economic Thought and Methodology*, 1, pp. 113-30.

[564] Pigou, A.C. (1922) Empty economic boxes: a reply. *Economic Journal*, 32, pp. 458-465.

[565] Pigou, A.C. (ed.) (1925) *Memorials of Alfred Marshall.* London: Macmillan.

[566] Pigou, A.C. (1928) An analysis of supply. *Economic Journal*, 38, pp. 238-57.

[567] Pigou, A.C. (1932) *The Economics of Welfare*, 4th ed. London: Macmillan.

[568] Pigou, A.C. (1944) Review of F.A. Hayek, *The Road to Serfdom. Economic Journal*, 54, pp. 217-19.

[569] Pigou, A.C. (1949) Mill and the wages fund. *Economic Journal*, 59, pp. 171-180.

[570] Pigou, A.C. (1950) *Keynes's 'General Theory': A Retrospective View.* London: Macmillan.

[571] Pimlott, B. (1985) *Hugh Dalton.* London: Jonathan Cape.

[572] Plant, R. (1994) Hayek on social justice: A critique. In *Hayek, Coordination and Evolution* (ed. by J. Birner and R. van Zijp), pp. 164-77. London: Routledge.

[573] Political Economy Club (1882) *Proceedings, vol. IV.* London: Printed for the Club.

[574] Popper, K.R. (1935) *Logik der Forschung.* Translated as *The Logic of Scientific Discovery* (1959). London: Hutchinson.

[575] Popper, K.R. (1992a) The communist road to self-enslavement. *Cato Policy Report*, XIV, May/June 1992, pp. 1, 10-12.

[576] Popper, K.R. (1992b) Tribute. In *Meeting in Memory of Professor Friedrich von Hayek*, pp. 5-6. London: London School of Economics.

[577] Posner, R.A. (1974) Problems of a policy of deconcentration. In *Industrial Concentration: The New Learning* (ed. by H.J. Goldschmid, H.M. Mann and J.F. Weston), pp. 393-400, 414-16. Boston: Little Brown.

[578] Posner, R.A. (1976) *Antitrust Law: An Economic Perspective.* Chicago: University of Chicago Press.

[579] Presley, J.R. (1978) *Roberstonian Economics.* London: Macmillan.

[580] Presley, J.R. (1981) D.H. Robertson, 1890-1963. In *Pioneers of Modern Economics in Britain* (ed. by D.P. O'Brien and J.R. Presley), pp. 175-202. London: Macmillan.

[581] Prest, A.R. (1948) Notes on the history of the Giffen paradox: comment. *Journal of Political Economy*, 56, pp. 58-60.

[582] Price, L.L.F.R. (1889) Review of E. Cannan, *Elementary Political Economy. Oxford Magazine*, 23 Jan. 1889, pp. 155-56.

[583] Price, R. (1774) *An Appeal to the Public on the Subject of the National Debt.* London: T. Cadell.

[584] Quaritch, B. (ed.) (1895) *Contributions Towards a Dictionary of English Book-Collectors, as also of Some Foreign Collectors whose Libraries were Incorporated in English Collections or whose Books are Chiefly Met with in England: Part VI.* London: Quaritch.

[585] Rae, J. (1834) *Statement of Some New Principles of Political Economy.* Reprinted (1964), New York: A.M. Kelley.

[586] Rawls, J. (1972) *A Theory of Justice.* Oxford: Clarendon.

[587] Ricardo, D. (1815) An essay on the influence of a low price of corn on the profits of stock. In *Works and Correspondence* (ed. by P. Sraffa), IV, pp. 1-41 (1951). Cambridge: Cambridge University Press.

[588] Ricardo, D. (1817-21) On the Principles of Political Economy and Taxation. In *Works and Correspondence, vol. I* (ed. by P. Sraffa) (1951). Cambridge: Cambridge University Press.

[589] Richardson, G.B. (1955) Schumpeter's history of economic analysis. *Oxford Economic Papers*, 7, pp. 136-150.

[590] Richardson, G.B. (1959) Equilibrium, expectations and information. *Economic Journal*, 69, pp. 223-37.

[591] Richardson, G.B. (1960) *Information and Investment.* Oxford: Oxford University Press.

[592] Richardson, G.B. (1965) The theory of restrictive trade practices. *Oxford Economic Papers*, 17, pp. 432-49.

[593] Richardson, G.B. (1966) The pricing of heavy electrical equipment: competition or agreement. *Bulletin of the Oxford University Institute of Economics and Statistics*, 28, pp. 73-92.

[594] Richardson, G.B. (1967) Price notification schemes. *Oxford Economic Papers*, 19, pp. 359-69.

[595] Richardson, G.B. (1972) The organisation of industry. *Economic Journal*, 82, pp. 883-896.

[596] Richardson, G.B. (1975) Adam Smith on competition and increasing returns. In *Essays on Adam Smith* (ed. by A.S. Skinner and T. Wilson), pp. 350-360. Oxford: Clarendon.

[597] Rima, I.H. (1983) George J. Stigler as a historian of economic thought. *Research in the History of Economic Thought and Methodology*, 1, pp. 271-89.

[598] Rizzo, M.J. (1992) Afterword: Austrian economics for the twenty-first century. In *Austrian Economics: Tensions and New Directions* (ed. by B. Caldwell and S. Böhm), pp. 245-55. Boston: Kluwer.

[599] Robbins, L.C. (1927) The optimum theory of population. In *London Essays in Economics: In Honour of Edwin Cannan* (ed. by T.E. Gregory and H. Dalton), pp. 103-34. London: Routledge.

[600] Robbins, L.C. (1928) The representative firm. *Economic Journal*, 38, pp. 387-404.

[601] Robbins, L.C. (1929) Review of E. Cannan, *A Review of Economic Theory*. *Economic Journal*, 39, pp. 409-14.

[602] Robbins, L.C. (1930) The economic works of Philip Wicksteed. *Economica*, 10, pp. 245-58.

[603] Robbins, L.C. (1932) *An Essay on the Nature and Significance of Economic Science*. London: Macmillan.

[604] Robbins, L.C. (1933) Introduction. In *Philip H. Wicksteed: The Commonsense of Political Economy*, pp. v-xxx (1910), London: Routledge.

[605] Robbins, L.C. (1934a) Remarks upon certain aspects of the theory of costs. *Economic Journal*, 44, pp. 1-18.

[606] Robbins, L.C. (1934b) Introduction. In *K. Wicksell: Lectures in Political Economy*, pp. vii-xix. Translated by E. Classen. London: Routledge.

[607] Robbins, L.C. (1934c) *The Great Depression*. London: Macmillan.

[608] Robbins, L.C. (1935) A student's recollections of Edwin Cannan. *Economic Journal*, 45, pp. 393-398.

[609] Robbins, L.C. (1937) *Economic Planning and International Order*. London: Macmillan.

[610] Robbins, L.C. (1947) *The Economic Problem in Peace and War.* London: Macmillan.

[611] Robbins, L.C. (1952) *The Theory of Economic Policy in English Classical Political Economy.* London: Macmillan.

[612] Robbins, L.C. (1955) Schumpeter's history of economic analysis. *Quarterly Journal of Economics*, 69, pp. 1-22.

[613] Robbins, L.C. (1958) *Robert Torrens and the Evolution of Classical Economics.* London: Macmillan.

[614] Robbins, L.C. (1961) Hayek on liberty. *Economica*, 28, pp. 66-81.

[615] Robbins, L.C. (1963) *Politics and Economics.* London: Macmillan.

[616] Robbins, L.C. (1970) *The Evolution of Modern Economic Theory.* London: Macmillan.

[617] Robbins, L.C. (1971) *Autobiography of an Economist.* London: Macmillan.

[618] Robbins, L.C. (1976) *Political Economy Past and Present.* London: Macmillan.

[619] Robbins, L.C. (1998) *A History of Economic Thought. The LSE Lectures* (ed. by S.G. Medema and W.J. Samuels). Princeton: Princeton University Press.

[620] Robertson, D.H. (1926) *Banking Policy and the Price Level.* London: P.S. King.

[621] Robertson, D.H. (1931) Mr. Keynes' theory of money. *Economic Journal*, 41, pp. 395-411.

[622] Robertson, D.H. (1940) *Essays in Monetary Theory.* Reprinted (1956), London: Staples.

[623] Robinson, J.V. (1933) *The Economics of Imperfect Competition.* London: Macmillan.

[624] Robinson, J.V. (1972) The second crisis of economic theory. *American Economic Review*, 62 (Supplement), pp. 1-10.

[625] Robson, W.A. (ed.) (1972) *Man and the Social Sciences.* London: Allen and Unwin.

[626] Roll, E. (1945) Review of F.A. Hayek, *The Road to Serfdom. American Economic Review*, 35, pp. 176-80.

[627] Rosner, P. and Winckler, G. (1989) Aspects of Austrian economics in the 1920s and 1930s. *Research in the History of Economic Thought and Methodology*, 6, pp. 19-30.

[628] Rothbard, M. N. (1995) *Classical Economics.* Aldershot: Edward Elgar.

[629] Rothenstein, W. (1932) *Men and Memories.* London: Faber.

[630] Royal Academy of Sciences (1974) The Nobel memorial prize in economics 1974. *Swedish Journal of Economics*, 76, pp. 46-71.

[631] Rubinstein, A. (ed.) (1990) *Game Theory in Economics.* Aldershot: Edward Elgar.

[632] Rühl, C. (1994) The transformation of business cycle theory: Hayek, Lucas and a change in the notion of equilibrium. In *Money and Business Cycles: The Economics of F.A. Hayek, vol. II* (ed. by M. Colonna and H. Hagemann), pp. 168-202. Aldershot: Edward Elgar.

[633] Rutherford, M. (1989) Some issues in the comparison of Austrian and institutional economics. *Research in the History of Economic Thought and Methodology*, 6, pp. 159-72.

[634] Rutherford, M. (1994) Austrian economics and American (old) institutionalisation. In *The Elgar Companion to Austrian Economics* (ed. by P. Boettke), pp. 529-34. Aldershot: Edward Elgar.

[635] Saffran, B. (1996) Recommendations for further reading. *Journal of Economic Perspectives*, 10, pp. 181-88.

[636] Samuels, W.J. (1966) *The Classical Theory of Economic Policy.* Cleveland: World Publishing.

[637] Samuels, W.J. (1974) The history of economic thought as intellectual history. *History of Political Economy*, 6, pp. 305-23.

[638] Samuels, W.J. (1983) Introduction. *Research in the History of Economic Thought and Methodology*, 1, pp. xi-xii.

[639] Samuels, W.J. (1989) Austrian and institutional economics: some common elements. *Research in the History of Economic Thought and Methodology*, 6, pp. 53-71.

[640] Samuels, W.J. (1996) My work as a historian of economic thought. *Journal of the History of Economic Thought*, 18, pp. 37-75.

[641] Samuelson, P.A. (1947) *Foundations of Economic Analysis.* Cambridge, Massachusetts: Harvard University Press.

[642] Samuelson, P.A. (1948) *Economics.* New York: McGraw Hill.

[643] Samuelson, P.A. (1959) A modern treatment of the Ricardian economy I. The pricing of goods and of labour and of land services. *Quarterly Journal of Economics*, 73, pp. 1-35.

[644] Samuelson, P.A. (1966-86) *The Collected Scientific Papers of Paul Anthony Samuelson.* Vols. I, II ed. J. Stiglitz (1966); vol. III ed. R. Merton (1970); vol. IV ed. H. Nagatani and K. Crowley (1977); vol V ed. K.Crowley (1986). Cambridge, Massachusetts: MIT Press.

[645] Samuelson, P.A. (1980) *Economics*, 11th ed. New York: McGraw Hill.

[646] Samuelson, P.A. (1987a) Out of the closet: a program for the Whig history of economic science. *History of Economics Society Bulletin*, 9, pp. 51-60. Reprinted in *The Historiography of Economics* (ed. by M. Blaug), pp. 181-90 (1991), Aldershot: Edward Elgar.

[647] Samuelson, P.A. (1987b) The 1985 Nobel prize in economics. In *Macroeconomics and Finance: Essays in Honor of Franco Modigliani* (ed. by R. Dornbusch, S. Fischer and J. Bossons), pp. 29-36. Cambridge, Massachusetts: MIT Press.

[648] Samuelson, P.A. (1988a) Keeping Whig history honest. *History of Economics Society Bulletin*, 10, pp. 161-7. Reprinted in *The Historiography of Economics* (ed. by M. Blaug), pp. 202-8 (1991), Aldershot: Edward Elgar.

[649] Samuelson, P.A. (1988b) Mathematical vindication of Ricardo on machinery. *Journal of Political Economy*, 96, pp. 274-282.

[650] Samuelson, P.A. (1988c) The passing of the guard in economics. *Eastern Economic Journal*, 14, pp. 319-29.

[651] Samuelson, P.A. (1989a) Ricardo was right. *Scandinavian Journal of Economics*, 91, pp. 47-62.

[652] Samuelson, P.A. (1989b) Remembering Joan. In *Joan Robinson and Modern Economic Theory* (ed. by G. Feiwel), pp. 121-43. London: Macmillan.

[653] Samuelson, P.A. (1990) Revisionist findings on Sraffa. In *Essays on Piero Sraffa* (ed. by K. Bharadwaj and B. Schefold), pp. 263-83. London: Routledge.

[654] Samuelson, P.A. (1991a) Conversations with my history of economics critics. In *Economics, Culture and Education: Essays in Honour of Mark Blaug* (ed. by G.K. Shaw), pp. 3-13. Aldershot: Edward Elgar.

[655] Samuelson, P.A. (1991b) Thoughts on the Stockholm School and on Scandinavian economics. In *The Stockholm School of Economics Revisited* (ed. by L. Jonung), pp. 391-407. Cambridge: Cambridge University Press.

[656] Samuelson, P.A. (1992a) The overdue recovery of Adam Smith's reputation as an economic theorist. In *Adam Smith's Legacy* (ed. by M. Fry), pp. 1-14. London: Routledge.

[657] Samuelson, P.A. (1992b) The fitness maximised by the classical canonical economy: a theme from Houthakker and R.A. Fisher. In *Aggregation, Consumption and Trade: Essays in honour of H.S. Houthakker* (ed. by L. Phlips and L.D. Taylor), pp. 9-19. Dordrecht: Kluwer.

[658] Samuelson, P.A. (1993) Gustav Cassel's scientific innovations: claims and realities. *History of Political Economy*, 25, pp. 515-27.

[659] Samuelson, P.A. (1994a) The classical classical fallacy. *Journal of Economic Literature*, 32, pp. 620-39.

[660] Samuelson, P.A. (1994b) Richard Kahn: his welfare economics and lifetime achievments. *Cambridge Journal of Economics*, 18, pp. 55-72.

[661] Samuelson, P.A. (1994c) Two classics: Böhm-Bawerk's positive theory and Fisher's rate of interest through modern prisms. *Journal of the History of Economic Thought*, 6, pp. 202-28.

[662] Samuelson, P.A. (1995) Gottfried Haberler (1900-1995). *Journal of International Trade and Economic Development*, 4, pp. 409-15.

[663] Samuelson, P.A. (1997) Review of I. Steedman (ed.), *Socialism and Marginalism in Economics 1870-1930. European Journal of the History of Economic Thought*, 4, pp. 179-86.

[664] Samuelson, P.A. (1998a) How *Foundations* came to be. *Journal of Economic Literature*, 36, pp. 1375-86.

[665] Samuelson, P.A. (1998b) Land. In *The Elgar Companion to Classical Economics, vol. II* (ed. by H. Kurz and N. Salvadori), pp. 27-37. Cheltenham: Edward Elgar.

[666] Samuelson, P.A. (1998c) Samuelson, Paul Anthony, as an interpreter of the classical economists. In *The Elgar Companion to Classical Economics, vol. II* (ed. by H. Kurz and N. Salvadori), pp. 329-33. Cheltenham: Edward Elgar.

[667] Samuelson, P.A. (1999) The classical theory of commodity money under a microscope. In *From Classical Economics to the Theory of the Firm: Essays in honour of D.P. O'Brien* (ed. by R. Backhouse and J. Creedy), pp. 47-64. Cheltenham: Edward Elgar.

[668] Samuelson, P.A., Patinkin, D. and Blaug, M. (1991) On the historiography of economics: a correspondence. *Journal of the History of Economic Thought*, 13, pp. 144-58.

[669] Say, J.B. (1803) *Traité d'Economie Politique, ou Simple Exposition de la Maniere dont se Forment, se Distribuent, et se Consomment les Richesses.* Paris: Deterville.

[670] Say, J.B. (1817) *A Treatise on Political Economy, or the Production, Distribution, and Consumption of Wealth.* Translated by C.R. Prinsep, new translation by C. Biddle (1880). Philadelphia: Claxton. Reprinted (1971). New York: Kelley.

[671] Say, J.B. (1825) Examen critique du discours de M. MacCulloch sur l'economie politique. Reprinted in *Oeuvres Diverses*, pp. 261-79 (1848). Paris: Guillaumin.

[672] Say, J.B. (1828-9) *Cours Complet d'Economie Politique.* Reprinted (1844). Brussels: Société Typographique Belge.

[673] Scherer, F.M. (1970) *Industrial Market Structure and Economic Performance.* Chicago: Rand McNally.

[674] Scherer, F.M. (1980) *Industrial Market Structure and Economic Performance*, 2nd ed. Chicago: Rand McNally.

[675] Scherer, F.M. and Ross, D. (1990) *Industrial Market Structure and Economic Performance.* Boston: Houghton Mifflin.

[676] Schmalensee, R. (1983) George Stigler's contributions to economics. *Scandinavian Journal of Economics*, 85, pp. 77-86.

[677] Schmidt, C. (2002) Hayek, Morgenstern and game theory. In *F.A. Hayek as a Political Economist* (ed. by J. Birner, P. Garrouste and T. Aimar), pp. 53-63. London: Routledge.

[678] Schotter, A. (1994) *Microeconomics: A Modern Approach.* New York: Harper Collins.

[679] Schumpeter, J.A. (1908) *Das Wesen und der Hauptinhalt der theoretischen Nationalokonomie.* Leipzig: Duncker and Humblot.

[680] Schumpeter, J.A. (1912) *Epochen der Dogmen - und Methodengeschichte.* Translated as *Economic Doctrine and Method* by R. Aris (1954). London: Allen and Unwin.

[681] Schumpeter, J.A. (1946) Review of F.A. Hayek, *The Road to Serfdom. Journal of Political Economy*, 54, pp. 269-70.

[682] Schumpeter, J.A. (1952) *Ten Great Economists.* Reprinted (1962), London: Allen and Unwin.

[683] Schumpeter, J.A. (1954) *History of Economic Analysis.* London: Allen and Unwin.

[684] Seccareccia, M. (1994) Credit money and cyclical crises: the views of Hayek and Fisher compared. In *Money and Business Cycles: The Economics of F.A. Hayek, vol. II* (ed. by M. Colonna and H. Hagemann), pp. 53-73. Aldershot: Edward Elgar.

[685] Selgin, G. (1995a) The productivity norm versus zero inflation in the history of economic thought. *History of Political Economy*, 27, pp. 705-35.

[686] Selgin, G. (1995b) The case for a productivity norm: comment on Dowd. *Journal of Macroeconomics*, 17, pp. 733-40.

[687] Seligman, E.R.A. (1903) On some neglected British economists. *Economic Journal*, 13, pp. 335-63, 511-35.

[688] Seligman, E.R.A. (1925) *Essays in Taxation*, 10th ed. New York: Macmillan.

[689] Seligman, E.R.A. (1926) *The Shifting and Incidence of Taxation*, 5th ed. New York: Columbia University Press.

[690] Senior, N.W. (1836) *An Outline of the Science of Political Economy*. London: Clowes.

[691] Senior, N.W. (1843) Free trade and retaliation. *Edinburgh Review*, 88, pp. 1-47.

[692] Seton, F. (1957) The transformation problem. *Review of Economic Studies*, 24, pp. 149-60.

[693] Shackle, G.L.S. (1967) *The Years of High Theory*. Cambridge: Cambridge University Press.

[694] Shackle, G.L.S. (1972) *Epistemics and Economics*. Cambridge: Cambridge University Press.

[695] Shackle, G.L.S. (1981) F.A. Hayek, 1899-. In *Pioneers of Modern Economics in Britain* (ed. by D.P. O'Brien and J.R. Presley), pp. 234-61. London: Macmillan.

[696] Shove, G.F. (1944) Mrs Robinson on Marxian economics. *Economic Journal*, 54, pp. 47-61.

[697] Sidgwick, A. and Sidgwick, E. (1906) *Henry Sidgwick: A Memoir*. London: Macmillan.

[698] Sidgwick, E. (1938) *Mrs Henry Sidgwick*. London: Sidgwick and Jackson.

[699] Sills, D.L. (ed.) (1968/1978). *International Encyclopaedia of the Social Sciences*, vols. 1-17 (1968); vol. 18 (1978). New York: Free Press/Collier Macmillan.

[700] Singh, S. (1997) *Fermat's Last Theorem*. London: Fourth Estate.

[701] Skidelsky, R. (1983) *John Maynard Keynes, vol. 1: Hopes Betrayed 1883-1920*. London: Macmillan.

[702] Skidelsky, R. (1992) *John Maynard Keynes, vol. 2: The Economist as Saviour 1920-37*. London: Macmillan.

[703] Skidelsky, R. (2000) *John Maynard Keynes, vol. 3: Fighting for Britain 1937-1946*. London: Macmillan.

[704] Smith, A. (1759) *The Theory of Moral Sentiments* (ed. by D.D. Raphael and A.L. Macfie) (1976). Oxford: Oxford University Press.

[705] Smith, A. (1763) *Lectures on Justice, Police, Revenue and Arms* (ed. by E.Cannan) (1896). Oxford: Clarendon.

[706] Smith, A. (1776) *An Inquiry into the Nature and Causes of the Wealth of Nations* (ed. by R.H. Campbell, A.S. Skinner and W.B. Todd) (1981). Indianapolis: Liberty Press.

[707] Smith, V.L. (1982) Markets as economizers of information: experimental examination of the 'Hayek hypothesis'. *Economic Inquiry*, 20, pp. 165-79.

[708] Smithies, A. (1941) Professor Hayek on the pure theory of capital. *American Economic Review*, 31, pp. 767-79.

[709] Snowdon, B.A. and Vane, H.R. (1998) Transforming macroeconomics: an interview with Robert E. Lucas Jr. *The Journal of Economic Methodology*, 5, pp. 115-46.

[710] Snowdon, B.A., Vane, H.R. and Wynarczyk, P. (1994) *A Modern Guide to Macroeconomics*. Aldershot: Edward Elgar.

[711] Sobel, I. (1983) Joseph J. Spengler: the institutionalist approach to the history of economics. *Research in the History of Economic Thought and Methodology*, 1, pp. 243-70.

[712] Spadaro, L.M. (ed.) (1978) *New Directions in Austrian Economics*. Kansas: Sheed, Andrews and McMeel.

[713] Spencer, R.W. (1975) Inflation, unemployment, and Hayek. *Federal Reserve Bank of St. Louis Review*. Reprinted in *Friedrich A. Hayek: Critical Assessments, vol. 2* (ed. by J.C. Wood and R.N. Woods), pp. 230-8 (1991), London: Routledge.

[714] Spengler, J.J. (1945) Review of F.A. Hayek, *The Road to Serfdom*. *Southern Economic Journal*, 12, pp. 48-55.

[715] Spengler, J.J. (1959) Adam Smith's theory of economic growth - parts I, II. *Southern Economic Journal*, 25, pp. 397-415, 26, pp. 1-12.

[716] Spengler, J.J. (1965) Kinked demand curves: by whom first used? *Southern Economic Journal*, 32, pp. 81-4.

[717] Spengler, J.J. (1968) Economics: its history, themes, approaches. *Journal of Economic Issues*, 2, pp. 5-30.

[718] Sraffa, P. (1926) The laws of returns under competitive conditions. *Economic Journal*, 36, pp. 535-50.

[719] Sraffa, P. (1932a) Dr. Hayek on money and capital. *Economic Journal*, 42, pp. 42-53, Reprinted in *Friedrich A. Hayek: Critical Assessments, vol. 1* (ed. by J.C. Wood and R.N. Woods), pp. 86-96 (1991), London: Routledge.

[720] Sraffa, P. (1932b) A rejoinder. *Economic Journal*, 42, pp. 249-51. Reprinted in *Friedrich A. Hayek: Critical Assessments, vol. 1* (ed. by J.C. Wood and R.N. Woods), pp. 113-5 (1991), London: Routledge.

[721] Sraffa, P. (ed.) (1951-5) *The Works and Correspondence of David Ricardo*. Cambridge: Cambridge University Press.

[722] Stark, W. (1959) The 'classical situation' in political economy. *Kyklos*, 12, pp. 57-65.

[723] Steedman, I. (1994) On the pure theory of capital by F.A. Hayek. In *Capitalism, Socialism and Knowledge: The Economics of F.A. Hayek, vol. II* (ed. by M. Colonna, H. Hagemann and O. Hamouda), pp. 3-25. Aldershot: Edward Elgar.

[724] Steele, G.R. (1993) *The Economics of Friedrich Hayek*. London: Macmillan.

[725] Steindl, F.G. (1995) *Monetary Interpretations of the Great Depression*. Ann Arbor: University of Michigan Press.

[726] Stewart, D. (1854-60) *Collected Works of Dugald Stewart* (ed. by Sir W. Hamilton). Edinburgh: Constable.

[727] Stewart, I.M.T. (1979) *Reasoning and Method in Economics*. London: McGraw Hill.

[728] Stigler, G.J. (1941) *Production and Distribution Theories*. New York: Macmillan.

[729] Stigler, G.J. (1947) Notes on the history of the Giffen paradox. *Journal of Political Economy*, 55, pp. 152-56.

[730] Stigler, G.J. (1948) Notes on the history of the Giffen paradox: a reply. *Journal of Political Economy*, 56, pp. 61-2.

[731] Stigler, G.J. (1953) Sraffa's Ricardo. *American Economic Review*, 43, pp. 586-99.

[732] Stigler, G.J. (1955) The nature and role of originality in scientific progress. Reprinted in *Essays in the History of Economics*, pp. 1-15 (1965), Chicago: University of Chicago Press.

[733] Stigler, G.J. (1958) Ricardo and the 93 per cent labor theory of value. *American Economic Review*, 48, pp. 357-67.

[734] Stigler, G.J. (1960) The influence of events and policies on economic theory. *American Economic Review, Papers and Proceedings*, 50, pp. 36-45.

[735] Stigler, G.J. (1962) Marshall's *Principles* after Guillebaud. *Journal of Political Economy*, 70, pp. 282-6.

[736] Stigler, G.J. (1965a) *Textual Exegesis as a Scientific Problem.* Chicago: University of Chicago Press. Reprinted in *The Economist* as *Preacher*, pp. 68-71 (1982).

[737] Stigler, G.J. (1965b) *Essays in the History of Economics.* Chicago: University of Chicago Press.

[738] Stigler, G.J. (1969a) Does economics have a useful past? *History of Political Economy*, 1, pp. 217-30.

[739] Stigler, G.J. (1969b) Review of R.V. Eagly (ed.), *Events, Ideology and Economic Theory: The Determinants of Progress in the Development of Economic Analysis. Journal of Economic History*, 29, pp. 336-7.

[740] Stigler, G.J. (1970) Review of L. Robbins, *The Evolution of Modern Economic Theory. Economica*, 37, pp. 425-6.

[741] Stigler, G.J. (1971) Smith's travels on the ship of state. *History of Political Economy*, 3, pp. 265-77.

[742] Stigler, G.J. (1972) The adoption of the marginal utility theory. *History of Political Economy*, 4, pp. 571-86.

[743] Stigler, G.J. (1976a) Do economists matter? *Southern Economic Journal*, 42, pp. 347-54.

[744] Stigler, G.J. (1976b) The successes and failures of Professor Smith. *Journal of Political Economy*, 84, pp. 1199-1213.

[745] Stigler, G.J. (1976c) *The Scientific Uses of Biography, with Special Reference to J.S. Mill.* Reprinted in *The Economist* as *Preacher*, pp. 86-97 (1982), Chicago: University of Chicago Press.

[746] Stigler, G.J. (1978) The history of economics through Professor Hutchison's spectacles. *Minerva*, 16, pp. 596-9.

[747] Stigler, G.J. (1981) Review of S. Hollander, *The Economics of David Ricardo. Journal of Economic Literature*, 19, pp. 100-2.

[748] Stigler, G.J. (1982) *The Economist as Preacher and Other Essays.* Chicago: University of Chicago Press.

[749] Streissler, E.W. (1994) Hayek on information and socialism. In *Capitalism, Socialism and Knowledge: The Economics of F.A. Hayek, vol. II* (ed. by M. Colonna, H. Hagemann and O. Hamouda), pp. 47-75. Aldershot: Edward Elgar.

[750] Summers, L. (1983) Comment. *Journal of Monetary Economics*, 12, pp. 159-62.

[751] Swann, D. and McLachlan, D.L. (1963) Competition policy in the common market. *Economic Journal*, 73, pp. 54-79.

[752] Swann, D. and McLachlan, D.L. (1964) Programming and competition in the European communities. *Economic Journal*, 74, pp. 85-100.

[753] Swann, D. and O'Brien, D.P. (1967) Information agreements: a further contribution. *Manchester School*, 25, pp. 285-8.

[754] Swann, D., O'Brien, D.P., Maunder, W.P. and Howe, W.S. (1974) *Competition in British Industry.* London: Allen and Unwin.

[755] Szenberg, M. (1992) *Eminent Economists: Their Life Philosophies.* Cambridge: Cambridge University Press.

[756] Tarascio, V. (1975) Intellectual history and the social sciences: the problem of methodological pluralism. *Social Science Quarterly*, 56, pp. 37-54.

[757] Taylor, O.H. (1955) Schumpeter's history of economic analysis. *Review of Economics and Statistics*, 37, pp. 12-22.

[758] Thompson, S.P. (1910) *Calculus Made Easy.* London: Macmillan.

[759] Thornton, H. (1802) *An Enquiry into the Nature and Effects of the Paper Credit of Great Britain* (ed. with an introduction by F.A. Hayek) (1939). London: Allen and Unwin.

[760] Thweatt, W.O. (1976) James Mill and the early development of comparative advantage. *History of Political Economy*, 8, pp. 207-34.

[761] Thweatt, W.O. (1979) Adam Smith, James Mill and Ricardian economics. *Midsouth Journal of Economics*, 3, pp. 7-19.

[762] Torrens, R. (1815) *An Essay on the External Corn Trade.* London: J. Hatchard.

[763] Torrens, R. (1827) *An Essay on the External Corn Trade*, 4th ed. London: Longman.

[764] Torrens, R. (1834) *On Wages and Combination.* London: Longman.

[765] Torrens, R. (1837) *A Letter to the Right Honourable Lord Viscount Melbourne on the Causes of the Recent Derangements in the Money Market and on Bank Reform.* London: Longman.

[766] Toye, J. (1997) Keynes on population and economic growth. *Cambridge Journal of Economics*, 21, pp. 1-26.

[767] Triffin, R. (1941) *Monopolistic Competition and General Equilibrium Theory.* Cambridge, Massachusetts: Harvard University Press.

[768] Tsiang, S.C. (1947) *The Variations of Real Wages and Profit Margins in Relation to the Trade Cycle.* London: Pitman.

[769] Tsiang, S.C. (1949) Rehabilitation of time dimension of investment in macrodynamic analysis. *Economica*, 16, pp. 204-17.

[770] Turgot, A.R.J. (1769-1770) Reflections on the formation and the distribution of wealth. Translated by R.L. Meek. In *Turgot on Progress, Sociology and Economics*, pp. 119-182 (1973). Cambridge: Cambridge University Press.

[771] Uhr, C.G. (1962) *Economic Doctrines of Knut Wicksell.* Berkeley: University of California Press.

[772] Uhr, C.G. (1975) *Economic Doctrines of David Davidson.* Uppsala: Almqvist and Wiksell.

[773] Vaughn, K. I. (1980) Economic calculations under socialism: the Austrian contribution. *Economic Inquiry*, 18, pp. 535-54.

[774] Viner, J. (1930) Review of E. Cannan, *A Review of Economic Theory. Economica*, 10, pp. 74-84. Reprinted in *The Long View and the Short*, pp. 395-405 (1958), London: Allen & Unwin.

[775] Viner, J. (1937) *Studies in the Theory of International Trade.* London: Allen and Unwin.

[776] Viner, J. (1954) Schumpeter's history of economic analysis. *American Economic Review*, 44, pp. 894-910.

[777] Viner, J. (1961) Hayek on freedom and coercion. *Southern Economic Journal*, 27, pp. 230-6.

[778] Viner, J. (1965) Introduction to *John Rae Life of Adam Smith (1895).* New York: A.M. Kelley.

[779] Walker, D.A. (1970) Leon Walras in the light of his correspondence and related papers. *Journal of Political Economy*, 78, pp. 685-701.

[780] Walker, D.A. (1981) William Jaffé, historian of economic thought. *American Economic Review*, 71, pp. 1012-19.

[781] Walker, D.A. (1983a) William Jaffé, officier de liason intellectuel. *Research in the History of Economic Thought and Methodology*, 1, pp. 19-39.

[782] Walker, D.A. (1983b) Biography and the study of the history of economic thought. *Research in the History of Economic Thought and Methodology*, 1, pp. 41-59.

[783] Webb, B. (1928) *My Apprenticeship*. Reprinted (1938), Harmondsworth: Penguin.

[784] Webb, B. (1982) *The Diary of Beatrice Webb, vol. I, 1873-1892* (ed. by N. and J. MacKenzie). London: Virago with the London School of Economics.

[785] Webb, B. (1983) *The Diary of Beatrice Webb, vol. II, 1892-1905* (ed. by N. and J. MacKenzie). London: Virago with the London School of Economics.

[786] Webb, S. and Webb, B. (1935) *Soviet Communism: A New Civilisation?* London: Longman.

[787] Webb, S. and Webb, B. (1978) *The Letters of Sidney and Beatrice Webb* (ed. by N. Mackenzie). Cambridge: Cambridge University Press.

[788] West, E. (1815) *An Essay on the Application of Capital to Land*. London: Underwood.

[789] Wheatley, J. (1807-22) *An Essay on the Theory of Money and Principles of Commerce*. London: Cadell and Davies.

[790] Whitaker, J.K. (ed.) (1975) *The Early Economic Writings of Alfred Marshall*. New York: Free Press.

[791] Whitaker, J.K. (ed.) (1996) *The Correspondence of Alfred Marshall, Economist*, 3 vols. Cambridge: Cambridge University Press.

[792] Whitaker, J.K. (1998) Rummaging in the attic: a chapter of accidents. *Journal of the History of Economic Thought*, 20, pp. 311-27.

[793] Wicksell, K. (1934) *Lectures on Political Economy* (ed. by L. Robbins). Translated by E. Classen. London: Routledge.

[794] Wilson, D. (1976) *Penicillin in Perspective*. London: Faber & Faber.

[795] Wilson, J. (1826) *Some Illustrations of Mr. M'Culloch's Principles of Political Economy*. Edinburgh and London: Blackwood.

[796] Wilson, R.J.A. (1996) *Economics, Ethics and Religion: Jewish, Christian and Muslim Economic Thought*. London: Macmillan.

[797] Wilson, T. (1939-40) Capital theory and the trade cycle. *Review of Economic Studies*, 7, pp. 169-79.

[798] Winch, D. (1962) What price the history of economic thought. *Scottish Journal of Political Economy*, 9, pp. 193-204.

[799] Winch, D. (1983) Jacob Viner as intellectual historian. *Research in the History of Economic thought and Methodology*, 1, pp. 1-17.

[800] Withers, H. (1909) *The Meaning of Money*. London: Smith Elder. Reprinted (1917), London: J. Murray.

[801] Wolfe, G. (1995) *Malcolm Muggeridge*. London: Hodder and Stoughton.

[802] Wolpert, L. and Richards, A. (1988) *A Passion for Science*. Oxford: Oxford University Press.

[803] Wood, J. C. and Woods, R. N. (eds.) (1991) *Friedrich A. Hayek. Critical Assessments*, 4 vols. London: Routledge.

[804] Wright, D.M. (1964) D.H. Robertson: comment. *Quarterly Journal of Economics*, 78, pp. 324-7.

[805] Yeager, L.B. (1976) *International Monetary Relations: Theory, History, and Policy*, 2nd ed.. New York: Harper and Row.

[806] Young, A. (1913) Pigou's wealth and welfare. *Quarterly Journal of Economics*, 27, pp. 672-86.

[807] Zamagni, S. (1984) Ricardo and Hayek effects in a fixwage model of traverse. *Oxford Economic Papers*, 36, pp. 135-51.

[808] Zamagni, S. (1987) Ricardo-Hayek effect. In *The New Palgrave Dictionary of Economics* (ed. by J. Eatwell, M. Milgate and P. Newman), 4, pp. 198-9. London: Macmillan.

[809] Zandt, D.E.V. (1993) The lessons of the lighthouse: 'government' or 'private' provision of goods. *Journal of Legal Studies*, 22, pp. 47-72.

Index